John J Pool

Studies in Mohammedanism, Historical and Doctrinal, with a

Chapter on Islam in England

John J Pool

Studies in Mohammedanism, Historical and Doctrinal, with a Chapter on Islam in England

ISBN/EAN: 9783743313163

Manufactured in Europe, USA, Canada, Australia, Japa

Cover: Foto ©Thomas Meinert / pixelio.de

Manufactured and distributed by brebook publishing software (www.brebook.com)

John J Pool

Studies in Mohammedanism, Historical and Doctrinal, with a Chapter on Islam in England

CONTENTS

CHAPTER XXXIII.

PREFACE

INTEREST in the comparative study of Religions is becoming in Western lands more and more prominently a sign of the times, not only among students in our theological colleges, but among thoughtful laymen everywhere. The time has gone by when the religions of the East can be put on one side as myths and delusions not worthy even for a moment to be compared with the Christian religion.

Now that the religious books of the East have all been translated into European languages, and the religious beliefs and practices of Eastern people have been carefully examined and recorded by competent scholars, it has become clear that the comparative study of religions, and especially of Christianity with other religions, is a necessity of the age in which we live.

The present work deals exclusively with Mohammedanism, and is an attempt to provide a popular text-book on the wide field of Mussulman faith, practice, and history, and to show wherein the religion of Mohammed falls below the religion of Christ.

Strange to say, Mohammedanism has established itself in England of late years. The leader of this remarkable movement is a Liverpool solicitor named Quilliam, who in 1884 was converted to Mohammedanism while on a visit to Morocco. Soon after his return to his native city he began to teach the doctrines of Islamism privately and publicly, but for a long time without success.

However, at length a select few joined the new enthusiast, and Islam in England became an accomplished fact.

Mr. Quilliam, in an article contributed to the *Religious Review of Reviews*, says : " When four converts were made a small mission-room was taken, and meetings were held on Fridays for the faithful and on Sundays for strangers. It was hard work. Frequently we got no audience but ourselves, and oftener still the ragamuffins of the neighbourhood broke our windows with stones and pelted us with mud, garbage, or even more obnoxious kinds of filth, as we either entered or came out of the room ; whilst amongst their friends and relations the converts had to endure ridicule, and in some instances petty persecution. We consoled ourselves with those passages of the Koran which tell us that 'God loveth those who persevere patiently.' "

The little band of four has increased to fifty, and their leader is very sanguine that greater triumphs are in store for Islam in England.

Mr. Quilliam naïvely remarks—" Why should there be any astonishment at such a condition of things having come to pass ? Surely it is quite as justifiable for Moslems to endeavour to promulgate their faith in England as it is for Christians to mission India, China, and Africa, to make converts to Christianity. From the Cape of Good Hope to Tangiers, from Cape Spartel to China, the Moslem heart is beating with anxiety at this development of Islam. Five times a day, from millions of true believers' lips, from the monarch on the throne down to the poorest ryot in India, rises the solemn supplication to Almighty God—

'Allah, most Merciful and Great, bless Thy work in England.' "

Now what shall we who are Christians say to these things ? We cannot assume an attitude of indifference with Mohammedanism at our very doors. Rather let us be stirred up to the comparative study of our own and the Moslem faith, so that we may be able to give intelligent reasons for the hope that is in us.

I have dedicated this volume to Islam in England and to all Seekers after Truth ; and I most earnestly trust that the perusal of its pages may be instrumental in deepening the general faith of Christians in Christianity, and, perchance, in leading some of the members of the Moslem Institute at Liverpool back to the faith of their fathers.

JOHN J. POOL.

REIMS,, *15th June, 1892.*

STUDIES

IN

MOHAMMEDANISM

CHAPTER I

THE FOUNDER OF THE SYSTEM

MOHAMMED (*Lit.* "The Praised One") was born in
Arabia, at the famous city of Mecca, A.D. 570. His
father's name was Abdullah, and his mother's Amina. His
family, by birth, was one of the highest in the land, but his
father was poor, though some of his uncles were rich and
powerful.

Mohammed was never to know the blessing of a father's
love and care, for Abdullah shortly after his marriage started
on a trading expedition to Gaza, in Palestine, and on the
return journey was taken ill at Medina, about 250 miles
from Mecca, and died there before his wife or any of his
friends could visit him.

It was shortly after this event that Mohammed was born,
and tradition says that as soon as he came into the world
he exclaimed, "Allah is Great! There is no God but Allah,
and I am his Prophet!" Many other marvellous things
are reported to have happened at the same time in honour
of the advent of this Arabian Prophet, but I pass them by
to deal with more trustworthy matters.

B

It was the custom among ladies of high birth in Mecca to put out their little children to nurse, and Amina decided that her boy should be no exception to the rule, though the expense might be difficult to meet, as her husband had left behind him no richer legacy than four camels, a flock of goats, and a slave-girl. Mohammed therefore was committed to the care of a foster-mother named Halima, who took him away to her home in the mountains of Taif, where in the fresh, pure air the baby boy would have ample opportunity to develop his body and grow strong. For five years he remained in the hills, and then returned home to gladden his mother's heart. The joy was short-lived, however, for in the following year, on a visit to Medina, where her husband was buried, the poor widow was taken ill, and, as she was returning home, died by the wayside, leaving her little boy to the care of the faithful slave-girl. This girl took Mohammed back to Mecca, and conducted him to the home of his aged grandfather, who, for the next two years, cared for the little orphan with great kindness and fondness. Then the old man died, and Mohammed was passed on at the age of eight to his uncle Abu Talib, a chief of wealth, ability, and influence. One cannot but think with compassionate interest of the youth who, in his earliest years, was thus bereaved. Mohammed knew practically nothing of either a father or a mother's care, and was indebted for his upbringing to the kindness of strangers or friends. In consequence of all this unsettledness and moving about, Mohammed's education suffered in respect to reading and writing, and these grave defects were not remedied in his new home, though he was treated with consideration and kindness, having a seat at his uncle's table, being taught the use of arms, and allowed to accompany Abu Talib wherever he went.

Thus the days of childhood and youth passed, and Mohammed grew up into handsome manhood, and was withal of a grave and serious deportment, as, indeed, might have been expected from such a sombre childhood.

And the seriousness of his character was deepened by the occupation in which we find he was engaged at the age of twenty, viz., that of tending sheep, like Moses and David of old. Thinking of this occupation in after days, when he was a prophet and a prince, Mohammed is reported to have greatly rejoiced, and said that "there never was a prophet who was not once a shepherd." When he was twenty-five an important event happened to him. He was chosen by a wealthy widow lady named Kadija to take supreme charge of a caravan, which she was preparing to send with merchandise into Syria. Mohammed knew the route, as some years before he had travelled over it with his uncle in one of his trading expeditions. The new occupation gained for Mohammed the title of "the Camel Driver," and he was also called, on account of his steady conduct and fair dealing, "the faithful," "the trusty." For the greater part of a year Mohammed was away on this trading expedition, and then he returned eminently successful, having disposed of everything to the very best advantage, and added considerably to the wealth of the lady in whose service he was engaged. And his reward exceeded all expectations.

The fact was, Kadija had fallen in love with her handsome camel-driver, and negotiated, through her sister, a match with him; and before that eventful year closed Mohammed was married, and at the head of a household of his own. Kadija was a widow, who had already been twice married. Her former husbands had been rich men, who had left their all to her, and she had since added greatly to her income, so that when she was married to Mohammed, she was one of the wealthiest ladies of the land. She was forty years of age, while her husband was but twenty-five, yet the marriage proved a very happy one.. Kadija was a beautiful woman, and as good as she was beautiful, and the heart of her husband could safely trust in her. Mohammed at this time is described as being a little over the medium height, and of a commanding presence. Mr. Gilman in his very readable book on " The Saracens," writes thus of Mohammed :—" His wide chest and broad shoulders were surmounted by a long and finely moulded neck, and a massive head, from which looked out a frank, oval face, marked by a prominent aquiline nose, large, restless, and piercing black eyes, over which long, heavy lashes drooped, and a bushy beard fell upon his breast." Such was the striking appearance of Mohammed at the time of his marriage; and this event made, of course, a remarkable change in his outward circumstances. In a moment he had been raised from comparative poverty to great wealth, and from a position of comparative insignificance to one of very considerable importance and influence. Years of domestic happiness followed, during which there were born to Mohammed two sons and four daughters. The sons died very young, and only one of the daughters attained to any fame. Fatima was the name of this daughter, and she lived to become the mother of sons, the tragic story of whose life has given to the Mohammedan world a Passion Play, which, when it is enacted, moves the hearts of the stoical children of the East to their very depths. In a later chapter an account will be given of this play.

For some years Mohammed continued to travel to distant places with caravans of merchandise, but gradually such expeditions were given up, and the whole energies of the thoughtful man were turned into a channel which was to make him a name famous throughout the world. From his youthful days Mohammed had taken a deep interest in religious questions. His father's faith and the faith of the people of Mecca and the surrounding cities was a belief in gods many and lords many. The people were idolaters, and had in Mecca a famous temple, and a famous idol, about which the exigencies of our story require that I should now say something. The idol was a pure white stone, which the people of Arabia say fell from Heaven when Adam fell from Paradise. This sacred stone the people, certainly long before the time of Christ, embedded in the walls of a building which they called the Kaaba or Cube, around which a temple was built, and there for generations the people of Mecca worshipped, with the firm faith that the gods would be pleased with them, and would bless them, if they rendered due homage to the pure white stone which had come down from heaven. The stone still exists, and is regarded as sacred, though it is not now worshipped. A Mohammedan Mosque surrounds the Kaaba (*see* Frontispiece), and every year the Faithful from all parts of the world go on pilgrimage to see it, and to touch it. It is now reddish-brown, some say even black, because, according to the Mohammedans, it has wept so much for the sins of the world. The real reason for the change of colour, of course, is because it has been handled and kissed by tens of thousands, yea, millions, of devotees during hundreds of years. Abu Talib, Mohammed's uncle, was guardian of this sacred stone, and took an important part in the temple worship. Thus Mohammed was well acquainted with the religion of his own land. And in addition, through his travels in Syria and Palestine, he had become acquainted, though imperfectly, with the Jewish and the Christian religions. For some years Mohammed had been dissatisfied with the religion of his fathers, with its idolatries, and gradually the hope and ambition had taken possession of his soul that he might be able to lead his people on a path of reform, and make them better citizens of this world, and give them a brighter hope with regard to the next.

The more Mohammed thought about this possibility the more he withdrew himself from the cares of business life, and at length he retired for a time altogether from public view, and made his home in a cave on the side of a mountain called Hera, to the north of Mecca. There he gave himself up to fasting, meditation, and prayer, accompanied by his faithful wife Kadija, who sometimes was in great fear for the life of her husband, as his intense meditation brought on ecstasies and trances, in which he would lose all consciousness, and lie upon the ground as one dead.

Thus for weary months, even for years, the strife went on in the mind of Mohammed, and the life of the husband and wife was passed now in their home at Mecca, and now in the cave at Hera.   But all things, pleasant or painful, have an end, and in the year 610 of our era, and in the fortieth year of the life of Mohammed, the strain on his mind was relaxed, for he had, according to his own telling, a revelation from Heaven, which assured him that there was but one God, Almighty, All-merciful, who claimed the adoration of all hearts.

This revelation was given one night while Mohammed was sleeping on the hills along which he had been wandering and meditating all the day.   At midnight a voice came from the sky, calling "Mohammed, I am Gabriel!"   Then an angel held before the astonished eyes of the dreaming man a broad piece of silk covered with written characters addressed to Mohammed, exhorting him to preach a new gospel to his countrymen.   The command ran—

> " Cry ! in the name of Allah !
>   In the name of Allah who hath created man !
>   O arise and preach
>   And magnify Allah ! "

And Mohammed accepted the mission.

From that time Mohammed declared himself to be the Prophet of God, and his one cry to his countrymen was that they would give up idolatry and worship Allah.   Think of what this new departure meant !   Mohammed against a nation !   He who, perhaps, could not write his name was deliberately setting himself up as a teacher on the weightiest matters concerning the life of man ; and he who had no clan or followers to support him was opposing himself to tens of thousands who were men of war, and who were devotedly attached to the religion of their forefathers. There were 365 idols in Mecca, in addition to the sacred stone ; and a large revenue was realized by the people of the city through the tax which was imposed on the strangers who came up each year to worship in the Temple or Kaaba.

Thus vested interests, as well as tradition, were against Mohammed ; and as we think of his fixed determination to preach to his countrymen of Allah, and Allah alone, we are struck with the sublime faith of this Arabian Prophet, who, strong in his belief, could boldly face contumely and scorn and anger and hate in his endeavour to turn his countrymen away from idolatry to the worship of God.

And what success had this brave enthusiast ? At first, and for a long time, scarcely any at all. His wife was his first convert. It is touching to think of the wifely devotion of this noble woman. In good report and ill report she clung to the man she loved. Others might call him dreamer and madman ; but she knew him to be sensible and kind, and she believed in him—believed in him with a faith that nothing could shake—and she encouraged him to hold fast to his new views, and preach them boldly to all who would listen. And as further and fuller revelations were given to her husband by the Angel Gabriel, this good wife began to practise the rites and ceremonies of prayer, fasting, and almsgiving, which afterwards became the peculiar characteristics of Islamism, or, as Western people generally call it, of Mohammedanism. In a future chapter the Koran or Mohammedan Scriptures and the religious teaching of the Prophet will be dealt with. It must suffice at present to say that the new religion of Mohammed, the one he wanted his countrymen to accept, may be summed up, as the historian Gibbon put it—Faith in Allah, and then the hope that " prayer " would carry the true believer half-way to God, that "fasting" would bring him to the door of His palace, and that " alms " would gain him admittance. For some time the Prophet's wife was his only follower. Then his nephew, Ali, a son of Abu Talib, cast in his lot with him. Then Zeyd, who had once been a slave, and whom Mohammed had freed, and adopted as a son, became a member of the new religious community. Then Abd-el-Kaba, a prominent citizen, a man of zeal and enthusiasm, went over to the Prophet ; and thus the little company grew, but oh, so slowly, that it seemed as if the new faith would never become a living and mighty power.

For nine years the Prophet preached, but the people only smiled or mocked. And then, to add to Mohammed's distress, his wife, the faithful Kadija, died. That was in the year A.D. 619. It was a terrible blow to the Prophet, for in losing his wife he not only lost one dearly loved, but his wealth also. Her property went into other hands. To do Mohammed justice, however, it should be recorded that he thought little of the lost money—he was never at any period of his history an avaricious man—but he thought much of his lost wife, and mourned for her at the time as one who could not be comforted. There is a proverb that says, "Troubles seldom come singly." It was so with Mohammed. His wife was dead—his money was lost—and then his uncle died. It verily seemed as if Mohammed was not only forsaken of the gods, as his fellow-countrymen declared, but forsaken by Allah Himself. Dark, indeed, were those days, but the Prophet never lost his faith. At length, however, a glimmer of light was seen on the horizon of his life. The light came in the form of persecution. The people of Mecca passed from smiles and scorn of the new doctrines to persecution of its few followers. And persecution was all that the new faith needed to give it impetus. It is a fact all the world over that "the blood of the martyrs is the seed of the Church." As soon as the people of Mecca began to persecute Mohammed and his disciples, Islamism began to spread. Now, instead of converts going over singly, they went in companies, and ere long the Prophet had a devoted band of, say, three hundred souls. Persecution, however, raged so fierce that Mohammed urged his followers to "emigrate," and many of them went to Abyssinia to wait for brighter days. A few, however, would not be separated from the Prophet, and remained to sustain him as best they could.

And now a most extraordinary event occurred. How true it is that "a prophet is not without honour, save in his own country and among his own kindred." A little party of seven devout men from the city of Medina came up to Mecca to take part in the yearly worship of the sacred stone. To these men the Prophet spoke of Allah, and denounced idolatry. The words found a resting-place in the hearts of the pilgrims, and they returned to their own city full of news about a great prophet whom they had met, and who had urged them to worship God alone. The people of Medina generally were as much impressed by the new teaching as the seven citizens who had brought the tidings. Months passed by and gradually nearly all the inhabitants of the town except the Jews became converts to the faith of Mohammed, though they had never seen his face. At the end of a year the citizens met in solemn council, and decided to send seventy of their leading men to Mecca to see if the great Prophet could be persuaded to forsake the city of his fathers, and become the ruler and prophet of the city of Medina.

Few more extraordinary things than this have happened, I think, in the history of the human race. And Mohammed readily embraced the invitation, and in A.D. 622, in the month of June, there occurred what is known as " the flight from Mecca." The word was given by the Prophet to depart, and his followers cast the dust of their native city off their feet, and made their way, though not without difficulty and danger, to Medina. From that Hejira, or Flight, the Mohammedans count their era, just as Christian people count from the time of Christ. In Medina Mohammed was joined by his adherents, who had been in exile in Abyssinia, and at length Mohammedanism found a local habitation and a name. A new life opened out for the Prophet—a life of the highest earthly power and dignity— his word being law, and his influence greater than that of a king: for he was Prince and Prophet in one. He had only to exclaim " Thus saith Allah " to silence all opposition to his will with the people, who looked up to him with the greatest reverence and trust.

The fame of Mohammed now quickly spread in the land. The sword was brought into play, and the people of neighbouring towns who were not convinced by the Prophet's spiritual reasoning were soon brought to subjection by his temporal power. Thus city after city gave in allegiance to the new faith, and at length Mecca herself had to confess her weakness, and submit to the rule and the religion of him whom she had cast forth only a short time before with every sign of hate and scorn. What a reversal of fortunes! And what seems to me the most wonderful feature of the remarkable event is that these changes became binding and lasting. Mohammed lived to see the terror of his arms carried to far distant lands, and his creed firmly established over wide regions of country and over millions of people. Truth verily is stranger than fiction!

The latter years of this extraordinary man were not as noble as the earlier. He fell into polygamous ways; and also became a persecutor in his turn. His wives and concubines numbered, some say, eighteen; and he in various other ways showed that prosperity had spoiled him. He became fierce and cruel and bloodthirsty—a man to be feared rather than loved. And yet many loved him even unto the end. He lived to the age of sixty-two, and died, it is said, in great agony, with his head on the lap of his young and favourite wife, Ayesha. His last words were, "O Allah, succour me in the agonies of death! Gabriel come close to thy servant! O Allah, grant pardon—yes, pardon—and eternity in Paradise!"

Thus died one of the most wonderful men the world has ever seen. From obscurity and poverty, he rose to be Prophet, Priest, and King, and founded a religious faith which endures to this day, and which has 210 millions of adherents.

CHAPTER II

THE word Koran is derived from the Arabic verb "*karaa*," to read, and thus signifies "the reading," or more properly, "that which ought to be read." It is the chief name by which the followers of Mohammed describe their Scriptures. Other names are used, such as *Al Forkan* the Division, *Al Majeed* the Exalted, *Al Azeez* the Mighty, and *Al Kitab* the Book. I shall keep, however, to the term Al Koran, as the one in general use in the East, and the only one well known in the West.

Al Koran, or "the reading," is held by the Mohammedans to be a sacred book, and they affirm that it was revealed to Mohammed portion by portion by the Angel Gabriel. The orthodox belief is that God Himself composed the book, that it was kept from all eternity near the throne of God on a vast table called "the preserved table," and that it was revealed in the fulness of time to Mohammed for the salvation of all believers. The truth, of course, is that the Koran was the work of Mohammed himself, that he derived his material partly from the Jews, partly from the Christians, partly from the Arabs, and partly from his own thoughts, aspirations, and convictions. It is essentially a very human work. Yet I would not deny to Mohammed a certain Divine inspiration, for I believe that all truth, wherever it is found,—and there is much truth in the Koran,—comes from God. It is very probable that the Prophet thought out his revelations privately, and then dictated them to one or two of his intimate friends.   Some say that a Jew and a Christian from the first aided Mohammed with material. It may be so, but I think on all hands it will be acknowledged that the composition of the Koran is entirely the Prophet's own work.   The language is choice, at times eloquent, and always powerful.

The Koran is not a series of books like the Christian Scriptures, but is one book, with a series of divisions of unequal length, which are called Suras, *i.e.*, portions or chapters.   There are 114 in all, some very short and some very long.

The Mohammedans make a great point of numbering the words and even the letters of their Suras.   The Koran contains 77,639 words, and 323,015 letters.   If we compare these figures with our Bible, which has 773,746 words and 3,566,480 letters, we see that the Mohammedan Scriptures are in bulk about one-tenth the size of the Christian.   It is interesting to notice that every Sura of the Koran has a title.   The first is headed "The Preface," the second "The Cow," the fourth "Women," the sixth "Cattle," the fourteenth "Abraham," the sixteenth "The Bee."   Other titles are "The Poets," "The Spider," "The Cave," "The Night Journey," "The Hypocrites," "The Slanderer," "The Elephant," "The Pen," "Man," "Smoke," "The Daybreak," and so on.   Every Sura also, save one, the ninth, commences with the words, "In the name of the Most Merciful God."   Mohammed evidently wished to impress most deeply on the minds of his disciples the Divine origin of the Koran.   From the beginning to the end of this remarkable book everything is declared to be in the name of the Most High.

As it exists to-day, it is believed to be due to the pious zeal of Abu Bekr, Mohammed's immediate successor. When the Prophet died the sacred writings were not in book form, but were scattered about in fragments, some with one person and some with another; some written on palm leaves, some on scraps of parchment, some on shoulder-blades of mutton, and some on stones and other materials. The work of Abu Bekr was to gather these fragments together and make one book of them, and in doing so he arranged them very much at haphazard, so that there is little or no connection between the subject-matter of one Sura and that of another. Probably Mohammed himself had no intention of arranging for any continuity of thought in his revelations. He wrote both at Mecca and at Medina, as circumstances seemed to call for a revelation, either to make known an attribute of God, or to announce some judgment on his enemies, or to settle some dispute amongst his adherents, or to encourage and strengthen the Faithful. Thus we find in the Koran a strange medley of things temporal and things spiritual; of things high and things low; of things wise and things foolish; of things good and things evil; and yet withal the book has a decided aim, and has given to the world a new religion.

As might be expected, all Mohammedans hold the Koran in the deepest, the profoundest reverence. "They never touch it without previous purification; they never, if they can help it, allow it to pass into the hands of an infidel; they never hold it below their girdles; they swear by it; they take it with them to the wars, and consult it for omens on all important occasions; and when they can, they have it splendidly bound and adorned with gold and precious stones."

As regards *matters of faith*, the Mohammedan is called upon in the Koran to believe in God, in angels, in the Scriptures, in prophets, in a future life, and in predestination to good and evil.

1. Belief in God stands at the head of this list. In the second Sura it is written—"God, there is no God but He, the living, the self-subsistent. Slumber takes Him not nor sleep. His is what is in the heavens, and what is in the earth. Who is it that intercedes with Him save by His permission? He knows what is before them, and what behind them, and they comprehend not aught of His

knowledge but what He pleases. His throne extends over the heavens and the earth, and it tires Him not to guard them both, for He is high and grand."

Mohammedans say that the Koran gives God ninety-nine names, such as God the Great, the Powerful, the Eternal, the Wise, the True, the Bountiful, the Merciful, the Gracious, and the Judge of all.

2. To belief in God the Koran adds belief in angels and in genii. These are said to have been created of fire, and some are represented as good spirits and some as bad spirits.

3. Belief in the Scriptures is another article of faith. Here I would quote the words of Sale. He writes : "The Mohammedans are taught by the Koran that God in divers ages of the world gave revelations of His will in writing to several prophets, and every word of which it is absolutely necessary for a good Moslem to believe. The number of these sacred books is 104, of which ten were given to Adam, fifty to Seth, thirty to Enoch, ten to Abraham, the other four being the Pentateuch, the Psalms, the Gospels, and the Koran, which were successively delivered to Moses, David, Jesus, and Mohammed. All these divine books, except the last four, are entirely lost, and their contents unknown. And these three, the Pentateuch, the Psalms, and the Gospels, have undergone so many alterations and corruptions that though there may possibly be some part of the true Word of God therein, yet no credit is to be given to the present copies in the hands of the Jews and Christians." Thus practically the Koran limits the faith of Believers to the writings of Mohammed.

4. Similarly, while another article of the creed is " Belief in Prophets," such as Adam, Noah, Abraham, Moses, Jesus, and Mohammed, it is declared that the last is the highest and most illustrious of all. As Mohammedans put it, holding up one finger to emphasize the statement, "There is no God but God, and Mohammed is the Prophet of God."

5. With reference to belief in a future life, the Koran teaches that there will be a Resurrection, a Judgment Day, a Paradise for the good, and a Hell for the wicked.

In the twenty-second Sura it is written, "Many are worthy of chastisement. They who believe not shall have garments of fire fitted unto them, boiling water shall be poured on their heads, their intestines shall be dissolved thereby, and also their skins; and they shall be beaten with maces of iron. So often as they shall endeavour to get out of Hell because of the anguish of their torments, they shall be dragged back into the same, and their tormentors shall say unto them, 'Taste ye the pain of burning.'"

In contrast with the woes of Hell, let us place the joys of Heaven. The Koran says, "Paradise is promised to the pious, and therein are rivers of incorruptible water, and rivers of milk, the taste whereof changeth not, and rivers of wine pleasant unto those who drink, and rivers of clarified honey, and therein shall they have plenty of all kinds of fruits, and pardon from their Lord. Moreover they shall receive beauteous damsels as wives, having fine black eyes, and complexions like rubies and pearls. The reward of good shall be good."

6. Predestination is a prominent article of the Mohammedan creed. The Koran teaches that life and death are in the hands of God, and that nothing happens either good or bad but as God wills, and that consequently men should not immoderately grieve for the happiness which escapes them on earth, or immoderately be glad in the joy that comes to them.

Mohammed found this doctrine of predestination a great help in inciting his warriors to fight for the faith he had delivered to them, for if they were victorious they were assured they would be rewarded in this world, and if they were defeated and slain they would be rewarded in the next world. Thus did the Prophet fill the hearts of his followers with great hopes, and with a passionate fanaticism that knew neither danger nor fear.

Passing from matters of faith, let us glance at *matters of law*.

The Koran gives to Mohammedans not only a system of theology, but a system of jurisprudence. Church and State are regarded as one and indivisible. According to the Arab proverb, " Religion and country are twins."

1. Certain laws are laid down with regard to inheritance. These are, generally speaking, much more favourable to men than to women ; but otherwise they seem good and just.

2. In dealing with meats and drinks, the Koran forbids the use of the flesh of swine as food, and prohibits the drinking of wine and all other intoxicating liquors ; for according to Mohammed the evil properties of the latter exceed the good properties.

3. Games of chance are also denounced ; chess, however, being permitted, as it requires skill.

4. Faithfulness is enjoined in the performance of business contracts. A rigid adherence to truth is demanded when in a court of justice ; but nothing is said in the Koran about truthfulness in general.

5. Usury and debt are deprecated, and a true believer is urged to show mercy to those who owe him anything, and find it hard or impossible to pay.

6. In cases of theft the law is stern and even cruel. In the fifth Sura it is written : "If a man or woman steal, cut off their hands in retribution for that which they have committed. This is an exemplary punishment appointed by God, and God is mighty and wise."

7. As regards punishment for personal assault, the law runs : " We have commanded them that they should give eye for eye, nose for nose, ear for ear, and tooth for tooth, and that wounds should also be punished by retaliation."

8. Manslaughter is met with a heavy penalty, and the law for murder is as follows :—" Whoso killeth a believer

designedly his reward shall be hell : he shall remain there
for ever, and God shall be angry with him and curse
him."

9. The laws with regard to marriage and divorce I place
last because they are the worst. A Mohammedan may, if
he likes, have four wives, and he can divorce any or all of
them for the most trifling offence. The Koran has little
that is good to say of woman. Sad in consequence is the
condition of womankind in Mohammedan countries, as
will be made plain in a later chapter.

There are also *matters of religious practice*, for a good
Mussulman is expected to demonstrate his religion by
certain outward and visible signs, such as prayer, almsgiving, fasting, and pilgrimages.

1. The Koran is very emphatic as to the duty of praying
to God five times a day. Prayer is called " the Pillar of
Religion and the Key of Paradise." In another Sura I
find these words, "There can be no good in any religion
wherein is no prayer." And again it is written, " Pray, and
pray with patience."

Then certain definite rules and regulations are given with
regard to times of prayer, ablutions before prayer, and
attitudes during prayer.

2. In almsgiving liberality is enjoined. The faithful
must never forget the needy, but must succour those who
are in want. In the second Sura these words occur, " If ye
make your alms to appear it is well, but if ye conceal them
and give them to the poor, this will be better for you, and
will atone for your sins."

3. Fasting Mohammed called "a fourth part of faith,"
and said of it that it was "the gate of Religion," and that
"the odour of the mouth of him who fasteth is more grateful to God than that of musk."

Certain seasons of the year are set apart for fasting, the
chief of which is the month Ramadan, the ninth month of
the Mohammedan year. During the whole of this month,
from sunrise to sunset, a complete fast is enjoined from

meats and drinks. When the sun goes down, however, the Faithful are allowed to partake of whatever they choose.

4. Pilgrimages are incumbent upon every Mohammedan who can afford the expense, or who is not otherwise incapacitated. One pilgrimage, at least, ought to be made to the sacred city of Mecca, the birthplace of the Prophet, and the possessor of "the stone which came down from heaven." The person who makes this Haj, or pilgrimage, is held in great honour, and is thenceforward called by the title of Hajji.

Having now summarized the teaching of the Koran with respect to matters of faith, law, and religious practice, I would conclude this chapter by a few general remarks.

The Koran does not contain from beginning to end an account of a single miracle performed by Mohammed. The miracles mentioned, and they are few, are taken chiefly from Jewish or Christian sources. When spoken to about miracles, the Prophet invariably answered that Allah had granted him no power to work them.

The Koran contains much with which we are familiar through reading our own Scriptures. The lives of some of the Patriarchs and Prophets are given, though the stories associated with them are altered in some particulars, and are not improved by the alterations. We scarcely recognize Abraham, Joseph, or Moses when we read their lives as told by Mohammed.

Our Lord Jesus Christ is spoken of in the Koran as truly human, and the Christian belief in his Divinity is forcibly denounced as idolatry.

The Koran indulges in fierce language against unbelievers or infidels, and advocates the power of the sword for their conversion. The Faithful are exhorted to fight against their enemies, and to kill them wherever they find them.

The Koran is not without its beautiful truths beautifully expressed. He who searches for good in its pages will find good. Take the following short sentences as illustrations of the very best that the Koran can give us :—

"Trust in God, for God loveth those who trust in Him."

"God loveth the beneficent."

"Fear God, and know that ye must meet Him."

"Be ye perfect in knowledge and works."

"Behave yourselves patiently in adversity."

"Paradise is for those who bridle their anger."

"Persevere out of a sincere heart to please the Lord."

"Whoso resigneth himself unto God, being a worker of righteousness, taketh hold on a strong handle."

"Oh, true believers, when ye discourse privately together, discourse not of wickedness and enmity and disobedience towards the Apostle, but discourse of justice and piety, and fear God, before whom ye shall one day be assembled."

"Whoso is preserved from the covetousness of his own soul, he shall prosper."

"Oppress not the orphan, neither repulse the beggar, but declare the goodness of the Lord."

"Woe unto every slanderer and backbiter."

"Woe unto those who are negligent at prayer, and play the hypocrite."

"Do good, for God loveth those that do good."

"Be patient, and try to excel in patience, and be constant-minded and fear God, that ye may be happy."

Notwithstanding the foregoing true and beautiful sayings, however, the Koran, taken as a whole, repels, for there is a cold, stern, hard spirit about it.

The Bible, compared with the Koran, is as light to darkness; and one decided outcome of my study of the Mohammedan Scriptures is to increase my love and reverence for the Christian Scriptures, which are incomparably more beautiful and instructive, and more precious both in what they tell us of the life that now is and of that which is to come.

C 2

CHAPTER III

MOSQUES

THE term mosque is derived through the Italian "moschea," from the Arabic "masjid," which signifies "a place of prayer."

The first mosque was erected at Medina during the lifetime of Mohammed, and that building has been the model for all mosques in every part of the Mohammedan world since. The site for the first mosque was chosen in a somewhat remarkable way. It was on the occasion of the Prophet's public entrance into the city as its ruler in both temporal and spiritual things.

On a certain Friday in the month of July, A.D. 622, Mohammed, with his nephew, Ali, and his son-in-law, Abu Bekr, and a host of followers on horseback and foot, appeared at the gates of Medina. The Prophet had come from Mecca, which would have none of his teaching, and where the people had sought to take his life. The gates of Medina were at once opened to receive the illustrious visitor, and from tens of thousands of the inhabitants there went forth a glad shout of welcome.

And as Mohammed passed through the streets on his favourite camel, from one and another came the cry, " Alight here, O Prophet ! here is abundance ! here is room ! here is protection ! " Every one was anxious to have the honour of receiving under his roof the Prophet of God. But the far-seeing man declined each invitation, saying courteously, "Let the camel go free ; she will show the place at which Allah wills that I shall alight."

Slowly the procession moved on, until at length, in the eastern part of the city, the camel halted, and sat down in a large courtyard containing a number of date-trees. "This is the spot," shouted Mohammed. "Here I alight! Here I dwell! And here shall a house be built where prayer may be offered to Allah!"

And so it was. Refusing to accept the ground as a gift, the Prophet paid the full value for it, and then, with the aid of his friends, he set about erecting a mosque, which he called Al Haram, or "the Sacred."

Trees were cut down, walls of earth and brick were built, the trunks of the trees were used to support a roof which was framed of their branches and thatched with their leaves. The mosque thus erected was very primitive in structure, but it was commodious, and answered the purpose for which Mohammed designed it.

There he gathered his followers together by thousands; there he instructed them in the new religion; there he led them in their devotions to God, and taught them what to say and what to do in the services of their House of Prayer.

Subsequent mosques, I have said, were imitations of the sacred building at Medina. Yet in time, though the original shape was almost invariably kept, there were improvements added, particularly in the way of minarets, or towers.

At the present day, wherever you go, you can distinguish at a glance a Mohammedan mosque from a heathen temple or a Christian church, by its square shape, its central dome, and its two or more minarets, which give it a picturesque and pleasing appearance.

Of course, mosques differ very greatly in size and in material, according to the population and the wealth of the people. I have seen in India mosques that would not hold a hundred people, and which were made of common bricks and mud, with whitewashed walls; and I have seen in the same country, and also in Egypt and Syria, buildings that would hold 15,000 people, and which were made of beautiful marble, some of them interlaid with precious stones.

Let us approach a mosque with thoughts of entering it. It is only of very recent years that Christians have been allowed to step over the threshold of Mohammedan places of worship. And even now, as a rule, our presence is regarded as an intrusion, and evil glances are directed towards us.

I was made somewhat unpleasantly aware of this in the great Mosque of Mohammed Ali at Cairo, where an official followed me about wherever I went, and seemed to be watching keenly for me to do something that would justify him in showing me the door.

Again in the Great Mosque at Damascus it was my lot to enter the building with others while the Mohammedans were at prayer. I stood at one side to watch them in their devotions, but my presence was felt to be a constraint, and I was warned by the angry glances cast at me by the worshippers that it would be well to withdraw, which I accordingly did.

Mohammedan fanaticism is a passion which it is unsafe to arouse. Whatever mosque a Christian may enter, he should, as a matter of prudence as well as of good taste and feeling, walk therein with circumspection, and be constantly on his guard against hurting the *amour-propre* of those to whom the building belongs, who are extremely sensitive to feel and quick to resent what they consider to be a slight or disrespect or insult.

As you approach a mosque you will notice that the building is surrounded probably by a high stone wall. The entrance-gate is always on the latch, and there are no locks, bars, or bolts. A mosque is meant for the worship of God, and it would be regarded by the Mohammedans as a very sad thing indeed if one of the Faithful, rich or poor, were unable, night or day, to obtain admittance.

Passing through the gateway, the visitor finds himself as

a rule in a large courtyard, in the centre of which is a tank or reservoir, and at the extreme end of which stands the House of Prayer.

Very often in warm climates the courtyard is used for worship, the people not entering the mosque at all. In India this is quite common. It seems to be considered sufficient that the mosque is there, and the courtyard is supposed to partake of the sanctity of the sacred building. Custom in this matter varies, and I have watched Mohammedans at their devotions both inside and outside their places of worship.

After walking round the courtyard, which contains nothing but the tank already mentioned, we enter the mosque. In many places a fee has to be paid for this privilege, and in all places it is incumbent upon the visitor to take off his shoes or boots, or draw over them certain large felt slippers which are kept for the purpose. As a rule the boots or shoes have to be taken off.

You will notice at once on entering that the House of Prayer is kept scrupulously clean and neat. Seats are conspicuous by their absence. A Mohammedan would not know how to use them, and they would be in the way in his form of worship. The floor is of stone or of marble, usually bare, though sometimes covered with matting.

We look at the walls, and find that they are perfectly bare, beyond perhaps a sentence or two from the Koran, for not even the slightest ornament is allowed on them. There is a pulpit, a plain wooden one, and a desk on which rests a copy of the Scriptures ; and these are absolutely the only articles of furniture that the majority of mosques contain.

What about windows ? Generally speaking there are none. Most mosques are lighted by a great doorway, which reaches almost to the roof. In many cases the front of the mosque is entirely open to the light, but in a few cases, as in the Mosque of Omar, at Jerusalem, there are windows.

That magnificent and famous mosque contains fifty-six stained glass windows of great brilliancy and beauty; but, all the same, the interior is so gloomy and dark that care has to be exercised in moving about therein.

But the Mosque of Omar is not used for worship, as the greater part of the building is filled up with an immense rock, which is said to be the very rock on which Abraham sought to offer up his son Isaac as a sacrifice. At Jerusalem the Faithful offer their prayers in the courtyard; and there also the great pulpit is placed, from which, on special occasions, sermons are preached.

Another point should be specially noticed in the interior of a Mohammedan mosque. The wall of the building facing the entrance will be seen to have a niche in it. That niche is an indication that in that direction lies Mecca, the sacred city of the Mohammedans. All worshippers when engaged in their devotions must turn their faces towards Mecca; and the niche in the wall is an indication to them of the right direction, and a constant reminder also of their religious duty.

There was a time, in the early days of Mohammed's teaching, when he exhorted his disciples to follow the example of the Jews, and turn their faces towards Jerusalem. But the Jews offended the Prophet, and he decided no longer to conform to their custom, but to institute for Mohammedans a new "kiblah" or place towards which to look when praying; and the new kiblah was, of course, Mecca.

To give the new practice special importance, and to make the matter binding on his followers, Mohammed declared that the Angel Gabriel had appeared to him in a vision of the night, and given him special instructions.

These instructions are embodied in the Koran, and are, I find, as follows:—

"The foolish man will say, What hath turned them from their kiblah towards which they formerly prayed? Say: Unto God belongeth the East and the West; He directeth whom He pleaseth in the right way. Thus have we placed you, O Arabians, an intermediate nation, that ye may be witnesses against the rest of mankind. . . . Every sect hath a certain tract of heaven to which they turn themselves in prayer. . . . We have seen thee turn about thy face towards heaven with uncertainty, but we will cause thee to turn thyself towards a kiblah that will please thee. Turn thou thy face towards the holy temple of Mecca ; wherever ye be, turn your faces towards that place."

When the above revelation had been made known to Mohammed, he called his followers together into the mosque at Medina, and in the midst of public worship acquainted them with the instructions of Gabriel ; and then asking them to look at him, the Prophet with great solemnity prostrated his body twice towards Jerusalem, and then, turning deliberately round, he faced Mecca, and said, "Jerusalem is behind us ; Mecca is in front of us. Mecca is henceforth our kiblah !" And from that day till this Mohammedans in their devotions have turned their faces towards Mecca.

Almost any day when you enter a mosque you will find a few worshippers therein ; but, like Christians and like Jews, Mohammedans have one special day in the week set apart for public worship. The Prophet in the Koran calls it "The Day of the Assembly."

In order probably to be different from others, Mohammed fixed upon Friday. Some say, however, that Friday was chosen because on that day God finished the work of creation. Still, others say that the choice of the day was decided by the remembrance of the fact that it was on a Friday that Mohammed publicly entered Medina, and decided to build the first mosque. Whatever the reason for it, it remains true that throughout the Mohammedan world Friday is the day which is set apart as the " Day of the Assembly."

This sacred day is not very strictly kept, however. It is not allowed to interfere very much with business pursuits.

As a rule, Mohammedans on their Sunday make a point of bathing and changing their apparel. They also consider it a meritorious thing to be more liberal in almsgiving on Sunday. They usually, moreover, spend a little more time over their prayers.

It is not absolutely incumbent upon Mohammedans to visit the mosque on Friday or on any other day, but they are exhorted so to do by their spiritual guides, who instance the example of Mohammed himself, and a good Mohammedan usually complies with such request, and conforms to the generally recognized custom.

Let us now make our way to a mosque on a Friday, and see of what character the worship is.

The call to prayers on Friday, as on other days, is by the human voice. An official called a Muezzin ascends one of the tall minarets of a mosque, and calls out in a loud, clear, distinct voice an invitation to the Faithful to worship God either in their homes or in the mosque, or wherever they may be at the moment.

There are five times in the day for prayer. "Glorify God," says the Koran, "when the evening overtaketh you, and when you rise in the morning, at sunset, after sunset, and when you rest at noon."

I remember well one day resting at noon on the banks of the Sea of Galilee, near the town of Tiberias. As I rested I heard the sound of a convent bell, which was sweet and pleasant. And it was immediately followed by a very different sound—viz., the call of a human voice from the minaret of a mosque which was close at hand.

And I preferred the Mohammedan voice to the Christian bell. Many a time had I heard a similar call in India, but never before had its impressiveness particularly arrested my attention. As the clear, sonorous notes fell upon my ear I listened with interest and delight.

And this was what the Muezzin was saying, "God is great! God is great! God is great! I bear witness there is no God but God! I bear witness that Mohammed is the Apostle of God! Come to prayers! Come to salvation! God is great! Prayers are better than sleep!"

It is a grand sight to witness, say, ten thousand Mohammedans assembled for worship in a mosque, and this I was privileged to see once in the Great Mosque at Delhi, in Northern India. I stood at the entrance to the courtyard, and watched the worshippers go in.

The first thing a Mohammedan does is to take off his shoes as a sign of respect, just as Christians take off their hats. The shoes are carried in the left hand, sole to sole. The worshipper also is very careful to put the right foot first over the threshold as he enters. Then he makes his way to the tank in the centre of the courtyard, and performs the necessary ablutions.

The Koran says, "O true believers, when ye prepare yourselves to pray, rub your heads and hands unto the elbows, and your feet up to the ankles." Where water cannot be got, sand may be used as a substitute ; and failing sand, fine dust. On no account must these ablutions be omitted, as, according to Mohammed, " The practice of religion is founded on cleanliness, which is one-half of the faith and the key of prayer."

After ablutions, the worshippers all meet together and arrange themselves in rows, standing, of course, and with their faces turned towards Mecca. A religious official, called an Imam, then leads the assembly in their prayers.

It will be noticed by the attentive onlooker that all the worshippers are plainly attired. It is altogether against the creed of the Mohammedans for any to address themselves to God in sumptuous apparel. The rich, when they enter a mosque, lay aside their costly habits and ornaments, lest they should seem proud and arrogant.

Verily amongst the Mohammedans the rich and the poor meet together in public worship, and it would be difficult to distinguish the one from the other. In prayer all are held to be equal, and no places are reserved for any.

There is a great deal of formality in a Mohammedan

service.   Look at those worshippers as they stand in rows in their hundreds and thousands.   At a given signal they hold themselves very erect, with hands lifted up, the palms being held out towards heaven ; while the eyes are supposed to be turned with expressions of adoration and praise to God.

For a few moments that attitude lasts ; then at another signal the worshippers prostrate themselves to the very ground in willing subjection to the power of the Almighty. Their foreheads must touch the floor.   Then at another signal the whole assembly assumes once more the erect posture.

These genuflections are gone slowly through, at least three times, often five times ; and always with the greatest reverence and solemnity.   Usually a signal is also given to sit or to kneel ; and then certain prayers are recited, some-times aloud, sometimes with a mere movement of the lips.

I find that it is not much that Mohammedans say during prayers.   Most of the time is taken up with genuflections, which may or may not have a meaning for those who indulge in them.

One explanation of these movements is, that man, as head of the creation, should praise the Creator on behalf of all—standing like a tree, stooping like quadrupeds, prostrate like reptiles, and sitting like mountains and hills.

The words of prayer are usually such as these, taken from the Koran : "God is great," "God is merciful," "I fly for refuge unto the Lord of men, the King of men, the God of men, that He may deliver me from the mischief of the whisperer who whispereth evil suggestions into the breasts of men," "This present life is no other than a toy and a plaything ; but the future mansions of Paradise are life indeed," "God is He who seeth and heareth," "God is great ; God is good !"

Then, very often prayers end with an ascription of praise to God, which is held in great reverence by Mohammedans ; and corresponds somewhat to our " Lord's Prayer."   It is very beautiful, and is as follows :—

"Praise be to God, the Lord of all creatures, the Most Merciful, the King of the Day of Judgment. Thee do we worship, and of Thee do we beg assistance. Direct us in the right way, in the way of those to whom Thou hast been gracious, not of those against whom Thou art incensed, nor of those who go astray."

When prayers are over, sometimes on a Friday in a Mohammedan mosque, a sermon will be preached. If so, some passage of the Koran is taken and expounded, and applied to the needs of the people.

Moreover, the Christian doctrine of the Trinity is a fruitful topic for discourse, the preacher often waxing eloquent over the idolatry of the followers of Christ. A favourite text is: "They say, God hath begotten children: God forbid!"

Preaching is not greatly practised in mosques. Mohammedan worship is chiefly prayer, and it is apt to degenerate into attention to the mere forms and ceremonies.

I have endeavoured to be strictly impartial and fair in my description of mosques or Mohammedan places of worship. There is something attractive about them. Their simplicity is charming. Whenever I have been in them I have felt that they were truly houses of prayer.

But taking them altogether in connection with their worship, I think that no Christian would hesitate a moment in saying that Christian churches, with their singing of hymns, their reading of God's Word, their prayers, and their sermons, are infinitely to be preferred to Mohammedan mosques.

CHAPTER IV

WOMEN

"WOMEN" is the title of the fourth Sura of the Koran, and therein is to be found a great deal of information as to the position which females occupy in the Mohammedan world.

The opening words of the chapter are : "O men, fear your Lord, who hath created you out of one man, and out of him created his wife, and from these twain hath multiplied many men and women ; and fear God, by whom ye beseech one another ; and respect women, who have borne you, for God is watching over you." "Respect women !" is the best of counsel to give to men. Happy the people who listen to it ; and blessed the country where such a precept is put into practice ! The interpretation of such a word as "respect" differs, however, in different lands. I am afraid amongst Mohammedans that the term does not mean very much ; at any rate, it does not keep them from treating their women as an inferior creation to men, and of exercising over them a despotic power. Mohammedan women labour under many disabilities and hardships of which Christian women, happily, have little or no experience.

It is a significant fact that in Mohammedan countries the birth of a girl is counted a matter of sorrow, while the birth of a boy is a matter for unbounded thankfulness and joy. "Few girls and many boys" is the universal motto, for more honour is said to be attached to a house where there are many sons. So woman, at the outset, is at a discount. There is no discharge of artillery or musketry when a little girl is born, as is the case when a boy is born. On the fourth day after the daughter's birth there is no gathering of friends to rejoice with the parents, as in the case of a son. And when the little girl's birthday comes round each year, there is no party to commemorate the day, as is the case with a boy. No! a girl is a girl—a source of anxiety, care, and sorrow—and parents and friends alike treat her appearance on the scene as an occasion, at the very least, for regret. This, surely, is a bad beginning in the carrying out of the Prophet's aphorism, " Respect women."

Nor does the passing of time improve matters. In the household economy the girl is taken little notice of, while the boy is ever to the front. If the parents decide to educate their children at all, it is their son that is put to school, while their daughter's education is almost entirely neglected. It is a startling fact that out of 9,000,000 Mohammedan females in the Bengal Presidency, only 9,000 can read and write. The want of education in general amongst Mohammedans is a crying evil, but that women in particular should be so sadly neglected is a shame and a disgrace.

Another wrong also under which women suffer in Mohammedan countries is that of early marriage. It is true that in Eastern lands girls become women sooner than in Western lands; but, all the same, the age of ten or even under is altogether too early to commence the duties, responsibilities, and trials of married life. In this matter Mohammed himself set a very bad example. His third wife, whose name was Ayesha, was a mere child of seven years when the Prophet espoused her, and she was only nine when he married her, and took her away from her father's house. It is said that the little girl had her playthings in her hands when the Prophet called for her; and doubtless she carried them with her to her new home. Mohammedans, when expostulated with about early marriages, have the example of their Prophet to point to. Yet I think some of the more thoughtful amongst them regret the general custom, because it is injurious to the manhood and womanhood of the community. It should be borne in mind also in connection with Mohammedan early marriages, that the young people have no choice in the matter, but do what is arranged for them by their parents.

As with Christians, so with Mohammedans, there are certain marriages which are forbidden, owing chiefly to close relationship. The law runs : " Marry not women whom your fathers have had to wife, for this is an evil thing. Ye are forbidden to marry your mothers, and your daughters, and your sisters, and your aunts both on the father's and mother's side ; and your brother's daughters, and your sister's daughters, and your foster-mothers, and your foster-sisters, and your wives' mothers, and your daughters-in-law ; and ye are also forbidden to take to wife two sisters ; for God is gracious and merciful."

The Mohammedan law is, unfortunately, generous as to the number of wives a true believer may possess. This is another wrong under which Mohammedan women suffer. The words of the Koran are : " Take in marriage of such women as please you, two, or three, or four, and not more. But if ye fear that ye cannot act equitably towards so many, marry one only, or the slaves which ye shall have acquired. This will be easier, that ye swerve not from righteousness." I believe that many Mohammedans, constrained by poverty or right feeling, content themselves with one wife, but there are millions of men who take the Prophet at his word, and have two, or three, or four wives. And hence springs a fearful amount of discord and misery. The first wife of a Mohammedan is, as a rule, the only one who receives the honour of a public marriage display. The first wife is also always considered the head of the female establishment, and takes precedence in all matters where dignity is to be observed. Except amongst the poor, each wife has a separate room. When the several wives meet, all the rest pay to the first wife that deference which superiority exacts from inferiors.

The son of the first wife, if she be so fortunate as to have one, becomes the undisputed heir, and is allowed a little latitude in lording it over his brothers by other mothers. When these points are kept in mind, it is easy to see that a plurality of wives is not likely to add to the peace or comfort of a household. Yet polygamy has a firm hold on the Mohammedan world, and will have as long as the verbal inspiration of the Koran is maintained as an article of Mohammedan faith. The argument is that whatever the Koran permits cannot be wrong, or even unwise. Experience goes for nothing, for is it not written "Take in marriage of such women as please you, two, or three, or four."

For refractory wives Mohammed has arranged certain punishments. In the 4th sura of the Koran, at the 33rd verse, these words occur: "Men shall have pre-eminence above women, because of those advantages wherein God hath caused the one to excel the other, and for that which they expend of their substance in maintaining their wives. The honest women are obedient and careful in the absence of their husbands. But those whose perverseness ye shall be apprehensive of, rebuke, and remove them into separate apartments and chastise them." What power to put legally into the hands of a husband! The fault of the poor wife may have been trivial, and may have been provoked by the words or actions of another wife, and for that fault she is at the mercy of her husband. He can take her apart and chastise her, and though the chastisement may be altogether beyond her deserts, the suffering creature has no redress. In defence of his conduct the husband can point to the words of the Koran, and say, "The mouth of the Lord hath spoken it."

By the Mohammedan law a man is allowed a divorce from his wife for very slender reasons; but the wife, before she can obtain a divorce, has to establish the fact of absolute neglect or very serious cruelty.

If a wife be unfaithful, and it can be proved, death is the penalty. Failing proof, a man can obtain a divorce, if he be willing to swear four times that he believes his wife to have been unfaithful, and then be prepared to imprecate God's vengeance on his head should he be swearing falsely. This latitude in the matter of divorce is very greatly taken advantage of by some Mohammedans. Stobart, commenting on this subject in his book, "Islam, and its Founder," says: "Some Mohammedans make a habit of continually changing their wives. We read of young men who have had twenty and thirty wives, a new one every three months; and thus it comes about that women are liable to be indefinitely transferred from one man to another, obliged to accept a husband and a home wherever they can find one, or in case of destitution, to which divorce may have driven them, to resort to other more degrading means of living." Thus while keeping the strict letter of the law, and possessing only one or certainly not more than four wives, unscrupulous characters may yet by divorce obtain in a lifetime as many wives as they please.

In another way also a Mohammedan may really have more than four wives, and yet keep within the law. This is by means of living with concubines, which the Koran expressly permits. In that sura which allows four wives, the words are added, "or the slaves which ye shall have acquired." Then, in the 70th sura, it is revealed that it is no sin to live with slaves. The very words are: "The slaves which their right hands possess, as to them they shall be blameless." At the present day, as in days past, in multitudes of Mohammedan homes, slaves are found; and as Muir says, in his "Life of Mahomet," "so long as this unlimited permission of living with their female slaves continues, it cannot be expected that there will be any hearty attempt to put a stop to slavery in Mohammedan countries." Thus the Koran, in this matter of slavery, is the enemy of mankind. And women, as usual, are the greatest sufferers.

It is interesting to notice that Mohammed, who, as he said, was commissioned by God to limit the number of legal wives which True Believers might possess to four, himself had sixteen, if not eighteen. About two months after the death of Kadija, his first wife, the Prophet married a widow named Sawda, for whom, it is said, he had little affection. Soon after, he married Ayesha, the little girl already referred to. Ayesha became his favourite wife, and played an important part in the Prophet's life, and in the after-history of Mohammedanism. Haphsa, the daughter of Omar, a brave warrior, was the fourth wife of Mohammed. Om-Salma was the fifth; and the sixth was the divorced wife of his adopted son, Zeyd. Thus the Prophet added wife to wife until the number reached four times the limit he had himself fixed by command of God. Such inconsistency was, of course, noticed by his enemies, and made much of; and even his devoted followers were perplexed at the behaviour of the Prophet. Mohammed, however, was equal even to such an occasion, and got over the difficulty and trouble by a special revelation which permitted him privileges which others could not possess. The words are to be found in the 33rd sura of the Koran, and are as follows:—"O Prophet, we have allowed thee thy wives, unto whom thou hast given their dower, and also the slaves which thy right hand possesseth of the booty which God hath granted thee; and the daughters of thy uncle, and the daughters of thy aunts, both on thy father's side and on thy mother's side; and any other believing woman if she give herself unto the Prophet in case the Prophet desireth her to wife. This is a peculiar privilege granted unto thee above the rest of the true believers." This revelation settled the matter. All grumbling ceased. The Prophet was allowed to be a law unto himself.

The wives of Mohammed received the honourable title of Mothers of the Faithful. This was a spiritual designation, as by none of them did the Prophet have any children, save by the first, Kadija. The only child that was born to him after his first wife died was a boy, the offspring of a Coptic slave-girl, named Mary. This little lad, who was the idol of his father's heart, died, however, at the age of fifteen months. His death was a great blow to the Prophet, for he had fondly hoped through the son of his old age to have transmitted his name to posterity. Mohammed is said to have borne this great trouble with the patient resignation of a man of faith.

Another peculiarity of the treatment of Mohammedan women is that which may be characterized as seclusion. The liberty of action which Christian women, especially Englishwomen, enjoy is a thing denied to their Mohammedan sisters. In India, seclusion is carried to an extreme. There Mohammedan women are scarcely ever permitted to go abroad, and when they do so they must be very carefully veiled. This strict seclusion is due, I believe, to an edict of the great Tamerlane, who, in 1398, entered Hindustan as a conqueror. He issued a proclamation to his followers to the effect that "as they were now in a strange land of idolatry, and amongst a strange people, the females of their families should be strictly concealed from view."

While Tamerlane is to blame for the strict seclusion of Mohammedan women, Mohammed is to blame that they are secluded at all. A strange story is told as to the first introduction of the custom. It is said by the Mohammedans themselves that one day the Prophet entered suddenly the house of his adopted son, Zeyd, and beheld there the handsome wife of the latter, whose beauty so captivated Mohammed's fancy that nothing would satisfy him but to have her for a wife.

When Zeyd heard of this he did not become indignant, but, remembering all the kindness the Prophet had shown him, he expressed his gratitude by divorcing his wife, and handing her over at once to Mohammed.

The Prophet received her with joy, and when the sense

of propriety of the people of Medina was scandalized by this union, Mohammed met it by a revelation, which gave him Divine sanction for the step he had taken.

In the 33rd sura of the Koran it is written : " When Zeyd had determined the matter concerning his wife, and had resolved to divorce her, we joined her in marriage unto thee. No crime is to be charged on the Prophet as to what God hath allowed him." And thereat the people were satisfied.

This episode, however, set Mohammed thinking about the seclusion of women, and as he would not have fallen in love with his adopted son's wife if he had not seen her face, he made a law with regard to his own wives—that whoever should have occasion to speak to them, should address them " from behind a curtain."

Very soon this regulation was followed by another to the effect " That all females belonging to the Faithful should be compelled to wear a close veil over their face and figure whenever they went abroad." Thus the practice of seclusion was started. The very frailty of the Prophet himself was the occasion of the bringing in of a custom which has restricted the freedom, hindered the education, and limited the natural enjoyments of Mohammedan women.

It must not be thought, however, that Zenana life is altogether gloomy. The ladies therein have their daily employments, and occasional amusements, which help to cheer them on their way. Mohammedan women, it should be borne in mind, are not debarred from the society of their own sex. They are very fond of company, and arrange as often as possible for social reunions. On the occasions of births and marriages especially the monotony of life is broken for them, and they are provided with food for thought, and with topics of conversation for many a long day.

In her book on the " Mussulmans of India," Mrs. Meer Hassan Ali, an English lady, who married a Mohammedan, says : " At first I pitied the apparent monotony of the lives of Mussulman ladies, but this feeling has worn away by intimacy with the people who are thus precluded from mixing generally with the world. They are happy in their confinement : and never having felt the sweets of liberty, they would not know how to use the boon if it were granted to them. As the bird from the nest immured in a cage is both cheerful and contented, so are these females."

Mrs. Meer Hassan Ali may be right, but all the same there is something wrong about the system that thus makes a prison of a home.

Mohammedan women, like all other women of the East, are excessively given to love of finery. And in this matter they are indulged by their husbands. The wealth of a family may, as a rule, be judged by a single glance at the principal lady of the house, who does honour to the establishment by a wonderful display of jewellery. Sterling metal is generally employed for the chains of gold and silver which encircle the neck or waist, for the bangles or bracelets which glitter on the arms and ankles, for the nut or ring which, in the case of married ladies, is inserted in the nostril ; for the innumerable rings which are put on fingers, thumbs, and toes, and for the ornaments which grace the hair. This love of finery in some wealthy families is carried to such an extreme, that ladies dress even their female slaves superbly; and on occasions of marriage ceremonies or scenes of festivity, proudly exhibit their attendants in their handsome attire with the idea of adding to their own consequence by the rich display.

I find that Mohammed issued one or two stern warnings against the Eastern love of ornaments and show. The Prophet was a plain man, and wished his followers to live in a simple way also. Once when his wives asked for more liberal allowances to be expended on sumptuous clothes and jewellery, that they might support with increasing dignity their exalted position as Mothers of the Faithful, Mohammed got very angry with them, and threatened them with serious punishments, and finally asked them to

choose between contentment and divorce. The Prophet
declared that he had received a Divine command on the
matter, which he proceeded to lay before his discontented
womenfolk. It is to be found in the 33rd sura of the
Koran, and runs: "O Prophet, say unto thy wives, if ye
seek this present life and the pomp thereof, come, I will
make a handsome provision for you, and I will dismiss you
with an honourable dismission : but if ye seek God and
His Apostle, and the life to come, verily God hath prepared for such of you as work righteousness a great
reward." It is recorded that these words brought
the Mothers of the Faithful to instant submission, and
Mohammed had no further trouble in his household on the
score of finery. But Mohammedans generally do not
follow the Prophet in this one particular. His rules and
regulations on dress are quietly but firmly put on one side,
and Mohammedan ladies, with the exception of widows,
clothe themselves as grandly as they please, and are
encouraged therein by their lovers and husbands. Considering the few interests these ladies have in their secluded
lives, and bearing in mind that they are not encouraged to
cultivate their intellects by reading and study, we cannot
very strongly denounce their passionate love of finery, which
undoubtedly gives them occupation, and affords them considerable pleasure.

Passing to more serious things, it is generally affirmed
that Mohammedan women are dutiful daughters, obedient
wives, affectionate mothers, and devoted servants of God
and of the Prophet. As far as they are taught, they are
zealous in performing their religious duties. The pity is
that in Mohammedan communities so little is done to
assist women in the formation of a religious character.
They are not much encouraged to cultivate the habit of
prayer, and they are scarcely ever to be seen in attendance
on the worship of God in mosques. I believe that women
are absolutely excluded from the majority of Mohammedan
places of worship, and are frowned upon if they venture to

appear in others, at any rate while men are there, for the men-folk declare that "the presence of a woman in a mosque is not conducive to devotion to God." During the years I was in India, and in my travels in other Mohammedan countries, though I entered hundreds of mosques, I never once saw a woman at public prayers. How different from our Christian custom! With us the two sexes meet in the House of God on a footing of equality, and we should regard our churches poor indeed if, for any cause, the refining and elevating influences which women exert there were withdrawn.

The conclusion I have come to, after a close study of the Mohammedan laws with regard to women, and after considering what I have seen and heard of their lives, is that the lot of our Eastern sisters is a hard one, as far as this world is concerned. And what about the next world? What hope does Mohammedanism hold out to women in the life that lies beyond the grave?

There is a pathetic story told of an old woman who came to Mohammed on one occasion, and told him that she had heard that he had promised untold joys in Paradise to all believing men. "Cannot something be done for us women also?" was the cry of the supplicant. "Will not the Prophet intercede with God that I may be admitted into Paradise?" And what did Mohammed answer? He gruffly responded, "No old woman will enter that glorious abode!" But, then, seeing the anguish of the almost broken-hearted creature, he was moved to compassion, and added, gently, "God will make thee young again!" Perhaps that interview set the Prophet thinking about the subject, and led to the insertion in the Koran of just two or three saving clauses, which assert the doctrine that women as well as men may enter into the joys of the redeemed of the Lord. In the 14th sura I find these words, "Whoso doeth evil shall be rewarded for it, and shall not find any patron or helper beside God; but whoso doeth good works, whether male or female, and is a true believer, will be admitted into Paradise, and will not in the least be unjustly dealt with." Then, in the 16th sura, these words occur : "Whoso worketh righteousness, whether male or female, and is a true believer, we will raise to a happy life, and we will give them their reward according to the utmost merit of their actions." There the revelation stops — advisedly, Gibbon says. Beautiful, "heavenly wives" without number are promised to believing men, but no "heavenly husbands" are promised to believing women. Nor is it said they will ever see again their earthly husbands.

The Mohammedan Paradise is without doubt primarily for men. To admit women at all was a kind of afterthought, and must be regarded in the light of a special favour. Yet it is something that women are admitted. And doubtless the hope of something better farther on—of rest and peace and joy "within the veil"—alleviates a little the oppression and pain of this present life to multitudes of God's creatures who have the misfortune to be born Mohammedan women.

CHAPTER V

THE FOUR PERFECT WOMEN

STUDIES in Mohammedanism would be incomplete which did not deal with the subject of the Four Perfect Women of the Faith. It is a remarkable fact that the religion which speaks of women in general in anything but complimentary terms, bestows unmeasured praise upon four ladies. The Prophet is reported to have said, "That among men there had been many perfect; but not more than four of the other sex have attained perfection—to wit, Asiyah, Mary, Kadija, and Fatima."

1. Asiyah, according to Mohammed, was the wife of the Pharaoh of the Exodus. This lady was of an enlightened spirit, and when she saw the wonders of Moses in Egypt, she forsook the faith of her fathers, and adopted that of Moses and of Abraham. For her change of faith she was persecuted by her husband, who sought to force her to a recantation. Failing, however, in that, he resolved to slay her, and by slow means, so as to make her suffer terrible agonies. He commanded that she should be thrown on the ground, and that her hands and feet should be fastened to stakes. Next, a large millstone was placed upon her breast, so that it was absolutely impossible for her to move. Then, with uncovered face, she was left exposed to the scorching rays of the Eastern sun.

Mohammed says that though persecuted and forsaken of mankind, the noble lady was remembered by God, who sent His angels to shade her with their wings, and to give her strength to be faithful even unto death. In the 66th sura of the Koran the last words of Asiyah are recorded.

They are, " Lord, build me a house with Thee in Paradise ; rescue me from Pharaoh and his doings, and deliver me from the unjust people." That prayer, we are told, was heard, and the martyred Queen was released from her anguish, and was taken by the angels into Heaven, where she ever liveth as an example of suffering affliction and of patience. Asiyah was the first perfect woman.

2. The second, Mary, was the mother of Jesus. Of her wonderful things are related, the most marvellous thing being that she was absolutely without sin. The Moham-medans have a tradition that every person who comes into the world is touched at birth by the Devil, and thereupon cries out. When Mary was born, however, God interposed a veil between her and the Evil One, so that the touch of the latter did not reach her ; and, as a consequence, she did not cry, and afterwards throughout her life committed no folly or sin.

It is interesting to notice here that some scholars think that in all probability the Roman Catholic Church took its doctrine of .the immaculate conception of the Virgin Mary from the Mohammedans. Soon after her birth, Mary, it is said, was given into the charge of Zacharias, the father of John the Baptist, and by him she was placed in the inner chamber of the Temple at Jerusalem, where she remained during the years of childhood and youth. As a conse-quence of those early Temple associations, Mary grew up learned in the Scriptures, and became eminently pious, so that she was worthy of that great honour which was con-ferred upon her of becoming the mother of Jesus, the very soul of God. In the 66th sura of the Koran it is written, " Into Mary we breathed of our Spirit ; she believed in the words of her Lord, and was a devout and obedient person." And, again, in the 3rd sura it is written, " O Mary, verily God hath chosen thee, and hath purified thee, and thou shalt bear the Word, and His name shall be Christ Jesus. . . God hath chosen thee above all the women of the world."

3. The third perfect woman of the Mohammedan Faith was the first wife of the Prophet, the beautiful and faithful Kadija, who in good report and ill report was the devoted helpmeet of him whom she sincerely and fondly loved. Of Kadija, and with good reason, Mohammed declared that she was "a Princess amongst women." Well would it have been for Mohammedanism if this lady had been spared to the Prophet until the close of his life! While she lived Mohammed was a true man, earnestly trying by fair means to win his countrymen over from idolatry to faith in God alone. During Kadija's lifetime also he seemed perfectly content with one helpmeet. But when she died he became a changed character. Force took the place of moral suasion in the propagation of the Faith; and then began that declension of soul which allowed Mohammed to take unto himself wives many, and which permitted him to turn his divine inspiration to the lowest and basest account, to satisfy his selfish aims and unnatural desires.

Mohammedanism has nothing but good to say of Kadija, and the Prophet was never weary of singing her praises and holding her up before the Faithful as a model wife and mother. It is related that Ayesha, Mohammed's girl-wife, a spoiled beauty, was jealous of the dead Kadija, and spoke disparagingly of her to her husband on one occasion, but only on one, for she was ever afterwards in fear of the Prophet's anger. Ayesha had said, "O my husband, was not Kadija, thy first wife, old, and has not God given thee a better in her place?" "No! by Allah!" was the indignant reply. "No! Kadija believed in me when men despised me: she relieved my wants when I was poor and persecuted by the world! No! by Allah! there can never be a better! She was one of the four perfect women of the world!"

Thus warmly did Mohammed defend the memory of the dear one dead. And thus was the occasion given him to exalt her to whom he owed so much. And in so doing he bore a noble testimony.

4. We come now to Fatima. She was the favourite
daughter of Mohammed, born to him in the early days of
his happy married life, when he was only known to his
countrymen as the " Camel Driver." Fatima is considered
by the Mohammedan world as the greatest of the illustrious
four. The Prophet himself drew no comparisons between
them. This lady was married to Ali, a nephew of Mohammed, and one of his earliest and most trusted followers.
Two children were the issue of the marriage, named Hasan
and Hosein, whom the Prophet dearly loved. Fatima, as
daughter, wife, and mother, seems to have won great praise.
From all accounts she was truly a model character. She
was renowned for her wisdom, her holiness, her religious
zeal, her domestic virtues, the meekness of her behaviour,
and her unselfishness, which constantly found expression
in generous gifts to the poor and needy. With regard to
her deeds of extraordinary charity, innumerable tales are
told, of which the shortest and the best, I think, is the
following :—It happened that Hasan and Hosein fell ill,
and one day when the Prophet called to see them, he suggested to the sorrowing parents, Ali and Fatima, that they
should, as was customary on such occasions, make a vow
to God for the recovery of their children. They willingly
assented, declaring in case the little ones got well they
would perform a strict fast of three days in gratitude for
the goodness of God. Shortly after the boys recovered,
and then the parents, along with their one maidservant,
Fidda, began their fast. From morning till night of the
first day not a morsel of bread or a drop of water crossed
their lips. When the sun went down, however, it was
permitted to partake of refreshment. For the three days
Fatima had provided herself with three measures of barley,
and it was arranged that one measure each evening should
be made into cakes and eaten. On no account would they
seek other or better food. The first evening arrived, the
cakes were prepared, and the family, having attended to
their devotions, assembled round the homely meal with

thankful hearts and contented spirits. They were just about to partake of the cakes and break their fast, when a voice of distress caught their ears. It was the cry of an old man at the door—"Give me, O give me," said the voice, "for the love of God, something to relieve my hunger, and to save my famishing family from perishing."

Fatima, glancing at her husband, said, "How can we, the Prophet's children, refuse that cry?" In a moment, gathering together all the cakes, and hurrying to the door with them, she gave them, with her blessing, to the old man. Ali, looking on, approved the self-sacrifice, and even the maidservant heaved never a sigh, though that night neither she, nor her master and mistress had bite or sup.

The next day was passed in useful occupation, and when evening drew nigh the same humble fare of five barley cakes was placed on the table, and the little household sat down to it with appetites made doubly keen by the lengthened abstinence. Again, as they were about to partake of it, came the cry, "For the love of God!" Fatima hurried to the door to see what was the matter, and found there two orphan children pathetically praying for food. The sight moved the compassionate mother, whose own children were so well off, and who had so mercifully been spared to her when she had feared to lose them. Returning to her husband, she said, "It is surely the will of God and of His Prophet that we should succour the needy! Let the little ones have our meal!" Ali, struck with the self-denying zeal of his wife, answered, "As thou wilt, and as God will!" Thus for a second night the household went without food. With feebleness of body, and yet with brave spirits, they attended to the duties of the morrow, and on the third evening sat down with glad hearts to partake of the simple provision that remained. This story was made public by Fidda, the servant, for Ali and Fatima were so accustomed to performing such deeds of charity that they never referred to it. When Mohammed heard of it, he was filled with joy, and said that all generations would call him blessed for being the father of such a noble woman as Fatima, the wife of Ali. Fatima lived for many years after that event, and was the admiration of the Faithful, both at Medina and at Mecca.

The lives of Asiyah, Mary, Kadija, and Fatima, "the Four Perfect Women," were placed by the Prophet before the women of Mohammedanism as examples of what good women should be. Everywhere the story of the lives of these excellent ladies has been told and retold. There is not a single respectable Mohammedan home in which some mention is not made almost daily of the virtues and good works of "the faithful four." And the great ambition of Mohammedan women is to follow in the footsteps of those perfect ones, that they may also haply be renowned for their goodness, and receive the favour of God and His Prophet. It seems to me that the one redeeming feature in connection with the dark picture of the treatment of women in Mohammedan countries lies in this doctrine of "the Four Perfect Women." It places an ideal, a worthy ideal, before the down-trodden and oppressed. It shows them how even in the darkness of their secluded lives they may make their light shine. It raises within their breasts a glorious ambition. It leads them to feel that a good woman is the noblest work of God. Mohammed rendered a great service not only to Mohammedanism, but to humanity, when he formulated his theory of "the Four Perfect Women."

There are instances on record in Mohammedan countries of both rich and poor who have earnestly striven to be like "the four" in every womanly grace and virtue, and have in large measure succeeded. I have heard of one poor, humble imitator who lived in Turkey, whose devoutness, holiness of character, and self-denial were most marked, and earned for her great renown. At length this widow woman, poor in goods but rich in faith, resolved to go on a pilgrimage to the tomb of her Prophet, and also to the far-famed tombs of Hasan and Hosein, the sons of

Fatima. Medina was reached after months of weary travelling, but the devoted soul felt amply repaid for all her toils when she was able to bend her knees and kiss the stone which covered the remains of the Prophet of God. And then she started off again to the tombs of the martyrs, Hasan and Hosein. There a heavy fee was required for permission to enter. At that time one hundred gold pieces was the amount fixed, though now it is but a trifle. The old woman was, however, quite prepared to meet the demand, and went boldly up to the wicket-gate, and requested to be let in. The custodian of the tombs looked at her, and judging from her appearance that she was one of the poorest of the poor, scoffed at her presumption, and bade her, in a harsh voice, be gone. She gave him a meek reply, and fumbling in her dress, brought forth the full price of admission, and laid it down before the astonished gatekeeper. Now the man supposed that he had to do with a thief, and calling others to his side, began to interrogate the poor old woman, intending at the close to hand her over to the Cadi, or Judge.

But the replies he received to his questions led him to change his mind. With dignity and some warmth of feeling the good woman answered him that she was no thief, but a true servant of God and of the Prophet. "As to this money," she said, "is it a great thing that I should freely give one hundred gold pieces out of my poverty for such an object? Know ye, my brothers, that I have laboured these thirty years at my spinning-wheel, and have debarred myself many things, while I have not forgotten those poorer than myself, that I might at length have sufficient money to realize the dearest wish of my life—to visit the tombs of the children of the blessed Fatima. Here, take at once the fruits of my labour, and let me in, for every moment's delay is an agony. I wish to pray and weep over the dust of the martyred ones." Such an appeal was irresistible. The saintly woman had her heart's desire, and the story of her love and zeal was that night told

round many a pilgrim's watch-fire, and has been handed
down the centuries for the encouragement of those who
are like-minded, and as an incentive to all the women of
Islam.

The scene changes.   Let us go in thought to India.   It
is the reign of Shah Jahan, that famous Emperor who
erected so many magnificent buildings to the glory of
Mohammedanism, and that lovely tomb, the Taj Mahal,
at Agra, in memory of his idolized wife, Mumtaz.   The
power of Shah Jahan seemed unshakable, and yet his own
son, Aurangzebe, dethroned him, and condemned him to
lifelong imprisonment.   Then it was that, though the aged
and unfortunate Emperor had lost a kingdom, he found a
daughter.   When all of his courtiers and friends forsook
him and fled, his eldest daughter, the beautiful Jahanara,
clave to him, and vowed that nought but death should part
them.   For seven long years the father and daughter were
immured in the strong fortress at Agra, and had nothing to
cheer them but each other's love and the consolations of
their religion.

Their conversation often turned on the Four Perfect
Women of their creed, and the aged monarch loved to
compare the devotion of his own daughter Jahanara with
the devotion of Fatima, the daughter of the Prophet.
" Was there ever," he would exclaim,—" was there ever
truer love than this, which keeps a beautiful woman away
from the pleasures of a Palace that she may share with me
the sorrows of a prison ? "   At length relief came ; the
imprisoned Emperor died, and Jahanara was at liberty to
enter the busy world once more.   Her seven years, however, of seclusion and devoted service had weakened her
frame, and ere long she also was laid in her last resting-
place.

Her tomb is at Delhi.   Miss Gordon Cumming, in her
book " In the Himalayas and on the Indian Plains,"
speaks of having visited the spot.   She says, " Here,
beneath the green turf, sleeps Jahanara, the beautiful

E

daughter of Shah Jahan, who voluntarily shared his captivity, and, after a life of such purity and holiness as earned her a place among the Mohammedan saints, desired on her death-bed that she might be buried without pomp or splendour."

It was my good fortune, also, in the spring of 1888, to visit that tomb. Many other sepulchres lie around, being plain, square, marble structures, about six feet long and two feet high, surrounded by screens of that exquisite marble trellis-work which is so beautiful a feature of Mohammedan architecture. The tomb of the faithful daughter, I noticed, differed from the others in one particular—it was not covered with a slab. And on the plain headstone was this inscription, " Let no rich canopy cover my grave. Grass and flowers are the only coverings meet for the tomb of the poor in spirit, the humble, the transitory Jahanara, the daughter of the Emperor Shah Jahan." That dying request has been religiously kept. The grass grows over her grave to this day ; and all who look down upon it are touched, as they think of the simplicity and beauty of the character of one who, though born to very high estate, was of such a gentle and humble spirit.

Noble Jahanara ! A bright example of a good Mohammedan woman wast thou ! A worthy successor of Fatima, and the other perfect three !

I could give additional examples, but enough, I think, has been said to show that Mohammedanism, with all its bad laws with respect to females, with its restrictions of their liberty, its neglect of their education, and its denial to them of the public means of grace, can yet produce women of exalted goodness, of estimable virtues, and of saintly character.

What might not the women of the East become if only their lives were passed under the elevating and benignant sway of the Christian religion, and with the one " Perfect Man, Christ Jesus," ever before them as their great Exemplar and present Saviour !

CHAPTER VI

THE Princes who in succession to Mohammed are supposed to have exercised during the last 1,200 years supreme temporal and spiritual authority amongst the Mohammedans have been described by various names, which practically mean the same thing, viz., successor or ruler. Out of the names Caliphs, Imams, and Commanders of the Faithful, I have chosen the last as the preferable title. It is, of course, impossible, if it were desirable, to give in this volume a history of all the Commanders of the Faithful, but it will be wise just to glance at this subject, and deal with the early successors of Mohammed, for in the first twenty years after the Prophet's death there occurred a great schism in the ranks of the Faithful, which remains to this day, and which seems likely to be perpetuated as long as Islamism exists. The schism arose out of the choice of the first three Commanders of the Faithful.

When Mohammed, the Prophet of Allah, was gathered to his fathers, as already related, there was great sadness in Medina. The people generally were loth to accept the tidings, hoping against hope, and saying one to another, through their tears, "How can he be dead, our witness, our intercessor, our mediator with God?" Even some of the leaders of the people, the dead man's most intimate friends, were so carried away by their grief and fanaticism that they joined in the general cry that Mohammed was not really taken from them. It is recorded that the warrior

Omar ascended the great pulpit, and proclaimed with a loud voice, "Let the Faithful know that the Prophet is not dead! No, no, he is not dead! He has but gone, like Moses, to talk with Allah! We shall see him among us again in a little while!" There was, however, one sorrowful, but calm spirit in Medina who was not deceived. Abu Bekr, on hearing the tumult in the city, hastened to the house of mourning, placed his hand upon the cold cheeks and quiet heart, and then, knowing the worst, made his way to the very centre of the grief-stricken and excited crowd, and exclaimed, "O Moslems, is it Mohammed or the God of Mohammed you worship? If ye would adore the Prophet, know that he is dead! If ye would adore Allah, know that He is alive for evermore! Be not deceived, O Moslems! Listen to this word of the holy Koran, which says, 'Mohammed is but a man with a mission;' and this other word, which says, 'Verily, O Mohammed, thou shalt die, and they shall die!'"

Thus was the tumult stilled; and the people, convinced that the Prophet was, indeed, dead, resolved, ere they buried him, to choose his successor. But whom to choose was a grave and difficult question. Unfortunately, Mohammed had not specially designated any one to take office after him. Indeed, so far as I can gather, the subject had never been raised in the lifetime of the Prophet. Of the great Princes of the Faith, there were, at least, four who were head and shoulders above their fellows, and with one of these practically the Commandership lay.

1. Ali was the nearest of kin to the dead man, for he was his nephew, and had married, also, his favourite daughter, Fatima, one of the "perfect women." This Prince was a man of mild and forbearing character, wise in counsel, and bold on the field of battle. Mohammed had given him the surname of "the Lion of God." One great fault, however, Ali had, and that was indecision of character.

2. Abu Bekr was another strong claimant for the vacant

leadership. He had been Mohammed's companion in the Flight from Mecca, and from that day had received the title of "the Other of the Two," a name of which he was exceedingly proud. Mohammed had also called him Al-Siddik, The Truthful, because his word could always be relied upon. Abu Bekr, it should be noted also, was the father of Ayesha, the favourite wife of the Prophet.

3. The redoubtable Omar was another mighty Prince. He had been a man of war from his youth up, and Mohammed had spoken of him as his "right hand." Undoubtedly Islamism owed much of its success in arms to the courage and daring of Omar. As we shall see directly, he was also as humble as he was brave.

4. The fourth claimant was Othman, who had married in succession two of Mohammed's daughters. He was a man of great wealth and influence. With regard to this chief, the Prophet had once said, " Each thing has its mate, and each man his associate ; my companion in Paradise is Othman."

When the people had such choice of worthy men to succeed Mohammed in the leadership, it is easy to understand that there was much difference of opinion and warm debate, which, though for the moment reverence for the Prophet might suppress, would eventually lead to trouble and schism. Many felt very strongly that Ali had the prior claim, while others thought and said differently. Some then suggested that Ali should take the Governorship of Mecca and the region round about, and that one of the other three Princes should be appointed Governor of Medina, with its adjoining territories. This summary division of the Empire was deprecated, however, by the majority, and at length the protracted debate was brought to a close by Omar rising and walking up to the aged Abu Bekr, and declaring, as he seized his hand, " Here is the successor of the Prophet." On the morrow, in the great Mosque, Omar again proclaimed that he gave in his allegiance to Abu Bekr. " The Apostle of Allah," he said,

" has been taken from us, but the Koran remains. Allah gave the Book as a guide to the Prophet, and it will guide us in the right way. To-day Allah has placed at our head the best man amongst us. Come, then, take with me the hand of Abu Bekr, and solemnly swear obedience to him ! " The people, moved by the nobility of Omar, who thus put his own claims on one side in favour of the one whom he styled " the best man amongst us," responded heartily to the call, and pressed forward to take the oath of allegiance. Thus was the first Commander of the Faithful chosen.

The choice made was a good one. Of the new leader, Gilman, in his book on the Saracens, says : " The form of Abu Bekr was spare, and he stooped. His face was thin, and his countenance gave the impression of a man of resolution and wisdom ; but his expression was mild, truly representing his disposition, though on account of the firmness of his faith in the Prophet he had become one of his most resolute and unyielding disciples. His handsome features were smooth and fair, and his thin beard and hair, though naturally white, were, in accordance with an Oriental custom, dyed red." All the experience, wisdom, courage, and faith of the Commander of the Faithful were needed in the struggle which now lay before the followers of Mohammed. When the news of the Prophet's death reached the provinces, there was as great astonishment as in Mecca and Medina, but not any grief. Mohammed, outside the circle of his relatives and fellow-citizens, was more feared than loved, and so immediately it was known that he was dead, the tribes whom he had subjugated by the power of the sword had dreams and hopes of recovered liberty. Soon all Arabia was ripe for insurrection, and the question which passed from city to city and from district to district was, " Can Islam be shaken off ? " Abu Bekr, the mild but the forcible, answered " No ! " Without delay, after the remains of the Prophet had been reverently and lovingly buried, the new commander divided the entire territory of Arabia into eleven sections, and sent an army into each section, with instructions to summon the tribes to allegiance. The troops carried all before them, and ere the year A.D. 633 closed the world knew that though Mohammed the Prophet of Islam was dead, Mohammedanism still lived, and gave promise of becoming one of the mighty powers of the world. The next year saw the arms of the Commander of the Faithful carried as far as Chaldea and Babylonia, and in September, A.D. 634, a great battle was fought with the Romans for the possession of Upper Syria, and the Mohammedans gained the victory. When the glorious tidings of success reached Medina, however, Abu Bekr was no more. At a good old age, though after only two years of sovereignty, he fell asleep.

Ere Abu Bekr died he called around him some of the great princes of the State, and prepared to nominate a successor. Ali was again passed over, though his friends strenuously pressed his claims. The choice fell on Omar. "But," said the latter, who, though brave, was of a lowly spirit, "I have no occasion for the place!" The dying man replied, solemnly, "That may be; but the place has occasion for thee! A strong man is needed, and thou art the man. Take the leadership! Only temper thy natural severity with moderation!" And Omar took it. Ali, upon this second disappointment, retired into private life; but, with true nobility of character, did nothing to cause dissension or trouble in the State. Omar, feeling strong sympathy for his rival, sought to comfort him for the loss of empire by the most flattering marks of confidence and esteem. The new Commander of the Faithful was a man of simple tastes, like his predecessor, and like the Prophet. Gilman says of him: "Humble as the most lowly, he was accustomed to sit on the steps of the Mosque at Medina, eating his barley-bread and dates, and he often slept on its porch or in a tree, while wielding a sceptre that the most powerful nations of his time felt and feared."

During Omar's reign Mohammedanism went forth conquering and to conquer. The distant kingdoms of Persia

and Egypt were added to the growing kingdom. Mesopotamia and Palestine bowed the knee to the successor of
the Prophet.   Such strong cities as Damascus, Antioch,
Alexandria, and Jerusalem fell, after desperate fighting,
before the might of Islam.   It seemed, indeed, as if ere long
the whole world would become subject to the Commander of
the Faithful, that stern, but humble man, who never stirred
out of the city of Medina.   In one conquest, that of
Palestine, we, as Christians, take special interest, and of
this I will therefore give just a few particulars.

In the spring of A.D. 636 the armies of Omar converged
towards Jerusalem, after having taken possession of other
parts of the country.   The sacred city was then a Roman
possession, and was for a time defended by a Roman army.
The inhabitants were chiefly Christians, and were under the
rule of a patriarch of the Greek Church.   The Roman
troops, fearing the power of the Moslems, quietly withdrew
one night, and left the city to its fate.   Still, the Patriarch
held out, until it seemed folly to do so any longer, when he
asked terms of peace from the invaders.   In the negotiations
that then ensued, he stipulated that the Commander of the
Faithful should come in person to receive the capitulation,
as there was a tradition that the keys of the city should
only be given up to a King having but three letters in his
name, and that of the successor of the Prophet comprised
no more in the Arabic tongue—Omr.   Omar, when he
heard of the strange request, acquiesced in it, and without
delay made arrangements to start for Jerusalem.   He was
the first Commander of the Faithful to journey beyond the
limits of Arabia.   It might have been expected that this
ruler, who was more powerful than the King of Persia or
the Emperor of the Romans, or, indeed, any other
monarch of his times, would have made the long journey
from Medina in great state.   But no ! Having the reality
of power, he cared nothing about its form.

The day Omar left Medina on his notable journey " he
was clad in the plainest of clothes, and rode a strong camel,

over the back of which rough saddlebags were thrown, containing parched grain in one pouch and dates and dried fruit in the other. Before him hung a skin for water, and behind a platter of wood, out of which he and his few companions ate together. At night he laid himself down beneath a tree, or under a tent. In the morning he bowed towards Mecca, and offered his devotions before proceeding on his way ; and he stopped as occasion demanded to dispense the primitive justice that his subjects called for. Sometimes he varied the monotony of the journey by dismounting and walking, while a slave took his seat upon a camel." In such simple state the Commander of the Faithful drew near Jerusalem ; and when within a day's journey some of his generals rode forward to meet him. These leaders of his armies were a great contrast to Omar, for their beasts and themselves were decked out in the richest silks of Damascus. We can imagine their astonishment and dismay, when their Master, addressing them sharply, said, "Is it thus that ye come to meet me ? Have two years effected such a change? Are ye women or men ?" Tearing off their rich garments, they showed underneath their armour, well worn with the strife of many a battle. At that sight Omar was better pleased, and in a few genial words expressed his satisfaction with all that had been done.

The next day Omar entered Jerusalem as a conqueror, being escorted through the streets by the Patriarch, in his gorgeous robes of office. They went on foot, and, as they moved slowly along, the intelligent Commander of the Faithful asked questions about this building and that, being evidently anxious to gather what information he could of the history of the city which, next to Mecca, was, perhaps, held in greatest veneration by the followers of Mohammed. The Patriarch answered him, it is said, with scant courtesy, for in his heart he loathed the son of the desert, with his coarse garments, soiled by the long and weary journey from Medina. Omar, however, in the grand simplicity of his character, was indifferent as to what the Patriarch thought about him. When at last the Church of the Holy Sepulchre was reached, and Omar sat down in the Patriarch's own throne of State, the latter exclaimed in the bitterness of his spirit, "Verily, this is the abomination of desolation, predicted by Daniel the Prophet, standing in the holy place."

Omar spared the lives of the inhabitants of Jerusalem, both Christians and Jews. However, as a memorial of the conquest to subsequent generations, and as a visible proof of the superiority of Islamism, he asked to be shown the site of the ancient Jewish Temple, and then ordered that on that spot should be erected, regardless of expense, a mosque, to the honour of Mohammed, and to the glory of Allah. The command was obeyed, and that beautiful structure was erected which is known as the Mosque of Omar. Thus, in the land of our Saviour's birth, and in the very city of his crucifixion, that power was established which afterwards took the "crescent" as its symbol, and which has, until this day, hurled defiance at the Cross of Christ.

When matters had been settled in Jerusalem, and the amount of "tribute"—which Omar declared was "better than spoil, for it continueth"—had been settled, the Commander of the Faithful said good-bye to his generals, and set off on the return journey to Medina, where he was received with demonstrations of delight. From Medina, with quietness and yet with a strong hand, Omar for twelve years directed the affairs of his vast Empire, even to the movements of his armies in the field; and nothing gave the grand old man greater pleasure than to hear that another city or another country had been added to the kingdom of Allah and of his Prophet.

Omar's death was a violent one. It occurred in November, A.D. 644. One day a slave who worked for his master at the carpenter's bench came to see the Commander of the Faithful, and complained to him of being overworked, and badly treated by the citizen that owned

him. Omar listened attentively, but arriving at the conclusion that the charges were false, sternly dismissed the
carpenter to his bench. The man retired, vowing to be
revenged. The following day was Friday, "the day of the
Assembly." Omar, as usual, went to lead the prayers of
the assembly in the great mosque. He opened his mouth
to speak. He had just said "Allah," when the keen
dagger of the offended slave was thrust into his back, and
the Commander of the Faithful fell on the sacred floor,
fatally wounded. The people, in a perfect frenzy of horror
and rage, fell upon the assassin, but with superhuman
strength he threw them off, and rushing about in the
madness of despair he killed some and wounded others,
and finally turning the point of his dagger to his own
breast, fell dead. Omar lingered several days in great
agony, but he was brave to the end. His dying words
were, "Give to my successor this parting bequest, that he
be kind to the men of this city, Medina, which gave a
home to us, and to the Faith. Tell him to make much of
their virtues, and to pass lightly over their faults. Bid him
also treat well the Arab tribes, for verily they are the back-
bone of Islam. Moreover, let him faithfully fulfil the
covenants made with the Christians and the Jews! O
Allah! I have finished my course! To him that cometh
after me, I leave the kingdom firmly established and at
peace!" Thus perished one of the greatest Princes the
Mohammedans were ever to know. Omar was truly a
great and a good man, of whom any country and any
creed might be proud. He was buried by the side of the
Prophet, whom in life he had so warmly loved, and whose
memory he had all along so fondly cherished, and whose
fame, as the Prophet of Allah, he had made to ring
throughout all the world. Omar was the first Commander
of the Faithful to die a violent death. Hundreds of his
successors have shared the same fate. Specially amongst
the Mohammedans is the adage true, "Uneasy lies the
head that wears a crown."

How often in human life men say, " Peace, peace ; when there is no peace." Omar's dying words were of peace, and yet, ere his body was placed in its tomb, yea, even before the breath had departed from it, there were heard the smothered cries of party strife, which soon broke out into a flame. The friends of Ali felt that now at any rate their leader should become Commander of the Faithful. But Othman was aspiring to the office, and had many adherents who contended on his behalf. However, the general feeling was in favour of Ali, and he was offered the throne on certain conditions, viz., that he would agree to govern in accordance with the precedents established by Abu Bekr and Omar. After consultation with his friends, Ali, however, to the surprise of the people, declined, saying that he could not bring himself to accept a position in which he would not be a free agent. Thereupon Othman was elected to the vacant commandership.

Now commenced days of darkness and sorrow for Islam at home, though abroad her arms were still conquering provinces and kingdoms. It was not so much that Ali stirred up strife, for he was too noble a man for that, though his spirit chafed sorely under his frequent rebuffs and disappointments. It was Othman himself who was unable to keep peace in his vast dominions. Though a brave and well-meaning man, he was weak and narrow-minded withal. His relations and friends, by whose aid mainly he had reached his exalted position, clamoured for positions of power and influence, and, regardless of their fitness for such posts, he made them generals of his armies, and governors of provinces and States. By so doing, of course, the new Commander of the Faithful raised up a host of enemies, and ere eighteen months had passed away, Othman, like Omar, had fallen beneath the assassin's knife.

Othman's death was on this wise. Conspirators from Egypt and Mesopotamia came up to Medina to seek redress of real or fancied grievances. The Commander spoke them plausibly, and they pretended to be satisfied, and withdrew ostensibly to return to their homes. However, three days later, while Othman was leading the prayers of the Faithful, news was brought that the discontented ones had returned, and this time were in strong force. The factious bands, unfortunately, were admitted into the city. They made at once for the Mosque, and insulted Othman in his pulpit, calling out for his abdication. The poor old man, unable to still the tumult, retired to his Palace. Later, the rebels stormed it, and entering the private room of the Prince, seized him by the beard as he sat with the Koran open before him, and smote him with their daggers. It was a dastardly deed! "Deeply wounded, the Commander of the Faithful fell, pressing the leaves of the sacred book to his bosom, and staining them with his ebbing life-blood." Then anarchy reigned at Medina.

The insurgents, for a successor to the vacant throne, turned their eyes towards Ali, as, indeed, did most of the Faithful. But Ali was weary of strife, and sick of the shedding of blood. When a deputation waited upon him and requested him to become the new Commander of the Faithful, he mournfully shook his head, and said, "Once I desired the office, but now I think the most comfortable position in life is that farthest removed from power. Elect whom you will." But the people would not be refused, and at length Ali, moved by their pathetic entreaties, consented to go to the great Mosque to receive the oaths of allegiance. All the factions in the city were represented, and the leaders promised to be faithful to the new Commander. However, this peace was deceptive, and ere long civil strife was renewed. Eventually, appeal was made to force of arms, and a battle was fought outside the city, in which "Ali, the Lion of God," was victorious.

Now, if prompt and energetic measures had been employed, the rebellion might have been stamped out. But Ali procrastinated. The fact is he was too mild a man for the stirring times in which he lived. He was too slow in

resolve, and too undecided in action.   At any time he preferred compromise and delay to energy and promptness,
and with fatal results.

Ali had a lieutenant in Egypt of the name of Amr, who
was ambitious, and determined to make capital out of the
troubles at Medina.   At Damascus, also, was a lieutenant
named Muawiya, who was like-minded.   These two joined
their forces against their Commander, and being men of
ability and action, they made considerable headway.   Still,
Ali, the brave and the skilful in war, would probably have
subdued his rebellious vassals if he had lived to prolong
the struggle.   As it was, however, he shared the fate of his
two predecessors.

In the year A.D. 660, three fanatics met by appointment
in the Mosque at Mecca, to talk over the disturbed affairs of
the kingdom.   The result of their deliberations was that
they conceived that they were called by Allah to rid the distracted state of Amr, Muawiya and Ali, and thus give Islam,
as they thought, the chance of a fresh start.   It was a mad
scheme, and could only add to the troubles of the unhappy
kingdom.

One fanatic started for Egypt, but stabbed the wrong
man ; so Amr escaped.   The other made for Damascus
and wounded Muawiya, but not vitally.   The third reached
Kufa, and with a poisoned dagger stabbed Ali to the heart.
It was characteristic of the gentle-spirited Ali that his last
words should be on behalf of his murderer.   He forgave him
freely, and asked that he might not be slain.   " At any rate,"
he said, " if by way of example he must be killed, let him
not be tortured."   Thus, with a prayer of forgiveness on
his lips, the much sinned-against Commander of the Faithful passed into the presence of God.

The death of Ali was an epoch-making event.   We come
now to the parting of the ways.   Henceforward the Commanders of the Faithful ceased to be elected by the votes
of the people of Medina or Mecca.   Arabia was no longer

to be the seat of the temporal power. For the future in Islam might was to take the place of right. And the spiritual power also underwent a change. The followers of Ali forced a great schism upon Mohammedanism. Maddened by the murder of their leader, and magnifying all the wrongs he had suffered from the time of the death of the Prophet, his father-in-law, they made a martyr of him, and almost worshipped his memory. And the intensity of their love for Ali was the measure of their hate for all who had in any way done him wrong. The adherents of the new sect called themselves Alyites; but the name they are known by in history is that of Shias, or Sectaries. They asserted that the first three Commanders of the Faithful—Abu Bekr, Omar, and Othman—were usurpers; and that Ali was the only lawful leader; or, as they preferred to call him Imam, a word that is found in the Koran. From that time until this the Shias have existed, and have ever looked to a lineal descendant of Ali as their spiritual head. Those who do not agree with them are called Sunis or Sonnites, or Traditionists. This matter may seem to us a little one to differ about; but to Mohammedans it is of vast importance. The difference between Shias and Sonnites is even more marked than that between Roman Catholics and Protestants. And the unfortunate schism has led to the shedding of rivers of blood.

Generally speaking, at the present day the Persians are Shias and the Turks are Sonnites. In India and Afghanistan many adherents of both sects are to be found. Taking the world as a whole, the Sonnites greatly outnumber the Shias; but the latter make up in hate what they lack in numbers. The Sonnites look to the Sultan of Turkey as the Commander of the Faithful. The Shareef of Mecca, however, who is a descendant of Ali, disputes the honour with the Sultan. Thus the strife is kept up. It seems to me a cruel irony of fate that one of the gentlest and most forgiving of men,—for such was Ali,—should have become,

through the mad zeal of partisans who profess to be his
followers, the innocent cause of so much bad feeling, strife
and bloodshed.

Commanders of the Faithful—the Faithful themselves—
we all—need to learn that "To err is human, to forgive
divine ;" and that " Greater is he that ruleth his spirit than
he that taketh a city."

CHAPTER VII

PARABLES

MOHAMMEDANISM is not great in parables, which is remarkable, as the people of the East are peculiarly susceptible to them, and Eastern language readily lends itself to figures of speech.

I have been astonished in reading the Koran to find how few parables Mohammed composed, and of what a commonplace character they are. Christ, it will be remembered, often addressed his fellow-countrymen in parables, so that it was said of him, "Without a parable spake He not unto them." It was different, however, with Mohammed. He but seldom spake in parables; and when he did, it was only half-heartedly. He either did not realize the power there is in well-told parables for the enforcement of truth, or he was unable to compose them. I am inclined to think the latter was the case. The Prophet put the best face on the poverty of his parabolic resources, however, for in the 39th sura it is written : "Now have we proposed unto mankind in this Koran every kind of parable, that they may be warned, and that they may fear God." And, again, in the 29th sura it is written : "These similitudes do we propound unto men, but none understand them except the wise." May we be numbered amongst the wise !

The first parable to which I would call attention might be characterized "the parable of a word." It is given in the 14th sura of the Koran, as follows :—"Dost thou not see how God putteth forth a similitude representing a good word as a good tree, whose root is firmly fixed in

F

the earth, and whose branches reach unto heaven, which bringeth forth fruit in all seasons by the will of the Lord? And the likeness of an evil word is an evil tree, which is torn up from the face of the earth, and hath no stability."

Some Mohammedan commentators regard "the good word" as meaning the Koran, and "the bad word" as referring to heathen scriptures, which speak of gods many and lords many. It is every way preferable, however, to think that Mohammed, by "a good word" meant any word spoken by man that was kind, truthful, pure, and helpful. Like a good tree, a good word would strike down its roots, spread out its branches, and bear abundant and rich fruit. And, like a bad tree, a bad word would inevitably lead to withering and to death. Herein the Prophet spoke wisely. The power of a word for good or for evil is quite incalculable.

In the 16th sura of the Koran it is written : " God also propoundeth as a parable two men, one of them born dumb, who is unable to do or understand anything, but is a burden to his master. Whithersoever he shall send him, he shall not return with any success. Shall this man, and he who hath his speech and understanding, and who commandeth that which is just, and followeth the right way, be esteemed equal?" The dumb man referred to would appear to have been deaf as well as dumb, for it is said, "He was unable to do or understand anything." The point of the parable evidently is, to emphasize the blessings of speech and hearing. How helpless the deaf and dumb are ! the Prophet says. How burdensome to others ! Can such men be regarded as the equals of those who hear and speak, and who seek to turn their talents to good account ? The Koran answers "No !" and exhorts men who are not afflicted to praise God for His mercies. But what about those who are afflicted ? One could have wished that the parable had expressed a word of sympathy on behalf of those who suffer under the deprivation of the powers of speech and hearing. For such Mohammedanism has no amelioration but almsgiving. It is a matter of rejoicing, however, that Christianity has exerted itself by means of Deaf and Dumb Asylums to cause, as far as possible, the deaf to hear and the dumb to speak. Thus those whom Mohammed regarded as utterly useless and burdensome are being taught in Christian lands, not only to provide for their own wants, but to be of service to the community.

Amongst Mohammedans almsgiving seems to be regarded as the panacea for all the ills that flesh is heir to, so that it is no surprise to find that there are at least three parables in the Koran which enforce the duty of generous charity. These parables are designated respectively, " A grain of corn," " A flint covered with earth," and " A garden on a hill." They appear in the 2nd sura of the Koran.

The first is as follows :—" The similitude of those who lay out their substance for advancing the religion of God is as a grain of corn, which produceth seven ears, and in every ear a hundred grains."

The second reads :—" O true believers, make not your alms of none effect by reproaching or mischief, as he who layeth out what he hath to appear unto men to give alms. The likeness of such an one is a flint covered with earth, on which a violent rain falleth and leaveth it hard. They cannot prosper in anything which they have gained."

The third reads—" Those who lay out their substance from a desire to please God, or for an establishment for their souls, may be compared with a garden on a hill, on which rain falleth, and it bringeth forth its fruits twofold. And if rain falleth not on it, yet the dew falleth thereon. God seeth that which ye do."

The first and the third of these parables afford great support to generosity in almsgiving. The Faithful are assured by them that Allah will give increase to the open-handed—that, in fact, " the liberal soul shall be made fat "—the grain of corn producing a hundred grains ; the garden on a hill well-watered bringing forth fruit abundantly. In the second parable sincerity is enforced. What is given must be given readily, heartily, and with sincere good-will. If men give alms simply to be seen of men, and not from love, then, just as a flint covered with earth when the rain descends is shown to be a flint, so the heart of such men will be laid bare and shown to be as hard as a stone. Thus high motives are enjoined in charity. A Mohammedan writer, Abdul Kadir, has well said, "The miser who refuses to give in charity, and the man who gives to make a show of giving, are equally hateful in the sight of God."

In the 24th sura of the Koran there occurs a curious parable, which compares God to a lamp in a glass-case. It runs :—

"God is the Light of heaven and earth, and the similitude of His light is as a niche in a wall wherein a lamp is placed, and the lamp enclosed in a case of glass. The glass then appears as a shining star. It is lighted with the oil of a blessed tree, an olive, neither of the East nor of the West ; it wanteth little but that the oil thereof would give light although no fire touched it. This is light added unto light. And God will direct into His light whom He pleaseth."

This parable is a puzzle, and it would take a very wise man indeed to unravel it. One is inclined to think that Mohammed himself must have felt, when he had propounded it, that it was "a dark saying." Various attempts have been made to explain it, but with poor success. However, two things are clear enough, and are instructive. The one is that God is Light, and the other that He giveth light to whom He will. The moral of the parable probably is that men should continually wait upon God, that they may be guided and directed in all their ways.

There is a short parable in the 11th sura of the Koran which is intended to show the great difference between believers and unbelievers. It reads : "The similitude of the two parties is as the blind and the deaf, and as he who seeth and heareth. Shall they be compared as equal? Will ye not consider?" The matter is certainly worth considering. I suppose, generally speaking, we agree with Mohammed that he who can see and hear is to be preferred to him who is blind and deaf. Just so, says the Prophet, is it with believers and unbelievers! The former are to be preferred to the latter. Unbelievers, the parable hints, are spiritually blind and deaf. Having eyes they see not, and having ears they hear not, and do not understand.

The folly of those who fear not God, but who trust in idols or in themselves, is enforced by a parable called "The Spider's House." It occurs in the 29th sura of the Koran, and reads:

"'The likeness of those who take other patrons besides God is as the likeness of the spider, which maketh herself a house; but the weakest of all houses surely is the house of the spider, if men but knew it."

This parable reminds one very forcibly of an eloquent passage that occurs in the Book of Job. Bildad the Shuhite, speaking to the Patriarch, said, "Can the rush grow up without mire? Can the flag grow without water? Whilst it is yet in its greenness and not cut down it withereth before any other herb. So are the paths of all that forget God, and the hypocrite's hope shall perish: whose hope shall be cut off, and whose trust shall be a spider's web! He shall lean upon his house, but it shall not stand: he shall hold it fast, but it shall not endure." Thus the Book of Job and the Koran agree in stating that to be wicked is to be weak; and they both enforce the truth by the same illustration, viz., a spider's web or house. How frail the airy fabric is! With the sweep of his hand a child can destroy it, though it be woven never so cunningly and skilfully! Truly, " the weakest of all houses is the house of the spider, if men but knew it."

As a further illustration of the folly of sinful men, and as

a warning in particular to the covetous, a parable, entitled
" The Destroyed Garden," is given in the 68th sura of the
Koran.   It is as follows :—

"Verily we have tried the Meccans as we formerly tried
the owners of the garden when they swore that they would
gather the fruit in the morning, and added not the exception, if it please God : wherefore destruction from the Lord
encompassed it while they slept, and in the morning it was
like a garden whose fruits had been gathered.   And the
men called to one another as they rose in the morning,
saying, 'Go out early to the plantation.'   So they went on,
whispering to one another, 'No poor man shall enter the
garden this day.'   When they saw the garden blasted and
destroyed they said, 'We have certainly mistaken our way,'
but when they found that it was their own garden they exclaimed, 'Verily we are not permitted to reap the fruit
thereof.'   Then the worthier of them said, 'Did I not say
unto you, will ye not give praise unto God?'   Thereupon
both cried out, 'Verily we have been unjust doers! Woe
be unto us! Verily we have been transgressors! We earnestly
beseech our Lord to pardon us.'"

This parable is a little confused in thought, but Mohammedan commentators explain it thus :—The garden referred
to was, they say, a certain plantation of date-trees belonging
to a charitable man, who, when he gathered his dates,
always gave public notice to the poor, and informed them
that they might take away such fruit as the knife missed,
such as was a little spoiled by the wind, and such as fell to
the ground from the trees.   When the good man died, however, his two sons, the men of the parable, who were now
the owners of the garden, and whose hearts were filled with
covetousness, resolved that the poor should have nothing.
Acting on this resolution, they arose one morning very
early, and went out of the town to the garden, to gather
their dates before any one was astir.   When they arrived,
however, they found to their great surprise and grief that
the plantation had been blasted and destroyed.   At first

they thought that in the dim light they must have mistaken their way and got to the wrong place, but as soon as they could see clearly they convinced themselves that they were really in their own garden. Then it was revealed to them that this disaster had come upon them on account of their covetousness. Seeking to possess all, they lost everything. The path of wisdom, as well as of righteousness, they were shown, lay in doing what their father had done, viz., in sharing their goods with the poor. The men, convinced of their sin and folly, repented, and prayed to be forgiven, saying, " Peradventure God will give us in exchange a better garden than this."

This parable, with its commentary, conveys sound teaching in a pleasing form. Mohammedanism, as well as Christianity, evidently teaches that " there is that scattereth and yet increaseth, and there is that withholdeth more than is meet, but it tendeth to poverty." I wonder if Mohammed had ever read the words of Christ, " Take heed and beware of covetousness, for a man's life consisteth not in the abundance of the things which he possesseth."

I have been surprised to find that the Koran contains one parable, and one only, which has been taken from the Bible, and altered and not improved in the transference. It is the one called the Ewe Lamb, recorded in the Second Book of Samuel, which Nathan, the Prophet, related to convict David of the heinousness of his sin with Bathsheba, the wife of Uriah the Hittite. Mohammed tells the story as follows :—

" Hath the tale of the two adversaries come to thy knowledge ?—how they ascended over the wall and entered the presence of David, who was afraid of them ? They said, ' Fear not ! we are two adversaries who have a controversy. The one of us hath wronged the other, wherefore judge thou between us with truth, and be not unjust, but direct us in the even way. This my brother had ninety and nine sheep, and I had only one ewe lamb, and he said, ' Give her to me to keep,' and he prevailed against me. David answered, 'Verily he hath wronged thee in demanding thy ewe as an addition to his own sheep, and many of those who are concerned in business wrong one another, except those who believe, and do that which is right, but how few are they!' And David perceived that he had been tried by this parable, and he asked pardon of his Lord, and he fell down and bowed himself, and repented. Wherefore We forgave him his fault; and he shall be admitted to approach near unto us, and shall have an excellent place of abode in Paradise."

That is how the Koran tells the story of the fall of David, and of how his transgression was brought home to him. Happy would it be for Mohammedan, Jew, and Christian, if the parable were remembered throughout life!

There is a short parable in the 16th sura which is worth considering. It refers to that humble but useful little creature the bee. It is written very quaintly :—

"The Lord spake by inspiration unto the bee, saying, 'Provide thee houses in the mountains, and in the trees, of those materials wherewith men build hives. Then eat of every kind of fruit, and walk in the beaten paths of thy Lord.' There proceedeth from them a liquor of various colour, wherein is a medicine for man. Verily herein is a sign unto people who consider."

Just as Solomon said to the Jews, "Go to the ant, thou sluggard, consider her ways and be wise," so Mohammed said to the people of Islam, "Go to the bee."

And the lessons to be learnt from the bee, according to the parable, are industry, skill, and usefulness. The home which the bee makes for itself is truly a beautiful construction, which no geometrician can excel. And how ceaselessly the work of filling the hive goes on. And how useful honey becomes in the service of man!

And man has to imitate the bee in industry and skill. Like the bee, also, he must spread an atmosphere of sweetness all around him, and redeem the time.

In the 18th sura of the Koran it is written :

" Propound a similitude of this present life. It is like water which we send down from heaven ; and the herb of the earth is mixed therewith ; and after it hath been green and flourishing, in the morning it becometh dry stubble, which the winds scatter abroad, and God is able to do all things. Wealth and children are the ornament of this present life ; but good works, which are permanent, are better in the sight of thy Lord, with respect to the reward, and better with respect to hope."

Mohammed in this parable wished by the similitude of water to show that life is a good thing, a precious gift of Allah, which, however, may become either a blessing or a curse to humanity, according as it is wisely or foolishly used. The Prophet wished the Faithful to choose the better part, that their lives might be " as rivers of water in a dry place" to others, and bring prosperity and fruitfulness to themselves both here and hereafter.

Here, strictly speaking, the parables of Mohammed and the Koran end. Sale, however, in a long and learned introduction to his translation of the Mohammedan Scriptures, relates a story which is too good to be omitted ; and with this I would conclude this chapter on Mohammedan Parables. It has reference to the righteous judgments of God.

A matter of grave inquiry amongst the followers of Islam at one time was, whether the body or the soul of man would be punished for sin. The argument was conducted thus, with great subtlety.

The soul said, " O Lord, my body I received from Thee, for Thou didst create me without a hand to lay hold with, foot to walk with, an eye to see with, or an understanding to apprehend with, until I entered into this body : therefore punish my body eternally, but not me."

Then the body, fearing the anger of God, exclaimed, "O Lord, Thou didst create me like a stock of wood, having neither hand that I could hold with, nor feet that I could walk with, till this soul, like a ray of light, entered into me, and my tongue began to speak, my eye to see, and my foot to walk: therefore punish my soul eternally, and not me."

The disputants were silenced by the parable of the blind man and the lame man, which runs :—

"A certain King, having a pleasant garden, in which were ripe fruits, set two persons to keep it, one of whom was blind and the other lame, the former not being able to see the fruit nor the latter to gather it. The lame man, however, seeing the fruit, persuaded the blind man to take him up upon his shoulders, and by that means he easily gathered the fruit, which they divided between them. The Lord of the garden coming some time after, and inquiring about his fruit, each began to excuse himself, the blind man saying that he had no eyes to see with, and the lame man that he had no feet to approach the trees with. But the King, ordering the lame man to be set on the back of the blind, passed sentence on, and punished them both.

"Hear ye this parable. In the same manner God will deal with the body and the soul. It will be vain of man on that day to deny his evil actions, since men and angels, and his own members, yea the very earth itself, will be ready to bear witness against him."

Thus is the truth enforced that man cannot dissociate himself from himself. Islamism and Christianity agree in this: "Be not deceived; God is not mocked; for whatsoever a man soweth that shall he also reap. For he that soweth to his flesh shall of the flesh reap corruption; but he that soweth to the Spirit shall of the Spirit reap life everlasting."

CHAPTER VIII

MIRACLES

MOHAMMEDANISM, like other religions, has its recorded miracles, but these are of a childish and utterly foolish character. We have but to compare them with the noblest of the Jewish miracles, and with the miracles of Christ, to see how far below Judaism and Christianity Islam is in its conception of a miracle.

Mohammed's attitude towards this subject was a credit to him, for he uniformly denied that he possessed the power to work miracles. When he first claimed to be the Prophet of Allah his friends and enemies alike urged him to give proof of his calling by performing some marvellous deeds such as the Prophets of old had wrought. But Mohammed felt that he had no such power, and was honest enough to say so.

In the 2nd sura of the Koran it is written: "They who know not the Scriptures say 'Unless God speak unto us, or thou show us a sign, we will not believe.' So said they before them. We have already shown abundant signs. We have sent thee in truth a bearer of good tidings, and a preacher, and thou shalt not be questioned."

But the people continued to question, urging Mohammed vehemently to do some mighty work, that they might believe on him. In the 17th sura some of the words of these cavillers are recorded. They run: "We will by no means believe on thee until thou cause a spring of water to gush forth for us out of the earth, or thou have a garden of palm-trees and vines, and thou cause rivers to spring forth from the midst thereof in abundance, or thou cause the heaven to fall down upon us, or thou bring God and the angels to vouch for thee, or thou have a house of gold, or thou ascend by a ladder to heaven."

These factious demands troubled Mohammed sorely, and he, at times, fain wished that he had the power to meet them, but, knowing that he had not, he answered always in the same strain, " Verily I am a preacher only. Allah hath not called me to work miracles."

The nearest approach to a miracle that Mohammed allowed to be associated with his name was an event that occurred on the famous battle-field of Badr, when the Prophet and his adherents of Medina, though only 319 in number, defeated an army of more than 1,000 Meccans. The event is referred to in the 3rd sura of the Koran, where it is written : " Ye have already had a miracle shown you in two armies which attacked each other. One army fought for God's true religion, but the other for infidelity."

Mohammedan commentators say that the miracle of the field of Badr consisted in three things. Firstly, Mohammed, by angelic guidance, took a handful of gravel, and threw it towards the enemy, saying, " May their faces be confounded ;" and thereupon the Meccans turned their backs and fled. Secondly, by the grace of God, the eyes of the infidels were made to see double, so that they imagined a host was encamped against them, and consequently were discouraged at the outset. Thirdly, the Angel Gabriel appeared on the scene with thousands of attendants, and really did the fighting, though the little army of the Faithful seemed to do it. The whole story is ridiculous. What happened doubtless was that Mohammed threw a handful of dust in the faces of his foes as emblematic of what he sought to bring them to, and then led his followers to the attack with his accustomed bravery, and the day was carried by enthusiasm, skill, and hard fighting. The idea of the miracle was probably an after-thought, when the Prophet came to consider the wonderful fact that 300 men had put 1,000 to flight.

Though Mohammed, according to the Koran, never laid claim to the power of working miracles, his fanatical and credulous adherents, in all the generations since his death, have maintained that he had the power, and that he used it too. Mohammedans cannot bear the thought that their Prophet should be a whit behind any other prophet the world had seen, so they have invented innumerable instances of miraculous occurrences in association with his life. Even at Mohammed's birth, it is said, some very wonderful things happened, such as a violent earthquake, shaking the palace of the King of Persia to its very foundations, and the sacred fire going out, which for a thousand years had burned incessantly on the altar of Zoroaster, under watch of the Magi. These and other remarkable events which happened at that time in all parts of the world must be regarded, we are told, as signs and wonders announcing the birth of the last and greatest of all the Prophets of the Lord.

Gibbon, who, in his description of Mohammedanism, does not seem to have overlooked a single point of interest, says: "The votaries of Mohammed are more assured than himself of his miraculous gifts, and their confidence and credulity increase as they are farther removed from the time and place of his spiritual exploits. They believe, or affirm, that trees went forth to meet him, that he was saluted by stones, that water gushed out of his fingers, and that he fed the hungry, cured the sick, and raised the dead: that a beam groaned to him, that a camel complained to him, that a shoulder of mutton informed him of its being poisoned, and that both animate and inanimate nature were equally subject to the apostle of God."

Arnold, in his book on "Islam and Christianity," also enumerates some of the Mohammedan miracles, as follows: "A camel weeps, and is calmed at the touch of Mohammed; the hair grows upon a boy's head when the Prophet lays his hand upon it; a horse is cured from stumbling; and the eye of a soldier is healed, and made better than the other."

Thus the credulous add miracle to miracle, and some doctors of Islamism have actually computed that at the least Mohammed wrought 1,000 striking miracles, while of other not quite such marvellous, and yet very wonderful deeds, he performed 3,450.

In the 54th sura of the Koran a few words occur around which a strange story has gathered. The words are : "The hour of judgment approacheth, and the moon hath been split in sunder ; but if the unbelievers see a sign, they turn aside, saying : This is a powerful charm ; and they accuse thee, O Mohammed, of imposture." Any one would think that the Prophet was referring to something that would come to pass on the day of judgment. I believe he was. But Mohammedans explain the passage another way, associating it with what they call a truly marvellous miracle. The story goes, that one evening when Mohammed was talking to a group of his fellow-townsmen of Mecca, and urging them to forsake their idols and worship God only, that they turned upon him, and demanded a sign from Heaven in support of his claims. "You shall have a sign," the Prophet is reported to have answered. "Do you see yonder moon ? Well, at my word it shall be cloven in two ; one part vanishing and the other remaining." The word was spoken, and, to the surprise of all, it happened as Mohammed had predicted. But that was not all. The Prophet spoke again, commanding the moon to come down from her place in the heavens, which she at once proceeded to do. Arriving at Mecca, she is said to have made seven revolutions round the sacred temple of "the pure white stone," then to have saluted Mohammed in the Arabian tongue, and finally, after contracting her dimensions, to have entered at the collar of the Prophet and come out at his shirt sleeve. After these astonishing tricks, she returned to her proper station in the sky, saying as she went, that now perchance men would believe that Mohammed had power with God, and could prevail.

Turning from the ridiculous moon story, which one

would think was too stupid even for the most vulgar to believe, let us glance at another so-called miracle which is of considerable human interest. It is in association with a cave, and has reference to a stirring incident in the life of the Prophet. On the eve of that ever-memorable Hejira, or Flight from Mecca, Mohammed was in great danger of losing his life. His enemies in the town, having learnt that he proposed departing to Medina, though for some reason he delayed to start, met in solemn council to consider what should be done. With one voice the chiefs of the city decided that the peace of the community could only be secured by the death of Mohammed.

It was resolved that a man from each principal family should be chosen, and that at a given signal the house of the Prophet should be surrounded, and that every dagger should be buried in his heart. Mohammed, however, was warned by some one of his danger—the Faithful say by the Angel Gabriel—and leaving Ali, his son-in-law, in his place, he escaped by the back of his house to his faithful adherent, Abu Bekr, with whom he made for the mountains. When the conspirators arrived at the house of the Prophet, they, of course, found only Ali there, who disclaimed all knowledge of the whereabouts of his leader. Rushing out, the duped chiefs sought high and low for their prey. Meanwhile Mohammed and his companion had reached the mountains ; and there, on a rocky summit, approached by a rugged and difficult path, they crept through a low opening that admitted them into a cave called Thor.

In this cave they remained for a few days, as the pursuit was prompt, and the search in all the neighbourhood thorough. So great was the strain on the nerves of the hunted men that the brave Abu Bekr almost gave way to despair. He is said to have whispered tremblingly in the ear of the Prophet, "What if our pursuers should find our cave ? We are but two !" "Nay !" was the noble answer, "Thou dost mistake, Abu ! We are three ! Allah is with us !" Thus did Mohammed cheer his fainting follower.

And that saying of his was perhaps the grandest of his whole life. Whatever faults Mohammed might have, he believed implicitly in God, and, according to his faith, it was done unto him. He was not found by the Meccans, and eventually he reached Medina, and entered upon that way of life which led to the highest earthly power and glory. But the miraculous part of the incident has not been mentioned. Briefly, it was this. Mohammedans say that the Prophet's enemies, in their search, arrived at the mouth of the cave, and that but for the special intervention of Allah they would have entered, and found Mohammed. God, it is affirmed, caused several things to happen in a moment of time, which completely deceived the search party. A tree grew up in front of the cave, some branches of which just covered the mouth, and on these branches a wild pigeon built its nest, and laid two eggs. A spider also wove a most wonderful web all over the entrance.

When one of the pursuers said, "Perhaps Mohammed is hiding in this cave," others, stooping down, remarked, "Nay, not so! Look at that spider's web! And mark that bird's nest with eggs in it right over the mouth! Nay! Mohammed is not in the cave! Why, a mouse could not have crawled in without breaking the web; and certainly no human being, without upsetting the nest! Come away! Let us search elsewhere!" Thus, by a miracle, was the Prophet's life saved.

The other miracles of Islam, besides those associated with Mohammed, are all of a stupid and frivolous character.

For example, there is the case of Ezra and his ass. This is referred to in the 2nd sura of the Koran. It is said that Ezra the Scribe was riding one day on his ass by the ruins of Jerusalem after the holy city had been destroyed by the Chaldeans. As the rider went slowly along he fell into a meditation about the ruined city, and doubted in his mind whether God could ever raise such a deserted and miserable place to anything like its old grandeur again.

As a punishment for his doubts, and to show him that

all things are possible with God, the Scribe, by a Divine decree, was deprived of life on the spot. However, his body was not allowed to crumble to dust. For a hundred years it remained on the roadside near Jerusalem, and then all at once by another Divine decree life came into it again, and Ezra stood upon his feet.

Thinking he had only been asleep for a short time, and feeling hungry, he stretched out his hand to the basket he had with him, and partook of some figs and a cruse of wine. These things, marvellous to relate, had not been spoiled or corrupted by the passage of time. Having satisfied his hunger, it occurred to Ezra that before he went to sleep he had been astride his faithful ass. Where was she now?

It was in vain the Scribe looked around. Not a trace of the animal could be seen. But what was that at his feet? The skeleton of an ass it seemed to be! Then was it revealed to the astonished man that he had been dead a hundred years as a punishment for his want of faith in the power of God, and that the dry bones lying before him were indeed all that was left of his ass.

But the wonders were not yet over. As Ezra gazed in sorrow at the skeleton, he was startled to notice that the dry bones began to move, and lo! they gathered themselves together and stood up, and flesh grew over them, and they became clothed, and life entered into the animal, and with a loud bray it announced in no uncertain manner that the Scribe had recovered his useful servant again.

Then, as the Koran puts it, a voice was heard from the most excellent glory declaring, "Look on thy food, and thy drink, they are not yet corrupted; and look on thine ass." Ezra looked, and considered, and devoutly answered, "I know now that God is able to do all things."

On the Kaaba or Cube House at Mecca there is fixed a golden spout, about which a curious story is told by

Mohammedans. Mrs. Meer Hassan Ali in her book on the "Mussulmans of India," relates it at great length. I will simply give the outlines of it.

Once upon a time a certain poor man of great sanctity went on a pilgrimage to Mecca. When he arrived at the sacred city he was without a coin in his pockets, and to beg he was ashamed.

Being in a very depressed state of mind on account of his poverty, the poor fellow thought that he would approach the Holy Temple and pray to God for assistance. As he drew near the edifice his eye was caught by the evidences of its wealth. Everything about it seemed to be made of, or covered with, the precious metals, or cloths of gold and silver.

One thing in particular attracted his attention, and that was a water-spout which was composed of solid gold. Thereupon he reasoned thus with himself: " This is the dry season of the year, and that water-spout is not needed where it is at present ; why should it not deliver me out of my distress? Further, it is not right that I should be famishing here while that gold remains there."

But how was the coveted treasure to be gained? It would be a sin and a sacrilege to steal it, but how could it be got without? The good man had recourse to prayer. "O God," he said, "I cannot steal, and to beg I am ashamed. I desire that spout of gold which hangs there to relieve my necessities. With Thee nothing is impossible. Command that the spout descend into the skirt of my garment which I now hold out to receive it." The prayer, so the story says, was answered, and the poor man walked away quickly with his prize.

However, in seeking to dispose of the spout for ready cash, the vendor was accused of theft and taken before the Cadi. While protesting his poverty and innocence, the magistrate suggested to him dryly that the two did not go well together, and advised him to confess that want had driven him to crime. But the good man held with dignity to his first statement, and explained fully how the spout had come into his possession.

Starting up from the judicial bench, as an idea flashed through his mind, the Cadi said : " Come with me," and he led the way to the Holy Temple. The spout was fixed securely in its old place, and then the judge said to the poor man, " What has been done once can doubtless be done again. Call for that spout to come to thee." The man called, in the name of Allah, and to the consternation of the Cadi and the assembled thousands of spectators the mass of gold descended into the arms of the man of prayer and faith.

" A miracle ! A miracle !" was the cry that went up from tens of thousands of voices at that marvellous sight. The poor man became a saint on the spot, and the people sought to touch if it might be but the hem of his garment.

The Cadi extolled his virtues also, and in lieu of the golden spout, which could not be parted with, he bestowed upon the saint its weight in the current coin of Arabia, thus raising him from poverty to affluence.

There is a miracle often told by Mohammedans in association with the life of Omar the second Commander of the Faithful, which I will next relate. It is said that by the sternness of his temper, though he was a just man, Omar raised up many enemies, and that he was often in danger of assassination, but by miraculous intervention he was for a long time preserved from all harm, though he fell at last by the dagger of a fanatic.

The most popular of the miraculous deliverances is one that runs thus :—A man who had resolved to slay Omar followed him about for days watching for an opportunity. At length he thought the chance had come. The Caliph was alone in a quiet garden meditating on the letters he had received that day, of events that were happening in far distant provinces of the Empire, and looking to Allah for counsel and guidance in his multiform and anxious duties.

The assassin was watching the Commander of the Faithful, and was about to spring from his hiding-place upon him, when suddenly a fierce lion appeared on the scene, and began to walk round and round Omar as if to protect him from threatened danger.   The Caliph looked up. The would-be murderer fled.   As he fled he threw a rapid glance back, and saw that the lion was licking the feet of Omar, and that the latter was patting it affectionately on the head.   Then the lion vanished into space.

The man spread the story far and wide, and it was ever after believed that a special Providence watched over the Commander of the Faithful, and that miracles occurred to protect his life from the hatred of his enemies.

Many other so-called miracles might be recorded, but I will close this chapter by a reference to only one more.   It is associated with Abraham, the Friend of God, whose son Ishmael is regarded as the progenitor of the desert Arabs.

The Mohammedans say that the mind of Abraham was often exercised with thoughts of the resurrection of the dead.   It was a subject which he could not thoroughly grasp or understand.   In the 2nd sura of the Koran it is written : "Abraham said, O Lord, show me how Thou wilt raise the dead. God said, Dost thou not yet believe?   He answered yes : but I ask this that my heart may rest at ease."

Thereupon God instructed the Patriarch, so the story runs, to take four birds—an eagle, a peacock, a raven, and a dove—and kill them. Abraham did so, pounding the birds in a mortar, and mingling their flesh and feathers together.   Then he divided the mass into four parts, and laid the parts on so many mountains, keeping the heads however in his right hand.

"Now," said the Lord, "call for the birds by name." The Patriarch called, and immediately the pieces came flying together, and the birds recovered their first shape, and when Abraham placed their heads upon their respective bodies they all signified their gratitude by making the peculiar noise appropriate to their kind.

It was thereupon made known to Abraham that the miracle he had seen wrought was just a type or emblem of things to come in the great day of the Resurrection of all mankind. By a word God would make the dead to live; and in a moment, in the twinkling of an eye, bodies would assume their old and well-known earthly appearance.

Abraham was satisfied, and so are all faithful Mohammedans. As for myself I can only wonder that men can have any faith in such childish and ridiculous miracles.

It is greatly to be regretted that Mohammedans have not had the wisdom to accept their Prophet's disclaimer of all power to work miracles. It is a pity, also, that Mohammed himself should have felt it necessary to invent such puerile stories in connection with the Old Testament characters he has introduced into the Koran. In the matter of miracles, as of parables, Mohammedanism cuts a sorry figure.

CHAPTER IX

In 1890 I attended the Christian Passion Play at Ober-Ammergau, and as in India I was a spectator of the Mohammedan Passion Play four or five years in succession, I am in a position to draw comparisons between the two. In deep human interest, as well as in beauty of conception and skill of management, the Western play exceeds the Eastern. Yet the latter is truly impressive, and most touching in its delineation of the sufferings and sorrows that are related.

To trace the origin of the Mohammedan Passion Play we must let our thoughts go back almost to the time of the Prophet. Already in these studies the names of Ali, Fatima, and their two sons, Hasan and Hosein, have been mentioned, and it is with these relatives of Mohammed rather than with the Prophet himself that the Passion Play deals.

In the chapter on the Commanders of the Faithful the story is related of the sad death of Ali by the assassin's knife in the mosque at Kufa, near Bagdad, whither he had removed the seat of government from Medina. That was in A.D. 660. Fatima had died some time before, in the year 633.

At Ali's death Muawiya, of Damascus, assumed the title of Caliph, or Commander of the Faithful, but the people of Arabia held aloof from him, and chose Hasan as their leader. This Prince, like his father, however, lacked decision of character, and allowed the precious days to slip by without making a decided move to win for himself the full inheritance of the Caliphs. In less than half a year his following fell away, and he retired into private life at Medina, where, in A.D. 669, he died of poison administered to him, some writers say, by his wife, at the instigation of his enemies.

Hosein was then the only pretender to the throne left, but Muawiya, feeling that he had nothing to fear from him, treated him with kindness. In the spring of A.D. 680 Muawiya died, and was buried at Damascus, and his son Yezid reigned in his stead. Now came the opportunity of Hosein to revolt, instigated thereto by the inhabitants of Kufa. But the rebellion was carried out in the half-hearted manner characteristic of the family of Ali, and was of course doomed to failure. Hosein was slain by the spear of a foe under painful and distressing circumstances.

The whole history of the house of Ali was a chequered one. There is something very pathetic about the fate of the near relatives of Mohammed—his son-in-law stabbed, one grandson poisoned, and the other speared. Little wonder that those who really loved the Prophet and his children should have given way to a madness of grief which led to schism, as they thought of the fearful events that had followed one another so rapidly.

The Mohammedan Passion Play records those events. This famous play, which is acted every year with astonishing enthusiasm in Persia, India, and Afghanistan, is the striking form in which the Shias perpetuate the story of the wrongs which their Imams suffered in the early days of the Faith.

The time of year when the Passion Play is performed varies according to our Western reckoning of time. The Mussulman year is lunar. It is during the first ten days of the first month of their year that the Mohammedans celebrate the Passion Play or Moharram, as it is called in the East. The ten days are kept as a sacred and solemn feast. The Faithful are expected to be specially liberal in almsgiving during this season, and to concentrate their thoughts as much as possible on the tragedies which are commemorated by the Play or Plays, which take place at least once, and in some places twice, on every one of the ten days. The last day, "Ashura," is considered the most important of all, for it is kept as the anniversary of the death of Hosein, whose untimely martyrdom was the culmination of the woes of the family of the Prophet.

Many Mohammedan families keep the Moharram in the privacy of their own homes. When that is the case there is no actual Passion Play performed, but the story of the Passion is read to the inmates by the head of the household. And to make the recorded events still more solemn, and the impression still more lasting, Tazias are set up in the home. The term Tazia signifies " grief," but the thing itself is a model of the mausoleum which was erected at Kerbelah, in Arabia, over the remains of Hasan and Hosein. Tazias are formed of every variety of material, according to the rank, wealth, and fancy of the family. Some that I saw in India were made of silver, and others of bamboo, covered with mica in sheets, and still others simply of paper. I have heard of their being made of ivory, ebony, and sandalwood. In addition to the Tazias that are prepared for the house, which are usually fixtures, others can be got which are intended for public processions, and especially for that procession which takes place on the tenth night of Moharram, when tens of thousands of people march through the streets, carrying these models of their martyred Imams' tomb. The Tazias thus carried are eventually deposited with funereal rites in the burial-grounds outside the towns or villages.

The Passion Play proper is enacted in large buildings called in Persia " Tekyas," and in India " Imambaras." Some of the finest I have seen are in Lucknow. One in particular is a magnificent edifice, which will hold, probably, over 20,000 people. An Imambara, like a mosque, is usually a square building with a dome or cupola top.

Unlike the mosque, however, an Imambara is superbly decorated within. The floor is carpeted, the walls are covered with mirrors, the reading-desk or pulpit is trimmed with cloth-of-gold or broadcloth of black or green ; handsome and costly banners are arranged here and there, and from the ceiling hang beautiful chandeliers, which light up in the evening the brilliant and impressive scene. A Mohammedan, when asked on one occasion why mosques were so plain, and Imambaras so grand, answered, "Mosques are devoted to the service of God, and consequently there should be nothing therein in the way of ornaments or worldly attractions calculated to draw off the mind or divert the attention from sacred things ; but Imambaras are erected for the purpose of doing honour to the memory of the Imams, and therefore a grand show is permissible and right." There is a magnificent building which I saw at Cairo, closely associated with Hosein, for it is said to contain his head, and is called after him. In that building, I am told, some very fine representations of the Passion Play are given. It is in Persia, however, that the Play is to be witnessed at its best ; and therefore Matthew Arnold, in his well-known description of it, styles it "the Persian Passion Play." In some of the Imambaras of India, however, excellent representations have been given ; and as regards the events on the closing day, I do not think it would be possible for any people to surpass Indian Mussulmans in the magnitude of their gatherings, or in the impressiveness of their displays.

The stage of the Tekya, or Imambara, is commonly in the centre of the building. There is nothing elaborate about it, as there is at the Passion Play at Ober-Ammergau. There is no skilfully-arranged mechanism to aid the acting, and to make the scenes portrayed appear the more real. All is open to the gaze of the audience, who advance even to the steps of the stage, and help the actors up and down. The performers are men and boys. Women take no part in the Mohammedan Passion Play other than as spectators.

Children, some of whom are very young, appear in the place of women. Count Gobineau, in his long but charming description of the play as performed in Persia, says: "Nothing is more touching than to see these little things of three or four years old, dressed in black gauze frocks, with large sleeves, and having on their heads small, round black caps, embroidered with silver and gold, kneeling beside the body of the actor who represents the martyr of the day, embracing him, and with their little hands covering themselves with chopped straw for sand, in sign of grief."

The chief director of the Play is called the Oostad, who answers to the Greek choragus, or, as we would say, the Master of the Ceremonies. Nothing comes amiss with this man. He is always on the stage, with the book of the piece in his hand, ready to give the actors their cue, or, in case of need, to act himself. Sometimes he will make an audible commentary on what is passing, and ask the compassion and the tears of the audience on behalf of the martyrs. At other times he busies himself with dressing the actors, or encouraging the children to speak out, and do their best with the parts assigned to them. All this by-play goes on in full view of the audience, but does not seem to interfere in the least with the general enjoyment. The fact is there is such an intense feeling of earnestness in the minds of both actors and spectators that they have no thought for anything but the tragedies enacted. Stanley Lane Poole, in his "Studies in a Mosque," speaking of the earnestness of the actors in Persia, says: "Nowhere else on earth can we see such passion of grief, such grandeur of selfless sympathy, as here, where the people forget the passing of time, and the changing of place, and taking the rude platform for the real scene of the martyrdom, and the actors for those they represent, furiously stone the soldiers of Yezid, and drive them from the stage; and the murderer-actor so loses himself in his part that he thinks he sees the real Hosein in the man before him, and actually beheads him before all eyes."

As the Play takes ten days to enact, it will easily·be seen that it is impossible in this chapter to give a complete account of it. Besides, it varies greatly in different countries and in different towns, so that no one description would give a perfectly accurate idea of it. I shall therefore content myself with just glancing at a few of the more important points. The introductory act is sometimes, strange to say, a scene taken from the Jewish Scriptures. Joseph and his brethren appear on the stage, and the old Bible story is portrayed at great length. There is the consultation of the brothers as to what they shall do with "this dreamer and babbler," the resolution to throw him into a disused pit or well, the taking him out again to sell him to the Midianitish merchants, the producing of the blood-stained coat before the eyes of the sorrowful father ; and then Jacob is depicted as left alone with his grief, refusing to be comforted by either sons or daughters. But lo, the Angel Gabriel visits him, and draws near to comfort the sorrowful old man ! And the method that the heavenly visitor adopts to administer consolation is that which has been used in like circumstances all the world over. Gabriel declares that what has happened to Jacob is just what happens to others, and that there is no household without its bereavements and sorrows. "Yea," says the comforter, "I foresee in the future a much more distressing case even than thine, O Jacob, a case that will make heaven and earth to weep." The Patriarch doubts it, and in the bitterness of his spirit moans, "Was there ever sorrow like unto my sorrow !" Gabriel thereupon causes some ministering angels suddenly to appear, and orders them to perform a Passion Play before Jacob, to convince him of the fact that the future has in store a tragedy which will surpass all others in painful and sad details.

Thus the Mohammedan Play is skilfully introduced. It has now really commenced. And the next act takes us to Medina, the city of the Prophet, and we are asked to enter the house of Mohammed's son-in-law, and look upon the

Holy Family, viz., Ali, Fatima, and their children, Hasan and Hosein. It is morning, and Fatima is seated with the little Hosein on her knees, dressing him. She combs his hair, talking to him meanwhile in cooing accents, which mothers only can adopt. Suddenly the comb is caught in a knot, and as it goes through it a hair comes out, and the little fellow starts. Fatima is distressed at having given her son even a moment's trouble, and looks at him tenderly, and soothes him fondly. While she is so doing, an angel appears before her, and reproves her weakness, saying, " A hair falls from the child's head, and you weep. What would you do if you knew the destiny that awaits him, the countless wounds with which that body shall one day be pierced, the agony that shall rend your soul?" Shortly after Fatima and Ali go out to visit their father Mohammed, and leave the children, Hasan and Hosein, to play in the garden. Some little friends join the young people, and all goes merrily. They amuse themselves with digging holes in the ground, and building mounds. Hosein, in particular, throws himself with great enthusiasm into the occupation ; so much so indeed that by the time Fatima and Ali return, he has scooped out a big hole that has all the appearance of a grave. The mother, looking at it, has a foreboding of trouble. In the afternoon the parents go out again, and the children resume their play ; but ere long they are interrupted in it by some big, fierce boys, who begin to pelt them with stones. A companion shields Hosein as well as he can ; but both are struck on the temples, and fall to the ground senseless. Then the tormentors turn and flee. And who are they? The audience in the Imambara at once perceive, with a shudder, that they are the future murderers of the Imams.

With the illness of little Hosein the second or third act ends ; and on another evening, and in another act, attention is drawn to certain noble deeds in the life of his brother Hasan. The time is many years later. Mohammed is dead. Ali and Fatima are gone also. It is a period of national turmoil and anxiety. Hasan has renounced his claim to the Commandership of the Faithful, which has been usurped by Muawiya, and lives in dignified seclusion at Medina. There the people almost worship him for his many noble traits of character, and call him Hasan the Good. Two instances of his greatness of soul we will now consider:—

1. Behold that actor representing Hasan as seated at table in his own house. It is the time of the evening meal. A slave waits upon him with a hot, savoury dish, and in a careless moment upsets it right over the Prince. The slave drops on his knees in terror, and cries out to his master in words taken from the Koran, "Paradise is for those who bridle their anger." Hasan, who has taken the mishap in good part, answers quietly, "I am not angry." The slave proceeds,—"and for those who forgive men." "I forgive thee," answers Hasan. But the slave finishes the quotation,—"for God loveth the beneficent." "Thou sayest truly," exclaims Hasan; "and since it is so, I give thee thy liberty, and four hundred pieces of silver."

2. The scene changes. Behold Hasan lying on his death-bed. The spectators in the Imambara still their very breath to hear the words of the departing saint. His brother Hosein bends over him, and says, "O my brother, and thou art about to leave me alone! Cruel the foe that gave poison to thee, the most gentle of all mankind! But I will find him out and punish him as he deserves, and avenge thy death!" The pathos of the incident is that neither brother suspects that it was Hosein's wife, a tool in the hands of their enemies, who had done the sinful deed! When he hears the vow to avenge his death, the dying man raises himself up, however, and, speaking earnestly, in feeble tones, utters these memorable words: "Beloved brother, let my murderer alone. He and I will meet some day before the throne of God. It is for us to bear no malice, but to forgive." Then the spirit of Hasan the Good wings its

flight to Paradise. And sobs are heard in every corner of the Imambara.

Another act takes the story of the Passion Play rapidly on. The men of Kufa, when Muawiya was dead and Yezid on the Throne, are represented as sending messengers to Hosein at Medina, urging him to come to them, and set up the standard of the Commander of the Faithful. Against the advice of his best friends, who knew the fickleness of the Kufians, Hosein assented and set out on the rash expedition, accompanied by his wives, his brothers, and his children, with only forty horsemen and a few foot-soldiers as an escort. News of the rebellion reached Yezid at Damascus, who post-haste sent troops to strengthen the garrison at Kufa, and a little army of four thousand to intercept the march of Hosein. When the latter was within twenty-five miles of his destination he was stopped, and as there was no possibility of retreat, he had to choose between surrender and death in battle. The attitude of Yezid towards the unfortunate Prince may be judged from the contents of the letter which he sent to the Governor of Kufa, the General of his Arabian armies. Yezid wrote : " If Hosein and his followers submit, and take the oath of allegiance, treat them kindly ; if they refuse, slay them, ride over them, trample them under the feet of your horses." Thus was Hosein brought face to face with death ; and in succeeding acts we shall see how bravely he met it.

A most touching act is that which is styled " The Family of the Tent." Hosein, when he saw that he must either surrender or fight, called his relatives and few soldiers together, and said to them : " These troops seek no life but mine ; hasten ye to a place of safety, and leave me to my fate." But not a soul would leave him, for they loved him better than life. " Nay," they answered, " we will die with thee." With tears streaming down his cheeks, Hosein thanked them, saying, " May Allah recompense you !" Then the gallant chief prepared himself and his people for the coming struggle. Bringing all their tents together, he

caused a trench to be dug around them, which was filled
with logs and brushwood. "At any rate," he said, "if die
we must, we will die like heroes." The morning of the
10th day of Moharram dawned, and saw a determined
band of less than a hundred souls, resolved to defend
themselves against four thousand. But ere the strife could
begin Hosein mounted a camel, and riding out before the
army of his foes, addressed the Kufians who were there,
reminding them of the invitations they had sent him, and
of the promises they had made, and calling upon them
now, even at the eleventh hour, to join his standard.
Overawed by the other troops, the Kufians as a body gave
no response, but thirty of their number could not resist the
appeal of Hosein, and sprang to his side and returned with
him to the Family of the Tent.

Thereupon the battle commenced, and from the beginning to the end it was, of course, nothing but a slaughter.
Prodigies of valour were shown on that famous field of
Kerbelah; but ere the sun went down scarce a soldier of
Hosein's remained alive. Let Gibbon tell the rest, for
no one has told it better: "Alone, weary, and wounded,
Hosein seated himself at the door of his tent. As he
tasted a drop of water he was pierced in the mouth with a
dart; and his son and nephew, two beautiful youths, were
killed in his arms. He lifted his hands to heaven; they
were full of blood; and he uttered a funeral prayer for the
living and the dead. In a transport of despair his sister
issued from the tent, and adjured the General of the
Kufians that he would not suffer Hosein to be murdered
before his eyes. A tear trickled down the venerable beard
of the General, and the boldest of his soldiers fell back on
every side as the dying hero threw himself among them.
The remorseless Shamar, a name detested by the faithful,
reproached their cowardice; and the grandson of Mohammed was slain with three-and-thirty strokes of lances and
swords." Thus perished Hosein, in the flower of his days
—a noble but unfortunate prince, whom Mohammedans

regard as a martyr, and who is the central figure of their famous Passion Play.

The closing act of the Play moves every spectator to a paroxysm of grief. The body of Hosein is represented as being trampled on and mutilated. When the head is struck off, a thrill of horror passes through the audience. The bloody trophy is held aloft, and then carried away to the castle of Kufa, and the inhuman Governor is depicted as striking it on the mouth with a cane, while an aged Mussulman standing by exclaims, "Alas! on those lips I have seen the lips of the Apostle of God."

Here the sad story ends; the Passion Play is over. It has been one long-drawn-out scene of tragedy and emotion, peculiarly Oriental. And the main characters are not unworthy of the grief that their sufferings have called forth. Ali and his sons, Hasan and Hosein, were truly noble men —men of righteousness—men of a brave, a humble, and a forgiving spirit. Their lives deserved to be commemorated in a Passion Play; for there was a peculiar pathos about them, and they were not spent selfishly or in vain. As Matthew Arnold very beautifully says, in "Essays in Criticism," "It is a long way from Kerbelah to Calvary; but the sufferers of Kerbelah hold aloft to the eyes of millions the lesson so loved by the Sufferer of Calvary, 'Learn of Me, for I am meek and lowly in heart, and ye shall find rest unto your souls.'"

CHAPTER X

LEGENDS AND SUPERSTITIONS

In all Mohammedan countries there is gross ignorance amongst the masses of the people, and consequently there is to be found a very general belief in the marvellous. Legends and superstitions abound, and many a chapter might be filled with chronicling them. I shall content myself, however, with giving a short account of some of the most noted.

Mohammed, it should be mentioned, by prohibitory laws, at the commencement of his public career, discountenanced certain superstitious practices, such as divining by arrows, and letting cattle loose in honour of the gods. It is questionable, however, whether those laws of the Prophet did not spring rather from his hatred of idolatry than from any disbelief in occult powers. Judging from certain passages in the Koran, and from a story which the faithful themselves tell of Mohammed, I am inclined to think that he was almost, if not quite, as superstitious as any of his followers.

The story is as follows :—Mohammed, it is said, by the severity of his treatment of the Jews round about Medina, incurred their hatred. Those persecuted people, unable to reach the Prophet by force of arms, had recourse to a famous necromancer amongst them, who was urged to compass the death of Mohammed by mystic enchantments. The task was set about in a peculiar fashion. The first thing the magician did was to make a small waxen image

H

of Mohammed, which was counted by all who saw it a
good likeness. Round this image he wound certain hairs,
which had been procured from the Prophet's beard, and
then pierced it with eleven needles. Now taking a bowstring, he tied a certain number of knots in it, and blew
upon each knot the breath of the mouth. By means of
this bowstring the wonderful image was let down a well,
and left there, the opening being covered with a large
stone. "Now," said the necromancer, "notice what will
happen to the Prophet!"

And we may be sure that the vengeful Jews did notice
with intense eagerness the appearance of Mohammed, who,
it is said, in a day or two showed signs of illness. The
spell worked marvellously, for the needles that had been
stuck into the waxen image were letting out the life-blood
of the Prophet. Day by day he wasted away, and his
followers began to despair. The physicians could not tell
what was the matter, and no remedies tried seemed to be
of any use. At length, when hope was at its lowest ebb,
the angel Gabriel interfered, and revealed to the Prophet
in a vision of the night that he was the victim of a magician
amongst his enemies the Jews. The next day Ali discovered the image in the well, and Mohammed, weak as he
was, was carried to it, and repeated over it the following
words, which are given in the 103rd sura of the Koran :—
" I fly for refuge unto the Lord of the daybreak, that he
may deliver me from the mischief of those things which
he hath created, and from the mischief of the night when
it cometh on, and from the mischief of women blowing on
knots, and from the mischief of the envious when he
envieth." It is recorded that as these words fell from the
Prophet's lips, the needles fell from the waxen image, and
the knots loosened themselves from the bowstring, and
thereupon Mohammed began to revive, and ere long was
quite well again. This strange story is very generally
believed amongst Mohammedans; and to-day, as in days
past, the words of the Koran are written out and worn as

LEGENDS AND SUPERSTITIONS

99

an amulet, or committed to memory and repeated as a charm in case of need.

The most wonderful, and the most popular, of all the legends connected with Mohammed is the one that tells of a certain visit that the angel Gabriel paid him, and of a famous ride he took on the heavenly steed, the Burak. One night, so the story goes, Mohammed was mysteriously awakened out of his sleep. "One stood before him with a face as white as snow; his forehead was serene and unruffled; hair of radiant beauty, plaited finely, hung in graceful curls about his shoulders; dazzling brightness made the many hues of his great wings illuminate the precious stones with which his robes were strewed; and gracious perfumes from ten thousand scent-bags filled the air with fragrance." This visitor was Gabriel, who bade Mohammed stand up upon his feet, and then mount a new kind of steed called the Burak, a name that signifies lightning. The Burak is represented as having the body of a horse, the face of a man, and the wings of a bird. The Prophet, not daring to disobey, got astride the wonderful beast, and found himself rising gently into the upper air, and passing like lightning towards the north. The destination of the little party was Jerusalem. On the way two stoppages were made. The first was at Sinai, to permit Mohammed to pray on the spot where God once communed with Moses; the second was at Bethlehem, to permit of prayer also where Jesus the son of Mary was born.

As the Burak and its riders rose into the air from the hill of Bethlehem, the Prophet heard a voice crying, "O Mohammed, tarry a moment, I pray, that I may speak with thee; thou art he to whom of all created beings I am most devoted." But Mohammed tarried not. Soon another voice was heard exclaiming, "Stop!" But with like result. Then a damsel of the most marvellous beauty appeared in front of the Prophet, and with bewitching smiles and charming voice sought to stay his onward

H 2

career. But Mohammed was as adamant. And when
Gabriel saw that his companion was not to be moved from
the path of duty, he congratulated him, saying : " The first
appeal came from a Jew ; if thou hadst listened to it, all
thy people would have become followers of Moses. The
second came from a Christian ; if thou hadst hearkened to
it, thy people would have become followers of Christ. The
third was from the world ; if thou hadst yielded, thy people
would have won earth, but have lost heaven. Verily, thou
hast done well ! " As Gabriel finished speaking, lo, they
were at Jerusalem, and the Burak descended into the
courtyard of the Temple. There she was fastened to a
ring, and the Angel and the Prophet entered the sacred
edifice, and the latter spent, as it seemed to him, much
time in prayer.

But the adventures of that wonderful night were not
over. They had, indeed, only just begun. The legend
goes on to tell how that, as Mohammed prayed in the
Temple, it was revealed to him that he might, if he would,
ascend into the heavens, and behold things that no other
man had seen, and lived to relate. Mohammed gladly and
eagerly assented. A ladder of light afforded him the
means. In a moment he found himself, with Gabriel at
his side, standing without the silver walls of the first
heaven. A voice bade them enter, and as they did so a
venerable form approached and did reverence to Mohammed. It was old Father Adam, who spoke of the Prophet
as the greatest among the sons of men. Mohammed was
shown all the glories of the place, and he noticed particularly that the city was lighted by means of stars that were
suspended by chains of gold. Then he rose higher, and
with Gabriel entered the second heaven. There the
Patriarch Noah stepped forward to greet him, and hailed
him as the greatest and last of the Prophets. Rising still
higher, Mohammed entered the third heaven, where he
was welcomed by Joseph. In this place he saw the Angel
of Death writing in a book the names of all who were born,

and blotting out the names of those who had lived their allotted years.

To heaven after heaven the Prophet ascended, meeting respectively Aaron, Moses, and Abraham, until the seventh heaven was reached. There Gabriel said that he himself must stop, as no angel was permitted to approach nearer to God; but Mohammed might go on into the very presence of his Maker. Alone, with his heart full of awe and reverence, the Prophet proceeded up the ladder of light, through vast spaces, until he reached the throne of Allah. What exactly passed at that interview between God and His Prophet no mortal knows, the Faithful say; but Mohammed returned to this earth a holier and a wiser man, and embodied afterwards in the Koran many of the sublime truths that had been revealed to him by the mouth of God. So runs the legend.

Mohammedans are very superstitious about lost rings. They say that to lose a ring is an omen of evil, and that it portends in the near future other losses of property, influence, or relatives. No time and efforts are spared to recover, if possible, the lost article, so that disaster may be averted. In support of this superstition an incident is related in connection with a ring that once belonged to Mohammed. The ring in question was that famous one that the Prophet in the zenith of his temporal and spiritual power caused to be engraved with the words, "Mohammed, the Apostle of Allah." At the death of the Prophet this signet ring passed to Abu Bekr, the first Commander of the Faithful. From him it descended to Omar, and became the recognized symbol of the royal power. At Omar's death the unfortunate Othman wore it. It was while it was in the possession of Othman that something happened to it that roused the superstitious fears of the Faithful. One day while the Prince was superintending the deepening of a well just outside the city of Medina, he had occasion to point to a particular stone, and as his finger was out-stretched, the famous ring dropped off and disappeared.

Instant search was made for it in the mud, the sand, the water, and the well itself, but all in vain. Large rewards were offered to induce the workmen to look most diligently for the missing relic, and the search was continued for many a day. Never more, however, was the ring seen! It had been lost beyond recovery! The event caused a profound sensation in Medina, and in the region round about. Othman was saddened by the loss. The people spoke of it as a fearful omen, portending great disasters to the State. And ere long those doleful prophecies were fulfilled, for Othman was cruelly murdered in his palace, and anarchy reigned throughout the kingdom. The loss of the signet ring of Mohammed was contemporaneous with the loss of the sovereignty to the cities of Mecca and Medina. Thus the coincidence was certainly a remarkable one, and it has served, and does serve the people of Islam well as an illustration, to justify them in their superstitious belief that it is nothing less than a calamity to lose a ring.

A belief in witchcraft is universal in Mohammedan communities. I have heard and read many a story of the cruel treatment of poor women who have been suspected of "the power of the evil eye." Here is an example:—A party of well-dressed, respectable people, when passing along a road in the suburbs of an Eastern city, met a white-haired woman, bent double with age. Almost immediately a cry of distress arose from a man of the party, who was carrying a child in his arms, "Seize her! seize her!" he shouted; "she has bewitched me!" The old woman was seized and beaten by the other members of the party. It availed nothing that the poor body asserted her innocence. "Do you not see that our friend is in pain? You have cast an evil eye upon him!" the enraged people exclaimed; and the beating was resumed.

At length some one suggested that perhaps a cure might be wrought if the possessed man pulled a few hairs from the head of the old woman. It was regarded as a happy thought! Without a pang of remorse, or a feeling of pity for the aged one, the man stepped forward, and grasping roughly the white hairs, dragged out a handful, and then went quickly on his way, to all appearance completely cured. It was a heartless and shameful deed. But superstition, when it takes the form of belief in witchcraft, is ever cruel. Many such deeds are done in the East.

Another superstition that enthrals many minds is that of lucky and unlucky days. Friday, "the day of the Assembly," is counted the most lucky day in the week. Works of any importance are generally commenced on this day, whether it be building a house, planting a garden, writing a book, negotiating a marriage, making a garment, or going a journey. Truly amongst Mohammedans the old adage, "The better the day, the better the deed," is firmly believed and acted upon ! Birthdays are usually regarded as "lucky days," and so are days which have been marked in the past by some striking and fortunate event. But, on the other hand, the days of the anniversary of their Imam's martyrdom, and days which have been marked in the past by some special disaster, either national or personal, are looked upon as "unlucky days." From time immemorial this superstition of lucky and unlucky days has prevailed in the East. Sale, in the "Preliminary Discourse" to his translation of the Koran, relates a story of the past which is worth repeating, both for its own sake and because it forcibly reminds us of the power that can alone free Islam from the enslavement of superstition.

A certain Arab chief, it appears, in a fit of madness brought on by indulging too freely in intoxicating drinks, caused one day two of his dearest friends to be buried alive. Grieving over their death afterwards, he erected a monument to their memory, and set apart two days of the year in remembrance of their untimely death. One of these days was called "the lucky" and the other "the unlucky," and the chief vowed that whoever met him on that unlucky day should be slain, and his blood sprinkled on the monument of his dead friends ; but whoever met him on the lucky day should be greeted with gracious words and sent away with magnificent gifts. It chanced on an unlucky day that the chief met a former acquaintance, who had shown him great kindness in an hour of need. To kill this man at once was more than the chief could do ; but to let him off altogether would be to annul his vow. As a compromise, therefore, he dismissed the prisoner with many presents to his home, on the condition that he returned at the end of twelve months to meet his doom. The unfortunate man agreed ; and one of the chief's own escort proffered to stand as surety. The twelve months quickly passed. Mid-day arrived, but not the condemned man. The chief, angry with this apparent failure to keep a solemn promise, ordered the surety to prepare himself for death. Those who were by urged their leader to patience, however, saying that the day had not yet expired. That was true ! And ere the sun went down the man appeared.

The chief, greatly pleased at the nobility of character of his former acquaintance in keeping his promise, complimented him, and asked him who had taught him such fidelity. The unexpected answer was : "Christ ! I am a Christian !" The chief inquired further concerning this matter, and at length came to the conclusion that a religion that could fill a man with such courage and nobility of soul was a religion to be desired. Thus was the will of the Arab conquered, and the episode ended by the prince becoming a convert to Christianity, by releasing his prisoner, by giving up his barbarous vow, and by renouncing all faith in lucky and unlucky days.

And what is needed everywhere in the East is the light of the Gospel of Christ. Superstitions die hard ; but they cannot live where pure Christianity abides. As the truth as it is in Jesus spreads, the power of superstition wanes. Christ is the light of the world, and his light chases away every form of darkness from the lives of men. When all Mohammedans come, like the Arab chief, to appreciate Christianity, and to learn of Christ, then may we hope to see the end of the thousand and one superstitions which now rule the lives and debase the manhood and womanhood of the people of the East !

CHAPTER XI

DAMASCUS is said to be the oldest city of the world. Be that as it may, it can certainly lay claim to being one of the most beautiful.

I shall never forget the day that, crossing Mount Hermon, from Cæsaræa Philippi, I caught my first view of the famous city. It was in the month of May, and nature all around was at her loveliest. Our little party stood on the brow of a hill, and looked over a perfect sea of foliage, which, miles in depth and leagues in circuit, girdles Damascus, and saw in the distance high walls, massive towers, white buildings, and innumerable minarets of mosques glittering in the rays of an Eastern sun. As we gazed at the lovely vision, we could appreciate the favourite saying of the people of Damascus, who in poetical language describe their city as "a pearl set in emeralds." We could understand also the feelings of Mohammed, the prophet of Islam, who when he was but a camel-driver is said to have gazed with rapture upon the fair city, which he refused to enter, exclaiming, "Man can have but one Paradise, and I seek mine above."

At the time Mohammed uttered those striking words he little thought that the city of Damascus would ever become the capital of an empire that would be called after his own name. And yet so it happened. On the death of Ali, the fourth Commander of the Faithful, in A.D. 660, Muawiya, who usurped the sovereignty, as related in an earlier chapter, moved the seat of government from Arabia to Syria, thus

making Damascus the most important city in the Mohammedan Empire.   And it retained that high position for
about 100 years, under the rule of Caliphs who are known
in history as the Omiades of Damascus.   The term Omiades
was taken from Omia, the father of Muawiya.   Omia had
been a Prince of note, and a firm adherent of the Prophet,
and as the name had come to be regarded as a famous and
honourable one, it was adopted by the new dynasty as the
family patronymic.

So far in the story of Mohammedanism we have seen
that the Commanders of the Faithful were elected by the
voice of the people ; but when Muawiya took forcible possession of the sovereignty great changes occurred in Islam.
He held the government by the power of the sword ; and
by force and bribery he succeeded in upsetting established
custom, and so arranging matters that the throne should
become hereditary in his family.   We have seen how, at the
death of Muawiya and the accession of Yezid, his son,
Hosein, the grandson of Mohammed, sought to overthrow
the Omiades' rule, but in vain.   The attempt ended in the
tragedy of the Moharram, and every competitor was removed
out of the way.   But though the Omiades thus obtained
and kept, for a long period of time, the Commandership of
the Faithful, by might rather than by right, their rule was, on
the whole, good for Mohammedanism.   The Princes of the
Royal House were, generally speaking, men of ability and
character; and victory followed their arms in all the struggles
in which they engaged.   The glory of the Omiades reached
its highest point in the reign of Walid, A.D. 705.   This
ruler was a man of elegant tastes, and delighted to adorn
the capital of his kingdom with costly and beautiful buildings.   Damascus was never so lovely as when Walid reigned
there in all his glory.

Walid, while loved by his Moslem, was, however, hated
by his Christian subjects.   There were many Christians in
Damascus, for the city, during the rule of the Romans, had
been an important centre of the Christian faith.

Even when the Mohammedans, under the Caliph Omar, had conquered Damascus, Christians were allowed to dwell in the city, and by a special arrangement their great cathedral, the Church of St. John the Baptist, was preserved to them for worship. The arrangement was that the building should be divided by a partition into two parts, and that one should be used by the followers of Christ, and the other by the followers of Mohammed. This remarkable settlement of a difficult question could not be expected to be a permanent one, however. The wonder is that it lasted as long as it did. For seventy years the adherents of the two great religions worshipped under the same roof; but in the reign of Walid the Mohammedans resolved to be sole masters. When, by order of the Caliph, the whole building was demanded, the Christians showed their treaty-rights, but they were only laughed at; and one morning Walid, with a company of soldiers, entered the sacred edifice and gave the order that every Christian priest should be turned out, and that every image of Christ, the Virgin Mary, the Apostles, and saints—of which there were many in the great building—should be destroyed.

Standing on the high altar, the Caliph himself directed the work of spoliation, and urged on his followers to make a speedy and thorough end of every vestige of Christian worship. Close by Walid, as he stood on the altar, was a figure of Christ. One of the fanatical but superstitious soldiers, noticing the proximity of the image, called out in a loud voice, "Prince of the Faithful, I tremble for your safety. The power of that image near which you stand may be exerted against you." "Fear not for me," replied the stern, proud Moslem; "for the first spot on which I shall lay my battle-axe will be that image's head." Even as he spoke he lifted his weapon, which descended with resistless force on the figure of Christ, and dashed it to pieces. A cry of horror rose from the Christians, who, from a distance, were looking on; but such expressions of sorrow were drowned in the glad shouts of victory which the Mohammedans raised when they saw that their Caliph's arm was more powerful than the image of the Christ. Thus the Christians of Damascus lost their ancient church ; and from that date we may count the rapid decline of Christianity in Syria. Walid reigned ten years, and during that time not only strengthened his empire at home, but increased it abroad. It was Musa, one of his most famous generals, that conquered for him the kingdom of Spain, and established the Moslem power in Europe. This great conquest is just mentioned now, in its legitimate place in the order of time, but it will be dealt with more fully in a subsequent chapter on the Moors in Spain. When Walid died, in the year 715, the Mohammedan rule in the East extended beyond the Oxus almost to the borders of China, and in the West beyond the Pillars of Hercules to the confines of France.

In the reign of Omar the Second, the successor of Walid, the Moslem arms received their first great check. The new Caliph ordered an advance on Constantinople, the capital of the Greek Empire, and that city would probably have fallen, so determined was the onset made upon it, if the Mohammedans had not been demoralized and dispersed by that terrible and mysterious weapon of war called "Greek Fire." Edwin A. Freeman, in his "Outlines of History," speaking of the disaster, says : "This defeat of the Saracens is really one of the greatest events in the world's history, for if Constantinople had been taken by the Mohammedans before the nations of Western Europe had at all grown up, it would seem as if the Christian religion and European civilization must have been swept away from the earth."

Excluded from the eastern entrance of Europe by the defeat at Constantinople, the Mohammedans sought to push their way by the western entrance, which was open to them through the conquest of Spain. But they had reached the limits of their power. The Divine command had been issued, "Thus far shalt thou go, and no further."

When, in the reign of the Caliph Hisham, the Moslems crossed the Pyrenees, it seemed at first as if they would carry everything before them ; but in the year 732, they received such a defeat that they never again turned their thoughts to the conquest of France.

This result was due to the genius of one man, who is known in history by the significant name of Charles Martel, or Charles the Hammer. This chief was the Mayor of the Palace in the Frankish monarchy, and in the hour of supreme danger to the State, was called to the front. When his countrymen clamoured to be led against the Moslems, Charles gave them this weighty advice : " If you follow my counsel you will not interrupt their march, nor precipitate your attack. They are like a torrent, which it is dangerous to stem in its career. The thirst of riches and the consciousness of success redouble their valour, and valour is of more avail than arms or numbers. Be patient till they have loaded themselves with the incumbrance of wealth. The possession of wealth will divide their counsels, and assure your victory." And so it came to pass. When the Mohammedans had ravaged many parts of the country, and were laden with booty, the Mayor of the Palace, joining his forces with those of the Duke of Aquitaine, attacked them near Tours, and, after a terrible struggle, defeated them, with a very great slaughter. Charles that day wrought prodigies of valour with his own right arm, and so powerful were the blows that he rained upon the heads of the Moslems, that they were spoken of as the blows of a sledge hammer, and thus did he earn for himself the name of Martel. The bodies of 300,000 Saracens are said to have been left on the field of battle ; and the Christians also had to mourn the loss of a host of valiant men. Still, that battle at Tours was a famous victory for the Franks. It gave Europe rest from the attacks of the followers of the Prophet in the West, as the victory at Constantinople had given her rest, at any rate for a season, in the East.

These disasters abroad were followed by the Wars of the Colours at home, and the power of the Omiades of Damascus began to totter to its fall. The fact is, the Omiades were popular nowhere out of Syria. The Arabians, who secretly were adherents, either of the descendants of Ali, the son-in-law of Mohammed, or of the descendants of Abbas, the uncle of Mohammed, had for years been nursing rebellion, and when they heard of the disasters in Europe they thought the time was ripe for revolt. The Alyites chose as the badge of their party a "green" flag, the Omiades had always used a "white" flag, and the Abbasides adopted a "black" flag. Thus were there three factions in the State seeking supreme power. Two of these factions, the green and the black, united their strength, to be revenged on the common enemy, the Omiades, who, for a century or so, had usurped the throne of the Commander of the Faithful. The whole Mohammedan world was, of course, convulsed by this struggle, which at length ended in the complete overthrow of the dynasty of the white flag.

The last of the Omiades was Mervan, a well-meaning and brave Prince. To this Caliph came one day a letter from the Governor of Korassan, which opened his eyes to the abyss on which he stood. He found that his kingdom was undermined on every side. The Governor wrote : "I see some sparks scintillating under the ashes, and from them a great fire may be kindled ; let us hasten to extinguish these sparks if you wish to avoid the conflagration ; why must I ask if the children of Omia are awake, or if a leaden sleep shuts their eyes?" The hour of doom had come, however, and nothing could turn it back. Mervan sent orders for the rigorous treatment of all traitors, and started in person to assist the Governor of Korassan. But this move on the part of the Commander of the Faithful was the signal for insurrection to break out in every part of his dominions. And soon the news reached him that Abu Abbas had been proclaimed

Caliph by the black faction in the city of Merv, the capital of Korassan.

Mervan, excited by the tidings, pushed on with the greater vigour, and at length joined issue with his rival on the banks of the river Zab, in January, 750. This spot was about thirty miles south-east of ancient Nineveh, and was close by Arbela, a place already made famous by the defeat of Darius, of Persia, by Alexander the Great. Here, after a struggle of two days' duration, Mervan was utterly defeated, and the sceptre of the Moslems fell from the grasp of the Omiades. The Caliph fled, and at Harran found his wife and children, and with them he went to Kinnesrin, and thence to Emesa, and on and on in wild flight to Damascus. But the gates of the beautiful city were closed against the unfortunate man, and he turned away with a broken heart, and once more resumed his flight, not caring much whither he went. He reached Egypt before he was overtaken, but there he was captured by his foes, and slain without mercy. Thus perished Mervan, the last of the famous line of Princes which for 100 years had, from Damascus, ruled the Mohammedan world with a strong hand.

The sun of the Omiades went down in darkness. Abbas, the new Commander of the Faithful, was a man of cruel deeds. Almost his first act when he reached Damascus was a perfidious one. He invited all the Omiades in the city to a banquet as his guests, and in the middle of the feast called in his guards, and massacred those who had confided in his word. The bodies of the murdered men were thrown under the table, the feast was continued, and the Abbasides made merry over the overthrow of their enemies, whose death made the settlement of Abu Abbas on the throne of the Caliphs a comparatively easy affair.

And with the Omiades fell also Damascus from her proud position of the Queen of Cities. The dynasty of the Abbasides founded a new capital city on the banks of the Tigris, and the Mohammedan power was thenceforth for centuries centred at Bagdad. In a later chapter we shall glance at the meridian splendour of the Moslem faith and rule by Bagdad's shrines. Meanwhile we cannot but think with regret of the eclipse of the power, the influence, and the grandeur of Damascus. What vicissitudes of fortune the oldest city in the world has experienced! It has been possessed in turn by Heathen, Jewish, Christian, and Mohammedan rulers. In the Middle Ages it was torn again and again from the grasp of the Moslems, but only to return to them again ; and at the present day it is essentially a Mohammedan city. The Pashalic of Damascus is now an important one, and the city has regained something of its former greatness, but it will never again under Moslem rule be fully what it was in the time of the Omiades, either in beauty, grandeur, or power. The century of Omiadian rule was altogether a glorious one for Damascus, and for Mohammedanism.

CHAPTER XII

THERE are many peculiar beliefs held by Mohammedans, which we need to consider if we would clearly understand and estimate fairly the Faith of the followers of the Prophet.

With regard to the creation of mankind, the strangest stories are told. It is said that God, having resolved to create man, sent an angel to bring seven handfuls of earth of different colours, which, being brought and examined and declared suitable, was taken to Arabia, and there first kneaded by the angels, and afterwards fashioned by God Himself into a human form. This form was then left for forty days to dry in the sun. While it was drying the angels are represented as visiting it, and passing their remarks about its appearance and wondering what God intended to do with it. Amongst the rest came Iblis or Satan, who immediately he saw it took a violent dislike to it, and kicked it with his foot till it rang. At the end of the appointed time God returned to the clay image, and breathed into it the breath of life and endued it with an intelligent soul, and carried it away to a place neither in heaven nor on earth, called Paradise. And there Eve was taken from Adam's side.

The enmity that Satan had shown to the senseless clay was continued and deepened when the creation was completed and man was made a living soul. And this enmity, it is declared, was the chief cause of the fall of Satan from

I

heaven.   It angered God that Satan should so proudly hold
himself aloof from man, or when he came near him express
nothing but ill-will and hatred towards him.   Matters were
brought to a crisis, the Koran tells us, by an edict from
God, that all the angels should worship the new creation.
Let me give the passage just as it stands in the 7th sura.
It runs : " We created you, and afterwards formed you,
and then said unto the angels, Worship Adam, and they all
worshipped him except Iblis.   God said unto him, What
hindered thee from worshipping Adam, since I had commanded thee ?   He answered, I am more excellent than
he ; thou hast created me of fire, and hast created him of
clay.   God said, Get thee down therefore from Paradise,
for it is not fit that thou behave thyself proudly therein :
get thee hence, thou shalt be one of the contemptible."
Then was Satan driven forth, and he became a wanderer in
space and the ruler of the powers of darkness.

    The fall of man, according to Mohammedan belief, quickly
followed the fall of Satan.   Indeed, as the Devil was leaving Paradise he is said to have hurled a defiant threat in
the very face of God.   He shouted : " Because Thou hast
depraved me, I will lie in wait for men in Thy strait way :
then will I come upon them from before and from behind,
and from their right hand and from their left ; and Thou
shalt not find the greater part of them thankful."   The
story of man's fall is probably taken from the Jewish
Scriptures.   The Koran tells of the forbidden fruit just as
the Bible does, only with greater brevity and less poetic
force.   The passage is worth quoting for the sake of comparison.   It is as follows :—" O Adam, dwell thou and thy
wife in Paradise, and eat of the fruit thereof wherever ye
will ; but approach not this tree, lest ye become of the
number of the unjust.   And Satan suggested to them
both that he would discover unto them their nakedness
which was hidden from them ; and he said, Your Lord
hath not forbidden you this tree for any other reason
but lest ye should become angels, or lest ye become

immortal. And he sware unto them, saying, Verily, I am one of those who counsel you aright. And he caused them to fall through deceit." After the fall God banished man from Paradise, and condemned him to live upon the earth and to die there.

When our first parents began their life on this earth, they found other creations, for God had peopled the world with all manner of things which were to be subject to man. In such creations, and in all creations, Mohammedans say the little word " Be " played an important part. The teaching on this point is most quaint. In the 36th sura of the Koran it is written : " The Lord is the wise Creator : His command when He willeth a thing is only that He saith unto it, Be, and it is." This striking and famous passage has led to all manner of controversies and divisions amongst the Faithful. " Be, and it is," the Arabic for which is " Kun fayakuna," is the watchword of the orthodox party. Their argument is that God created the world, and all that therein is, by means of the word " Be." " But," say others, " unless Be was from all eternity, then one created thing must have created another; and if Be was from all eternity, then there are two Eternals, God and Be." One would think that such an argument would close the controversy. But no ! The orthodox have always an answer ready. " Granted," is the reply, " that there are two Eternals, God and Be, it does not necessarily follow that there are two Gods, for Be can do nothing until it receives the command to do." So the discussion is continued with considerable subtlety ; and Mohammedans take the greatest delight in it, though we all probably think that it is a case of " much ado about nothing."

The story of Cain and Abel, as told by Mohammedans, is most curious. It is said that the brothers had each a twin sister, and that God ordered Cain to marry Abel's twin, and Abel to marry Cain's. Abel agreed, but Cain refused, because his own twin sister was the handsomer of the two. Father Adam being appealed to to settle the dispute, instructed the brothers to make each an offering unto the Lord, and that the acception or rejection of the respective offerings might be taken as conclusive of the will of God. Cain's offering was a sheaf of the very worst of his corn ; but Abel's was a fat lamb of the best of his flock. And Abel's offering was accepted, and Cain's rejected. Thereat Cain was exceeding angry, and purposed in his heart to slay his brother. But not knowing how to accomplish this resolve, he invoked the aid of Satan, who promptly appeared, and showed him how to proceed. Satan, Mohammedans say, took a bird, and laying its head on a stone, smote it with another stone ; and lo ! to the delight of Cain, it was killed. And that very night he did the same thing with his brother Abel as he lay asleep in the field. But when the awful deed had been committed, Cain repented him, and taking up the body of his brother, carried it about on his shoulders, weeping as he went. Then God, taking pity upon him, sent a raven, which killed another raven, and buried it by digging a pit with its claws and beak. This was done in the sight of Cain, who, quick to perceive the lesson, put his brother's body on the ground, and at once digging a grave for it, buried it out of his sight. Mohammedans affirm that in the Judgment Cain's punishment will be equal to half the punishment of all the rest of mankind.

Another peculiar belief is that in Genii. In the 55th sura of the Koran these words occur : "God created man of dried clay, like an earthen vessel ; but he created the Genii of fire clear from smoke." And in many other places in the Koran the Genii are referred to. Mohammed believed implicitly in their existence ; and so do the Faithful to the present day. Mohammedans say that the Genii inhabited the world for many ages before man was created, that they fell into sin, and were driven by command of God into a remote part of the earth, whence, however, they came out at times when called by the power of man. The Genii are said to be something like angels, only of a grosser fabric. They are believed to eat and drink, and to have offspring, and to die like human beings. Of all men who have ever lived, Solomon, King of the Jews, is said to have possessed the greatest control over the Genii. He could make them do just what he chose. If he wished to go on a journey, for instance, he was wont to spread on the ground a carpet of green silk, and sitting on it, give the word of command to the Genii, who would transport him in a moment of time to the place he desired to be at. The Temple of Solomon is believed by Mohammedans to have been the work of Genii.

The Prophet refers to this in the Koran, and states that Solomon died ere the Temple was completed, but that the building went on all the same, for the Genii did not know the King was dead. I remember, when in Jerusalem, a place was pointed out to me as the spot where the King died, and the following strange story was told me in connection with it. My guide said: "Before the Temple was completed Solomon, perceiving that his end drew nigh, begged of God that his death might be concealed from the Genii, who were busily engaged in the wonderful enterprise. God, recognizing the wisdom of the request, so ordered it that the King died in the court-yard of the Temple as he stood at his prayers, leaning on his staff, which supported his body in that position a full year. The Genii, supposing him to be alive and watching them, continued their work with energy, and at length completed the magnificent edifice. Thereupon a worm, which had found its way into the staff of Solomon, ate it through, and the corpse fell to the ground, and discovered the King's death." Mohammedans delight in such tales, and constantly introduce Genii into their literature. One can but wonder at such credulous beliefs!

Another belief, called the doctrine of the Two Watchers, is not without its attractiveness, and is certainly ingenious. The statement is that every human being from birth is

attended by two angels, one resting on the right shoulder
and the other on the left. The business of the two watchers
is to register in a book every action of man, so that at the
last day a man's good and evil deeds may be found fully
recorded and be used as evidence for or against him. It
seems, however, that the angel who sits on the right
shoulder, noting good actions, is more powerful than the one
who sits on the left shoulder, and that he is always inclined
to exercise his power on the side of mercy. Directly a
man does something good, the good angel writes it down,
not once merely, but ten times. And if the man does
anything evil, the same angel stays the hand of the other
angel who is about to record it, saying, " Forbear ! Do
not set it down for seven days : peradventure the offence
will be repented of!" I like the doctrine of the Two
Watchers, and fain wish that all the peculiar beliefs of the
Mohammedans had as much sense and good feeling in them.

I would mention next a most gloomy belief. It is connected with the action of two other angels, who are called
Munkar and Nakir. These angels are represented as being
black as ink, and of a frightful appearance in other
ways. Their mission is to examine the dead. Directly a
corpse is laid in the grave, Munkar and Nakir appear before
the terrified person, and tell him to sit up. Mohammedans
do not enclose the dead in coffins, nor do they usually fill
in, but only cover, the grave, so that if a corpse can sit up
it has room to do so. The questions put by the examiners
are : " Who is thy God ? Who is thy Prophet ? What is
thy faith ? Which is thy book ? Where is thy Kiblah ?
Who is thy leader?" If the dead man answers satisfactorily, his body is suffered to rest in peace, and he is
refreshed, until the Resurrection, by a breeze from Paradise.
If he does not answer satisfactorily, terrible is the treatment
that he receives. The angels at once seize hold of him,
and beat him on the temples with iron maces till he roars
out with anguish so loud that he is heard in the lowest hell.
Then earth is thrown on the corpse, and ninety-nine

dragons are let loose upon it, and they are commissioned to gnaw it and sting it, day and night, without ceasing, until the day of Judgment, when still more terrible torments await it. This is altogether a horrible doctrine, and shows Mohammedanism in a bad light.

The teaching of Islam with regard to the Resurrection is replete with peculiarities. The immediate signs of the Resurrection will be three blasts of a great trumpet. The first is called the " Blast of Consternation," at the hearing of which all creatures in heaven and earth will be struck with terror. The heavens will melt, the sun be darkened, the stars will disappear, the sea will dry up, and everything on earth will fall into chaos and ruin. Then will be heard the " Blast of Death," at which everything with life in heaven and earth will die, in a moment, in the twinkling of an eye, with the exception of God, and those beings created before the world. Forty years later the third blast will be blown, which is called the " Blast of Resurrection." At the sound thereof all souls will come to life, and fill the space between heaven and earth, whence, at the Divine command, they will wing their flight to their respective bodies, which the opening earth will suffer to arise.

Then cometh the Judgment, at which both Genii, men, and animals must appear. The length of the Day of Judgment is variously estimated by Mohammedan commentators, some saying that it will last 1,000 years ; while others affirm that it cannot be expected to come to an end under 50,000 years. At the Judgment, the Faithful say, God will appear in the clouds, surrounded by angels, and, being seated upon the Great, White Throne, He will declare the time has come for all flesh to answer for the deeds done in the body, whether good or evil. An Intercessor will be called for, who, it seems, will be Mohammed. Adam, Noah, Abraham, and Jesus will in turn be asked, but all will refuse, saying that Mohammed is the most worthy to fill the honourable post. Then the Books will be opened, and the Recording Angels will give an account of the following items :—Time, how spent; wealth, how acquired and used ; the body, how treated ; knowledge and learning, how employed.   To show how exact justice will be, Mohammedans state that the Angel Gabriel will produce a pair of scales, of size so vast that one of the scales will completely cover Paradise, and the other completely cover Hell.   In these scales the good and bad actions of all created beings will be weighed in turn, and judgment given accordingly.   It is generally thought that animals, after being judged, will be permitted to punish each other at once for the wrongs they may have done each other, and that then every one of them will be blotted out of existence.   Some say that the Genii will share the same fate.   As for mankind, however, they are reserved for future bliss or woe.   Those who turn the scale on the right side are allotted to Paradise, with all its marvellous joys ; and those who turn it on the left are doomed to Hell, with all its awful torments.

The Judgment being over, and the assembly dissolved, Mohammedans teach that then the righteous will turn their faces at once towards Paradise, while the unrighteous will march towards Hell.   All, however, must pass over a wonderful bridge called "The Bridge of Sirat," which is placed over the mouth of Hell.   This bridge is said to be finer than a hair, and sharper than the edge of a sword. And on either side of it briars and thorns are placed. "Nothing, however, will be an impediment to the good, for they shall pass with wonderful ease and swiftness, like lightning or wind, Mohammed and his Moslems leading the way ; whereas the wicked, what with the slipperiness and extreme narrowness of the path, the entangling of the thorns, and the extinction of the light which directed the former to Paradise, will soon miss their footing, and fall down headlong into the bottomless pit, which is gaping beneath them."

Such are some of the Peculiar Beliefs of the followers of Islam.   They are a strange mixture of wisdom, and folly, of truth and error. It is a mystery that Moslems of intelligence can be content with such teaching. It is said that many are not, and that at the present day there is, in all Mohammedan countries, amongst the educated classes, a growing desire to throw overboard the musty traditions of the Fathers. However, the common people of Islam have to be reckoned with, for they are the majority, and they cling with fanatical earnestness to everything that the Prophet once taught, or that received, even in the remotest way, his approval or sanction.

CHAPTER XIII

ABBASIDES OF BAGDAD

BAGDAD, the name of a province and a city in the south-west of Asiatic Turkey, is one of the most famous names in the history of Mohammedanism. It was at Bagdad, on the banks of the Tigris, that the Abbasides, or descendants of Abbas, the uncle of Mohammed, fixed the seat of government, when they had dethroned the Omiades of Damascus, in the year 750.

Damascus, as the capital of the late dynasty, notwith-standing its admirable situation and marvellous beauty, was considered unworthy of the line of Abbas, relatives of the Prophet. With the new dynasty, it was resolved to begin altogether a new era. So, in the year 762, the Caliph Mansur, the second of the Abbasides, erected Bagdad, or the "City of Peace." And in this new capital, which the genius of the architect and the skill of the painter and gilder combined to make one of the most magnificent in the world, the powerful house of Abbas reigned for some centuries as successors of the Prophet of Allah. And Bagdad is almost as well known to the people of the West as to the people of the East, for it was the scene of many of those romantic tales described in that fascinating book called "The Arabian Nights' Entertainment."

Though Bagdad was called the City of Peace, it was not because at the time it was built there was peace in the Mohammedan Empire. It was meant as a prophecy of the future rather than as a statement of the then existent state of things. In fact, when Bagdad was built, there was strife in almost every province; and peace was not secured until the power of the Caliphate was divided. It happened thus:—From the massacre of the Omiades at Damascus, by Abbas, as related in a previous chapter, one intended victim, named Abd-er-Rahman, somehow managed to escape. This Prince, after marvellous adventures, reached Egypt, and for a time lived amongst the wandering Berbers of the Desert, whose respect and esteem he won by his noble origin, princely appearance, and manly virtues. And from Egypt Abd-er-Rahman eventually made his way to Spain, and after a while, in that country he won the allegiance of the Moors from the Caliph of Bagdad, and founded, at Cordova, the Royal house of the Omiades of Spain, which endured for 250 years. Thus was Spain, in the eighth century, lost to the Successor of the Prophet : and the Mohammedan world was divided into two great sections. In fact, from this time there were two Caliphs or Commanders of the Faithful, one ruling at Cordova, and the other at Bagdad.

But this disunion of the Empire was a source of strength rather than of weakness. Spain was too far away from the banks of the Tigris to be governed from thence with comfort. The loss of the kingdom of the West allowed the Caliph of the East to concentrate his powers, and the result was great gain. Mohammedanism, indeed, was never so strong as in the eighth and ninth centuries, when it was worthily represented both at Cordova and at Bagdad. The meridian splendour of the Eastern Empire was reached during the reign of Harun-al-Rashid, or Aaron the Just. His name is familiar to us as the hero of the Arabian Nights. He it was who went about disguised in his own city in search of adventures; he it was who did the many wonderful things which now astonish and delight childhood ; and he it was who used the whirling scimitar in such a marvellous way to rescue friends and to punish foes. Harun was truly a great Prince ; noted for his skill in war, his wisdom in council, his encouragement of learning, and his righteousness as judge. Far and wide he was known as Harun the Great, the magnificent, and the just; the only blot on his fair fame being his treatment of his great Ministers, the Barmecides, whom he destroyed root and branch, suspecting them, rightly or wrongly, of treason to the throne.

But though Harun raised so high the name of Moslem, and made the followers of Mohammed to be feared on every hand, it was during his reign that the most insulting letter a Caliph ever received came from the Greeks of Constantinople, the inveterate foes of Islam. Irene, the Queen of the Greeks, had for a few years, for the sake of peace, paid tribute to the Moslems; but when Nicephorus usurped her power, he decided that such payments should cease, so he sent the following extraordinary letter to the Caliph :—

"From Nicephorus, King of the Greeks, to Harun, King of the Arabs :—The Queen considered you as a rook, and herself as a pawn; she submitted to pay tribute to you, though she ought to have exacted twice as much from you. A man speaks to you now, therefore send back the tribute you have received, otherwise the sword shall be umpire between us."

The Ambassadors who bore this message to the Caliph threw at the foot of his throne a bundle of swords to emphasize the threat of their Sovereign; but Harun only smiled at their zeal, and bade them return to the Emperor. And he sent this stinging message back with them :—
"In the name of Allah, most merciful! Harun-al-Rashid, Commander of the Faithful, to Nicephorus, the Roman Dog! I have read thy letter, O thou son of an unbelieving mother! Thou shalt not hear, but behold, my reply!"
Thus did the Moslem render to the Greek scorn for scorn, and railing for railing. And in the war that followed Harun earned the name of the Victorious, for he utterly defeated the powerful armies of Nicephorus, and forced that proud monarch to make an ignominious peace, in which he agreed to pay tribute twice as often as Irene had

done before him. Thus ended for the time being the war between Moslem and Greek; and thus did Harun-al-Rashid show that he had some right to be considered the most powerful monarch of his time.

But peace abroad was followed by strife at home. Indeed, for some years, the Alyites, or descendants of Ali, who had assisted the Abbasides to dethrone the Omiades, had been plotting against the Caliphs, and causing trouble in the land. Matters came to a head at the death of Harun. The latter left two sons, who quarrelled over the vacant throne, and though Mamun, the younger brother, eventually proved the stronger and became Caliph, yet the Royal power had been so weakened by the fratricidal strife that the Alyites lifted their heads, and in the year 814 made a bold snatch at the Commandership of the Faithful. At first this rebellion seemed as if it would prosper, but at the end of ten months its leader died, or fell by poison, and the country had rest. But in less than two years the Alyites again gave serious trouble to the State, and the dazed Caliph, scarcely knowing what to do, resolved, by a bold and self-denying stroke, to bring, if possible, permanent peace to the distracted kingdom. His idea was to surrender completely to the descendants of Ali. Gilman, in his book on the Saracens, describes the decision thus : " Mamun called to him at Merv in 817 one of the great-grandsons of Ali, Ali ben Musa el Rida, a man well known for his learning, piety, and good life, to whom he gave his daughter in marriage ; he then promised him the throne after his death : coined money in his name ; exchanged the black garments of the tribe of Abbas for the green which marked the descendants of the Prophet, and sent out letters commanding that the same change of colours should be made by all the civil and military officers of the kingdom." By a strange freak of fortune, it thus seemed as if the children of Ali and Fatima would, when they least expected it, secure the supreme power in Islam, which was rightly theirs.

It was not to be, however. Mamun had reckoned without his people. When the inhabitants of Bagdad heard of the treaty their Caliph had made with the Alyites, they repudiated it with indignation, and so great was their wrath that they actually deposed Mamun, and chose in his stead Ibrahim, the son of a former ruler. When Mamun, who was still at Merv, was informed of events at Bagdad, he saw that he had made a mistake in leaguing himself with the Alyites, and at the eleventh hour he broke the alliance, and, with true Oriental baseness, caused Ali ben Musa to be poisoned, ordered other eminent personages to be made away with, and marched straight for the capital, to call the inhabitants to account for their disloyalty. Such daring and energetic measures had the desired result. The people saw that Mamun was not to be trifled with, and they quickly made their peace with him. Continuing in the same stern course, the Caliph ere long put down every foe, and obtained for the State that internal rest of which it stood sorely in need. The Alyites were suppressed, and the Abbasides were once more successful and all-powerful.

Mamun reigned over Islam for many years, and added even to the prosperity and glory of the previous Caliph. One writer says: " Mamun was not so accomplished a general as his father, but he continued and increased the enlightened cultivation of letters that Harun had begun, and his reign has been compared to the times of the De' Medici in Italy, and of Louis XIV. in France. Mamun was succeeded by his brother Motasim, who was nicknamed the Octave, because he reigned eight years and eight months, and left behind him eight sons, eight daughters, eighty thousand slaves, eight million dinars, and eighty million dirhems. Motasim's period of rule was chiefly taken up in waging war with the Greeks ; and it is notorious for the capture of Armorium, the most populous and the richest city in the Greek Empire. Theophilus was at the time reigning at Constantinople. This Emperor hated the Mohammedans with a deadly hatred, and in 836 he threw a large army upon the borders of Syria, and carried his arms far and wide, giving no quarter, and devastating a region almost up to the limits of Mesopotamia. He even made use of ferocious wild beasts to help him in desolating the countries of the Moslems. But in these mad acts the Emperor overreached himself. When Motasim heard of them, he resolved on a swift and terrible revenge. He put himself at the head of an army of 200,000 men, and advanced upon Armorium. Each soldier was supplied with a buckler, with the word "Armorium" stamped on it, as an evidence of the terrible determination with which the expedition set out. Arrived in front of the city, after months of journeying and fighting, the Moslems laid siege to it, and eventually took it. It was full of people and full of spoil. The former the enraged conquerors massacred without mercy, and the latter they carried off to enrich their own city on the Tigris. Armorium is said to have been stripped bare, to have been left utterly desolate, and afforded a terrible proof of the power and enmity of the Moslems. It is said that the massacre at Armorium has few if any parallels in Saracenic history.

With Motasim, the eighth Caliph of Bagdad, the glory of the Abbasides culminated. Elements of weakness now entered into the life of the nation, and gradually undermined the Empire. For instance, under the Caliphate of Motawakkel, in 842, stringent laws were passed against all Christians and Jews living in Mohammedan countries. So far the adherents of these two great religious sects had been tolerated by the Abbasides, and treated with some show of justice. Henceforward, however, they were to be treated harshly, and so were forced into an attitude of enmity. Of Motawakkel it is written: "He persecuted the Jews and the Christians, ordering that they should never ride on horses, but only on asses and mules, and that without stirrups; that their dwellings should be marked by figures of dogs and monkeys; and their persons always known by yellow dresses. He refused them the right to enter the baths frequented by Moslems, or to occupy any office of public service. They were restricted in regard to their schools and places of worship; their taxes were doubled; and the very indications of their graves were obliterated."

Thus was begun in the Mohammedan Empire that system of the persecution of subject races, especially Christian, which has continued till this day, and which has ever been one of the serious errors of Moslem Princes, and the occasion of the loss to them of many a fair province and country. The Abbasides of Bagdad were the first to reap the fruits of such an iniquitous system.

Another element of weakness in the sovereignty of the Abbasides was the establishment of a system of Guards in the Royal city and palace. In their wars with the people of Turkestan the Caliphs made many prisoners, and these they formed gradually into a body-guard. The idea thereby was to strengthen the personal influence of the Commanders of the Faithful, and for a time doubtless that object was gained; but eventually the Guards saw that they were indispensable, and realizing their power, they used it despotically. For three centuries or more the actual rulers of Bagdad and the Mohammedan Empire in the East were the Turkish Guards, some 50,000 strong; and history has nothing good to say of them. They were bloodthirsty and cruel, and would commit any deed of darkness to maintain their hold over the Caliphs. If a Commander of the Faithful, more independent or braver than the rest, ventured to oppose the will of the Guards, his doom was dethronement or death. Gibbon, writing of these things, says: "As often as the Turks were influenced by fear or rage or avarice, the Caliphs were dragged by the feet, exposed naked to the scorching sun, beaten with iron clubs, and compelled to purchase by the abdication of their dignity a short reprieve of inevitable fate."

The Guards chose one of their own number to represent them, and this leader was called the Prince of Princes; for the Caliphs, acting under compulsion, legally placed all the temporal power of the State in his hands, only reserving for themselves the spiritual power. As Gilman says : " The Prince of Princes usurped an authority not unlike that possessed in Rome by the Praetorian Guards, in France by the Maires du Palais, and in Constantinople for five hundred years by the terrible Janizaries." With the death of the Caliph Radi, in the tenth century, the rule of the Commanders of the Faithful practically came to an end, though the dynasty of the Abbasides nominally governed in Bagdad until the thirteenth century. After Radi, "never more did a Caliph write poems that were collected into a volume ; no longer did a Caliph politely harangue the Faithful of a Friday in the mosque ; nor did another hold train and table after the olden style of magnificence ; no other one disposed the armies and the finances after his own will ; nor ever held familiar companionship with his friends ; for all power was henceforth lodged in the hands of the Prince of Princes, and of those who gave that officer his supremacy."

It would be dreary work to trace in detail the fall of Bagdad, and with it the house of Abbas. For years the Turkish Guards, who, though cruel, were brave and gallant soldiers, upheld the power of the State against foreign foes, both Greek and Barbarian. There came a time, however, when the Guards quarrelled amongst themselves, and then the streets of Bagdad ran with rivers of blood ; and the whole Caliphate felt that the day of doom was not far distant. Yet it lingered. However, in the year 1258 the end came. The Tartars, under their Prince Hulaku, the grandson of that scourge of the East, Jenghis Khan, swept like a torrent upon the distracted Empire, and there was no power to withstand them for more than a brief space.

Mustasim was Caliph, and he made a brave stand for his kingdom, but it was in vain. After keeping the besieging army at bay for two months, Bagdad opened her gates to the foe, who swarmed in like locusts to devour all they

K

could find. The savage Tartar Prince at once ordered Mustasim to be put to death, and along with him, it is said, sixteen hundred thousand inhabitants of the captured city. Thus fell Bagdad, the most famous of Eastern cities, and thus miserably perished the last of the Caliphs of the dynasty of the Abbasides, which had endured for full five centuries! How the Tartars were won over to the faith of Islam, and what dynasties rose on the ruin of the Abbasides, will be shown in subsequent chapters. The fall of Bagdad did not mean the death of Islamism. It simply meant another change of capital, and the onward march of Mohammedanism to greater and still greater victories, both in the East and in the West.

Bagdad was rebuilt in course of time, and is at the present day an insignificant city of 60,000 inhabitants. It has from the outside an extremely picturesque appearance; but within, it is mean-looking, dirty, and poverty-stricken. What a contrast the present city must present to the city that the Tartars destroyed, to the city of Harun-al-Rashid, to the city of the Arabian Nights! And yet Bagdad in its poverty, dirt, and meanness will ever be dear to lovers of the old and the romantic; for its very name is fascinating, and the sight of it leads all who gaze upon it and enter within its walls to say with the poet—

> So I wander and wander along
>   And for ever before me gleams
> The shining city of song
>   In the beautiful land of dreams.

MOHAMMEDANS, like many Christians, have one period of the year which they set aside specially for fasting and prayer. This Lent season is called by the Moslems Ramadan.

The term Ramadan has exercised the ingenuity of many writers as to its meaning. It is evidently derived from the Arabic *ramadh*, which signifies to burn. But what connection has burning with fasting? The generally accepted explanation of the meaning and use of the term is that the first institution of the ceremony of fasting in Arabia occurred during one of the hottest months of the year, and so the "fasting month" was called and known ever afterwards by the name of the "hot month." Ramadan is the ninth month of the Moslem year, but as the months are variable, owing to the fact that they are lunar, sometimes this particular month is in the summer and sometimes it is in the winter. All the same, it is "the fast month;" and to speak of Ramadan is now equivalent to speaking of "fasting," though, as I have said, the meaning of the term is something entirely different, viz., "burning."

What, it may be asked, are the motives of Mohammedans for enduring a month of fasting? One of our poets has said—

> The poor man fasts because he wanteth meat ;
> The sick man fasts because he cannot eat.
> The miser fasts, with greedy mind to spare ;
> The glutton fasts to eat a greater share.
> The hypocrite, he fasts to seem more holy ;
> The righteous man, to punish sinful folly.

K 2

I think that in the case of Moslems of the present day the chief reasons for fasting are that it is the custom so to do, and that therein they are obeying the commands of their Prophet, who taught that the due performance of certain rigid vows of fasting would be an acceptable service from man to God. Mohammed went as far as to affirm that Fasting is a fourth part of Faith, and that without fasting it is impossible to please God. He called it also "the gate of religion," and declared that "the odour of the mouth of him who fasteth is more grateful to God than that of musk." Doubtless devout Moslems believe these things. And while I would say, generally speaking, that "custom" accounts for the practice being kept up so widely, yet in particular cases there can be no doubt that it is the desire to do God service that prompts to the performance of the act.

The words of the Koran with reference to the duty of fasting occur in the 2nd sura. They are: "O, true believers, a fast is ordained you that ye may fear God. A certain number of days shall ye fast. And those who can keep it and do not must redeem their neglect by maintaining a poor man. And he who voluntarily dealeth better with a poor man than he is obliged, this shall be better for him. But if ye fast it will be better for you, if ye knew it. The month Ramadan shall ye fast, in which the Koran was sent down from heaven, a direction unto men, and declarations of direction, and the distinction between good and evil. Therefore fast the same month."

It may be asked, "Where did Mohammed get his idea of fasting?" And the answer, I think, must be "From the Jews." Muir, in his "Life of Mahomet," conjectures that fasting was not observed by the followers of the Prophet at the very beginning of his ministry; probably not until after the settlement at Medina. "Two or three months after his arrival in Medina Mahomet observed the Jews, on the tenth day of their seventh month, keeping the great fast of the Atonement, and he readily adopted it for his own people. Prior to this, fasting does not appear to have been a prescribed ordinance of Islam. It was established at a period when the great object of Mahomet was to symbolize with the Jews in all their rules and ceremonies." However, in course of time, as has been already intimated in these studies, Mohammed quarrelled with the Jews. Thereupon he altered the date of fasting, as he had altered the Kiblah towards which the Faithful should turn in worship. The fast of the Jewish Atonement ceased for Islam, and in its place was put the fast of Ramadan. And although the new ordinance was professedly similar in principle to that of the Jews, yet in duration and in the mode of its observance it was entirely different.

The fast of Ramadan, according to Mohammedan divines, is threefold in its character :—

1. The restraining of the appetite.

2. The abstaining of all the members of the body from sin.

3. The withdrawal of the heart from worldly cares, and of the thoughts from everything besides God.

The first rule is so rigidly carried out that during fasting hours nothing whatever is allowed to pass the lips in the way of food, whether fluid or solid. The fast moreover is considered null and void if perfumes are inhaled, or a pipe is smoked, or a bath is taken, or the spittle is consciously swallowed. There are some good Mussulmans so exceedingly good that they are observed even to open their mouths with fear and trembling lest peradventure they should permit the air to enter too freely. It can easily be seen therefore that the month Ramadan, though such a holy month, is not characterized as either pleasant or happy. It is a month of trial, of discipline, and of considerable privation.

The Moslem fast is at least thirty days in duration—from one new moon to another. Many of the Faithful extend the time to forty days, in imitation of the Prophet

and his family.   The prohibitions already mentioned, at
any rate those with regard to food and drink, it must be
understood, apply only to the day, not to the night.   The
Koran says that the fast ends with the setting of the sun,
and that then believers may partake of that which God has
ordained for them, "until ye can plainly distinguish a
white thread from a black thread by the daybreak."   The
duration of the fast then, by the day, is practically from the
rising of the sun to the going down thereof.   The quaint
idea of discerning the black thread from the white was
taken by Mohammed from the Jews, for the latter determine
the time when they shall begin the religious duties of the
day by their ability to discern the blue threads from the
white threads in the fringes of their garments.

The severity of the Mohammedan fast can only be understood by those who have experienced it, or who have
watched the subjects of it very closely.   When I was a
householder in Calcutta I had opportunities of testing the
reality of the fasting and seeing the effects of it, for I
had two or three Moslem servants.   I always dreaded the
season of Ramadan coming round, for the sake of the
domestics themselves and for the general discomfort of the
house.   It was a time of great upset in every way, for
though the pangs of hunger and thirst were generally
bravely borne, yet the individuals who underwent the fast
were weakened in body, distracted in mind, and altogether
out of trim for the tasks of the day.   How longingly the
evening was looked forward to, when the ordeal would be
over and the fast might be broken !   I have noticed with
much sympathy the servants go up to the roof of the house
to watch feverishly for the departure of the last rays of the
setting sun, or to hear the voice of the crier from the
minaret of the neighbouring mosque declare that the day
was past and over.   I have little hesitation in saying that
the fast of Ramadan, though borne with an appearance of
stoical patience, is in reality to the multitude not only a
severe strain on the flesh, but a weariness and an injury to

the spirit. Generally speaking, I should call the institution a curse rather than a blessing.

Yet doubtless to some fasting is a savour of life unto life, but such are people of a choice spirit. Mrs. Meer Hassan Ali, a writer whom I have frequently quoted, mentions in her book on the "Mussulmans of India" the case of her father-in-law, Meer Hadjee Shah. This gentleman was over seventy years of age when Mrs. Hassan Ali first made his acquaintance, and yet, she says, he never failed as the season of Ramadan came round to undergo the severity of that ordinance day by day during the full period of thirty days. He declared that it was to him a season of great gain, and that he ever looked forward to it with delight. His daughter-in-law says of him: "It was even a source of uneasiness to my venerable friend when, two years prior to his decease, his medical advisers, aided by the solicitude of his family, urged and persuaded him to discontinue the duty, which by reason of his great age was considered dangerous to health, and perhaps to life.

Meer Hadjee Shah seems to have been an exceptionally fine character, and some of his remarks on "fasting" are well worthy of our consideration. He declared that the great secret of a fast, to be beneficial, was to employ time well, and thus both body and soul would be benefited. He also asserted that if the temper were soured, either by abstinence or by the petty ills of life, the good effects of a fast would go with the ruffled spirit, and that the person thus disturbed had much better break his fast since it ceased to be of any value in the sight of God. This wise old Mussulman was constantly telling his younger friends that the institution of Ramadan had for its objects the humbling of the pride of man and the subjection of the spirit of man to the spirit of God. "Therefore," he said, "be watchful and prayerful and zealous in the observance of the fast." It is refreshing, amidst the dry ceremonialism of the creed of Islam, to meet with such a devout and spiritual character as Meer Hadjee Shah! Peace be to his memory!

The laws of Ramadan are as binding on women as on men, and it is said that women, as a rule, observe the fast days with zealous rigidness. And where in the Zenanas the females are not fortunate enough to possess a knowledge of books, or a husband or father disposed to read to them, the hours pass very heavily on their hands. I remember a poor old woman, the servant of a neighbour, who was in but feeble health, yet on no account would she be excused the performance of the fast. Ere the month had expired she was in a pitiable plight, but she persevered with a brave spirit even to the end, saying that if the Prophet had not meant women to undertake the task he would have said so, and that she was sure God would give her strength to go through with it. The faith and patience of the dear old soul were very commendable, but I could not help wishing that such virtues had been shown in a more righteous cause.

One of the greatest curses of the East is the free use of opium by both men and women, and there is a real and close connection between fasting and the spread of the opium mania. I do not know whether the opponents of the opium trade have sufficiently considered the influence that the month Ramadan has over the use of the drug. It seems it is permissible during the thirty or forty days of fasting for Mohammedans to partake of medicine, if there be need ; and tens of thousands take advantage of this rule to relieve somewhat the sufferings of the days, especially towards the close of the fast. Now opium undoubtedly has medicinal properties, so that I have not been surprised to find that multitudes have had recourse to this drug to appease somewhat the cravings of hunger and to impart support to the failing strength. The Rev. J. Ewen, in his racy little book on " India : Sketches and Stories of Native Life," speaking incidentally of Ramadan, says : " Few are exempted, while many who might be prefer to endure the torture for the sake of the accruing merit. Among these must be included the great majority of women. I well remember one I had occasion to see frequently during the fast; she could hardly stand, she was so exhausted and emaciated by disease, yet when I ventured to suggest that, under the circumstances, she ought to resume her ordinary mode of life, she replied, ''There will be no need to do that. *I take opium freely*, and if you will give me liquid medicine I shall be able to dilute it, and thus refresh myself several times during the day.'" And that one case of flying to opium to alleviate the pains of fasting is just typical of what is being done by tens of thousands in Eastern lands; and the craving for the poison grows upon the poor victims. The Fast of Ramadan has much to answer for in the way of inducements to evil, and yet, in the foolishness of man's judgment, the institution was designed to produce good. The fact of the matter is, a month of fasting is a wrong to Nature, and the people who endure it are bound to suffer for it sooner or later.

Some few persons are exempted from the claims of Ramadan, *e.g.*, those who are very ill, the aged, women giving nourishment to children, and very young people. A certain latitude is allowed also in the case of travellers, which, however, is seldom taken advantage of. Most of these exceptions are only temporary, however. When the people are able they are expected to make up for lost time. In the 2nd sura of the Koran it is written: "In the month Ramadan a certain number of days shall ye fast; but he among you who shall be sick, or on a journey, shall fast an equal number of other days." And farther on in the same sura this command is repeated, in slightly different words, thus making the rule doubly binding. Only children are really exempted from the requirements of Ramadan; and even in their case some Moslem parents are so foolish as to go beyond both the letter and spirit of the law, and actually exhort the little ones to imitate their elders. A very sad instance of such stupidity I heard of lately, which resulted in the death of two promising children, who were unable to stand the ordeal. Too late the parents saw their folly, and their only consolation in their bereavement was that the boy and girl had died in what is called "the path of duty," or "the road of God."

At sunset every evening, as has been said, the fast of the day ends. Then the Faithful are allowed to partake of what refreshment they choose. After so many hours of abstinence it is dangerous to health to take a full meal at once, so that there has sprung up a custom called " Breaking the fast," which is usually the taking of a cooling draught. In India this draught is composed of the seeds of lettuce, cucumber, and melon, with coriander, all well pounded together and diluted with cold water. When strained through a muslin and flavoured with syrup of pomegranate, oranges, &c., this concoction is very pleasant. It is drunk eagerly by the famished people. Aged folk and the delicate prefer the juice of spinach only, or a little boiling water to sip. Some people choose a cup of tea, and others declare that the best thing possible with which to break the fast is simply a good pinch of salt. All feel that something light must be taken as a preparation for more substantial things to follow. In the majority of cases I fear the hours of night are given up to feasting. It is a case of turning night into day, and of eating and drinking to satiety. One writer well acquainted with the inner life of Mohammedans says that "at night they make up for their previous self-denial by an unbridled indulgence in the pleasures of the palate, and spend the hours that should be given to sleep in feasting, music, and merrymaking."

And then, as a grand finale to the fasting, when the thirty or forty days are completed, there occurs an Eade, or festival. This is called the Goat Festival. The people turn out in their thousands in gay apparel, and march to the mosques to render praise and thanks to Allah for all His mercies. I can well conceive that the worshippers are in earnest, for all, even the most saintly, must be heartily glad that Ramadan, with all its trials, is over. Goats are carried in the procession—a goat for each little party or group—and these animals are sacrificed as an atonement to God for sin, the people who offer them saying : "Its blood for our blood, its flesh for our flesh, its bones for our bones." In the streets, at the mosques, and in their houses the excited people keep "holy day." They seem to be beside themselves with joy. They give themselves up with perfect abandon to merriment and good living, and act as if the feast would last for ever.

But, prolong the festival as they will, it ends at length; and the joy of a few days cannot make up for the deprivations of a month. No! Ramadan leaves its sad after effects in the way of weakened constitutions, unstrung nerves, uncertain tempers, and altogether a very depressed condition indeed of body, soul, and spirit. Ramadan, instead of being a means of grace to Mohammedan communities, is nothing less than an undermining of the general health, morals, and happiness !

CHAPTER XV

THE story of the Moors in Spain is a romance from the beginning to the end; and it is a story that reflects great honour on Mohammedans. Spain is the one country on the face of the earth in which Moslem rule has been really beneficial to the people of the land. The Moors made Spain prosperous; they made her a great nation; they made her the home in the Middle Ages of science, art, and civilization. And all this was done without injustice to the Christian inhabitants. Indeed, while Mohammedans held supreme sway in Spain, Christians, Jews, and Moslems lived together in amity, and combined their talents and energies to the one common end of exalting their country in the eyes of the whole world.

The conquest of Spain, which took place in the year 711, while the Omiades were Caliphs at Damascus, was a comparatively easy affair. The country was in the possession of the Visigoths, or West Goths, who had ruled the land for two hundred years, but had not been able to consolidate their power. They were nominally Christians, but were without the virtues thereof; and one writer, speaking of them, says: "The vices of the Goths rivalled if they did not exceed the polished wickedness of the pagans." The last of the Gothic Princes was Roderick, around whose memory there has gathered a halo of romance, of which he was totally unworthy. He was the son of a Duke of Cordova, and in A.D. 708 he revolted against his Sovereign, Witica, whom he dethroned and banished, and whose Government he seized.

The ill-gotten kingdom was only retained two years, however, for the Mohammedans of North Africa, to whom has been given the name of Moors, then crossed the Straits of Gibraltar, at the invitation of some of the disaffected noblemen of Spain, and tried their strength with the Goths. The Battle of Xeres decided the struggle in favour of the Moors, though they were only 12,000 in number, while the Goths were 80,000 strong. The fact is, the invaders were bold and hardy men, inured to war, and led by a hero called Tarik; but the Spaniards were a crowd of ill-treated slaves, officered by treacherous noblemen, at whose head was a recreant King. The battle lasted a week, and prodigies of valour are recorded on both sides; but at length the army of Roderick was utterly defeated, and the remnant of it left the field in wild flight.

One of the numerous ballads recording the event gives a graphic picture of the ill-fated King looking in dismay upon his scattered army :—

> He climbed into a hill top, the highest he could see,
> Thence all about of that wide rout his last look took he ;
> He saw his royal banners where they lay drenched and torn ;
> He heard the cry of victory, the Arab's shout of scorn.
>
> He looked for the brave captains that led the hosts of Spain,
> But all were fled except the dead, and who could count the slain?
> Where'er his eye could wander, all bloody was the plain,
> And while thus he said, the tears he shed ran down his cheeks like
>   rain ;
>
> Last night I was the King of Spain—to-day no King am I ;
> Last night fair castles held my train—to-night where shall I lie?
> Last night a hundred pages did serve me on the knee,
> To-night not one I call my own—not one pertains to me.

Thus was Roderick defeated, and Spain conquered. One battle decided the fate of the kingdom. What became of the King remains a mystery to this day. His horse and sandals were found on the banks of the river Gaudalete, and it is supposed he was drowned therein ; but no man knoweth.

Tarik, the Moor, from whose name, the word Gibraltar (*Gebel Tarik* = Rock of Tarik) is derived, followed up his first success vigorously, capturing city after city, including Cordova and Toledo the capital, until the whole land was at the feet of the invaders. The pacification of the country was effected by Musa, another great Arab leader, the superior of Tarik, who joined his subordinate in the summer of A.D. 712, with 18,000 men. In little more than twelve months Spain was completely incorporated with the Mohammedan Empire, and there was peace in the land. Then Tarik and Musa, between whom there was much jealousy, were both recalled by the Caliph Walid to Damascus, to receive their reward. The Commander of the Faithful died, however, before Musa, who was proceeding slowly with a train of 30,000 captives, and immense quantities of booty, could reach the capital of the Empire.

The Moors, not content with the possession of the fine country of Spain, cast covetous eyes towards France. Indeed, Musa, ere his recall, had conceived a magnificent scheme, which, had it been carried out, would have given quite a different complexion to subsequent European history. This scheme was nothing less than to "make his way back to Damascus by the way of Constantinople, thus possessing himself of Europe from the west to the east, surrounding the Mediterranean with a connected series of Moslem allies, and ranging the entire ancient world under the standard of the Prophet." And probably this bold design would have been successfully carried out if the plans of the gallant General had not been upset by the order of the Caliph to resign his command. Subsequent Governors of Spain were without the military genius of Musa, or his lieutenant, Tarik ; and the numerous campaigns which were undertaken against France with indifferent success were ended at last by an overwhelming defeat near Tours in

732. From that "Blow of the Hammer," as has been related in a previous chapter, dates the cessation of the Mohammedan invasion of Western Europe.

As a rule, in Moslem countries, when there are no foreign wars to keep the active, intriguing spirits busy, there are dissensions at home. It was so in Spain. It has to be borne in mind that the Moors were a mixed race, though of one creed, and the different parties and factions amongst them were constantly at strife. Yet the country prospered. Religious toleration was granted to Christians and Jews; trade was encouraged; waste lands were reclaimed; the laws were justly administered; and the outlook generally was very bright. It was felt that if only all the jarring factions could be united under one strong ruler, immeasurable possibilities lay before a land like Spain, so richly endowed by nature.

And in A.D. 755 the strong ruler appeared, in the person of Abd-er-Rahman. And who was he? He was an Omiadis of Damascus, almost the sole survivor of that horrible massacre by the Abbasides which took place in Syria when the Caliphate of Damascus was overthrown. Abd-er-Rahman was but twenty years of age when he fled for his life. He is said to have been blind of one eye, but he had the advantage of a noble stature, and great physical energy and courage. His mental powers were considerable, and though almost penniless, he was full of hope and ambition. Seeing that there was no chance for him to recover the lost possessions of the Omiades in the East, he resolved to turn his eyes to the West, and see if he could not detach the province of Spain from the Caliphate, and found there a new monarchy in his own person. It was a bold scheme to undertake, with no following at his back; but his princely name, and the dissensions in Spain held forth just a prospect of success.

The landing of Abd-er-Rahman on the shores of Spain in 755 was as romantic an episode as the arrival of the Young Pretender in Scotland in 1745, only it had a more prosperous ending. The news of the arrival of the Prince spread like wildfire throughout the country, and many of the old adherents of the Royal family flocked to the standard of the Omiades. Others admiring the bold bid of the young hero for power, rallied to his side. And with a mere handful of soldiers Abd-er-Rahman gallantly, attacked the forces of the Governor of Spain, and routed them. By degrees he captured city after city, until the capital, Cordova, was in his hands, and then he announced himself as King of the whole land. The Caliph of Bagdad sent an army against his rebellious vassals, but it met the fate of previous armies; and at length Spain was acknowledged to be lost to the Commander of the Faithful. It was the first country ruled by Mohammedans to cut itself adrift from the parent authority.

Abd-er-Rahman, who took the title of Sultan or Caliph of Cordova, was a great king, and he established a powerful dynasty in Spain, which endured for nearly three centuries. The land prospered marvellously under him and his successors, and Spain had never reason to rue the day that she threw off the authority of the Abbasides, in favour of the Omiades.

The chief city in Spain was now Cordova, and the Sultans did all in their power, and with success, to make it the rival of Bagdad. Abd-er-Rahman early in his reign began to beautify the city, and in addition to erecting magnificent buildings, he planted the streets with trees. He is said to have imported a date-tree from Syria, to remind him of his old home. It was planted in a garden which he laid out in imitation of the one in which he used to play when a child in Damascus. Other Sultans continued the work of adorning the Royal city, until in the tenth century it was considered everywhere as a metropolis to be proud of. One writer says:—"Except, perhaps, Byzantium, no city of Europe could compare with Cordova, in the beauty of her buildings, the luxury and refinement of her life, and the learning and accomplishments of her inhabitants." This city was delightfully placed on the banks of the Guadalquivir. It was ten miles in length and five in breadth. It contained "more than fifty thousand houses of the aristocracy and official classes, more than a hundred thousand dwellings for the common people, seven hundred Mosques, and nine hundred public baths." Truly Cordova must have been a delightful place in the heyday of Moorish rule; and we can quite understand an Arab writer speaking of the city in the following grandiloquent strain :—"Cordova is the pride of Andalusia. To her belong all the beauty and the ornaments that delight the eye or dazzle the sight. Her long line of Sultans forms her crown of glory; her necklace is strung with the pearls which her poets have gathered from the ocean of language; her dress is of the banners of learning well knit together by her men of science; and the masters of every art and industry are the hem of her garments."

Beautiful as Cordova was in palaces and gardens, she had, as has been hinted, still greater claims to renown. The city was the abode of all that was best in the world of science and letters. Stanley Lane-Poole, in his charming book on the "Moors in Spain," says: "The mind was as lovely as the body. Her professors and teachers made her the centre of European culture; students would come from all parts to study under her favourite doctors. . . . Astronomy, geography, chemistry, natural history, all were studied with ardour at Cordova; and as for the graces of literature, there never was a time in Europe when poetry became so much the speech of everybody as when the Moors ruled Spain." In the Arts also Spain was pre-eminent. Her architects were renowned for the majesty of their conceptions, and her workpeople for the skill with which they executed even the finest work. Silk-weaving was a cherished industry. Pottery was carried to great perfection. Ivory-carving was much in vogue. Chasing in bronze was exquisitely done. The delicacy of open filigree-work was marvellous. Moorish jewellery was not

L

to be surpassed anywhere. And every one has heard of the famous sword-blades of Toledo and the chain-armour of Seville. In arts, sciences, and civilization generally, Spain, under the rule of the Moors, was *facile princeps.*

If any one is tempted to envy the greatness of the Sultans of Cordova, it would be well for him to study almost the last words of the most prosperous, the wealthiest, and the most renowned of the many Moslem Monarchs that sat on the Throne of Spain. This was Abd-er-Rahman the Third, who began to reign at the age of twenty-one, and who lived to be an old man of seventy. His description of life was practically that of Solomon, that "all is vanity." One writer, speaking of this great Sultan, says : "Never was Cordova so rich and prosperous as under his rule ; never was Spain so well cultivated, so teeming with the gifts of nature brought to perfection by the skill and industry of man ; never was the State so triumphant over disorder, or the power of the law more widely felt and respected. Ambassadors came to pay him court from the Emperor of Constantinople, from the Kings of France, of Germany, of Italy. His power, wisdom, and opulence were a by-word over Europe and Africa, and had even reached to the farthest limits of the Moslem Empire in Asia." And yet the Sultan of whom all these gracious things are spoken, has left it on record that "all is vanity." After his death, in the year 961, a paper was found in his private desk, on which were written these remarkable words : "I have now reigned above fifty years in victory or peace, beloved by my subjects, dreaded by my enemies, and respected by my allies. Riches and honours, power and pleasure, have waited on my call; nor does any earthly blessing appear to have been wanting to my felicity. In this situation I have diligently numbered the days of pure and genuine happiness which have fallen to my lot. They amount to fourteen ! O man ! place not thy confidence in this present world !"

The Moors were not fated to maintain their mighty

kingdom of Spain many more centuries. Christians in the outlying provinces of the kingdom, such as Leon, Castille, and Navarre, slowly but surely gathered power, and when they had the wisdom to unite their forces, they in time became the rivals of the Sultans of Cordova. For three hundred years or more a desultory war was kept up by the Moslems and Christians, in which the former usually were the victors; but in the eleventh century the tide began to turn, and it steadily set in in favour of the Christians. Rodrigo Diez of Bivar, commonly called the Cid or "Champion," did much to weaken the Moorish power. He was the idol of the Christians for his bravery, dash, and success in hand-to-hand conflicts with the foe. Even the Moslems described him as "a miracle of God."

The experiences through which this famous chief passed in love and war would fill a volume. I merely mention his name, and hint at his exploits here, because the story of his life is for ever linked with that of the Moors.

Between the years 1238 and 1260 the provinces of Valentia, Cordova, Seville, and Murcia were lost to the Moslems, and their rule was thenceforward, until the end, restricted to the town and province of Granada. Granada seems to have been almost as beautiful a city as Cordova, and for some time it had been gradually taking the place of the latter as the home of the arts and sciences. No city in Spain is more favoured than Granada, in site or climate, for a capital city, and it was a metropolis that the Moors dearly loved. In Granada the Sultans had built the famous Alhambra, or "Red Palace," the ruins of which to-day are the admiration of artists, and are regarded as one of the wonders of the world. At Granada the Moors made their last stand. And their strength even in the period of their decline may be judged from the fact that for two hundred years they held their own against their numerous and determined foes. When, however, Ferdinand of Arragon married Isabella of Castille, and the two Christian kingdoms were thus united, the Moorish power was doomed. It then became a question of only a few years.

The last King of Granada was called Boabdil, a Prince who was a strange union of strength and weakness, of cowardice and courage. On the 25th November, 1491, he surrendered his capital, and with it his kingdom, to their Catholic Majesties of Arragon and Castille, who had invested Granada for months, and made the fair city suffer the rigours of a prolonged siege. Boabdil and his followers were allowed to depart in peace. Historians describe the unfortunate monarch as taking a farewell look at his lost kingdom from the brow of a neighbouring hill. And as he gazed at the beautiful land stretched out before him, and as he looked upon the towers of the Alhambra, the chief ornament of the city, which had been so long the pride and glory of Spain, he is said to have exclaimed, "Allahu Akbar!" "God is most great!" Then he burst into tears, and wept as one who would not be comforted. The mother of Boabdil stood by—Ayesha, a woman of a stern spirit. The only words she addressed to her sorrowful son were, "You may well weep like a woman for what you could not defend like a man!" The spot where Boabdil took his last, sad farewell of his fair kingdom is called to this day "the last sigh of the Moor."

CHAPTER XVI

PILGRIMAGES

AMONGST the religious duties binding upon Mohammedans, that of going on pilgrimage to certain sacred
places, and especially to Mecca, the birthplace of the
Prophet, is one of the most prominent. Tradition says
that Mohammed once declared that a Moslem who died
without performing "the great pilgrimage" might as well
die a Jew or a Christian.

In the 3rd sura of the Koran the law is very plain on
the matter. It is written, "Verily, the first house appointed
unto men to worship was that which is in Mecca : blessed :
and a direction to all creatures. And it is a duty towards
God, incumbent on those who are able, to go thither, to
visit this house." Ability thus involves responsibility.
The phrase "those who are able" has, however, given rise
to much difference of opinion. Sale sums up the rival
theories thus :—"According to an exposition of the phrase
attributed to Mohammed, that person is supposed to be
able to perform the pilgrimage who can supply himself with
provisions for the journey and a beast to ride upon. Al
Shafa'i has decided that those who have money, if they
cannot go themselves, must have some other to go in their
room. Malik Ibn Anas thinks that he is to be reckoned
"able" who is strong and healthy, and can bear the fatigue
of the journey on foot, if he has no beast to ride, and can
also earn his living by the way. But Abu Hanifah is of
opinion that both money sufficient and health of body are
requisite to make the pilgrimage a duty."

There is great need of some binding rule on the matter, for the present uncertainty leads in many instances to serious results. A commander of a steamer plying between Bombay and Jeddah during the pilgrim season, in a letter to the *Times of India* some time ago, wrote: " Many pilgrims leave India with a passage-ticket obtained by begging, a few dirty rags, and perhaps two days' food. What becomes of these people? Why, they starve to death. That many pilgrims die every year through starvation is a well-known fact. And, again, there are amongst the pilgrims the very old and weak—people who are hardly able to come on board. Why should these people be allowed to undertake a voyage for which they are totally unfit? Eventually the end of these old people is painful in the extreme." This plain-spoken sea-captain then goes on to suggest that the Indian Government, at any rate, which has control over a large contingent of pilgrims to Mecca, might insist upon a money guarantee before giving out passports. He states that the French and Dutch Governments, in the countries where they have control over Mohammedans, are very particular to insist upon every pilgrim having in his possession a sum of money which is considered sufficient to take him to Mecca and see him back home again. The Indian Government, however, refuses to adopt any method so drastic, and contents itself with merely advising, in a paper of official rules, every pilgrim to have with him, say, not less than £30. Unhappily, very few pilgrims from India, or elsewhere, count the cost before starting. A blind faith leads them on, and they imagine they will be miraculously helped in the journey which they call " the road of God."

Ages before the time of Mohammed, Mecca was a sacred city, and had its sacred temple, which contained "the pure white stone which came down from heaven." And from all parts of Arabia the tribes met in "the Mother of Cities" to worship at certain seasons of the year. It was of course after the Prophet had conquered Mecca, and made it the centre of the new faith, that Mohammedan pilgrimages commenced. The idols of the city were destroyed, but the temple was converted into a mosque, and the sacred stone was commanded for the future to be " honoured," but not " worshipped." It is thought that the Prophet would have liked to have put a stop to pilgrimages altogether, regarding them as heathenish, but the general feeling in favour of their continuance was too strong for him, and so he made a virtue of necessity. The probability is that the financial aspect of the question weighed heavily with all parties concerned. The people of Mecca, in fact, lived on what gains they made by taxing, and trading with, pilgrims. To have abolished such a profitable source of income would have caused great discontent, and increased the personal enmity to the Prophet, which was already deep enough, amongst the Meccans; but to countenance the old system, and make pilgrimages part of the faith of Islam, would be a politic move which would go a long way towards reconciling the people of Mecca to Mohammed's conquest of their city, and his rule over them. Thus the matter presents itself to many students of Mohammedanism, and, I think, with justice.

1 Mecca is the chief place of pilgrimage. This famous city is about 65 miles east of Jeddah, a port on the Red Sea, and lies in a narrow, barren valley, surrounded by bare hills and sandy plains, simply watered by a brook. At the present time Mecca has a settled population of about 40,000; but in seasons of pilgrimage this is more than quadrupled. The principal building of the city—indeed, the only fine building—is the great mosque where the pilgrims worship, a structure that will hold, it is said, about 35,000 people. The townsfolk are reputed lively, polished, and frivolous, and "spend their time in nothing else but either to tell or to hear some new thing." And to-day, as in days past, they are absolutely dependent upon pilgrims, whom by one means or another they contrive to drain of

their pecuniary resources ere permitting them to depart on their homeward way.

2. Medina is also visited by many of the Faithful, as it contains, or is supposed to contain, the body of the Prophet ; and the bodies of three of the early Commanders of the Faithful. Medina is about 270 miles north of Mecca, and about 140 miles from the nearest port on the Red Sea. It is a difficult place to reach, and the journey thereto wearies the pilgrim ; but it is a meritorious act to visit it ; and the devotee who includes Medina in his tour feels well repaid for his pains by a sight of the tomb of the Prophet, and by the after-praise of all who hear of his deed.

3. Kerbelah, in Turkish Arabia, is also a place of pil-grimage, owing to the fact that there lie buried Hasan and Hosein, the unfortunate grand-children of Mohammed. The pilgrims to Kerbelah are chiefly of the Shia sect. The Sunis are in possession of Mecca ; and as they tax Shia pilgrims more heavily than those of their own particular creed, the Shias often take their revenge by declining to go to Mecca, and by contenting themselves with worship-ping at Kerbelah.

4. Damascus, as the home of Mohammedanism under the Omiades for a century, is also visited by a vast number of pilgrims.

5. Jerusalem, also, is not overlooked. Indeed, perhaps next to Mecca, no place is a greater favourite with pilgrims generally than the Holy City of the Jews. The Mosque of Omar is the great attraction ; and the spot is shown therein, where Mohammed prayed that night, just before he made his famous journey to heaven, as related in the chapter entitled " Legends and Superstitions."

Pilgrims can be divided into three classes. One class may be described as professional beggars. The giving of alms in charity is part of the faith of Islam ; and certain lazy fellows take advantage of this custom, and go on pilgrimage avowedly to see the sacred places ; but really to impose upon their more devout companions. Another class may be described as merchants in a small way. Those from India are called Box-Wallahs.

Almost any trifling article may be obtained from these vendors, who go on pilgrimage to get gain, and not so much spiritual gain as temporal. I have been told that a pretty brisk trade is carried on by the way, as the wants of the pilgrims, though few, are constant. The third class comprises the Hajees, or pilgrims proper, who are journeying to the sacred places out of zeal for their religion, however mistaken that zeal may be. This class constitutes, of course, the bulk of the pilgrims.

Certain qualifications are considered necessary in the case of true pilgrims, or the pilgrimage will be of none effect. The more thoughtful Mohammedans subject themselves to the following tests. It would be well if all pilgrims were equally solicitous on such matters, but I fear they are not. The tests are :—

1. A true pilgrim must be a sincere believer in God, and in Mohammed as the Prophet of God.

2. He must consistently conform to all the regulations of the Koran with respect to faith, law, and practice.

3. He must be free from the world ; that is, all his debts must be paid, and his family and dependents provided for, during the period of his absence from home.

4. He must freely forgive his enemies ; and if he has given any one cause of offence, he must confess his fault and seek reconciliation.

5. Finally, he must repent of every evil thought, word, and deed, against his fellow-men or against God.

Thus prepared, the pilgrim feels that he may start upon his journey, be it short or long, with a clear conscience and a contented spirit, believing that a Divine Providence will watch over him, and bring him back to his country and home again in peace.

While the duty of pilgrimage is as binding upon women as upon men, yet, as a matter of fact, but few women go on pilgrimage. And the reason is not far to seek. It is not that they shrink from the length of the ourney or the hardships of the way. Such things count for little with women of any religion when duty calls them. But there is something from which Eastern women greatly shrink, and that is to be seen by the public. With the poorer classes this does not so much matter, for they do not keep up seclusion or Zenana customs. But with the middle and higher classes, the rules of the Zenana are a formidable barrier in the way of pilgrimage. It would never do to be seen of men even while on "the road of God," so that the desired enterprise has to be given up. But what cannot be done in person may be managed by proxy, and, as a rule, it will be found that female pilgrims are of the lower classes of the people, and that their expenses are borne by the rich who feel constrained to stay at home.

While Mecca is the great goal of the pilgrims, yet that goal is reached by different routes. Devotees are on their way from all parts of the world—from China, India, Afghanistan, the Malay Peninsula, Egypt, Central Africa, the Cape, Syria, Turkey, Persia, Mongolia, and various places of Central Asia. Truly, a motley gathering—different races, speaking different languages ! These people, however, will form themselves, as they draw near to Arabia, into groups, parties, and caravans. Cairo is the meeting-place for Africa ; Jeddah for India ; and Damascus for Turkey and Western Asia generally. There are probably one or two other converging points about which I have not heard ; but the three mentioned are the most famous ; and from these celebrated places every year great caravans start on the pilgrimage to the sacred city of the Mohammedan faith.

I would dwell for a moment on the Indian pilgrims, about whom Messrs. Thos. Cook and Son, the tourist agents, have supplied me with much interesting and important information. In 1886 the Government of India appointed this world-famed firm " Pilgrim Agents " for the whole of India, and the arrangement has worked admirably. It may seem, on the face of it, a strange anomaly that a Christian firm should be so prominent in helping Mohammedans on their pilgrim way to Mecca; but the action is certainly a humane one. Indian pilgrims have from time immemorial either taken the long and trying land journey *via* Persia, or the shorter but even more trying sea journey from Bombay to the port of Jeddah, on the Arabian coast. And they have been the victims of lodging-house keepers and crimps at Bombay ere they get on board ship; and even when on the latter they have too often suffered terribly from over-crowding and defective sanitary arrangements. At the Jeddah port also pilgrims have always had to put up with much bad treatment from boatmen and local agents on shore.

Most of these evils have been altogether removed, and the rest greatly ameliorated, by the appointment of Thos. Cook and Son as "Pilgrim Agents." In a letter which I received from them lately, in answer to certain inquiries which I made, they say: "So far as the boatmen at Jeddah are concerned, we have succeeded in a great measure in putting a stop to their ill-treatment of the pilgrims; but as the territory is Turkish, it is a very difficult matter to get any further. If the pilgrims would report any case of cheating or fleecing to the British Consul, they would always obtain the best assistance and advice; but, unfortunately for themselves, they do not wish to make any complaints during the Haj; and a great many of them think that the greater the hardship they may have to submit to, the more efficacious their pilgrimage."

On the general success of their special agency, Messrs. Thos. Cook and Son remark: "We think we may say that there can be no doubt that our arrangements have had a good result in protecting pilgrims; and the fact that the Government of India asked us to continue the arrangement after the expiration of the term first agreed upon between us shows that they are satisfied with the results."

As has been intimated, when pilgrims from India reach Jeddah, and enter Arabian territory, and actually tread the road to the Sacred City, no outside aid can help them, and the Turkish Government gives itself no trouble in the matter. Pilgrims on every route and of every nationality suffer dreadfully from the imperfect means of conveyance, from the bad roads, from the difficulty at times of obtaining food, from robbers and armed gangs of marauders, and from the most terrible enemy of all, the cholera or plague, which is constantly breaking out amongst them. In the year 1890 the cholera was very bad, and it is estimated that in three weeks, when it was at its height, there were no fewer than from 25,000 to 30,000 deaths. However, notwithstanding all drawbacks and hindrances, the people, by the different routes, plod on their weary way along " the road of God," and the majority at length reach the sacred territory or confines of Mecca.

The month called Dhu'l Hijjah, the last month of the Mohammedan year, is the great month of the pilgrimage. The caravans usually arrive in the vicinity of Mecca some time in advance. When within, say, ten miles of the city, a halt is called. The pilgrims are about to tread on holy ground, and they must make the necessary preparations. On the sacred territory it is not lawful to attack an enemy, or to hunt game, or even to cut a branch from a tree. Sale says that some of the Faithful are so particular about not taking life that " they will not kill even a louse or flea if they find them on their bodies." A special garment is now put on, called " the Ihram," which consists of two woollen wrappers, one of which is fastened round the body, and the other is thrown over the shoulders. This must be worn until all the rites of the pilgrimage are over. It seems, also, that the head must be left bare, the hair being shaved off, that the nails must be trimmed, and that the feet must be shod with a peculiar kind of slipper, which " covers neither the heel nor the instep." With regard to the beard, which every good Mussulman is always supposed to wear, it is a *sine quâ non* when he goes on pilgrimage; it is, indeed, a badge of the Faith, none being admitted at the "Holy House" who has not this passport on his chin.

Properly habited, the pilgrims now push on their way, and enter Mecca, the goal of their journeyings, at last. We can imagine the satisfaction and joy of all, and especially of those who have come from the ends of the world, and have scarcely dared to hope for such a happy conclusion to their travels. The appearance of Mecca is rather mean, the roads are very dusty, and the crowds jostle each other somewhat rudely; but no one cares. It is Mecca! The feet of the pilgrims stand within the gates of the far-famed city, and there is no room in their hearts, for the time being, for anything but thanksgiving and praise. There is usually a great rush for lodgings, which are not easy to obtain, as the Meccans drive a hard bargain. But all are settled down after a while, and their thoughts are turned to the due observance of the necessary rites of pilgrimage.

The ceremonies which are prescribed for the Faithful in Mecca in the month of Dhu'l Hijjah are many and elaborate. Let me briefly enumerate them.

1. The first thing to be done is to compass the Kaaba, or Holy House, seven times, beginning at the corner where "the sacred white stone" is placed. At each turn the stone must be gravely kissed by the worshippers, to show their reverence for it.

2. Another important thing is to have a view of a footprint of Abraham, which is kept locked up in an iron chest. The Koran, referring to this precious relic of the past, exhorts the Faithful to pray over it.

3. The well Zam-Zam must also be visited. It is within the Temple grounds, a little to the east of the sacred stone. Mohammedans say that this well is the very spring from which water gushed out for the relief of Ishmael when Hagar, his mother, wandered with him in the desert.

To drink of the water of Zam-Zam is considered a panacea for most of the ills of life ; and bottles of the precious fluid are carried by returning pilgrims to every part of the Mohammedan dominions.

4. The next ceremony is partly to run and partly to walk seven times between Mounts Safa and Marwa, two slightly elevated spots in the vicinity of the Temple. Idols used to be worshipped by the Arabians on these eminences, but now there is nothing to be done but to ascend and descend with what gravity the Faithful can muster for the occasion.

5. Then a visit must be paid to another mountain, not far from Mecca, called Arafat, which is sacred to the memory of our first parents, Adam and Eve. Pilgrims, when on this famous mountain, should, says the Koran, " Ask pardon of God, for God is gracious and merciful."

6. The ceremonies draw to an end in the valley of Mina, near Arafat. In this valley there are three pillars, at which all pilgrims must throw seven stones, in imitation of Father Abraham, who, meeting the devil in that place, and being disturbed by him in his devotions, drove him away with stones.

7. On the tenth day of Dhu'l Hijjah sacrifices are offered to God   " The victims must be either sheep, goats, kine, or camels ; males if of either of the two former kinds, and females if of either of the latter, and of a fit age."

8. The sacrifices being over, the pilgrims shave their heads and cut their nails, which have not been touched since the sacred territory was first entered.

9. These little matters having been attended to, and the hair and trimmings of the nails having been most solemnly buried in the valley of Mina, the pilgrimage is regarded as satisfactorily completed, and the people may now either visit other sacred spots, such as Medina or Jerusalem, or return at once to their homes. Probably the majority choose to go home ; and thenceforth amongst their kindred, friends, and neighbours they are known by the honourable title of Hajees, or pilgrims.

No sensible person can regard the pilgrimage to Mecca, with its silly and ridiculous rites, which are relics of idolatry, other than as an imposition upon the good faith of Mohammedans. And in time, doubtless, notwithstanding the injunctions of the Koran, the custom will be abolished, for there can be little doubt that the pilgrims, who go with joy and gladness, return with very different feelings. The pilgrimage is said to be a general disappointment ; and one cannot wonder at it when one thinks of the terrible hardships that are endured on the way to the Holy City, and of the poor return that the pilgrims receive for their pains. The whole thing is a mockery of religion, and no doubt earnest and devout Moslems feel it to be such. I have been told that of late years there has been a great falling off in the number of pilgrims. There was a time when a quarter of a million or more wended their way every year to the Mother of Cities ; but now the number is under 100,000, and of these over 11,000 are from India. The surest evidence of the decline is shown, I think, in the fact that the settled population of Mecca has fallen more than one-half during the last two or three decades of years. The zeal for going on pilgrimage has evidently considerably abated, and as knowledge increases in Eastern lands there can be little doubt that the custom, in its present form, at any rate, will fall into disuse. And the sooner the better !

CHAPTER XVII

FATIMITES OF EGYPT

THE title of this chapter refers to the most glorious period of Moslem rule in Egypt, between the years 953 and 1171; but ere touching on that period I would call attention to the original subjugation of Egypt by the followers of the Prophet, which occurred in the seventh century, in the reign of the Caliph Omar.

At the disruption of the Roman Empire, Egypt, the country of the Pharaohs, was left in the possession of the Greeks of Constantinople, and it was from the latter that Amr, a Moslem General, took it, after a struggle of one or two years' duration. Amr had borne a glorious part in the conquest of Syria, and especially in the capture of Jerusalem. He was a man of considerable mental ability, of determined courage, and of wonderful success in war. When in Medina on one occasion, Omar had asked to survey the sword which had cut down so many Christian warriors, and when Amr unsheathed a short, ordinary scymetar, the Caliph expressed surprise. The warrior smiled, and said, "A sword in itself counts for little; without the arm of its master, my sword is neither sharper nor more weighty than the sword of Pharezdak the Poet."

This was the man who in A.D. 638 marched towards the borders of Egypt, resolved to conquer the land for Islam. After a thirty days' siege he took possession of Pelusium, the key of the country, and then marched forward to the ruins of Heliopolis and the neighbourhood of the modern

Cairo. Memphis, the ancient capital, was soon after taken, and the forces of Amr being strengthened by the people of the land—the Copts—who hated their Greek rulers, by degrees drove the latter to the sea-coasts, and the war centred itself at Alexandria, which the Greeks had made their capital. Alexandria stood a siege of fourteen months; and but for the desperate valour of Amr and his Moslems, and the neglect of the Emperor of Constantinople to supply the besieged with provisions and munitions of war, the city would not have been taken at all, for it was a strong fortress, and was open to the sea. Amr lost 23,000 men in the prolonged struggle; but at length, on a Friday, in the year 640, he had the proud satisfaction of seeing the standard of Mohammed planted on the walls of the second city of the Greek Empire.

The victorious General sent off an express messenger to Medina to the Commander of the Faithful with the news. " I have taken," he wrote, " the great city of the West. It is impossible for me to enumerate the variety of its riches and beauty; and I shall content myself with observing that it contains four thousand palaces, four thousand baths, four hundred theatres or places of amusement, twelve thousand shops for the sale of vegetable food, and forty thousand tributary Jews. The town has been subdued by force of arms, without treaty or capitulation, and my soldiers are impatient to seize the fruits of their victory." The idea of pillage thus suggested was firmly rejected, however, by the Caliph, who, in reply, directed Amr to reserve the wealth and revenue of Alexandria for the public service and the propagation of the Faith.

Thus was Egypt conquered by the Mohammedans, and added to the dominions of the successor of the Prophet. And the new conquest was found to be even a richer prey than had been anticipated. The fertility of Egypt at once began to supply the dearth of Arabia, and "the string of camels laden with corn and provisions covered, almost without an interval, the long road from Memphis to Medina."

M

The Caliph Omar, pleased with these presents, and with his curiosity aroused by the news that reached him, requested Amr to write him a description of the conquered country, which the gallant warrior proceeded to do in his usual graphic and forcible style.   As a Moslem description of the singular land of Egypt, it is well worth recording.   It runs as follows :—

"O Commander of the Faithful, Egypt is a compound of black earth and green plants, between a pulverized mountain and a red sand.   The distance from Syene to the sea is a month's journey for a horseman.   Along the valley descends a river, on which the blessing of the Most High reposes both in the evening and morning, and which rises and falls with the revolutions of the sun and moon.   When the annual dispensation of Providence unlocks the springs and fountains that nourish the earth, the Nile rolls his swelling and sounding waters through the realm of Egypt; and the villagers communicate with each other in their painted barks.   The retreat of the inundation deposits a fertilizing mud for the reception of seeds; the crowds of husbandmen who blacken the land may be compared to a swarm of industrious ants ; and their native indolence is quickened by the lash of the taskmaster, and the promise of the flowers and fruits of a plentiful increase.   Their hope is seldom deceived ; but the riches they extract from the wheat, the barley, the rice, the vegetables, the fruit-trees, and the cattle are unequally shared between those who labour and those who possess.   According to the vicissitudes of the seasons, the face of the country is adorned with a silver wave, a verdant emerald, and the deep yellow of a golden harvest."

I do not know that Amr's description could be much improved, as far as it goes ; and, in its pleasant and painful particulars, it holds good of Egypt at the present day as in days past.

Egypt, once conquered by the Moslems, has ever since remained a Mohammedan State, and, as a general rule, has been a dependent province.   For many generations after

Amr's time the country was under the control of the Commanders of the Faithful. When the Omiades of Damascus usurped the sovereignty of the Empire, Egypt quietly acquiesced in the change, and gave no trouble ; and even when the Abbasides, a hundred years later, dethroned the Omiades, and set up the Caliphate at Bagdad, Egypt still remained a dutiful daughter of the successor of the Prophet. And in her dependent position she prospered, though the greater part of the wealth of the country found its way into the coffers of the Commander of the Faithful. So matters went on for centuries—indeed, until the tenth century, when, however, a great change occurred, which ushered in a period of unexampled power and glory for Egypt as an independent Moslem kingdom.

In the chapter on the "Abbasides of Bagdad," the Alyites were referred to, who were constantly causing trouble in the Empire, and seeking to put a Prince on the throne of the Commander of the Faithful ; but all such efforts invariably ended in failure. At length the Alyites, or, as they are also called, the Fatimites, from Fatima, the wife of Ali, accepted the inevitable, and instead of trying to dethrone the Caliph of Bagdad, they resolved, if possible, to follow the example of Spain, and detach a province from the Empire, and found an additional Caliphate. Egypt was the province fixed upon ; and in the reign of Moktader, a boy-Caliph, A.D. 909, the attempt was made. Moktader was a weak Prince, entirely under the control of his eunuchs and his wives. Gilman, in his book on the Saracens, says—"Moktader was incapable of maintaining order in his kingdom, or even of controlling his own palace ; and though he remained long on the throne, the record of his reign is crowded with accounts of the falling away from loyalty of cities and provinces, and the revolts of bold chiefs who made him tremble, in moments when he thought at all on the affairs of State." The attempt of the Fatimites on Egypt was not altogether successful, however, in the reign of Moktader. Only parts of Africa were taken possession of. But still a foothold was gained, and gradually the insurgents extended their power, until, in the year 969, they conquered the whole country, and the setting up of the new dynasty of the Fatimites was an accomplished fact.

Moez, who claimed direct descent from Fatima, the daughter of Mohammed, through Ismail, a grandson of Fatima, was the first Sultan or Caliph of the new Royal house of Egypt. He was a brave and skilful Prince, and all the power of the Abbasides of Bagdad was unable to dethrone him, or even to persuade him to render tribute. Moez took up the position of an independent Prince, and declared himself the equal, if not the superior, by virtue of his descent, of the ruler of Bagdad.

In the tenth century we see, then, the remarkable spectacle of three great Mohammedan powers ruling at the same time, and all claiming to be Commanders of the Faithful. We find the Abbasides at Bagdad, the Omiades in Spain, and the Fatimites in Egypt. The three flags—the black, white, and green—representing the three great factions of Islam, were, for the first and last time in the history of Mohammedanism, fluttering in the breeze at one and the same time, as representative of reigning powers. And this state of things lasted for fully two centuries. And of the three Caliphates, that of Egypt was not the least powerful. Sultan Moez was a remarkable man, and ere he died he added to his dominions Palestine and Northern Syria, even to and beyond Damascus. The Fatimites, in fact, just about divided the possessions of the Caliphate of Bagdad into two parts, and they retained perhaps the more fruitful.

The genuineness of the descent of the Fatimites of Egypt from the Prophet has been often called in question, but it was a matter about which the Princes themselves troubled little. The brave and impetuous Moez, when straitly questioned regarding the matter on one occasion, silenced his questioner effectually by drawing his scymetar and saying: "See, this is my pedigree; and these," casting a handful of gold to his soldiers, "and these gallant fellows are my kindred and my children."

The new dynasty founded Cairo on the right bank of the Nile, and near the point of the Delta, and made the city the capital of Egypt, and such it has remained ever since. And a very beautiful capital Cairo is. The city occupies about five square miles, and at the present day has some fine broad streets, some magnificent mosques and palaces, and a number of well and richly-supplied bazaars.

My first view of Cairo was early one April morning about four years ago. It was from a railway train. I had been travelling all the night in an over-crowded carriage from Suez, and was feeling in anything but a cheerful frame of mind. However, the sight which presented itself on a sudden turn of the line, as we drew near our destination, was so splendid that every trace of languor was thrown off, and I had eyes, ears, and feelings for nothing but the grand vision. Cairo, with its great fortresses, its lofty minarets, its splendid mansions, its beautifully laid-out gardens, and its background of the Nile, the mighty Pyramids, the mysterious Sphinx, and the far-reaching desert, was a sight such as my eyes had never before seen, though accustomed to the splendours of the East.

The situation of Cairo is unique, and though there are more beautiful capital cities in the world, there are few, if any, that make such a deep and lasting impression on the mind of the traveller. Cairo, in the time of her real greatness, in the days when the Fatimites ruled, must have been a capital to be proud of. And not only was the city famous for her unique situation and grandeur, but she earned renown in the East, as Cordova did in the West, for her encouragement of learning. Gibbon says : "The Royal library of the Fatimites consisted of one hundred thousand manuscripts, elegantly transcribed and splendidly bound, which were lent, without jealousy or avarice, to the students of Cairo."

The Fatimite rule in Egypt has gained a somewhat unenviable notoriety, through the vagaries of a prince called Hakem, the third of the Royal line. This Caliph's whole soul was given up to theological questions, and he had no time or thought for anything else, except to seek to enforce his views upon others. He was troubled—cursed, we might say—with "religious mania." At first Hakem posed as the most zealous of Fatimite Shias, and actually caused twelve hundred copies of the Koran to be transcribed in letters of gold. But wearying of the position of Defender of the Faith, he went to the other extreme, and questioned almost every religious practice that the Prophet had ever instituted. Finally, the Royal madman essayed to introduce a new religion of his own, which he fondly, but vainly, hoped would supersede that of Mohammed. However, though Hakem did not succeed in upsetting the creed of Islam, he did succeed in establishing a new religion, which has existed until the present day, and seems likely to endure for generations to come. I refer to the Druse religion.

The Druses inhabit a district in the North of Syria, where they have maintained for eight hundred years a distinct religious and political independence and nationality. The Druses of Mount Lebanon are well known in history. "They are industrious, brave, and hospitable. Their staple article of commerce is silk. Their population exceeds 200,000, and it is said that, in case of need, their Emir can assemble, in a very short time, 30,000 men armed with muskets." Their faith and doctrines are a wonderful mixture of the teachings of the Jewish Pentateuch, the Christian Gospels, and the Mohammedan Koran.

But the most extraordinary feature of their creed is the belief in Hakem, the Fatimite ruler of Egypt, as not only a Prophet, and the original creator of their Faith, but as an Incarnation—the tenth and the last Incarnation—of the Most High God. An able article in "Chambers's Encyclopædia" on the Druses puts the history of the origin of this singular faith in a nut-shell. I would quote one paragraph: "Hakem Bimar Allah, Caliph of Egypt, and a Nero in cruelty, was the author of the Druse system of religion. He affirmed that he was the representative of God, and having enlisted his confessor Darazi in his cause, he prepared to propound his doctrine. In the 407th year of the Hejira, or A.D. 1029, the divine nature of Hakem, or rather the incarnation of the spirit of God in him, was publicly announced at Cairo. The revelation, however, was unfavourably received by the mob. Hakem's confessor, Darazi, narrowly escaped the fate of a martyr to the impostures of his master. Retiring, however, to the fastnesses of the Lebanon, he there began to inculcate the principles of the new faith; and although he never acquired any mastery over the sympathies of the mountaineers, he at least left his name to them, for there can be little doubt that the name Druses is derived from that of Darazi." Thus a Fatimite Prince of Egypt, who was a madman and a tyrant, founded a new religion. Verily fact is stranger than fiction!

After the death of Hakem, from about the year 1076, Egypt knew no peace; for she was being constantly invaded, either by the rising Turkish power, to which reference will be made in a later chapter, or by the Franks from Europe, who began to think and dream of conquering the land of Christ from the followers of Mohammed. The Fatimites now gradually declined in power and influence. The first possessions to be torn from their grasp were the fair provinces of Syria. These were seized by the Turks, who made a bold dash at Egypt, but failed in the latter enterprise. The Turks, in turn, lost Palestine, for a time; for the Franks stepped in, and founded a Christian kingdom at Jerusalem. But such changes only made matters worse for the Fatimites, who were sorely pressed, on every side, by land and sea. Still, for a season, they bravely held on; though their power was tottering to its fall.

At length, in 1171, the end came. Amalric, the Christian King of Jerusalem, resolved to attempt the conquest of Egypt. Gathering together a large army, he set forth on his daring enterprise, which, however, was not fated to prosper. The proximity of the Franks, whose prowess was well known, filled the Fatimites with fear ; and, in their despair, they sent off to the Turks of Damascus, asking succour from them as brethren. The Turkish Prince Noureddin, the uncle of Saladin, who became so famous in history, was delighted at the request, and promptly responded to it. The troops that he sent reached Cairo just in time to save the city, for the Christians were at the gates. " Amalric prudently declined a contest with the Turks in the midst of a hostile country, and retired into Palestine, with the shame and reproach that always adhere to unsuccessful injustice." The Turkish Generals entered Cairo in triumph, and, once in, it was impossible to get them out. They saw the feebleness of the Fatimites, and they resolved to usurp their power. The revolution was a bloodless one. A word sufficed to effect the stupendous change, so low had the Caliphs of Cairo fallen. The reign of the Fatimites was over ! The lease of power of the Shias was ended ! The Alyites had to succumb to the might of their foes !

The new-comers were Sunis, and adherents of the Abbasides, and they gloried in their triumph. Gibbon says—" By the command of Noureddin, and the sentence of the doctors, the holy names of Abu Bekr, Omar, and Othman were solemnly restored ; the Caliph Mosthadi, of Bagdad, was acknowledged in the public prayers as Commander of the Faithful ; and the green livery of the sons of Ali was exchanged for the black colour of the Abbasides. The last of his race, Sultan Adhed, who survived only ten days, expired in happy ignorance of his fate, and his treasures secured the loyalty of the soldiers, and silenced the murmurs of the sectaries."

Thus fell the Fatimites of Egypt, and with them, or, at any rate, with the fall of the Mamelukes, who succeeded them, ended the position of Egypt as a great and independent power. The changes in the history of Egypt since the twelfth century have been varied and remarkable; but, through all, the country has remained Mohammedan, being tributary first to the Abbasides, and afterwards to the Ottoman Turks. To-day the Khedive of Egypt is more or less subject to the Sultan of Constantinople; and he is also, in some measure, under the control of England. And the arrangement is working well. It is all, I suppose, preliminary to the granting of absolute freedom and complete independence to the Egyptian Government. It is hoped, in the not very distant future, that Egypt will become once more a strong nation, and even surpass in power and glory the palmiest days of her Moslem history, under the brilliant but unfortunate dynasty of the Fatimites.

CHAPTER XVIII

MANNERS AND CUSTOMS

ALREADY in this series of studies some of the manners and customs of Mohammedans have been referred to; and others will be mentioned incidentally in later chapters. Consequently there is no call now to attempt to cover the whole ground. I shall, therefore, confine myself to a notice of certain matters which, unless dealt with in a special chapter like this, would be omitted altogether.

Amongst the better-class Mohammedans the mother very rarely nourishes her own infant. Mohammed, it will be remembered, was put out to nurse, and the custom prevails still amongst the wealthy. More often, however, a nurse is brought to the house, and is given entire charge of the child for two years or so. And when once a nurse is engaged in a family, she, as a rule, becomes a member of that house to the end of her days, unless she chooses to quit herself. Sometimes, when a nurse is not obtainable, an infant will be reared on goat's milk rather than that the mother should be obliged to fatigue herself with motherly duties. On the fortieth day after the child's birth the little one is submitted to the hands of the barber, who shaves the head, as commanded by the law. The mother dresses in her most costly attire, and makes the baby look as smart as possible, and then visitors arrive to present their congratulations and to offer gifts. The gift need not be a costly one, but it would be deemed an evil omen not to bestow something. The birthday of each son in a family is regularly kept as a day of annual rejoicing, to which friends and neighbours are invited. " Dinner is provided liberally for the guests, and the poor are not neglected. whose prayers and blessings are coveted by the parents, for their offspring's benefit ; and they believe the blessings of the poor are certain mediations at the throne of mercy, which cannot fail to produce benefits on the person in whose favour they are invoked." The birthday is called, in India, the Sal-girrah, from " sal," a year, and " girrah," to tie a knot. As the boy's anniversary comes round, the mother ties a knot on a string kept for the purpose. The girl's years are numbered by a silver loop being added to the neck-ring which she wears. These are the usual methods of registering the ages of Mohammedan children.

From their very earliest years Moslem boys and girls are exhorted to show great respect and reverence for their parents. Mohammed taught expressly that children should cultivate love, honour, and humility towards their mothers no less than towards their fathers. He said, beautifully, " The son gains Paradise at the feet of the mother." Parents entertain for their son the most tender regard, and as soon as possible the father makes him both his companion and his friend ; yet the most familiar endearments do not lessen the feeling of reverence a good son entertains for his sire. Common as smoking is in the East, a son can rarely be persuaded by an indulgent father or mother to smoke a hooka or nargileh in their presence, and that not because he is afraid of their displeasure, but from feelings of real, genuine respect. In these things I consider that Mohammedans are to be admired. From what I have seen of their lives, I believe that they earnestly strive to carry out the teaching of the Koran, which says, " The Lord hath commanded that ye show kindness unto your parents, whether the one of them or both of them attain to old age with thee. Wherefore speak respectfully unto them, and submit to behave humbly towards them, out of tender affection, and say, O Lord, have mercy on them both, as they nursed me when I was little."

As we have already seen in the chapter on "Women," Mohammedans seek to get their offspring married as early in life as possible. Girls are considered to have passed their prime when over sixteen years of age; even the poorest peasant would object to a wife of eighteen. The majority are married between the ages of eight and twelve. The task of fixing upon a desirable match for their sons and daughters is a source of constant anxiety to Moslem parents, and they know no rest till they have satisfactorily accomplished their purpose. Often before commencing negotiations, even when desirable parties have been discovered, the father will consult an omen, to make sure that Providence is guiding them in their choice. This singular custom is carried out as follows :—Several slips of paper are cut up, and on half of the number are written the words "to be," and on the other half the words "not to be." Armed with these, after they have been mixed together, the head of the household sallies forth to his evening devotions at the mosque. At the portion of the service when he bows down his head to God, he beseeches the Almighty to instruct and guide him for the best interest of his child. The prayer concluded, the parent seats himself with solemn gravity on the prayer-carpet, under which he has placed the slips of paper, and with his right hand proceeds to draw out slip after slip. If the omen be favourable, the papers first drawn will bear the words "to be," but if unfavourable the words "not to be." The result is at once made known to the anxious mother, who, in a state of great excitement, has been awaiting the decision at home. If the answer of that "wisdom which cannot err" is all that the parents could wish, no delay occurs in opening negotiations with the chosen parties, and in course of time the match is made.

Marriage ceremonies amongst Indian Moslems occupy three full days, and entail much expense, as well as a great deal of trouble. The work does not matter so much, as it is all in the way of enjoyment, but the expense sometimes hampers the parents through life in their circumstances. Everywhere in the East marriage customs financially need to be reformed, but so far reformers have met with little or no success. Unfortunately the feeling in favour of a grand display, even if useless, is so deeply embedded in the breasts of Mohammedans that if it be found impossible to meet properly the pecuniary demands of a marriage-ceremony the girl very often has to live out her days in single blessedness, which is considered a great disgrace. No licenses are required in the case of Mohammedans, nor is any registry kept of marriages in strictly Mohammedan countries. And any person who is acquainted with the Koran may read the marriage-service, but usually a professed Moolah, or Moulvi, a so-called priest, is engaged to do it. The day being fixed, the elders, male and female, of the two families, invite their several relatives, friends, and acquaintances, to be present to observe the ceremony, and to rejoice with them over the auspicious event. The invitations are written in the Persian character on red paper. Strange to say, a purdah, or screen, separates the bride and bridegroom while the service is being conducted, and they are not permitted to see each other until they are lawfully married. The priest calls on the young lady by name to answer a somewhat superfluous question, viz., "Is it by your own consent that this marriage takes place?" The answer always is, "It is by my own consent." Indeed, what other answer dare a Moslem bride make? A portion of that sura of the Koran entitled "Women" is then read, and the law of marriage, as laid down by Mohammed, is briefly explained. It is the young man's turn next to answer a question. He is asked to name the sum he proposes as his wife's dowry. The bridegroom mentions the amount. Everybody being satisfied, the priest declares the parties to be man and wife, and prays that the young couple may receive the blessing of Allah both in time and eternity. The taking home of the bride is the grand finish to the three days' rejoicings. A long procession accompanies the happy pair through the streets, and the guests make a perpetual din of noisy music until the bridegroom's house is reached. I have watched many such gay processions with great interest.

At weddings, and on many other occasions in their lives, Mohammedans are expected to give something to the poor. Alms-giving is, indeed, one of the binding customs of Islamism. Good Moslems never allow the voice to pass unheeded which applies " In the name of God," or " For the love of God." As one writer says : " They are persuaded that alms-giving propitiates Heaven, consequently this belief is the inducing medium for clothing the naked, feeding the hungry, supporting the weak, consoling the afflicted, protecting the fatherless, sheltering the homeless, and rendering the ear and the heart alive to the distresses of the poor in all situations." What is bestowed in charity is called Zakat, or God's portion. Alms may be given of five things—of cattle, of money, of corn, of fruits, and of wares sold. Of each of these a certain portion, equal to $2\frac{1}{2}$ per cent., is to be set aside for the poor. Mohammed instituted the custom, and ever since it has been kept up in every part of the Mohammedan world. The Koran says, " Alms are to be distributed to the poor and the needy, and to those who are employed in collecting and distributing the same, and unto those whose hearts are reconciled, and for the redemption of captives, and unto those who are in debt and insolvent, and for the advancement of God's religion, and unto the traveller." Alms-giving is carried to the extreme by Moslems, and undoubtedly encourages mendicity and pauperism. The indolent impose upon good nature, and from what I can gather, the bestowers of charity do not trouble themselves to find out deserving cases. The merit to the giver is the same whether the recipient is a deserving or an undeserving object. The general rule, I fancy, is " First come, first served, and no questions asked." Such a custom, in the long run, leads to more harm than it does good.

The practice of giving complimentary presents is universal amongst Mohammedans, as indeed, amongst other Eastern races. It is a custom that has sprung from selfish motives, for there is always an ulterior design in the apparently generous gift. Nuzzer is the name for such an offering, and it usually takes the form of a present of money. It is an inferior that makes the gift to some one that ranks above him in society, *e.g.*, a subject to a Prince, a soldier to an officer, a servant to his master. Mrs. Meer Hassan Ali, in her book on the " Mussulmans of India," gives from her own personal experience an excellent illustration of the custom. This English lady, who married a Mohammedan, says, " When we arrived in India, an old servant of my husband's family was sent to meet us at Patna to escort us to Lucknow. On entering the budgerow, or boat, he presented fourteen rupees to me, which were laid on a folded handkerchief. I did not then understand what was intended, and looked to my husband for an explanation. He told me to accept the Nuzzer; and when I still hesitated, remarking that it seemed more than a man in his situation could afford to give away, my husband smilingly silenced my scruples by observing : 'You will learn in good time that these offerings are made to do you honour, together with the certain anticipation of greater benefits in return. This servant tenders this Nuzzer to you, and it may be all the money he possesses, but he feels assured that it will be more than doubly repaid to him in the value of a khillut or present he expects from your hands to-day. He would have behaved, in his estimation, disrespectfully in appearing before you without a Nuzzer, and had you declined accepting it, he would have thought that you were either displeased with him, or did not approve of his coming.' " This Nuzzer custom must be a great nuisance at times, for the advantage is all on one side.

Who has not heard, when travelling in the East, the Mohammedan expression, " Shookur Allah ? " It means

"All thanks to God." Hearing this saying so frequently, one would think that Moslems were a most grateful people : and grateful they may be to God, and possibly to their fellow-creatures also for benefits conferred ; but to the latter, strange to say, they never express any thanks. In fact, the phrase, "Thank you," has no equivalent in most Eastern languages. A Mohammedan will, on receipt of a favour, probably make a bow, and say "Salaam"—"Peace be with you ;" but he will not say, "Thank you," or "I am very much obliged." The Moslem thanks God for everything, and man for nothing. At every turn it is "Shookur Allah ;" and while one says nothing against, but really admires, such a sentiment, one cannot help wishing that, more widely over the earth's surface, the good old English custom of saying "Thank you" prevailed.

The practice of dyeing the hair is very common among Mohammedans as they advance in life. The favourite colour is a dull, brick red. This dye is prepared from the plant "Lawsonia inermis." It is used in every grade of society, and by both sexes. Doubtless, by means of this red dye, a Moslem may preserve for many years a deceptive appearance of juvenility, but the natural colour would be infinitely more becoming. Hair-dyes, moreover, are not always to be depended upon.

I have heard of a Princess in Southern India who, as age crept on apace, and her hair turned grey, cast about her for a dye that would bring back the raven tresses of youth. At length she thought she had obtained one. It was highly recommended by her friends ; in short, it was guaranteed to produce the desired effect. The cautious Princess, however, resolved to try the new dye on a favourite white Persian cat before she applied it to her own hair. It was well that she did so, for the unfortunate cat, after a few applications of the mixture, became a wonder among the animal creation—it turned a beautiful peagreen.

Generally speaking, Mohammedans treat animals with

kindness. They are rather partial to cats, because they say Mohammed was very fond of them. The Prophet is reported to have taken a favourite pussy with him where-ever he went, and to have put himself to no little incon-venience at times to minister to its comfort. At Damascus there is a retreat or refuge for cats, where thousands are kept at the expense of the charitable. If asked as to the origin of the custom, the Damascenes will reply that the "Retreat" is kept open in memory of the Prophet's attachment to members of the feline race.

The story goes that Mohammed, when he once visited Damascus, though there is no proof that he ever did visit that famous city, had a cat with him, which slept in the sleeve of his garment, and which he carefully fed with his own hand. On one occasion, when he wanted to remove his garment, and saw that his little friend was asleep, he cut off the sleeve so that its slumbers would not be disturbed. Ever since the Faithful in Damascus and elsewhere have paid an almost superstitious regard to cats. Dogs have not been quite so fortunate. Indeed, with the exception of those which are trained for the chase, these animals are very generally despised and neglected. Dogs, dirty and mangy, are found about Moslem towns and villages, but not in the houses of the people. "Beware of dogs," Mohammedans say, and there is an Eastern proverb which affirms that "when a dog comes into the house all the good spirits fly away." Goats, asses, kine, horses, and, above all, camels are greatly valued, and are well looked after by the Faithful. I think Mohamme-dans will compare very favourably with Christians in their treatment of the animal creation.

A common custom amongst Mohammedans is that which is called Zikr, or the repetition of the names of God in many different ways. The Koran says, "God hath most excellent names, therefore call on Him by the same." Hughes, in his "Notes on Mohammedanism," remarks that "the most common form of Zikr is a recital of

N

the ninety-nine names of God, for Mohammed promised those of his followers who recited them a sure entrance into Paradise." A Moslem rosary contains ninety-nine beads, and as each name of God is mentioned a bead is reverently touched. Vendors of rosaries are to be found outside mosques and in the bazaars of the East, and an excellent trade is carried on in these peculiar aids to worship.

Moslems do not bury their dead in the vicinity of a mosque, for the sacred edifice, they say, would thus be polluted. They carry the departed to cemeteries quite outside the town. About six hours after death the body is taken away from the house, for interment. Before it is committed to the grave it is reverently wrapped in a winding-sheet of white calico, on which has been written particular chapters from the Koran. The truly religious generally prepare their own winding-sheet, keeping it always ready, and occasionally bringing it out to add another verse or chapter as a new train of thought occurs. The dead body being prepared, it is taken up with great gentleness, and laid in the grave on the side, with the face turned towards Mecca. The officiating priest then steps solemnly into the grave beside the corpse, and with a loud voice repeats the Moslem creed. Then addressing the dead man, he says: "O son of Adam, when the two angels come to question thee, answer them, 'God, greatest in glory, is my only Lord; Mohammed my Prophet; Islam my faith; the Koran my book; and the Holy House at Mecca my Kiblah.'" The priest then quits the grave, retires forty paces, turns round, and approaches once more. Now standing on the edge of the grave, he concludes the ceremonies by offering the following short prayer:—"O great and glorious God, we beseech Thee with humility, make the earth comfortable to this Thy servant's side, and raise his soul to Thee, and with Thee may he find eternal mercy and forgiveness." And all the people say, "Amen."

CHAPTER XIX

WHEN, in the thirteenth century, Bagdad fell, and the dynasty of the Abbasides perished, Mohammedanism, as a temporal power in the East, was at a low ebb. In the West also the outlook was very dark, for Spain was gradually passing into the hands of the Christians.

The next century, however, saw a great turn in the tide of affairs, and Islamism more than recovered her former greatness, though under different conditions. In the West, Spain was lost; but, as we shall see, the Greek Empire was won. In the East, no one Mohammedan dynasty ever again obtained complete and sole power over the whole of Islam, like the Omiades of Damascus, or the Abbasides of Bagdad; but from the wreck of one great Caliphate there arose similar mighty Moslem kingdoms in Persia, Afghanistan, India, and Turkey. So far, therefore, from suffering by the ruin of Bagdad's shrines, Mohammedanism really gained thereby in dignity, numbers, and influence. In this chapter, I purpose dealing with the history of that Mohammedan power which was the first to form itself into a distinct nationality after the fall of the Abbasides. I refer to the Ottoman Turks. The stories of the Shias of Persia, of the Afghans, and of the Moghuls of India will follow in due course.

The founder of the dynasty of the Othmanlis, or Ottoman Turks, which has existed till this day, was Othman, born A.D. 1258 to Ertoghrul, the prince of a wandering tribe of warriors from Turkestan, which had become converted to the faith of Islam. Ertoghrul established himself with his followers in Bithynia, on the borders of the Greek Empire, and sought to form his tribe into a nation. At his death, in 1288, all his possessions passed into the hands of his son Othman, who carried out most successfully the policy his father had inaugurated, and even dreamt of turning the nation into an empire. Othman is described as a man of strong physique, with arms reaching below his knees, of dark and prominent features, of stern aspect, and of heroic courage. He was called by his contemporaries " Black Othman "—not in any way as a reflection on his person or character, but as a compliment ; for, in the East, black is a colour of honour, and indicates strength of soul, as well as bodily vigour and energy.

Othman, whose small principality was contiguous to the territory of the Greeks of Constantinople, early in his reign set himself to harass the enemies of his faith, and to seek to win from the Christians additional land and towns. In most of these border expeditions the fierce chief was successful ; for small parties of the somewhat effeminate Greeks were unable to stand against the rude shock of Othman and his comrades, who rushed madly into battle, impelled by the desire of fame, and sustained by that heroic bravery which is the heritage of the Turk. In 1316 Othman resolved to make a great stride forward by seizing, if possible, the important city of Brusa, well within the Greek territory. Finding the city too strong to be taken by assault, he erected two forts over against it, and laid siege to it, determined to subdue it. For ten weary years the siege was continued ; but in 1326 Brusa capitulated, and Orkan, the son of Othman, planted the Ottoman flag triumphantly on its walls. These exploits made a deep impression on the Greeks, who now first began to fear for the safety of their Empire, which, for centuries, had withstood the might of Barbarians and Moslems. It looked as if it were reserved, as indeed it was, for the comparatively insignificant tribe of the Ottoman Turks to succeed where others had failed. Stanley Lane-Poole, referring to the warlike deeds of Othman, says, " Othman's flying cavalry ravaged the country as far as the Bosphorus and Black Sea ; the Emperor, standing on the towers of his palace at Constantinople, could see the flames of the burning villages across the Bosphorus ; the vessels of the Turk harried the coast ; the whole country trembled before his unwearied and ubiquitous onslaught."

But death put a stop to Othman's career of conquest. Soon after the capture of Brusa he sickened and died at the age of seventy, after a reign of twenty-six years. His last wish was to be buried in the captured city, which was now the capital of the little kingdom. Thither the body of the great man was reverently borne, and there, for generations, did his sepulchre stand, even long after his descendants had conquered Constantinople, and possessed the empire of which their first chief had but dreamed. The thirty-fourth lineal descendant of Othman in the male line now lives and reigns as Sultan of Turkey. It is a remarkable fact, and as one writer has said, " There is no such example of the continuous authority of a single family in the history of Europe."

Orkan, the son of Othman, carried on vigorously the war against the Greeks, wresting from them Nicomedia, Pergamon, and other important cities ; and in 1329 he defeated the Emperor Andronicus at Pelecanon. Then overtures were made for peace, which both sides gladly accepted. The Turks were allowed to keep their newly-acquired possessions, and their kingdom now comprised the whole of the north-west corner of Asia Minor, with the command of the eastern shore of the Bosphorus. In two generations all this had been accomplished—the small tribe had become a great nation. Peace, however, was needed to consolidate the Turkish power. Immediately Orkan had the opportunity and the time, he set himself to work to organize the State and the army. He also assumed the insignia of Royalty, and issued money in his own name as an independent Prince. From end to end of his compact territory he went, establishing courts of justice, encouraging agriculture and trade, and seeking to unite his somewhat heterogeneous subjects in the bonds of a common interest in local and national prosperity. Thus, with skill, foresight, and earnest labour, during twenty years of peace, were the foundations of the Ottoman power solidly laid.

About this time the Turkish Princes formed that famous body of troops called the Janizaries, which for centuries constituted the flower of the Ottoman armies, and by whose aid the most famous Moslem victories were won. And who were the Janizaries? Strange to say, they were Christians, who were forcibly converted to Mohammedanism. Out of the families of the Christians conquered in the campaign against the Greeks, Orkan chose a thousand of the finest boys, and formed them into a Royal Bodyguard. "Every year for three centuries a thousand Christian children were thus devoted to the service of the Ottoman power; and when there were not enough prisoners captured during the year, the number was made up from the Christian subjects of the Sultan; but, after 1648, the children of the soldiers themselves were drawn upon to recruit the force." When Orkan had chosen the first thousand, he led the boys before a saintly Dervish, and asked him to bless them and give them a name. The holy man, flinging the sleeve of his robe over the head of the leading youth, said, "Let them be called Janizaries (new soldiers), and may God the Lord make their arms strong, their swords keen, their arrows deadly, and give them the victory." The discipline of the new troops was severe, but their emoluments were great, and they were generally sure of the Royal favour, which, however, they in time greatly abused.

Sir E. Creasy, in his "History of the Ottoman Turks," says of the Janizaries, "Cut off from all ties of country, kith, and kin, but with high pay and privileges, with ample opportunities for military advancement, and for the gratification of the violent and sensual, and the sordid passions of their animal natures, amid the customary atrocities of successful warfare, this military brotherhood grew up to be the strongest and fiercest instrument of imperial ambition which remorseless fanaticism, prompted by the most subtle statecraft, ever devised upon earth." I might here mention the after-fate of the Janizaries. Formed into a body of troops in 1330, they, for five hundred years, were a mighty power in the Turkish dominions, but eventually they so horribly abused their powers by assassinations and atrocities of every kind, that at the beginning of this century, in 1826, Sultan Mohammed resolved on their destruction. By one stratagem or another, he got their officers to desert them, and then he attacked them with other troops. Seven thousand of the ill-fated Janizaries perished by the sword, 8,000 were burnt to death in their barracks, which caught fire, and 20,000 were banished. A Royal proclamation then declared the force for ever dissolved. Thus does the Grand Turk sometimes execute summary justice on evil-doers !

The yearly drain of the Christians by the Mohammedans to recruit the corps of the Janizaries during the early years of the existence of the force greatly incensed all the Christian States on the confines of the Ottoman kingdom, and led to numerous wars ; but in almost every case the Turks were the victors, and they gradually increased their borders, and crossing the Hellespont, carried their arms into Europe, even advancing as far as the Danube. In 1394 the Pope declared a crusade against the Ottomans. Many nations responded, and some great battles were fought with the Serbians, the Bulgarians, the Franks, and the Hungarians, who rallied to the support of the Greeks ; but at Kosoro and Nicopolis, Sultan Bayezid, the great-grandson of Othman, defeated the allied Powers utterly. At Nicopolis the slaughter of Christians was frightful, tens of thousands perishing on the field of battle, and multitudes being afterwards slain in cold blood. Thus did the

Turks achieve conquest upon conquest, and the goal of their ambition, Constantinople, seemed to be at last within their reach.   Indeed, Bayezid was so carried away with his marvellous successes, that he boasted when once he reigned in the city of the Greeks, he would push on farther, and stable his charger at the altar of St. Peter's at Rome.

But the victorious and ambitious Turk, even while he was laying siege to Constantinople, was suddenly checked in his successful career, and that by an unexpected foe. " Just at the moment when the Sultan seemed to have attained the pinnacle of his ambition, when his authority was unquestionably obeyed over the greater part of the Byzantine Empire in Europe and Asia, when the Christian States were regarding Bayezid with terror as the scourge of the world, another and a greater scourge came to quell him, and at one stroke all the vast fabric of empire was shattered to the ground.   This terrible conqueror was Timur the Tartar, or, as we call him, 'Tamerlane."   Timur was a Turk also, only of another tribe than the Ottomans.   He was born at Samarkand in 1333, consequently he was an old man when, in 1401, he turned his arms against Bayezid. Though born only a petty chieftain, Timur, by his remarkable genius for war, quickly forced his way to the front rank of Eastern conquerors, subduing the vast country north of the Oxus, carrying his victorious arms into India, and becoming ruler of Persia and Syria to the borders of Egypt.   This marvellous Mohammedan power of mushroom growth resolved to try conclusions with the Ottoman power, which had proved itself no mean adversary.   It seems strange that Moslem should thus seek to destroy Moslem, but Timur's ambition, even in old age, could brook no rival.   It is wonderful to think of an old man of seventy leading forth his armies to such an enterprise as the conquest of the dominions of the Ottomans, just when the latter were flushed with their victories over the Greeks, and were seeking to establish themselves on the throne of the Cæsars.   And the Tartar won in the struggle with the

Turk. Bayezid withdrew his troops from the siege of Constantinople, and hurried to join issue with Timur. The outcome of the furious battle that was fought was irretrievable disaster to the Turkish Prince. On the field of Angora, A.D. 1402, the Ottoman forces were cut to pieces, and Bayezid, with one of his sons, was taken prisoner. It has been said that the unfortunate monarch was confined in an iron cage by his fierce Tartar captor, but that story is now denied, though it is generally acknowledged that Bayezid was kept a very close prisoner, and was carried about in the train of his conqueror in a barred litter. The hapless prisoner, after eight months of such indignities, died of a broken heart. "Seldom has the world seen so complete, so terrible a catastrophe as the fall of Bayezid from the summit of power to the shame of a chained captive."

Two years later, in 1405, Timur the Tartar, "the Wrath of God," passed away, and his vast dominions became the prey of his generals. Now was the chance for the Ottoman Turks to recover their independency, which, after various vicissitudes of fortune, they succeeded in doing. We cannot trace this Restoration in detail, but it was effected mainly by Mohammed the First, a son of the late unfortunate prince. The new monarch was a man of uncommon gifts—indeed, just the ruler for such an emergency. The Greeks described him as "persevering as a camel;" his friends spoke of him as "filled with wisdom;" and amongst friends and foes alike he was known, on account of the refinement and humanity of his character, as "Mohammed the Gentleman." In twelve years this prince reorganized his shattered kingdom, and at his death, in 1421, the Restoration was completed, and the Turkish power was almost as formidable as ever. An ominous step was now taken. The Ottoman capital was moved from Brusa, in Asia, to Adrianople, in Europe. Evidently the next move was to be Constantinople.

The inroad of the Tartars had only delayed the fall of

the Greek Empire for half a century, not saved it altogether. The Turks, under Murad the Second, a noble prince, who reigned thirty years, resumed their career of conquest in the West. That career was continued by his son, Mohammed the Second, an able, but violent and treacherous, ruler, who also reigned thirty years. It was by this prince that Constantinople was captured. It is a story that deserves a chapter to itself. We cannot linger over it now. The strong city stood a long siege, and was nobly defended by the last of her Christian Emperors; but all valour availed nothing against the might of the Ottoman arms; and the 29th May, 1453, saw the standard of Mohammed floating from the towers of the then grandest Christian city of the world. And ever since, Constantinople, which stands on the finest site in Europe, has been in the possession of the Turk, and has been the great seat of the Mohammedan power.

The Turkish Sultans were now ranked amongst the most powerful rulers of the earth. All Europe began to fear their strength, and to dread their onward march. For a while, however, after the fall of Constantinople, the West remained comparatively unmolested; for the Sultans had their thoughts turned towards the East, and, as soon as possible, marched to the conquest of the Moslem kingdoms of Syria and Egypt. They even tried, though vainly, to possess Persia, aspiring to universal dominion. Syria and Egypt, after a long struggle, succumbed to the Ottomans. In 1517 the Mameluke rulers of Cairo were defeated by Selim the Grim, and their kingdoms added to the Turkish dominions, which now, both in the East and West, had grown enormously. It seemed like a return to the early days of Mohammedanism, when the Caliphs ruled in all their glory. And the glory of the Ottomans even surpassed that of the Omiades, the Fatimites, or the Abbasides.

In 1518 the actual title of Caliph, or Commander of the Faithful, was assumed by the Sultans of Constantinople; for Selim acquired the right to it from no less a personage than a genuine descendant of the rulers of Bagdad, who was living in obscurity at Cairo. This degenerate Abbaside, for a consideration, made over to the Ottoman ruler the spiritual authority he still affected to exercise, and with it the symbols of his office, the standard and cloak of the Prophet. Stanley Lane-Poole says: "Selim now became not only the visible chief of the Mohammedan State throughout the wide dominions subdued to his sway, but also the revered head of the religion of Islam, whereso-ever it was practised in its orthodox form. The heretical Shias of Persia might reject his claim; but in India, in all parts of Asia and Africa, where the traditional Caliphate was recognized, the Ottoman Sultan henceforth was the supreme head of the Church, the successor to the spiritual prestige of the long line of the Caliphs. How far this title now commands the homage of the orthodox Moslem world is a matter of dispute; but there can be no doubt that it has always added, and still adds, a real and important authority to the acts and proclamations of the Ottoman Sultans."

The Turks reached the pinnacle of their greatness in the sixteenth century, during the long reign of Suleyman the Magnificent. By land and sea the Moslem arms were everywhere triumphant. A large slice of Eastern Europe, including Moldavia, Bulgaria, Serbia, Bosnia, Hungary, Greece, and innumerable other States passed under the sway of the Ottomans. What a change time and valour had wrought! The line of Princes which, under Othman, counted only a few hundred spears, could now march to war with a force of 500,000 veteran troops. And the territory which they possessed, once so circumscribed that it could have been crossed in a few hours' ride, was now so extended that it was difficult to estimate its length and breadth. As Sir E. Creasy says: "An empire of more than forty thousand square miles, embracing many of the richest and most beautiful regions of the world, had been acquired by the descendants of Ertoghrul, the father of

Othman, in three centuries from the time when their fore-
father wandered a homeless adventurer at the head of less
than 500 fighting-men."

It is a strange and remarkable story of human prosperity
and greatness. And in the arts of peace, as well as in
the trade of war, the Ottomans excelled in the reign
of Suleyman. That enlightened Prince encouraged the
aspirations of the learned, founded schools and colleges,
and sought amongst both high and low to elevate the tone
of general society. He rigorously punished evil-doers, and
especially officers and Pashas who were proved guilty of
corruption and partiality. His great object was to see
even-handed justice administered throughout the length
and breadth of his vast dominions.

But the palmy days of Ottoman rule were of short
duration. The death of Suleyman the Magnificent was
the climax. From the seventeenth century the Turkish
power has been gradually decaying. Under the walls of
Vienna, in 1682, the Moslems received a check which saved
Western Europe from all further alarm from the advancing
tide of Mohammedan invasion. And little by little, since
then, the Turks have been driven back, and their possessions
stripped from them. As the Russian Empire has increased,
that of the Ottoman has decreased. It is a singular thing
that all Mohammedan kingdoms, no matter how strongly
built up, soon, comparatively speaking, crumble to their
fall. What they lack is that righteousness which exalteth
a nation. The Ottoman dynasty is most surely going the
way of the Omiades, the Fatimites, the Abbasides, and the
Moors.

It is only a question of a little time. Even now the
Turkish Empire is designated "the Sick Man." And the
sickness is unto death ! The injustice, the oppression, the
cruelties, the vices of the modern Turk have turned
Christendom against him, as well as undermined his constitution. No one will shed a tear when the end comes !

It is sad that it should be so, but so it is! "There are some who believe in a great Mohammedan revival, with the Sultan-Caliph at the head; a second epoch of Saracen prowess, and a return to the good days when Turks were simple, sober, honest men, who fought like lions. There is plenty of stuff in the people still; but where are their leaders? Till Carlyle's great man comes—the hero who can lead a nation back to paths of valour and righteousness—to dream of the regeneration of Turkey is but a bootless speculation."

CHAPTER XX

PARADISE

THE Koran has a great deal to say about Paradise, and there can be no doubt that the teaching of Mohammed with respect to the marvellous joys of that blessed abode influenced public opinion greatly in his favour in the early days of the Faith. The Prophet not only promised in this present life rich rewards to those who followed his standard, but spoke of untold favours in store for true believers in the life hereafter. And the joys he spoke of, as we shall see, were of that character that they appealed strongly to the selfish passions of humanity, and thus drew over many eager converts to Islamism.

Though Mohammedans speak so much about Paradise, they are by no means agreed amongst themselves as to certain particulars with regard to it. The time of its creation, for instance, is a moot point. The Mutazilites and other sectaries assert that Paradise at present has no existence, but will be created in a moment of time by God after the great day of the Resurrection. The orthodox, however, maintain that the blessed abode of the Faithful was created even before the world, and was, indeed, the very place from which Adam and Eve by transgression fell. Then, as to the location of Paradise, various opinions are held; but all are agreed that it is not anywhere on this earth, nor under the earth. Nor must Paradise be confused with heaven, or the heavens, through which Mohammed passed when he made his famous night-journey up the ladder of light into the very presence of Allah. The general belief is that Paradise is above the heavens, and next under the throne of God.

This wonderful abode of the Faithful is said to be of such a size that no human standards of measurement can even approximately give any idea of it, so that the task is not essayed. It is believed to be surrounded by high walls, in which are placed eight beautiful gates, through which all seeking admittance must pass. So involved and contradictory, however, are Moslem ideas about everything connected with Paradise, that tradition says that another entrance has been found—even at Jerusalem. The story was told me on the spot. It seems that Mohammed, when on earth, delivered a prophecy that one of his followers should, while alive, enter Paradise.

And in the reign of Omar, the prophecy, we are assured, was fulfilled. It happened thus: A certain devout man, named Hayian, went up to the Mosque of Omar, in Jerusalem, to worship, and also to draw water from a well in the outer courts. While engaged in the latter task his bucket fell splash into the well. The man let himself down in the usual way to recover his utensil, but, to his surprise, when he got to the bottom, he saw a door standing partly open. Impelled by curiosity he pushed through it, and then found himself in a beautiful garden. Therein he wandered about for some time, eating of its delicious fruits, listening to the music of its fountains, and being charmed with the air of serenity and peace which everywhere prevailed. Reluctantly, remembering his daily duties, he withdrew from the happy place, but not before he had plucked a leaf to preserve as a memento of the visit, and as a token that there really was such a garden. Unfortunately, the next day, when he wished to repeat his delightful experience, he could not find the door. Nor has it been found since. Yet the leaf, which never withered, remained to testify to the veracity of the saintly explorer. And the well, to this day, is called the " Well of the Leaf," and as I stood beside it, I was gravely assured by a reverend Moulvi that, somewhere near

our feet, there was, most certainly, an entrance to Paradise ;
for the garden in which Hayian had wandered was none
other than the garden of the Lord, prepared for Mohammed
and the Faithful.

When, after the Judgment, as related in a previous
chapter, the righteous have safely crossed the Bridge of
Siraat, which is finer than a hair, and sharper than the edge
of a sword, they immediately wing their flight towards
Paradise.   And, even before they are admitted to that glad
abode, their pleasures begin.   The first delectation is to
refresh themselves at a pond, called the "Pond of the
Prophet."   This reservoir of water is said to be an exact
square, of a month's journey in compass ; and nowhere on
earth is there such a refreshing drink to be obtained.   "The
Pond is supplied by two pipes from one of the rivers of
Paradise, being whiter than milk or silver, and more
odoriferous than musk ; with as many cups set round it as
there are stars in the firmament ; of which water whoever
drinks will thirst no more for ever."   Wonderfully invigorated
by their rest and refreshment at the "Pond of the Prophet,"
the Faithful push on their way, and in due time reach the
gates of Paradise.   There two fountains are placed, and in
one the righteous must bathe, that every outward trace of
uncleanness may be removed from their persons ; and of
the other they must drink, that inwardly, also, they may be
purified, and made meet for the land into which nothing
unholy may pass.   And so delightful are the experiences
of these initiatory duties that they are regarded not in the
light of tasks, but as joys—a foretaste of the good things in
store.

Immediately the Faithful reach Paradise, the gates fly
open to admit them, and a voice, loud and sweet, bids
them welcome.   Thereupon two angels step forward—two
for each person—and give to the individual upon whom
they have to wait presents sent by God.   One gift is a
beautiful robe, called "the garment of Paradise," with
which the angels invest their charge.   The other is a ring

of surpassing value, with certain inscriptions engraved upon it, telling of the different felicities that await him. In addition to angelic attendants, each person has also a number of beautiful youths, whose duties are to run errands, to fetch and carry, and to acquaint the heavenly wives of the new-comer with the fact of the arrival of their lord. The total number of servants of every kind that the very meanest of the Faithful shall have in Paradise is estimated to be not less than eighty thousand. Thus there is really nothing that a man need do for his own personal comfort in the way of labour, for Allah, in His bountiful goodness, has placed at his disposal even a superfluity of able and willing attendants.

Very soon after the righteous have entered Paradise they will receive an invitation from the Almighty to sup with Him at His table. It is fabled that "the whole earth will then be as one loaf of bread, which God will reach to them with His hand, holding it like a cake ; and that for meat will be provided the ox Balam, and the fish Nun, the lobes of whose livers will suffice for all." Many favours will be shown the Faithful at this feast, and then they will be dismissed to the mansions prepared for them, where, throughout eternity, they will enjoy such bliss as was never dreamt of in the wildest fancy of human imagination. While all will be perfectly satisfied, there will be, however, diversity of enjoyment ; for "one star differeth from another in glory." Dr. James Cameron Lees, in his St. Giles' Lecture on "Mohammedism," says that Paradise consists of eight divisions. There is "the garden of eternity, the abode of peace, the abode of rest, the Garden of Eden, the garden of refuge, the garden of delight, the garden of the Most High, and the garden of Paradise." The garden or abode in which a believer shall dwell will depend upon his deserts. The highest, in which the most eminent degree of bliss will be experienced, is reserved for Mohammed and the Prophets; the next for the Doctors and Teachers of the Law ; and the next for the Martyrs. About the rest it does not so much

matter, for they differ little in the degree or variety of their
enjoyments.   When we come to inquire as to the character
of the supreme joys of Paradise, we are told that Mohammed
is reported to have said that " that believer will be in the
greatest honour with God who shall behold the Divine face
morning and evening, which sight will give such exquisite
delight that in respect thereof all other pleasures of Paradise
will be forgotten and lightly esteemed."

In the chapter on " Women " it was stated, it may be
remembered, that, contrary to the general belief, the Koran
speaks expressly of the admittance of women into Paradise.
In the 2nd sura it is written, "'The Lord says, I will not
suffer the work of him among you who worketh to be lost,
whether he be male or female," and in the 43rd sura, after
some remarks about the Day of Judgment, these words
occur : " O My servants, there shall no fear come on you
this day ; neither shall ye be grieved, who have believed in
our signs, and have become Moslems ; enter ye into Paradise,
ye and your wives, with great joy."   Nothing, however, is
told us in the Koran as to the section of Paradise that
women will occupy.   Some Mohammedans think that wives
will be reunited to their husbands ; but others say that
women will have a garden all to themselves.   It will not be
a large place, however, as not many women are esteemed
worthy of admittance into Paradise.   Yet those who do
obtain an entrance will be well treated.   " Dishes of gold
will be carried round unto them, and cups without handles ;
and therein shall they enjoy whatever their souls shall
desire, and whatever their eyes shall delight in."

The inhabitants of Paradise, whether male or female,
will enjoy, it appears, a perpetual youth.   Their features
will be the same as when they lived on earth, only cast in
a larger mould, for they will be as big as Adam and Eve.
And what size do Mohammedans make out our first parents
to have been ?   Of Adam it is said, " He was as tall as a
high palm-tree," and of Eve, that " When her head lay on
one hill near Mecca, her knees rested on two others in the

plain about two musket-shots away." The inhabitants of
Paradise will not be less than sixty cubits in height. If the
Faithful die in childhood or old age, it matters not ; for when
they appear in the Better Land they will be in their prime
and vigour, that is about thirty years of age, which age they
will never exceed. And to this age and stature their
children, if they shall desire any, shall immediately attain,
according to that saying of the Prophet—"If any of the
Faithful in Paradise wish for offspring, such shall be born
and grow up within the space of an hour." With respect to
the clothing of the Blest, it has been revealed that they
will have in rich abundance the finest silks and brocades,
chiefly of green, which will burst forth from the trees and
fruits of Paradise. They will be given also innumerable
bracelets and anklets of gold and silver, and on their heads
will be placed crowns set with pearls of incomparable lustre.
Indeed, in the matter of clothing, the Faithful can, if they
please, set off their fine persons in the gayest, richest, and
most attractive attire.

Mohammed, in his conception and description of
Paradise, has evidently sought to please all the senses of
man. A great deal is made of the sense of taste. Three
hundred dishes will be set before each believer at every
meal, containing each a different kind of food, the last
morsel of which will be as grateful as the first. Strange to
say, wine will be provided. Wine, of course, is forbidden
to the Mussulman in this life ; but it will be freely allowed
him in the life to come. Once a believer enters Paradise,
he can drink as much as he likes of every kind of liquor ;
and he will find as many kinds of beverages served up in
vessels of gold, as he does viands served up in dishes of
gold. But the wines of Paradise, it is significantly said,
though delicious to the palate, will not inebriate. A certain
tree, called Tuba, or the Tree of Happiness, is chiefly
instrumental in supplying the pleasures of the taste of the
blest. Sale, speaking of this remarkable tree, says : "Concerning this tree, Mohammedans fable that it stands in the

palace of the Prophet, though a branch of it will reach to the house of every true believer; that it will be laden with pomegranates, grapes, dates, and other fruits of surpassing bigness, and of tastes unknown to mortals. So that if a man desire to eat of any particular kind of fruit, it will immediately be presented to him; or if he choose flesh, birds ready dressed will be set before him according to his wish. They add that the boughs of this tree will spontaneously bend down to the hand of the person who would gather of its fruits; and that the tree is so large that a person mounted on the fleetest horse would not be able to gallop from one end of its shade to the other in a hundred years."

The sense of hearing is not overlooked. Every effort will be made by the minstrels and singers of Paradise to charm the Faithful through the pleasures of the ear. In this respect I do not think that Mohammedans, at any rate, while on earth, are difficult to please; for, as will appear in a later chapter on "Recreations," Moslem music, at the best, is very poor. In Paradise the Angel Israfil has the most melodious voice of all God's creatures, and it is his special mission to minister to the happiness of the righteous, by constantly giving them songs of surpassing beauty. Certain female singers, "the daughters of Paradise," form a choir, and assist Israfil in his delightful entertainments. Sale says: "Even the trees themselves will celebrate the divine praises with a harmony exceeding whatever mortals have heard; to which will be joined the sound of the bells hanging on the trees, which will be put in motion by the wind proceeding from the throne of God, as often as the blessed wish for music; yea, the very clashing of the trees, whose fruits are pearls and emeralds, will surpass human imagination, so that the pleasures of this sense will not be the least of the enjoyments of Paradise."

We come now to speak of the Houris, or black-eyed girls of Paradise, so famous in the Mohammedan system, and which other creeds, perhaps, have too strongly insisted upon as being the distinguishing feature of the Moslem Paradise. The following are the principal references to Houris in the Koran. In the 52nd sura it is written : "The pious shall dwell amidst gardens and pleasures, delighting themselves in what their Lord shall have given them. And it shall be said unto them, Eat and drink with easy digestion, and we will espouse them unto virgins having large black eyes." Again, in the 25th sura, it is written : "The pious shall be lodged in a place of security among gardens and fountains : they shall be clothed in fine silk and satin, and they shall sit facing one another. Thus shall it be : and we will espouse them to fair damsels having large black eyes." Once more, in the 56th sura, it is written : "The companions of the right hand, how happy shall the companions of the right hand be ! They shall dwell in gardens of delight, reposing on couches adorned with gold and precious stones, under an extended shade, near a flowing river, and amidst fruits in abundance. Verily, we have created the damsels of Paradise by a peculiar creation, and we have made them beloved by their husbands, of equal age with them, for the delight of the companions of the right hand." Each believer has seventy-two of these " Houris " of resplendent beauty to wife, and he is allowed a mansion and a garden all to himself, where he may keep his treasures. It is just carrying out in Paradise, only on a larger scale, the hateful Zenana system, so generally practised by the Faithful on earth.

The delights of Paradise, as I have described them, are very sensuous, at any rate as far as the words go. Of late years a few of the more refined and spiritual-minded amongst Moslems have revolted at such teaching, and would fain believe, and have striven to show, that it is a mistake always to take the literal meaning of the Koran ; and that the passages referring to Paradise should be regarded as metaphorical or allegorical. Some European scholars have supported, ably and strongly, the new movement, which, however, does not appear to make much progress, as the common sense of the Mohammedan world rebels against it.   Moslems, as a body, accept, and desire to cling to, the literal meaning of the words of the Koran.

They know themselves, and they know their Prophet ; and I have heard some boldly aver that Paradise, without its sensuous delights, would not be worth entering. Gibbon, who thoroughly studied Mohammedanism, holds to the literal interpretation, and speaks of those " modest apologists who are driven to the poor excuse of figures and allegories." Sale, also, who had years of familiar companionship with Moslems of every school and sect, maintains that the literal theory is so evident from the whole tenor of the Koran, " that, although some Mohammedans, whose understandings are too refined to admit such gross conceptions, look on their Prophet's descriptions as parabolical, and are willing to receive them in an allegorical or spiritual acceptation ; yet the general and orthodox doctrine is, that the whole is to be strictly believed, in the obvious and literal acceptation."   I do not see, however much we may desire to do it, that we can give Mohammed credit for only, or even chiefly, holding and preaching spiritual views of believers' joys in the mansions of the blest.   His own earthly life of sensuous enjoyment stands as a witness against him that can never be put on one side.

What, it may be asked, are the conditions of admittance into the Mohammedan Paradise?   Undoubtedly, first of all, acceptance of this creed : "There is no God but God, and Mohammed is the Apostle of God."   Then it is necessary to attend to all matters of faith, law, and practice, as laid down in the Koran.   The doctrine of works is clearly taught in that passage which says that "the angels shall say unto the righteous whom they cause to die, Peace be unto you, enter ye into Paradise as a reward for that which ye have wrought."   Yet salvation, after all, depends more upon the grace of God than the works of man, if we can give credit to a touching story of the last hours of the great Prophet. Tradition, well supported, says that, as Mohammed lay dying, with his head on the lap of his favourite wife, Ayesha, the sorrowful woman addressed to him this question : " O Prophet, does no one enter Paradise except by the mercy of Allah ? " " No one ! " was the answer. " But you, O Prophet," pleaded Ayesha, " will you not enter Paradise except by the compassion of Allah ? " Mohammed, placing his hand upon his head, said solemnly, thrice : " I shall not enter except Allah cover me with His mercy ! " The last prayer of all devout Moslems is like the Prophet's—a petition for pardon, and for admittance into Paradise, that they may have the companionship, and participate in the enjoyments, of the Blessed on high.

CHAPTER XXI

THE term Hell is one that is seldom used now amongst Christians, for of late years it has fallen greatly into disfavour. Doubtless future, as well as present, punishment for sin is regarded as certain, but Christians are not as ready to-day to speak of "the damnation of hell" as they were fifty years ago. However, amongst Mohammedans little, if anything, is known of such theological changes of thought. Hell is a word that Moslems do not shrink from using, nor do they mince matters with respect to the torments that are in store for unbelievers. Eastern language lends itself only too readily to vituperative expressions; and Eastern people, I am afraid, only too eagerly employ the coarsest and strongest expressions of the Koran to convey their bitter feelings towards their adversaries and the enemies of their Faith. Indeed, judging from some things I have heard and read, it would appear that Mohammedans think that their Hell, dreadful as it is, is altogether too good a place for those who are destined to dwell there throughout all eternity.

There is no difficulty in locating the abode of the lost; for the Mussulman belief is that it adjoins the abode of the saved—indeed, that there is only a thin, middle wall or partition between Paradise and Hell. And this space between the two abodes, it appears, is inhabited. It is called Al Urf, or "the place that parts." Some Mohammedans regard it as a kind of limbo for patriarchs and prophets, martyrs and saints, where they may bide

after death until the judgment and their admission into
Paradise. Others regard Al Urf as the abode to which
those go whose good and evil works are so equal that they
exactly counterpoise each other, and therefore deserve
neither reward nor punishment. While others, again, say
that "the place that parts" is the future state of all those
who have here disobeyed their parents, more especially in
going to war without their leave, and have fallen in battle.
Such, for their disobedience, are excluded from Paradise,
but are not relegated to Hell. In Al Urf they must
remain, knowing neither joy nor sorrow, neither anguish
nor bliss. There are not, however, many people in this
intermediate state ; for the great bulk of human beings are
either in Paradise or Hell. Al Urf, in fact, is so small a
place that the people therein can hold converse either with
the saved or the lost ; and even the voices of the inmates
of Paradise and Hell can be heard right across the gulf.

And who, it may now be asked, dwell in Hell ? The
answer is definite—" There are seven distinct classes, who
will be confined in seven separate rooms or places of
torment."

1. The first room, in which the lightest punishments
will be inflicted, will be the abode of wicked Mohammedans. This place will be the smallest of all the apartments of Hell, for the majority of the Moslems will go
straight to Paradise after the judgment. Moreover, nearly
all the inmates of this first room, it is affirmed, are women.
The Prophet is reported to have remarked, on one occasion,
that Allah had granted him a look into the future, and that
he had seen, from a view of Paradise, that the majority of
the inhabitants thereof were men who had been poor on
earth, and that the greater number of the wretches confined
in Hell were women, both rich and poor. However, there
is hope for all wicked Mohammedans, for the teaching of
the Koran is, that after enduring a course of punishment
proportionate to their crimes, they will eventually be
released, and granted admittance to one of the least

blissful abodes of Paradise. The time of the sojourn in Hell will not be less than nine hundred years, and not more than seven thousand. "As to the manner of their delivery," writes Sale, "they shall be distinguished by the marks of prostration on those parts of their bodies with which they used to touch the ground in prayer, and over which the fires of Hell will have no power ; and, being known by this characteristic, they will be relieved by the mercy of God, at the intercession of Mohammed and the blessed; and, thereupon, those whose bodies have contracted any sootiness or filth from the flames and smoke of Hell will be immersed in one of the rivers of Paradise called the River of Life, which will wash them whiter than pearls."

2. The second room of Hell, which is placed underneath the first, will be inhabited by Jews—and not merely Jews who have wrought evil, but all Jews. No Jew, according to Moslem belief, will ever enter Paradise, unless, of course, he renounces, while on earth, the religion of his fathers, and becomes a convert to Islamism.

Mohammed, in the Koran, has much to say about Jews ; for he was well acquainted with those who dwelt in Arabia, and at first hoped to win them over to his views of religion. Failing in that, however, he took a violent dislike to them, and made it part of his deliberate policy to treat them with harshness when he had the power.

It is related that when, on one occasion, a Jewish woman in Medina composed some couplets in which Mohammed was denounced as a false Prophet, the poor body paid the penalty of her rashness by death. "In the dead of night, surrounded by her little ones, this woman was stricken by the dagger of an assassin, who was, the next day, applauded by Mohammed in the Mosque for his hideous crime."

"The People of the Book," as the Prophet called the Jews, were difficult to suppress, however ; and after a time Mohammed declared open warfare against them, and sought to exterminate them. Mention is made of one town in

Arabia near Medina entirely in the hands of a Jewish tribe, called the Kuraizah. Mohammed laid siege to this town; and when, after a long defence, the inhabitants surrendered, the Prophet had the men executed by the hundred with the most heartless barbarities, and the women and children he caused to be sold into slavery in exchange for horses and harness.

The Koran speaks exultingly of those savage operations against the Jews; and Mohammed, not content with destroying all that he could in this world, doomed the whole Jewish race to perdition in the next world.

In the 58th sura it is written of the People of the Book: "God hath prepared for them a grievous punishment, for it is evil which they do. They have taken their oaths for a cloak, and they have turned men aside from the way of God: wherefore a shameful punishment awaiteth them; neither their wealth nor their children shall avail them at all against God. These shall be the inhabitants of Hell-fire. They shall abide therein for ever."

3. The third room in Hell, which is placed under the second, and is a degree hotter, will be inhabited by Christians. Mohammed spoke with respect of Jesus, as a Prophet of God, but he strongly denounced all Christians who believed that Christ was "God manifest in the flesh." In the 5th sura of the Koran it is written: "They are infidels who say, Verily, God is Christ, the son of Mary. Say unto them, And who could obtain anything from God to the contrary, if He pleased to destroy Christ, the son of Mary, and his mother, and all those who are on earth? For unto God belongeth the Kingdom of Heaven and earth, and whatsoever is contained between them: He createth what He pleaseth, and God is Almighty. The Jews and the Christians say, We are the children of God and His beloved. Answer, Why, therefore, doth He punish you for your sins?" As in the case of the Jews, the Prophet's animosity against Christians seemed to grow deeper as he grew older. He was glad of the support of Christian tribes in the hour of his weakness, but when he

had the power, he began to persecute them because they would not accept his teaching as superseding that of Christ. Moslems were exhorted to have no friendship with Christians, who were likened to idolaters.

The Koran says : " O true believers, take not the Jews or Christians for your friends : they are friends the one to the other : but whoso among you taketh them for his friends, he is surely one of them. Verily, God directeth not unjust people." Mohammedans very often, as a term of reproach or offence, call Christians " Nazarenes," " Infidels," and also " Christian dogs." The doom of the Christians is nothing short of eternal woe in Hell. The attitude which the Moslem takes up towards the Christian is well expressed in the saying of a Turkish general, who, on the borders of Egypt, was on one occasion skilfully effecting the withdrawal of his troops from a dangerous position. As the Turks defiled before their adversaries, and their leader closed the rear with a vigilant eye, and a battle-axe in his hand, a Christian presumed to ask if he were not afraid of an attack. The brave, though fanatical, reply was, " It is, doubtless, in your power to begin the attack, but rest assured that not one of my soldiers will go to Paradise till he has sent an infidel to Hell." No matter how holy the life of a Christian may be, there is, according to Moslem teaching, no escape for him from the damnation of Hell ; for the Koran, which cannot lie, says, " Whosoever followeth any other religion than Islam, it shall not be accepted of him, and in the next life he shall be of those who perish."

4. The fourth abode of Hell will be inhabited by the people called Sabians. At the time of Mohammed the Sabians had some political power in Arabia, but now they have none. In fact, very few Sabians exist at the present day. There is a small colony of them near Harran, in Mesopotamia ; and travellers who meet them generally speak of them as Christians of St. John the Baptist, whose disciples, indeed, they profess to be, " using a kind of

baptism, which is the greatest mark they bear to Christianity." Sale, speaking of the Sabians, says : "They pay an adoration to the stars, or the angels and intelligences which they suppose reside in the stars, and govern the world under the Supreme Deity. They offer many sacrifices, but eat no part of them, burning them all. They have a great respect for the temple of Mecca, and the Pyramids of Egypt, fancying these last to be the sepulchres of Seth, and of Enoch and Sabi, his two sons, whom they look on as the first progenitors of their religion. Besides the Book of Psalms, the only true Scripture they read, they have other books which they esteem equally sacred, particularly one in the Chaldean tongue, which they call the Book of Seth, and which is full of moral discourses. This sect say that they took the name of Sabian from the above-mentioned Sabi, though it seems rather to be derived from Saba, the host of heaven, which they worship." The Arabs were greatly influenced in religious matters by the Sabians, who lived amongst them, and, for a while, Mohammed tolerated the sect ; but eventually he persecuted its adherents, and condemned them to be punished both in this world and the next.

5. Now we come to the Magians, who are doomed to an eternity of punishment in the fifth abode, or apartment, of the Moslem Hell. By the Magians Mohammed meant, probably, not merely the Magi, or wise men, who were the priests of the ancient Persian religion, but all the followers of that religion, commonly called, not Magians, but Zoroastrians, Fire Worshippers, or, more recently, Parsees. Islamism is now the religion of Persia, and the Magians, or Parsees, driven from their own land by the Mohammedans in the seventh century, took refuge in India, where they have remained ever since. There are to-day, probably, about 90,000 Parsees in the Indian Empire. At one time the Magians were a mighty nation, and their spiritual leaders, the Magi, were famous for their learning, wisdom, and occult powers, as diviners, augurs, and astrologers.

The terms magic and magicians are derived from the name
Magi, only now the ideas associated with the words are not
learning or wisdom, but sleight-of-hand and the performance of conjuring-tricks.   Mohammedanism owes much to
Magianism, for Mohammed, there can be no doubt,
borrowed from the Persian religion many of his beliefs
with regard to God and Satan, Paradise and Hell, and
future rewards and punishments.   Yet the ungrateful
Prophet assigns all the Magians to an abode, the fifth
department of Hell, from which they can never escape,
and in which they will have to endure innumerable and
awful torments.

6. The sixth abode of Hell will be filled with idolaters,
against whom Mohammed was constantly hurling fierce
invectives.   The people of Arabia, generally, before the
advent of the Prophet, were idolaters.   Indeed Mohammed
himself, in his early years, worshipped idols in the famous
temple at Mecca.   But when the Prophet grasped the
truth that " There is no God but God," he was a determined opponent of idolatry.

At the capture of Mecca he is said to have ordered at
once the ignominious destruction of the 360 idols in the
sacred Kaaba ; and after the House of God had been purified, he made a law that no unbeliever or idolater should
be permitted thenceforward to set foot within the territory
of the Holy City.

Moreover, everywhere in his dominions the Prophet
sought to destroy idolatry root and branch, declaring that
he would brook no compromise with "the accursed thing."
For example, the leaders of a strong city called Taif, fearing
destruction at the hands of Mohammed, came to him and
offered to embrace the Moslem faith on certain conditions.
The principal condition was that they might be allowed to
worship their idols three years longer, so that they might
get used to the idea of relinquishing them.

Mohammed, however, would not listen to this, but said
sternly, " No !"   The trembling leaders then asked : " May

we not have a month's time in which to prepare the minds of the people?" "No!" was the reply; "Allah cannot be served by those who bow to idols." Then said the deputation, "May our people, at least, be absolved from the oft-repeated daily prayers?" The only answer they got was: "There is no true religion without prayer."

The surrender of the city was made, and Mohammed, to ensure the carrying out of his wishes, sent a messenger to destroy the famous idol of stone in the great temple of Taif. "It was left in fragments on the earth, surrounded by weeping women, lamenting the fall of their hopes."

The portion of idolaters here, according to Mohammedanism, is the sword, and hereafter there is reserved for them fearful torments in Hell. The Koran says: "Verily, God will not pardon the giving him a companion. The receptacle of these shall be Hell: they shall find no refuge from it." And again: "Verily, look ye, O men, and the idols which ye worship besides God shall be cast as fuel into Hell-fire: ye shall go down into the same, and remain therein for ever: in that place shall ye groan from anguish."

Indeed, so strong was Mohammed's feeling against idolatry, and so clear his teaching on the matter, that a Mussulman is not allowed to pray even for a lost relation, if that relation happened to be an idolater. The instruction on this point occurs in the 9th sura of the Koran, where it is written: "It is not allowed unto the Prophet, nor those who are true believers, that they pray for idolaters, although they be of kin, after it is become known that they are inhabitants of Hell."

A pathetic story is told of Mohammed himself in this connection, when he visited his mother's tomb in March, A.D. 630. It was when he was on his way back to Medina after the capture of Mecca. Amina, his mother, it may be remembered, died on the roadside between the two cities, when the Prophet was a little child, and she was buried where she fell. As Mohammed stood and looked at her grave, tears came into his eyes, and he longed to kneel down and pray for the peace of his mother's soul ; but the fact that she was an idolater forbade it. There was no hope for her, any more than for the rest of idolaters. Heavily did the Prophet sigh, and bitterly did he weep, saying through his tears, " I asked leave of God to visit my mother's tomb, and He granted it to me ; but when I asked leave to pray for her, it was denied me ! " No ! for idolaters there is, in the next world, no hope of mercy !

7. We come now to the seventh and last division of Hell. And in this bottomless pit are confined hypocrites of every clime and nation, of every language and creed. Above every other sin Mohammed placed hypocrisy, and his most awful warnings and threatenings are addressed to those who wear only the mask of religion—who approach Allah with their lips, while their hearts are far from Him. Of hypocrites, the Koran says, " Verily, God hath cursed them, and hath prepared for them a fierce fire, wherein they shall remain for ever. They shall find no patron or defender. On the day wherein their faces shall be rolled in Hell-fire they shall say, O that we had obeyed God, and had obeyed His Apostle ! "

Ere closing this chapter something ought to be said about the nature or character of the sufferings endured by the seven classes of the Lost in the Moslem Hell. It is a painful and unpleasant topic, and I shall make it as short as possible. Let it be borne in mind that those who will be the most lightly punished of all will be shod with shoes of fire, the fervour of which will cause their skulls to boil like a cauldron. Fire, however, is not the only agent employed to torment the damned. High winds, cold as well as hot, will at times rush and howl through the caverns of Hell, and the cold winds will be so intense that they will freeze the very marrow in the bones of the lost. Then other and still more dreadful means will be adopted to cause pain and horror and despair. A few quotations from the Koran will give a clear idea of what Mohammedans hold is in store for the wicked. In the 23rd sura it is written, " Fire shall scorch their faces, and they shall writhe their mouths therein for anguish." In the 56th sura these words occur, " And the companions of the left hand, how miserable shall the companions of the left hand be ! They shall dwell amidst burning winds and scalding water, under the shade of a black smoke, neither cold nor agreeable."

Then, in the 88th sura it is written, " Labouring and toiling, they shall be cast into scorching fire, to be broiled; they shall be given to drink of a boiling fountain ; they shall have no food but of dry thorns and thistles." And again, in the 44th sura, these dreadful words are recorded : " Verily, the fruit of the tree of Az Zaqqum shall be the food of the impious ; as the dregs of oil shall it boil within the bodies of the damned, like the boiling of the hottest water. And it shall be said to the tormentors, Take him, and drag him into the midst of Hell, and pour on his head the torture of boiling water, saying, Taste this ; verily, this is your punishment."

And these dreadful torments go on for ever and for ever, save, as already said, in the case of wicked Mohammedans, who will eventually be freed and enter Paradise. As Gibbon puts it, " The Prophet has judiciously promised that all his disciples, whatever may be their sins, will be saved by their own faith and his intercession from eternal damnation." Jews, however, and Christians, Sabians, Magians, and idolaters, will remain from everlasting to everlasting in the place which has been prepared for them. The Koran says that the abodes of the lost are guarded by nineteen fierce spirits or angels, and that past these there is no possibility of escape. The suffering ones may call out for pity, but no pity shall be shown them ; they may pray vehemently to be blotted out of existence, to be annihilated, but God will answer them, " Ye shall remain here for ever : speak not unto me to deliver you !"

Can anything more awful be imagined than the teaching of Islam with regard to Hell ? To all but a favoured few there is no hope of happiness in a future life ! Moham-

P

medanism is an utterly selfish religion ! The doctrines of
the Koran with regard to the torments of Hell are devilish !
That any thoughtful person can prefer Islamism to Christianity is to me a mystery ! Give me the religion whose
Sacred Book says: "Now is Christ risen from the dead
and become the first fruits of them that slept. For since
by man came death, by man came also the resurrection of
the dead. For as in Adam all die, even so in Christ shall
all be made alive." And again : "As by the offence of
one judgment came upon all men to condemnation : even
so by the righteousness of one the free gift came upon all
men unto justification of life ! "

CHAPTER XXII

CAPTURE OF CONSTANTINOPLE

It was in the year of our Lord 330—just 240 years before Mohammed was born—that Constantinople became an important city. Before that date it was known as Byzantium; but when Constantine the Great made it the capital of the Roman Empire it was re-named Constantinople. Henceforth it was the residence of the Roman Emperors; and at the division of the Empire it was retained as the residence and chief city of the Greek Emperors. And such it remained until its surrender to the Mohammedans in 1453, when it became the capital of the Ottoman Turks, and the great centre of the Mohammedan faith. The capture of Constantinople forms an epoch in the history of Islamism.

Constantinople, by reason of its commanding position on the borders of Europe and Asia, has always attracted a great deal of attention; and the city has also been so favoured by the glories of nature, and so beautified by the genius of men, that it has been ever regarded as one of the most charming and desirable capitals of the world.

Stanley Lane-Poole, speaking of this famous city, says: "Constantinople stands on the finest site in Europe. St. Petersburg, with its noble river, Stockholm, on its many islands, Venice, the bride of the sea, cannot rival the ancient city of the Eastern Cæsars. To see Rome and die is mere gratuitous suicide, when the other Rome, the beautiful city of Constantine, remains to be visited. There is hardly a scene in the world so replete with natural beauty, so rich in storied recollections, as that enclosed betwixt the Bosphorus and,—

> ' The dark blue water
> That swiftly glides and gently swells,
> Between the winding Dardanelles !'"

Even from the earliest days of Mohammedanism covetous eyes had been directed towards the beautiful and mighty city of the Cæsars.   Tradition says that Mohammed himself had dreams of possessing it, and though nothing came of them, he prophesied that in future years Constantinople would be the home of his religion.   And as an incentive to his followers to attempt the task, the Prophet promised plenary indulgence of all sins to all who should be counted in the first army to take the capital of the Greeks.

It was about the year 670 or 672 that the earliest Moslem effort was made to capture Constantinople.   It was in the reign of Muawiya, the first ruler of the Omiades of Damascus. That great Prince prepared a formidable army, officered by veterans, and sent the host forth with this war-cry: " Plant the banner of Islam on the walls of the capital of the Cæsars !" Hosein, the unfortunate grandson of Mohammed, was one of the leaders in this holy war against the Christians. However, the enterprise failed, though vigorously pushed both by land and sea.   For six or seven years the strife was carried on, and then Muawiya was glad to make peace with the Greeks by promising to pay a heavy yearly tribute. Only a remnant of the great army that had gone forth returned to Damascus.   They who had drawn the sword had perished by the sword !   Forty years later, in the summer of 716, another attempt was made on Constantinople by the Caliph Soloman, but again the Moslems were defeated, and the humbled Prince took his failure so much to heart that his sorrow carried him to his grave.   About A.D. 730 Caliph Hisham sent forth an army on the same holy warfare, but with no better success.   Thus, again and again, under the Omiades, and later also, under the Abbasides, did the Mohammedans seek to capture Constantinople; but through one cause or another all their efforts were in vain. Yet they never lost heart, for they trusted implicitly in the words of the Prophet, who had declared that the city of the Greeks would one day be inhabited by the people of the true Faith. Another consideration that reconciled the Moslems to their repeated failures was the belief that all who died in the wars with Christians undoubtedly obtained a great reward hereafter, according to the saying of the Koran: "As to those who fight in the defence of God's true religion, God will not suffer their works to perish; He will guide them, and will dispose their heart aright, and He will lead them into Paradise, of which He had told them."

For nearly 800 years the efforts to win Constantinople were continued, and at length they were crowned with success. And when we think about it we cannot but be struck with the faith and patience of the Mohammedans. The Omiades passed away; the Abbasides perished; the Fatimites rose and fell; the Moors entered and were about to be driven from Spain: all these things happened during the centuries the Moslems were seeking to win the capital of the Greeks! Defeat daunted not the courage of the followers of the Prophet; disaster weakened not their determined resolve; the passage of time did not change their steadfast belief in their destiny! And in the fifteenth century what was begun in the seventh was realized! All things come to the nation that waits! Under the Ottoman Turks the standard of the Prophet of God was erected on the walls of Constantinople, and the Cross went down before the Crescent.

Two great names are linked with this important event, viz., Mahomet, the Ottoman Prince, and Constantine, the Greek Emperor.

Mahomet, usually called Mahommed the Second, was a devout Mussulman from his earliest years, and is said to have carried his zeal or fanaticism for the Faith so far as to have always made a rule of purifying his hands and face even after any converse with a Christian. Under the tuition of skilful masters, this Prince advanced with early and rapid progress in the paths of knowledge ; and besides his own language, it is affirmed that he could speak or understand Arabic, Persian, Chaldean, Hebrew, Latin, and Greek. Much of his time was spent with cultivated men, and devoted to the making of verse, and the general study of literature.   His liberality towards poets, colleges, and private foundations, led to the bestowal upon him of the title of " Father of good works."   Great as he was in the walks of peace, Mahomet is said to have been even greater in the art of war, being a military genius of a high order ; and his almost invariable success earned for him the name of the " Conqueror."

Constantine, his great adversary, was also a scholar and a warrior.   Gibbon speaks very highly of the Emperor, calling him " The first of the Greeks in spirit as in rank." And certainly a memorable letter which he sent to Mahomet when the latter declared war against him shows his character in a fine light.   He wrote with the courage of a soldier and the resignation of a Christian, as follows :—" Since neither oaths, nor treaty, nor submission can secure peace, pursue your impious warfare.   My trust is in God alone.   If it should please Him to mollify your heart, I shall rejoice in the happy change.   If He delivers the city into your hands, I submit without a murmur to His holy will. But until the Judge of the earth shall pronounce between us, it is my duty to live and die in the defence of my people."

The task to which Mahomet was committed when he resolved to lay siege to Constantinople, and to win it at all costs, was a herculean one, for the city was surrounded by great walls, supported by strong towers, and had a population of more than a hundred thousand souls.   A strong fleet also defended the approaches to the city by the sea, and thus kept open the way for succours that might come from allied Christian States.   The Turkish Sultan knew these things, and did not make light of them, and was full of anxiety as to the issue of the struggle. It is related that one sleepless night he started from his bed, and commanded the instant attendance of his Grand Vizier, and when the latter responded in fear and trembling, not knowing what was in store for him as the result of such an untimely call, the Prince greeted him with this startling cry, " I must have Constantinople ! " The Vizier answered, " The same God who hath already given thee so much, will not deny thee the remnant, this capital ; for His providence and thy power assure thy success ; and be sure myself, with the rest of thy faithful slaves, will sacrifice, if necessary, our lives and fortunes in the struggle." Whereupon the Sultan spoke again, saying, " Seest thou this pillow ? All the night, in my agitation, I have pulled it on one side and the other. I have risen from my bed ; again have I laid down ; yet sleep has not visited these weary eyes. Beware of the gold and silver of the Infidels. In arms we are superior ; and with the aid of God and the prayers of the Prophet, we shall speedily become masters of Constantinople."

And what was the feeling within the walls ? The Greek Emperor, when he saw that the die was cast, set himself like a hero to the work of defence. One of his first efforts was to find out exactly how many of the people of the city could be depended upon to fight to the last. He caused inquiry to be made from street to street and from house to house, and, to his dismay, he discovered that he was dealing with a degenerate race, and that out of a population of 100,000 he could only obtain 4,970 willing to live or die with him in the defence of their city and of their homes. Fortunately the number was added to by 2,000 veteran soldiers, under the command of John Justiniani, a noble Genoese, who entered Constantinople in search of service. The besieging army is said, at the lowest calculation, to have numbered 250,000. Think of the scanty garrison of barely 7,000 men defending an extensive city against such a mighty host ! And yet so strong were

the defences of Constantinople, and so brave were the few
gallant Christians, that the apparently unequal struggle was
maintained day after day and week after week !

To add to the troubles of the besieged, religious strife
broke out in the city. The Greeks had sought, in their
deadly peril, the aid of their neighbours, and had even sent
to Rome, beseeching the Pope to declare a crusade against
the followers of "the false Prophet." This request provided an opening for the expression of religious jealousy
and ill-feeling. The Latin Church and the Greek Church
had always been at strife one with the other, and the
Pope had been trying for many years to bend the Greeks
to his will. Constantine knew this ; and when he sent for
temporal aid to Rome he hinted at spiritual obedience in
payment ; and the Vatican eagerly caught at the offer, and
despatched, at once, Cardinal Isidore and other priests, with,
however, only a small retinue of soldiers. The Emperor
received the envoy with respect, and subscribed to an act
of union which gave to the Latin Cardinal in the churches
of Constantinople a place by the side of the Greek
Patriarch. This measure on the part of the Emperor,
however, instead of promoting union, led to strife. Gibbon
says : "No sooner had the Church of St. Sophia been
polluted by the Latin mass than it was deserted as a Jewish
synagogue or a heathen temple by the Greek clergy and
people, and a vast and gloomy silence prevailed in that
venerable dome, which had so often smoked with a cloud
of incense, blazed with innumerable lights, and resounded
with the voice of prayer and thanksgiving. The Latins
were the most odious of heretics and infidels; and the first
Minister of the Empire, the great Duke Lucas Notoras,
was heard to declare that he had rather behold in Constantinople the turban of Mahomet than the Pope's tiara or
a Cardinal's hat." Thus quarrelled the Latins and the
Greeks within the walls, while the common foe of both was
thundering at the gates ! It was a miserable sight, and,
moreover, it was a dreadful source of weakness, for it

deprived the brave Constantine of the affection and support of many of his subjects, and served as an excuse for native cowardice.

Mahomet, meanwhile, was pushing the siege hard. He is said, by the help of a Dane or Hungarian, to have produced a piece of brass ordnance of stupendous magnitude. " A measure of twelve palms is assigned to the bore : and the stone bullet weighed alone six hundred pounds." With this great cannon, and with one hundred and thirty smaller guns, the Sultan hammered away at the walls of Constantinople. He sought also to fill the ditch that surrounded the city ; but what the Turks did in the daytime was undone by the Christians during the night. And in all his mining also he was undermined and countermined. So brave was the defence, and so great were the losses of the besieged, that, at one time, the Moslems were on the point of giving up the enterprise in despair.

A retreat was meditated, and only the genius of Mahomet prevented it. He resolved on the execution of a plan which involved great skill and labour, but which, if thoroughly carried out, promised immediate success. This scheme was nothing less than to transport the Moslem fleet overland to a point higher up the harbour than that at which the Greek fleet was stationed, or which, owing to the size of its vessels, it could reach. Then the city could be attacked simultaneously by land and sea. Absolute secrecy was necessary, but Mahomet was a master in that craft. This remarkable man never told any one his plans until he wanted them executed. On one occasion, when asked what were his arrangements for a certain campaign, he answered dryly and sternly, " If even a hair of my beard knew them, I would pluck it out, and cast it from me." The distance to be traversed by the vessels was about ten miles, and the ground was uneven and overspread with thickets ; but the skill of the Sultan triumphed over all difficulties. " The way was covered with a broad platform of strong and solid planks ; and to render them slippery and smooth, they were anointed with the fat of sheep and oxen. Four score light galleys and brigantines of fifty and thirty oars were disembarked on the Bosphorus shore, arranged successively on rollers, and drawn forwards by the power of men and pulleys. Two guides or pilots were stationed at the helm and the prow of each vessel; the sails were unfurled to the winds, and the labour was cheered by song and acclamation. In the course of a single night this Turkish fleet painfully climbed the hill, steered over the plain, and was launched from the declivity into the shallow waters of the harbour," almost under the walls of the city.

Now the end drew nigh. The evening of the 28th May was fixed upon by the Moslem Prince for the grand, and, as he rightly anticipated, the final assault. Mahomet exhorted his followers to prepare for the struggle by purifying their minds with prayer, and their bodies with seven ablutions. He instructed also a band of saintly dervishes to visit the tents, and remind the soldiers that immortal youth, with untold joys in Paradise, would be the portion of all who fell in the coming fight. Moreover, promises of earthly rewards were not overlooked, for the Sultan had it proclaimed: "The city and the buildings are mine, but I resign to your valour the captives and the spoil, the treasures of gold and beauty; be rich and be happy!" Fired with such promises, and with fanatical zeal, the Moslems rushed upon the doomed city like tigers hungering for their prey. It was in vain that Constantine and his few devoted adherents, filled with the courage of despair, fought like heroes! The Turks swarmed over the walls. They hewed and hacked like madmen! And as the Christians were only one to fifty, there could be but one end to the struggle, viz., destruction.

The Greek Emperor was seen everywhere in the thick of the fight, seeking death, and yet, for a long time, not finding it. In the agony of his despair, not wishing to fall into the hands of his enemies, he mournfully exclaimed, "Cannot there be found a Christian to cut off my head?" but no one answered him. Then he threw on one side his purple robes, and mixed as a stranger in the mêlée, and at length he met his death by an unknown hand, and his body was buried under a mountain of the slain. Then the struggle was over! The Greeks fled! The Moslems flocked into the streets! And soon the entire city was at the feet of the conquerors. Thousands of the inhabitants were massacred, but the majority were spared, made prisoners, and afterwards sold into slavery. We cannot linger over the details. It is enough to say that the morning of the 29th May, 1453, rose on the victory of the Moslems and the utter ruin of the Greeks.

At the eighth hour of the day the Sultan, who was received with acclamations, entered Constantinople in triumph. He was attended by his viziers, bashaws, and guards. As he passed slowly along the broad thoroughfare on his way to the church of St. Sophia, he gazed with satisfaction and wonder on the strange, though splendid, appearance of the domes and palaces, so dissimilar from the style of Oriental architecture. "In the hippodrome his eye was attracted by the twisted column of the three serpents ; and, as a trial of his strength, he shattered with his iron mace or battle-axe the underjaw of one of those monsters, which, in the eyes of the Turks, were the idols or talismans of the city."

St. Sophia, a massive and beautiful building, was the chief place of worship of the Greeks, and that building Mahomet determined to dedicate to what he conceived to be a better and nobler worship. Gibbon, writing about the remarkable event, says : " At the principal door of St. Sophia, Mahomet alighted from his horse, and entered the dome : and such was his jealous regard for the monument of his glory, that on observing a zealous Mussulman in the act of breaking the marble pavement, he admonished him, with his scimitar, that if the spoil and captives were granted to the soldiers, the public and private buildings had been reserved for the Prince. By his command the metropolis of the Eastern

Church was transformed into a mosque : the rich and portable instruments of superstition were removed : the crosses were thrown down : and the walls which were covered with images and mosaics were washed and purified, and restored to a state of naked simplicity. On the same day, or the ensuing Friday, the *muezzin* or crier ascended the most lofty turret and proclaimed the *ezan* or public invitation in the name of God and His Prophet : the Imam preached : and Mahomet the Second proclaimed the *namaz* of prayer and thanksgiving on the great altar where the Christian mysteries had so lately been celebrated before the last of the Cæsars."

Thus Constantinople passed from the hands of Christians into the hands of Mohammedans, and became the seat of the Caliphs or Successors of the Prophet. And, from the fifteenth century until now, Moslems, in all parts of the world, have been justly proud of the chief city of their Faith.

Visitors to the beautiful city, if they have sufficient influence, may enter a jealously-guarded building, and therein see the sacred relics of the Prophet of God, the possession of which give the Sultan of Constantinople his unique position as the supreme head of Islamism. These relics are simply the mantle of Mohammed, which he once threw over the shoulders of an Arab poet as a reward for an ode ; and the banner of Mohammed, that Holy Oriflamme with which he first led his followers to war and to victory. So long as these remain in the possession of the Ottoman Turks it is believed that Constantinople will remain in the hands of the Faithful.

Who can tell, however? Perhaps, before many more years have elapsed, the world will see another great siege of Constantinople, in which the aggressors will be Christians, and the defenders Moslems. The Ottoman power has fallen so low that it is now generally recognized that " the Turk will mount guard over the Bosphorus, and sit in the seat of the Cæsars only so long as Europe requires him there. Another power is quite ready to take his place, and, even in England, the impossibility of permitting a Tsar to reign at Constantinople is no longer quite an undisputed axiom."

There are some who think that the death-knell of Turkish dominion has already been sounded. Anyway, it seems a certainty that the next capture of Constantinople, whenever it may happen, will reverse the story of the fifteenth century, and that, once more, the Greek worship will be celebrated in the Church or Mosque of St. Sophia, and the Cross replace the Crescent on all the churches of the famous and beautiful city of Constantine.

CHAPTER XXIII

PROVERBS

THE East is the natural home of Proverbs, and Mohammedan countries have produced many sensible and instructive ones. A study of some of these cannot but be interesting, and will moreover throw much light upon Moslem religious beliefs, habits of thought, and customs of society.

How shall we define a Proverb? It is about the most difficult task a student could set himself! We all, doubtless, know a Proverb when we meet with one ; but how to define a Proverb is an altogether different thing. One of the most popular definitions is that given by Howell, who maintained that a sentence, to lay claim to be called a Proverb, must have "sense, shortness, and salt."

Bacon has left it on record that Proverbs are "the genius, wit, and spirit of a nation." Earl Russell wrote : "A Proverb is the wisdom of many and the wit of one." Cervantes said : "Proverbs are short sentences drawn from long experience." Aristotle held them to be "Remnants which, on account of their shortness and correctness, have been saved out of the wreck and ruins of ancient philosophy." Thus we might go on repeating definitions, all true, and yet no single one expressing all that we feel a Proverb is to us and to others. Dr. Johnson's definition is as good as any. He said : "Proverbs are short sentences frequently repeated by the people." At any rate we are sure of this, that no proverbial saying, however sensible, true, and clever it may be, will live unless it gain the ear of the common people of a country, and become a household word.

Trench tells us that the famous James Howell, who, in the seventeenth century, did such good work in collecting stray Proverbs into volume form, also composed five hundred Proverbs of his own. But who to-day knows anything about them? No! Proverbs cannot be made to order. If the people take them up, they will live; if not, they will die. It has been well said :—

> The people's voice, the voice of God we call;
> And what are Proverbs but the people's voice?
> Coined first, and current made by common choice!
> Then sure they must have weight and truth withal.

Suppose we begin with a few Arabic Proverbs. There is certainly wisdom in this one: "Alms are the salt of riches." Perhaps some people would question the enduring truth of the following, that "one sword keeps another in its scabbard." We all agree, however, in owning that "war has its vicissitudes," and that "forward lies honour." There is much shrewdness in the saying: "If I am master, and you are master, who will drive the asses?" also in that other assertion that "a scalded dog fears even cold water;" and again in that saying: "The ass knows well in whose face he brays." It may be a true, but it is rather a sad, view of life to say that "the world is a carcase, and they who gather round it are dogs." There is something more cheerful in the proverb about the lucky man, which asserts: "Throw him into the Nile, and he will come up with a fish in his mouth." And there is a pleasant ring in the saying that "Thou wilt catch more flies with a spoonful of honey than with a cask of vinegar." It is good advice also to counsel: "Hold the skirts of thy mantle extended when heaven is raining gold," which means, make the most and the best of spiritual advantages. We receive a needed warning by the proverb which assures us that "who chatters to you will chatter of you." There is something, however, very grim and terrible in the saying:

"There are no fans in hell." We would sooner hear about Paradise, and of this more blessed abode the Arabs say: "Paradise is for those who bridle their anger." There is something, moreover, for us to think about in the true saying: "Every day in thy life is a leaf in thy history."

It is not a far cry from Arabia to Persia, and in the latter country there are to be found many choice Mohammedan proverbs. There is that familiar one, which is so sensible that some people think it must needs be English, viz., "Speech is silvern; silence is golden." There is some point also in the saying, "Be not all sugar, or the world will gulp thee down." And there is a depth of meaning worth fathoming in the assertion that "Of four things, every man has more than he knows—of sins, of debts, of years, and of foes." Speaking of friends and foes, the Persians remark, "The whole world is too narrow for two foes; but a needle's eye is wide enough for two friends." In the following, the bad results of evil companionship are hinted at: "He that takes the raven for a guide shall light upon carrion." Again, it is said, "Who lies down with dogs will rise up with fleas." And referring to dogs, it is asserted that "If you bury a dog's tail for years, it will still remain crooked," which is as much as to say that evil propensities are difficult to eradicate.

It is also a common saying: "A bad tree, bad fruit!" The covetous are assured that "Two water-melons are not held in one hand." And the faint-hearted are told that "Cowardice saves no man from his fate." For the encouragement of the persecuted, it is affirmed that "Stones and sticks are flung only at fruit-bearing trees." To an army or a community sorely bereaved, the solace is given: "Captains die; God lives." But the grandest Persian proverb is probably that which announces that "A stone fit for the wall is not left in the way." Trench, commenting on the foregoing, says something to this effect—that if a man looks well to himself, and makes himself fit for noble duties, and a useful position in life, his time will come, though for a while, like a stone on the wayside, he may appear to be overlooked, neglected, and passed by. At last he will be picked up; sooner or later the builders will be glad of him; the wall will need the man to fill the place, and he will be found!

Many of the Turkish proverbs, as might be expected, are warlike. For instance, there is that one which asserts that "There is no argument like the sword." Another says, with sad truth: "No place is secret in the day of battle." Flattery is aptly hit off in the proverb: "He who has need of a dog calls him Sir Dog." And there is considerable insight into human nature displayed in the saying: "When once thy cart is overturned, every one will show thee the way." The liberties that some favoured domestics take with their master's property is rebuked by the proverb: "The King eats an apple; his servants cut down the tree." That familiar saying "Curses, like chickens, always come home to roost," is Turkish. The Turks say also, of unsatisfied covetousness: "Nothing but a handful of dust will fill the eye of a man." I suppose there is sound sense in the advice, though on the face of it it seems harsh, to the effect: "Feed thy horse as a friend, and mount him as an enemy." It was a suspicious nature, however, that coined this phrase: "Keep the dogs near when thou suppest with the wolf." Experience of life's hardships must have suggested the saying: "It is ill sport between the cotton and the fire." There is much good sense in the reminder that "It is not with saying honey, honey, that sweetness comes into the mouth." And we cannot but admire the profound wisdom of this assertion—that "He is the true sage who learns from all the world."

When we turn to India, we meet with perhaps the finest collection of Eastern proverbs. Doubtless it is hard in all cases to distinguish between Hindoo and Mohammedan proverbs, but the following are certainly in everyday use amongst the Mussulmans of India. How essentially Indian is this assertion: "Every one rakes the embers to his own cake."

Q

It speaks of that selfishness which is so often manifested amongst the servant classes, when a number of them are gathered round a common fire to prepare their evening meal. Then, again, how expressive is the saying, " Don't hang your troubles on my neck." It shows us the duty of self-help. The readiness of some people to lean unduly upon others, and to follow, whether for good or evil, the lead of others, is well shown by the proverb, " The thread follows the path of the needle." There is the teaching of experience in the advice, " In merchandise consider well ; in agriculture not at all." Also in the saying, " A living sheep is better than a dead cow." And I have been much struck with the thoughtfulness of this short sentence, " A crowd is not company." Women, of course, in the East have been made the butt of proverbs. It is said, " Should a woman scold, the earth will shake ;" again, " Better a night in the jungle, than a day in a palace with a jealous wife ;" and again, " Fear an angry woman more than an angry man." I can only recall one favourable proverb about women, but it hits all round. It is, " May her enemies stumble over her hair," meaning, " May she flourish so, may her hair, the outward sign of this prosperity, grow so rich and long, may it so sweep the ground that her detractors and persecutors may be entangled by it and fall." Of a thoughtless man the Mohammedans of India will say, " His eyes are in the nape of his neck." To a man who speaks bitter things, they will remark, " The tongue is not steel, but it cuts." And to all men this sensible advice is given : " Of thy word unspoken thou art master ; thy spoken word is master of thee." That is a noble proverb ! And so is this one, which beautifully exhorts to forgiveness of injuries, and to overcoming evil with good : " The sandal-tree perfumes the axe that fells it."

Leaving now the grouping of proverbs, let us deal with three or four single proverbs, and show their derivation or special application. For example, there is a proverb of Mohammed that well illustrates the connection between faith and works. The teaching of the Prophet on "predestination" was so strong that some of his followers imagined that the decrees of God absolved mankind from all effort, for do what they would the result would be the same. Mohammed, however, by a proverb, sought to win his disciples from their foolish belief. It is related that one evening when out with an army, after a weary march through the desert, just after the command was given to pitch the tents for the night, the Prophet overheard one of his people say: "I will loose my camel, and commit it to God!" The idea was that the Lord would take every care of the beast until morning. Such folly deeply grieved Mohammed, and he called the offender into his presence, and administered to him a sound rebuke, which ended with this advice: "Friend, tie thy camel, and commit it to God." Thus did the Prophet teach that the providence of God does not do away with the responsibility of man. Whatever is our part to do should be done, and then we may with comfort leave the issue in higher hands. "Friend, tie thy camel, and commit it to God!"

In India there is a well-known proverb to express that nothing is certain in this world. The saying, which had a tragic origin, is this: "Delhi is still far off," or, as an Englishman would say, "There is many a slip between the cup and the lip." The phrase, "Delhi is still far off" was first used by a Mohammedan saint named Nizam-uddin, and it was directed against his king, Tughlaq Shah, who reigned in Delhi at the beginning of the fourteenth century. The latter had somehow offended the holy man, who resolved on a terrible revenge. When the monarch was away from his capital, on an expedition against the people of Bengal, the saint conspired with the heir-apparent against the life of Tughlaq Shah. The scheme, which was kept secret, was arranged thus: The young Prince, by the advice of the Saint, caused a temporary wooden palace to be erected about six miles from Delhi, on the road along which the King would be sure to travel on his return home. The building was put up in such a way that if certain ropes were pulled the whole fabric would collapse and kill the inmates. Tidings of seditions at Delhi reached Tughlaq Shah in Bengal, and he was specially incensed at the news of certain predictions of Nizam-uddin that he would never see Delhi again. " Let me but have that holy man in my power," the King said, " and he will feel the weight of my anger." At once the monarch marched for his capital, and ere long the inhabitants heard that their Sultan was approaching in haste and wrath. Friends of the Saint, not in the guilty secret of the wooden palace, urged him, as the chief offender, to flee ere the incensed King arrived. To all such well-meant importunities the " holy man " had but one answer : " Delhi is still far off." Tughlaq Shah, to his great surprise, was met on the road by the Prince, his son, who humbled himself before him, and expressed great joy at his return. And to show his deep interest in his father's comfort, the heir-apparent told his sire that he had caused a temporary wooden palace to be erected for him, where he might stay a little while and take rest before marching in triumph into the city. The pleased King, suspecting no treachery, gladly assented. And that night the building fell, and buried the unfortunate monarch in its ruins ! It is a typical story of Moslem perfidy and filial ingratitude ! Such events have only been too common in the history of Mohammedan rulers, and of them in particular, while of mankind in general, the saying is felt to be true that nothing is certain, that " Delhi is still far off."

Asiatics are all too often " time-servers," and are particularly gifted in the disagreeable art of flattery. Moreover, they are well aware of their failing, and have many proverbs which aptly satirize their racial weakness. The best known and most popular of these proverbs is a Persian one, which says, " When the monkey reigns, dance before him." There is a story told of Mahmud of Ghazni, one of the most renowned of Eastern conquerors, which is a case in point. Mahmud was a man of gigantic frame, and could wield a mace or hurl a spear with the strongest and skilfulest in his army, but as regards his features, nature had formed them so plain that they approached ugliness. The Sultan often referred to his lack of good looks, and in tones of great regret. On one occasion it is recorded that he said to his Vizier: "I have re-polished my glass, and having looked in it steadfastly, I see so many faults in my face that I can easily overlook those of others. The face of a King should brighten the eyes of all beholders, whilst mine, alas! appears the picture of misfortune." But the obsequious courtier was equal to the occasion, and replied, in a cheerful tone: "Let not your Majesty be troubled. It is not one in ten thousand who sees your countenance, but your virtues are diffused over all!" This was a neat speech, and was none the less acceptable, doubtless, because it skilfully blended falsehood with truth. It was true that few saw the face of the King, but as for all knowing his virtues, that was a stretch of imagination, for, from what I can learn, the Sultan's moral character was no more attractive than his face. It suited the Vizier's purpose, however, to flatter his Sovereign, and it must be confessed that he did it handsomely. If necessary, such men can aver that black is white, and that they see the sun at midnight. And amongst both high and low in Mohammedan countries "time-servers" are common, and the practice of fulsome flattery prevails. Thus very often there is occasion for this sarcastic proverb, in the way of reproof: "Yes! yes! when the monkey reigns, dance before him!"

There is a very striking Arabic proverb quoted by thoughtful Mussulmans that is worth recording. It is, "Purchase the next world with this, so shalt thou win both." Some trace the first use of this proverb back to Omar, the second Commander of the Faithful. Certainly that famous Caliph seemed to act upon it, for though he had great riches, he did not set his heart upon them, and rebuked those who did. He ever cared more for character than for wealth, and was constantly exhorting the leaders of his armies and the faithful generally to seek first the kingdom of God and His righteousness, assuring them that other things would be added unto them.

During the wars which were waged in Omar's time against the Persians, the Arabs gathered great booty, and were in danger, so the Caliph thought, of being spoiled with their riches. One of his Generals, out of the wealth gained in those wars, built the town of Kufa, and erected therein a sumptuous residence for himself after the style of the White Palace of the Khosru, or ancient Royal house of Persia. When Omar heard of this extravagance he sent off a messenger at express speed with a letter addressed to his General, and instructions to deliver it to him, after the grand palace had been burnt to the ground. The messenger rode into Kufa, and, with the assistance of his escort, piled up a quantity of wood against the doomed mansion, and deliberately set fire to it. When the astonished General, in a rage, demanded what these things meant, the messenger quietly handed him the Caliph's letter, which ran thus : " I am told thou hast built a lofty palace like to that of the Khosrus, and decorated it with a door taken from the latter, with a view to have guards and chamberlains stationed about it, to keep off those who may come in quest of justice or assistance, as was the practice of the Khosru before thee. In so doing thou hast departed from the ways of the Prophet, on whom be benedictions, and hast fallen into the ways of the Persian monarchs. Know that the Khosru have passed from their palaces to the tomb, while the Prophet, from his lowly habitation on earth, has been elevated to the highest heaven. I have sent my messenger to burn thy palace. In this life two ordinary houses are sufficient for thee : one to dwell in, the other to contain the treasure of the Moslems. See thou to it ! Purchase the next world with this ; so shalt thou win both ! "

The Caliph Omar was a fine character, a worthy successor of the Prophet. And Christians as well as Moslems might wisely lay to heart his ever-memorable saying, " Purchase the next world with this, so shalt thou win both;" that is, " Live not selfishly ; do not accumulate wealth for the sake of accumulating it ; spend freely over good works ; think more of what you can do than of what you can get ; and in so doing it will be found that you will obtain manifold more in this present time, and in the world to come life everlasting." Verily, one of the noblest of Mohammedan proverbs is here !—" Purchase the next world with this, so shalt thou win both !"

CHAPTER XXIV

PERSIA or, as its inhabitants call it, Iran, an Independent Kingdom of Western Asia, is 700 miles in length, and 900 in breadth, comprising an area of 648,000 miles, but with a population of about five millions only.

Persia of to-day is nothing compared with Persia of the past. There was a time in her history, hundreds of years before the birth of Mohammed, when she was the most powerful kingdom of Asia, and indeed of the whole world. During the reigns of Cyrus, Darius, and Xerxes, Persia was the foremost of the nations of the earth, and the land was then densely inhabited with a hardy, valiant, and prosperous people. And even down to 636 A.D., when the Mohammedans conquered the country, the kingdom of the Persians was one that other nations feared, respected, and envied. The dynasty that ruled the land when the Moslems cast covetous eyes towards it was called the Sassanidæ, and for 300 years the Princes of that famous Royal house had reigned with wisdom and vigour, at least the equals if not the superiors of the Emperors of Constantinople, with whom they were perpetually at war.

The first mention of Persia in connection with Mohammedanism is contained in an historical letter which Mohammed himself sent to Shah Khosru the Second, exhorting him, as he valued his soul, to abjure the religion of his fathers—Magianism or Zoroastrianism—and embrace Islamism, the religion of all true believers. This extra-

ordinary letter reached Khosru just after he had returned
to Persia from a victorious foray into the domains of the
Greeks, in which foray he had captured Jerusalem, and
carried off in triumph the so-called Holy Cross of the
Christians. It was certainly a very inopportune moment
for Mohammed's letter to arrive! Who was Mohammed
that the victorious Khosru should obey his voice!

When the Prophet's envoy reached the Persian capital,
and begged or demanded an audience, it was grudgingly
granted; and when the letter was produced the Shah of
Shahs sent for his interpreter to read it. The epistle began
as follows:—"In the name of the Most Merciful God!
Mohammed, son of Abdallah, and Apostle of God! to
Khosru, King of Persia." But that was all that was ever
publicly read. The arrangement of the words had incensed
the monarch. "What!" cried Khosru, starting up in
haughty indignation; "does one, who is my slave, dare to
put his name first in writing to me?" Thereupon he seized
the letter, and tore it in pieces, utterly regardless of the
remaining contents. He then wrote to his viceroy in
Yemen, on the borders of Arabia, to this effect: "I am
told there is in Medina a madman, who pretends to be a
prophet. Restore him to his senses; or, if you cannot,
bring me his head." The Viceroy, however, knew that all
efforts against Mohammed in his own land would be futile,
so he did nothing; and the Prophet, when he heard of the
treatment his letter had received at the hands of the King
of Persia, was deeply incensed, and uttered the following
prophecy:—"As Khosru has torn my letter in pieces, even
so shall Allah rend his empire in pieces."

Though Mohammed designed to avenge himself by
undertaking a war against the Persians, yet through the
pressure of other events he was not able to do so, but he
left the resolve as a legacy to his followers. And in the
reign of Omar, the second successor of the Prophet, the
daring enterprise was begun.

It was entered upon, however, with great caution, for Omar

knew that the conquest of Persia was even a more difficult task than that of Egypt, which had cost many precious lives. The first move of the crafty Caliph was to send an Embassy to the court of the Shah, whose name was Yezdigird. The haughty Khosru was dead, but the Arabs soon found that his successor was just as proud, though not quite as powerful.

When the Embassy reached the magnificent city of Madayn, the chief members of it were ushered through the sumptuous halls and saloons of the great White Palace, which was crowded with guards and attendants, into the presence of the august Monarch, whom they found seated on a silver throne with his princes and nobles around him.

What a contrast the Arabs presented, dressed in their simple attire, to the Persians, who were decked out in silks with embroidery and jewels, as was the custom in that Eastern Court of pomp and luxury ! Yet the plain Moslems bore themselves with dignity, and feared not to deliver the message of the Caliph.

Some of the details of that famous interview are very interesting, as they throw light upon the then existing state of things in Persia, and also upon the habits and customs of the Arabs in the early days of the Mohammedan Faith.

The spokesman of the Embassy is represented as setting before the Persian monarch the alternatives of tribute or war, whereupon Yezdigird answered in indignation : "You Arabs have hitherto been known to us by report as wanderers of the desert ; your food dates, and sometimes lizards and serpents ; your drink, brackish water ; your garments, coarse hair-cloth. Some of you who by chance have wandered into our realms have found sweet water, savoury food, and soft raiment. They have carried back word of the same to their brethren in the desert, and now you come in swarms to rob us of our goods, and our very land. You are like a starving fox, to whom the husband-man afforded shelter in his vineyard, and who in return brought a troop of his brethren to devour his grapes. Receive from my generosity whatever your wants require ;

load your camels with corn and dates, and depart in peace to your native land; but if you tarry in Persia, beware the fate of the fox who was slain by the husbandman."

The Arabs replied with great gravity and decorum : "O King, all thou hast said of our forefathers is most true. The green lizard of the desert was their food; brackish water was their drink; their garments were of hair-cloth, and they buried their infant daughters to restrain the increase of their tribes. But all this was in the days of ignorance. Our parents knew not good from evil. They were guilty and they suffered. But Allah, in His mercy, sent our nation the Sacred Koran, and the Prophet Mohammed. Allah has caused us to be wise and valiant, and has commanded us to war with infidels, until all men shall be converted to the true Faith. It is in the name of Allah we come now, and all we demand of thee, O King, and of thy people, is to acknowledge that there is no God but God, and that Mohammed is His Apostle. Pay the customary tribute in proof of thy faith, and we shall depart in peace ! Refuse, and we shall declare a Holy war, and Persia shall be subjected by the sword."

Never before had the Shah of Shahs heard such bold language, but he bridled his wrath as best he could, saying to the Embassy : " Were it not unworthy of a Prince to put Ambassadors to death, you should be executed by my guards. Away ! away ! ye robbers of the lands of others ! Take with ye a portion of the soil ye crave ! "

Thereupon sacks of earth were bound upon the backs of the Arabs, and they were ordered to return to their master, and tell him that the King of Persia sent a present to symbolize the doom—earth to earth—that awaited all who should venture upon the mad enterprise of the invasion of the Shah's dominions.

The Arabs carried away the soil as directed, but when in the presence of their Commander, Saad Wakkas, they with ready wit represented it as being an omen for good. "As surely, O Saad," they exclaimed, "as we deliver to thee these sacks of earth, so surely will Allah deliver the Empire of Persia into the hands of the Faithful."

In 636 A.D. war was declared, and in the fierce struggle that followed the Arabs found the Persians foemen worthy of their steel. Indeed, it almost appeared in the first encounters as if the Moslems would be hopelessly beaten. The elephants of the Persians were more than the Arabs had bargained for, and struck terror into the bravest hearts. Horse and rider turned in dismay from such strange opponents, and victory inclined to the side of the Persians, who fought for home and fatherland with the enthusiasm of a brave and gallant people. But gradually the invaders showed their superiority over their opponents in endurance, and as they became accustomed to the huge elephants they attacked them so fiercely and vigorously, and wounded them so sorely, that the poor animals, mad with pain, rushed hither and thither in the ranks of the Persians, and caused great destruction of life. For months a desultory warfare was kept up, and though the Arabs were usually the victors, yet the country was by no means conquered. At length, however, a great battle was fought, which sealed the fate of the kingdom. It lasted four days and a night, and so dreadful was the struggle during the last night that it was ever afterwards spoken of as "the night of delirium." When the morning dawned a whirlwind of dust hid the combatants from each other, but it aided the Moslems, as it blew in the faces of the Persians. Disheartened by the awful carnage and by the storm, the Persians grew faint-hearted, and when the cry was raised that Rustam, their brave General, had fallen, a panic ensued, and the day was lost. It is said that 30,000 Persians fell in that battle, in 637 A.D., on the plains of Kadesia, which practically decided the fate of the country. The Arabs lost 7,000 of their bravest warriors. The booty that was taken was enormous, and amongst other precious things that fell into the hands of the Arabs was the venerated standard of Persia, the so-called "Leathern Apron," which was studded with jewels. There was a prophecy that whenever the day came that Persia lost her national standard on the field of battle, the doom of the country, as a free and independent kingdom, had come.

Shah Yezdigird the last of the royal race of the Sassanidæ, on receipt of the news of the disaster at Kadesia, sought to rouse the people of the land to renewed attempts to expel the foreign foe, but his efforts were in vain. The country was demoralized by the magnitude of the Arab victory, and the unfortunate King had to leave his capital to become the prey of his enemies, and flee for his life.

Taking refuge amongst friends in a distant part of his dominions, he in a little time, however, was able to gather together a small army, which rapidly increased in numbers as he advanced once more to try his fortune with the Arabs. Defeat followed defeat, and at length the almost heart-broken Prince had to give up the struggle in despair, and seek safety in a foreign land. Gilman, in his book on " The Saracens," says : " Yezdigird, overpowered, deprived of his kingdom and his fortunes, and deserted by his followers, finally died, in 651 A.D., a refugee in a miserable hut beyond the distant Oxus, whither he had fled, taking his way through Ispahan and Merv."

The conquest of Persia by the Arabs was followed by a period of prosperity, though the people of the country were compelled to adopt the religion of their conquerors, those who refused being slain or banished. Zoroastrianism was thus practically rooted out, and Islamism reigned supreme. During the sovereignty of the Omiades of Damascus, Governors administered the affairs of Persia ; but when the Abbasides became Caliphs, the Commanders of the Faithful themselves ruled the country, and they made Bagdad, within Persian territory, the capital of the whole Mohammedan Empire.

On the fall of the Abbasides, however, in 1258, Persia became the prey of adventurers and then followed centuries of disorder.   Wild hordes from Tartary overran the country, and dynasty succeeded dynasty in rapid succession, and it looked as if never again would the fair country be the home of peace and plenty.   Yet, strange to say, during those ages of misrule and misery, the Persian mind contrived to find expression in some noble literature, which lives to this day, and which is greatly admired by students of Asiatic learning.   Referring to these things, Mr. Benjamin, in his very readable book on " Persia," in the " Story of the Nations " series, says : " Then it was that the great poet Firdousee composed, in the pure language of Persia, the noble historical epic, or poetical chronicle, of the legends of Persia, prepared at the Court of Mahmoud of Ghuznee.   Soon after flourished Nizamee, the poet of the heart and the passions ; and the lyric poet Hafiz.   Then, too, Omer Khayam composed his celebrated philosophic verses ; and Djamee sang of the loves of Yusuf and Zuleika."   These, and other great authors, whose works were read throughout the Mohammedan world, and widely influenced the taste and style of subsequent Oriental writers, shed a ray of glory on the otherwise miserable record of Persian history during many generations.

In the fifteenth century brighter days dawned for the down-trodden country.   And the change was due to religious influences.   When the Persians first gave up Zoroastrianism, the creed of their fathers, and adopted the Mohammedan faith, it was because they were compelled to do so ; but being essentially a reasoning and a religious people, they soon saw the superiority of the new faith over the old, and ere long became Moslems from principle, and were reckoned among the most devoted and zealous adherents of Islamism.   And as time went on they had to choose between the two great sects which divided the Mohammedan world—viz., Sunis and Shias, already often referred to in these studies.   They cast in their lot heartily with the Shias, mainly because Hasan, the grandson of Mohammed the Prophet, had taken as one of his wives a

Persian lady—no less important a personage, indeed, than a daughter of Yezdigird, the last of the Persian Kings. That great lady had been made prisoner when her father had fled for his life across the Oxus, and she had been taken to Medina, and there chosen by Hasan to grace his harem. Through that marriage the Persians felt that they were brought as a nation very near to the originators of the Mohammedan Faith ; and so it was but natural, in the religious divisions and struggles that succeeded the martyrdom of Hasan and Hosein, that the people of Persia should declare themselves to be Shias, or followers of Ali and his unfortunate sons.

We have seen how again and again in the history of Mohammedanism the Shias—or, as they were also called, the Alyites and Fatimites—strove to obtain supreme power. In Egypt they succeeded in establishing themselves for a time, but they were eventually put down by their enemies, the Sunis. However, in the fifteenth century the persecuted sect gathered force in Persia, and, under Ismail, a gallant chief, took possession of the whole country, and established an independent kingdom.

It was in 1499 A.D. that Ismail was proclaimed Shah ; and with him a new era began. Persia was no longer an appanage of a foreign Prince, no longer a country overrun by greedy adventurers, no longer an oppressed province of some great empire, but free, strong, and great in herself. The Ottoman Turks, who have always been of the Suni creed, sought, in the reign of Selim the Grim, of Constantinople, 1514 A.D., to conquer Persia, and to destroy the power of the Shias ; but the attempt ended in failure. The so-called heretical sect continued to flourish ; and the deadly hatred of their religious adversaries only served to make the Persians the more determined to remain true to their own faith, and with it to preserve the independence of their country.

The Shias reached the height of their power and glory in the seventeenth century, under Shah Abbas the Great, who was crowned in the year 1586, and died in 1628, at the age of seventy, after a reign of forty-two years. Mr. Benjamin, speaking of this prosperous period, says : " Abbas was one of the greatest sovereigns who ever sat on the throne of Persia. He was great in war, as shown by his conquests in every direction, conquests which carried Persia to the highest pinnacle of renown. He was an able administrator, improving the revenues, regulating his armies, beautifying Ispahan, his capital, to a degree that has carried its fame to all lands ; and constructing good roads, bridges, and inns all over his dominions. He was a patron of letters, and by establishing schools of art he did more to cultivate the progress of the arts in Persia than any sovereign of whom we have any record. To crown all these qualifications that entitled him to the respect and love of his people to all time, Shah Abbas the Great was a Prince of wide and generous views, anxious to promote friendly and commercial relations with all nations ; and, unlike every other sovereign of his time, he was tolerant of all religions and beliefs."

At the death of Abbas, a weak ruler unfortunately succeeded him, and Persia again suffered from internal strife, and the country was once more overrun by foreign foes. Early in the eighteenth century Mahmood, an Afghan chief, invaded the land with an army of 50,000 men, and so weak had the empire become, that Ispahan, although it had a population of 600,000 souls, fell, almost without a struggle. That magnificent city never recovered from the blow. The Afghan dynasty was of short duration. It was destroyed by that soldier of fortune, Nadir Shah, who from an obscure station in life rose to be the ruler of Persia and the scourge of the East, carrying the terror of his arms as far as India. It was Nadir Shah who bore away from Delhi that famous peacock throne of jewels, the pride of the Moghul Emperors, valued at not less than three millions sterling, which is now in the Royal Treasury of Persia.

In 1794 the fortunes of the country once more revived.

Aga Mohammed Khan, a eunuch, the founder of the present reigning house, called the Khajar dynasty, crushed every rival, drove out the foreign princes and soldiers, and established a strong native Government. Teheran was chosen as the new capital in place of Ispahan. And since the close of the eighteenth century Persia has maintained her independence, though it has been threatened many a time by the progress of the Russian arms in Western Asia. In 1848 Nesr-ed-deen Shah, the present sovereign, ascended the throne. He is a prince of decided intelligence and excellent motives, and it is generally believed that he is sincerely desirous of improving the administration of his empire, that his people may be contented and prosperous. But the Shah occupies a peculiar position, owing to the situation of his country, which is the seat of the intrigues between Russia and England. The outlook just now is not very bright. Yet there are some who think that Persia will weather every storm, preserve her independence, and be in the future one of the greatest of the Mohammedan Powers in the East.

The Persians are still Shias, devoted to the memory of their Imams, passionately attached to their particular creed, and the somewhat strong and bitter opponents of the Turks, who return the ill-feeling with interest. It would seem that while Mohammedanism remaineth the Faithful will be divided into two great sects, and I think there can be little doubt that Persia will continue to be the stronghold of the much-hated, the much-persecuted Alyites, Fatimites, or Shias, whose tenacity of life is marvellous, whom, in short, it seems impossible to root out and destroy!

R

CHAPTER XXV

RECREATIONS AND AMUSEMENTS

TURNING from the graver matters of Mohammedanism, let us see what manner of people the inhabitants of Moslem countries are in respect of recreations and amusements.

Mohammedan children have few toys, and therein form a great contrast to Christian children, and also to the Buddhists of China and Japan. The little people of Islam are indeed to be pitied, for their parents do not put themselves to much trouble to make the days of childhood and youth pass pleasantly. A Turkish father, when spoken to and expostulated with by an English lady on this matter, answered, " Our religion forbids children to have toys. Studies must be directed towards religion and war, and for that reason they must ride and use the bow and gun, but nothing else." However, things are not quite as bad as that surly Turk made out, for Moslem boys are permitted to play with marbles, and Moslem girls are given a wretched apology for a doll made of bundles of rags, which they hug and kiss, and make much of. Children of both sexes, moreover, in the higher grades of society, have rattles, trumpets, and drums, which delight their hearts. Still it remains true that the lads and lasses of Mohammedan countries are a long way behind their Christian brothers and sisters in the matter of toys, and, indeed, in all things that minister to the amusement and enjoyment of childhood's days.

Of course, Moslem habits vary in different countries, and I think that perhaps the Mussulmans of India are more fortunate than their co-religionists in other lands, in the number and variety of their games. In India kite-flying is a very common amusement, and it is not confined to children or even to young people, but is indulged in by grave and reverend seniors. The same is true of the neighbouring country, Afghanistan. Indeed, both in flying kites and playing with marbles the old in the East vie with the young, without a thought crossing their minds that they are doing anything unbecoming their age or dignity. Elphinstone, in his "History of Cabul," says, "Most of their games seem to us very childish, and can scarcely be reconciled with their long beards and grave behaviour. Marbles are played by grown-up men through all the Afghan country and in Persia." I watched many a time, when in Calcutta, Mohammedan men and boys flying kites in the cool of the evening from the flat roofs of their houses, and to all appearance they immensely enjoyed the entertainment. Often the sport would take the form of a contest. Say, half a dozen or so of kites, with lines previously rubbed with paste and covered with pounded glass, would be let fly at or about the same moment, and the object of the different owners was to bring the kites together so that the lines might be rubbed against each other, with the result that the sharpest, if skilfully handled, would cut the others, and the disconnected kites would go tumbling to the ground, to the great glee of the winner and the little urchins who were watching the contest from the street below.

Mohammedans, generally speaking, are enthusiastic pigeon fanciers, and will spend much money and time over this amusement. The birds are confined in bamboo sheds or booths on the top of the house, and at early dawn the master of the house may be seen taking his station to feed his pets and give them an airing. The more particular fanciers are not satisfied with the possession of the ordinary kinds of birds, but seek rare breeds, and every variety of species, from different parts of the world. The late King of Oude, in his Palace at Garden Reach, on the banks of the Hooghly, had a wonderful collection of pigeons, numbering, it is said, at the least, fifty thousand, and some of them of almost fabulous price. It was a sight to witness the airing of those birds as they were let loose flock by flock, and soared up into the heavens, and made their beautiful evolutions, returning at a given call to their well-arranged, clean, and attractive-looking dovecotes. I do not suppose that any person has given more time and attention, and spent more money over pigeons, than did His Majesty of Oude. At the death of the King the marvellous collection was sold. The keeping of pigeons amongst Mohammedans, though a pleasant and harmless occupation, yet not infrequently leads to strife. As one of the Faithful is flying his flock, it may happen that a pigeon will join a neighbour's flock, and return home with it, in which case the strayed bird is considered a lawful prize, unless redeemed by money or by an exchange of prisoners. While many are the proofs of good breeding and civility elicited on such occasions between Moslem gentlemen, many also are the perpetuated quarrels, when such a collision of interest happens between people of quick temper and angry passions.

Apart from exercise on horseback, or on an elephant, and military exercises, of which I shall speak presently, a Mohammedan has not much recreation of a physical character. It is considered plebeian to walk much; and such Western games as football, cricket, and tennis are usually deemed too violent for gentlemen of the East. However, for the strengthening of the muscles and the expansion of the chest, recourse has been had to the use of "moghdhurs," or Indian clubs. These are used in pairs, each weighing from eight to twenty pounds, and are brandished in various ways over the head and round the body, with remarkable ease and rapidity by those with whom the art has become familiar by long use. There can be no doubt that it is a capital exercise, and one well suited to an Eastern climate. Moslem youths give themselves to it with great avidity. One writer says, "Those who would excel in the use of the moghdhurs practise every evening regularly, and after the exercise is finished they have their arms and shoulders plastered with a moist clay, which they suppose strengthens the muscles, and prevents them from taking cold after so violent an effort. The young men, who are solicitous to wield the sabre with effect and grace, declare the practice of the moghdhurs to be of the greatest service to them in their sword exercise ; they go so far as to say that they only use the sword well who have practised the moghdhur for several years."

The chief outdoor exercise of Mohammedans is riding, and, with the exception of the warlike Turks and Afghans, such exercise is taken very quietly. The swiftness of a good English hunter would be no recommendation to the natives of India or Persia, for they like a pace that seldom exceeds a gentle canter. Considerable pride is taken in the appearance of a riding-horse, and much pleasure seems to be derived from the healthy exercise. It is interesting to notice what Moslems conceive to be the good points of a horse. For instance, they have a great aversion to docking a horse's tail, for they consider that just as the glory of a man is a flowing beard, so the glory of a horse is a long tail. Then, they consider a horse " unfortunate " if the legs are not all of a colour, or if the movements are not easy and agreeable. With such matters we may have some sympathy; but the practice of colouring horses to improve their appearance is surely barbaric. Just imagine a pure white Arab steed with its legs stained yellow up to the knees, its mane and tail also coloured, and its haunches, chest, and neck all marked with divers stars and crescents ! It is a common sight in the East in Mohammedan countries.

The atrocious practice of training animals for so-called sport of the lowest kind is a serious blot upon Moslem life. Everywhere cock-fighting is in vogue. Gay young men spend much money in such low contests, and appear to delight in them. Besides cocks, a small bird called the " Buttairie," a species of quail, is trained for sport, with much care and attention. These poor little birds are said to be very game; and once brought to the contest fight until they die. Tigers and elephants are often made to combat for the amusement of spectators on gala-days; so also are buffaloes, and even alligators. I have been told that elephants are sometimes drugged, and actually intoxicated before they are made to fight, so as to add to the fun. Camels also are trained for sport. Elphinstone, speaking of sports in Afghanistan, says: "I have seen camels matched, and during their rutting season they fight with great fury. When the battle ends, the spectators had need to clear the way, for the beaten camel, who runs off at his utmost speed, is often pursued by the victor to a distance from the field of battle." Various other animals, such as stags, leopards, and cheetahs, are also kept for sport; and the fiercer the struggles, and the more deadly the results of the conflicts, the better pleased are the trainers, betters, and spectators. The whole business from beginning to end is unworthy of the human race, and the lesson needs to be taught in Moslem countries as well as in Christian that "a righteous man is merciful to his beast."

A Mohammedan is nothing unless he is a fighting man, as he believes that Allah has called him to propagate Islamism by might of arms, and that no more glorious death can be desired than to fall on the field of battle, according to that saying of the Prophet, "Paradise is under the shadow of swords." Military exercises, therefore, are popular amongst all classes of society, and the young are early trained in the use of the lance, the bow, and the sword. The Turks excel in such exercises, and even the less active Mussulmans of India can show surprising agility in the use of the lance. The Afghans and Persians also delight in warlike sports, even in time of peace. Elphinstone says of the Afghans: "It is a common amusement with the better sort to tilt with their lances in the rest at a wooden peg, stuck in the ground, which they endeavour to

knock over or to pick up on the point of their spears.
They moreover practise their carbines and matchlocks on
horseback; and all ranks fire at marks, with guns or with
bows and arrows. On such occasions there are often from
ten to twenty of a side, sometimes men of different villages
or different quarters of the same. They shoot for some
stake; commonly for a dinner, but never for any large sum
of money." By such popular games not only do Mohammedans obtain a measure of physical exercise, but they
foster the warlike and military spirit which has been in the
past the very breath of their nostrils.

But to turn to a pleasanter subject, I think we should
not overlook a favourite pastime of the women of Islam in
countries where it can be practised. It is that of freeing
captive birds. In India nothing gives a Moslem lady
greater pleasure than a present of cage birds, accompanied
by permission to let them go free if so desired. For
religious and humanitarian reasons, the fair sex of Mohammedan communities delight in giving birds their liberty.
It is considered a meritorious act so to do; and if any
member of a family is ill, the release of a bird, it is believed,
will incline the favour of Heaven towards the afflicted one.
But not only at periods of sickness, at all times the custom
of releasing birds from their cages is, in the East, a popular
one; and as the pretty little creatures effect their escape,
the ladies of the zenana clap their hands, and raise their
voices in pleasure and joy. Mrs. Meer Hassan Ali learnt
this pleasant custom from the women of India, and in her
book on the "Mussulmans of India" she says: "I am
annoyed whenever I see birds immured in cages. If they
could be trained to live with us, enjoying the same liberty,
I should gladly court society with these innocent creatures;
but a bird confined vexes me, my fingers itch to open the
wicket, and give the prisoners liberty. How I have been
delighted in seeing the pretty variegated parrots, minas, and
pigeons fly from the basket when opened in my verandah!
I have sometimes fancied in my evening walk that I could

recognize the birds again in the gardens and grounds which had been set at liberty in the morning by my hand."

It is an easy transition from birds to musical entertainments. What a singular thing it is that though the Mohammedans like to hear music, they do not as individuals cultivate the gifts either of playing or singing ! The giving of musical entertainments is left almost entirely to a special class, who, while valued for the pleasure they bestow, are looked down upon and despised by all respectable people. In saying this, I do not refer to those who act in theatrical performances in a public building, which is quite a new feature of Mohammedan social life, but to strolling minstrels, who, wandering about in small companies, are invited into the homes of the people, to sing in the men's quarters or to the ladies in the zenana. One would think, if the young people of Moslem families were taught to sing and play, that the monotony of zenana life would be agreeably broken ; but such studies are absolutely denied them. It would be considered a disgrace rather than an accomplishment for a Moslem young lady to be able to play the sitar (a stringed instrument) or to sing a song, such things being left to slaves and to professional classes. In Calcutta, Cairo, and Damascus I have been present at some of the best Mohammedan musical entertainments, but I cannot say that I have been impressed favourably by what I have heard.

And I find that most Europeans are of my opinion. Bishop Heber, in his "Journal of Travels in India," writes thus of an entertainment he witnessed in a certain native Court : "There was a great deal of Persian singing and instrumental music, the character of which does not seem a want of harmony, but dulness and languor. The airs were sung sotto voce, the instruments, chiefly guitars, were low-toned, and struck in a monotonous manner, and the effect intended to be produced seemed rather repose and luxurious languor than any more ardent or animated feeling. One man, a native of Lucknow, had a good natural voice, and two of the women sang prettily. The tunes had first parts only."

Many of the female professional musicians of the East are also Nautch Dancers, the two occupations being often combined. It should be noted, however, that Nautch Dancers, who are usually questionable characters, are excluded, as a rule, from the women's apartments of the better sort of people, as no respectable Mussulman would allow them to perform before his wives and daughters. Those who sing and dance within the pale of zenana life are called Domenies, and are girls of good behaviour. As with music, so with dancing: Mohammedans leave the pastime altogether to professionals, and are greatly surprised, and somewhat shocked, with Europeans for what they call their bad taste in this matter. When witnessing a station ball in India, Moslem gentlemen many a time have been heard to say: "Why do these Christians so fatigue themselves, when they can so well afford to hire dancers for their amusement?" A Mohammedan considers himself disgraced or insulted by the simple question, "Can you sing, play, or dance?" Nautch girls, though called dancers, are rather pantomimists and posture-makers. They are not, as a rule, handsome, or even pretty; but they dress well, and have an attractive appearance. They wear pyjamas, or trousers, of velvet, silk or muslin, which reach to below the ankle and trail on the ground, and are often made so loose that they contain fifteen or twenty yards of stuff. The upper part of the body is covered with a graceful "sari," wrapped many times round the person, and brought over the head. The colours of such dresses are usually green and red. Of course, much jewellery is worn, in the way of earrings, nose-rings, armlets and anklets. The bare feet of the girls are stained red with "henna," as also are the palms of their hands; and the languishing expression of their dark eyes is heightened by a border of antimony around the edge of the lids. Thus got up, Nautch girls, as may be imagined, are a pretty picture to behold; but as for their dancing, it is not, in my opinion, worth looking at. The dancing simply consists in moving the person backwards and forwards and from side to side, in throwing the arms about, and in gently waving the drapery.   It is a picturesque sight for once in a way ; but what pleasure Mohammedan gentlemen can find in constantly witnessing such insipid exhibitions, I cannot imagine.

There are various other recreations and amusements which need not be lingered over, such as tumbling men and women, jugglers, snake charmers, bird tamers, and so on. And the professional story-tellers should not be overlooked. Mohammedans, and, indeed, all Eastern people, dearly love a fairy tale, a ghost story, or an account of wonderful adventures in love or war. The listeners will sit by the hour simply entranced as the story-teller at great length, but with considerable skill, relates his yarn.

Thus the hours of leisure and ease of Moslems are passed !   In childhood's days they have few pleasures, but as they advance in years they obtain both in the zenana and outside a sufficiency of recreation and amusement.

CHAPTER XXVI

THE AFGHANS

WE are accustomed to speak of the people of Afghanistan as Afghans, but in reality only about half the inhabitants own that title, the rest being Tajiks, Afridis, and Hazarahs, probably the descendants of the original natives of the soil. The Afghans, however, are the most powerful and the ruling race, and they have given to the whole country its well-known name, so that we are justified in a general sketch like this in calling the people of the land Afghans. The population of Afghanistan at the present time is supposed to be about seven millions.

The early history of Afghanistan is involved in obscurity, and we only feel sure that we are on historical ground when we reach the thirteenth century, and find the present dominant race in the land, to which it is said they emigrated from a district called Ghor, to the east of Herat. The Afghans are supposed, in the days of their more tribal strength, to have become allies of the Prophet Mohammed, converts to Islamism, and enthusiastic propagandists of the Moslem faith. In the course of their warlike expeditions in Western Asia they are believed to have been attracted by, and finally settled down in, what is now called Afghanistan, but what was then named Zabulistan or Kabulistan.

The Afghans, strange to say, claim to be Bani Israel, or Children of Israel, and say that they are descended in a direct line from King Saul. The physiognomy of the Afghans, and some of their peculiar traits of character, all go to support their claim of Jewish origin, and I think that a much better case might be made out on their behalf as the genuine descendants of the Lost Ten Tribes than on behalf of the English.

Any way, because of their keenness after shekels, and their extreme shrewdness in making a bargain, they are often called "The Jews of the East." For centuries the Afghans, though brave soldiers and headed by gallant chiefs, were kept in a dependent position, for they were placed geographically on the borders of two great empires, the Persians and the Moghuls of India, who divided Afghanistan between them, the one Power occupying the districts round Herat and Kandahar, and the other the districts round Cabul and Ghazni.

The sympathies of the Afghans inclined more towards their Indian than their Persian neighbours, partly on account of race affinities, partly because of trade interests, but principally because of religious unity, for like the Moghuls they were Sunis, and consequently hated the Persians, who were Shias.

When early in the eighteenth century Persia, as related in a previous chapter, was weakened by bad government and internal strife, the Afghans thought their time had come to strike for liberty. Invoking therefore the aid of the Moghuls, they thrust out the Persian garrisons from their cities, and being flushed with their comparatively easy victories, they pushed on to attack the Persians in their own country.

A chief named Mahmood was the leader of this bold enterprise, and he had with him an army of 50,000 men. Such were the daring and courage of the invaders, and such the feeble condition of the Persian empire, that Mahmood in 1722 had but little difficulty in capturing Ispahan, the capital, and making himself master of the whole country. Thus at one stroke the dependent Afghans not only freed themselves from bondage, but completely turned the tables on their oppressors, and became masters in their turn. But this sudden rise to power was not fated to endure. A deliverer and an avenger rose for the Persians in the person of a soldier of fortune named Nadir Kuli.

The Afghans, while masters in Persia, sadly abused their power, for they slaughtered nearly all the male members of the dethroned Royal house, and pillaged the capital Ispahan, and slew tens of thousands of the innocent inhabitants of the country. For five years such atrocities were endured, and then the Persians rose in their might·under Nadir Kuli, and defeated their oppressors with a very great slaughter, and sent the remnant flying back to their own land.

The victorious Nadir now assumed the Persian crown himself, and was ever afterwards known as Nadir Shah. And this fierce chief, not content with the punishment he had already inflicted on the Afghans, resolved to follow them with fire and sword into their own mountain fastnesses.

In 1737 he took Kandahar after a protracted siege, when he razed the grand old city to the ground, massacred its inhabitants, and ploughed up its interior. Then he advanced to Ghazni and Kabul, which he also conquered. All Afghanistan trembled at his terrible work, for he granted no mercy to his foes, but burnt and destroyed everything that came in his way. Sir Edward Sullivan graphically puts it, "Plucking the muzzle of curbed license from his troops, Nadir Shah hounded them on to slaughter, and for seven months the wild dogs of Persia did flesh their teeth in every innocent of Afghanistan."

Some of the leaders of the Afghans managed to flee their country and obtain a refuge at the court of the Great Moghul at Delhi, but even there the enmity of Nadir Shah followed them, demanding that the Emperor Mohammed should put them to death, and when met with a refusal he was so incensed that in 1738 he crossed the Indus with an army of 270,000 men, and slaked not his fury until he had given the magnificent city of the Moghuls to the sack, and slaughtered all the Afghans he could find therein, and 100,000 of the inhabitants besides. Thus terribly did the Persians avenge themselves on their foes.

The fortunes of the Afghans were now at the lowest ebb, and it seemed as if for generations they might be ground under the heels of foreign masters. But to their surprise, and to the astonishment of the whole Eastern world, the day of their humiliation was to be the day of their independence. How often the unexpected happens in this life !

In 1747 Nadir Shah was assassinated, just as he reached the borders of Persia laden with untold spoil. His end had become a necessity to his subjects, for so insatiable was his thirst for human blood that no one felt safe in his presence.

An Afghan prince, named Ahmed Khan, was the first to benefit by the death of the tyrant. By a bold stroke he, with his following of 10,000 horse, captured one of the treasure convoys of the Persians when it was near the ruins of Kandahar, on its way to Ispahan. With the immense wealth thus fortuitously acquired he bought over the other chiefs of his native country, and by their unanimous consent was proclaimed king, the first king of independent Afghanistan.

This was towards the close of the year 1747. And Ahmed Shah proved himself worthy from an Eastern point of view of the high dignity to which by force of character and good fortune he had attained. In the second year of his reign he took Kabul, and drove out the Persians, and thus established his authority in every corner of the land. He soon became renowned and feared far and wide, and during his brilliant reign of twenty-six years he had no equal or rival in Afghanistan or the neighbouring kingdoms.

Dr. Bellew, in his book on the " Races of Afghan- istan," speaking of Ahmed Shah, says : " 'This great prince repeatedly replenished his leaky coffers by successive in- vasions of India : he raised the name of his nation to a high pitch of renown, opened a career for the ambition and greed of his hungry and luxurious nobles by foreign conquests, and at his death left an empire extending from the Sutlej and the Indus on the East to the Persian desert on the West, and from the Oxus on the North to the Arabian Sea on the South."

Notwithstanding all these victorious wars and outward grandeur, the condition of the people of Afghanistan was very pitiable in the eighteenth century. Only the chiefs and their more fortunate retainers possessed any wealth. The poorer people were ground down with enforced military service and unjust taxation. There were no roads; there was no certainty of even-handed justice, no security for life or property, no encouragement of trade, no patronage of learning, no proper cultivation of the soil of the naturally fine country. Indeed, everything that civilized nations consider essential to the true prosperity and genuine happiness of a nation was conspicuous by its absence. Even Mohammedanism, which had raised many Eastern peoples from a state of heathen degradation, had as yet done little for the Afghans.

The successors of Ahmed Shah had not the strength of character of that great chief, and but very little of his military genius, so that very soon the extensive kingdom gave signs of falling to pieces. Taimur, the son of Ahmed, was a perfect contrast to his father. He removed the capital from Kandahar to Kabul, and gave himself up to a life of ease and pleasure, utterly neglecting all the affairs of the State, with the result that province after province was snatched from the Crown by disaffected chiefs.

Zaman Shah, the next ruler, who ascended the Musnud in 1793, had to dispute the succession with a score or so of brothers, who were all eager to seize supreme power, and, failing that, to grasp what prizes they could in the way of towns and villages and slices of country. Zaman was dethroned by his brother Mahmud after a reign of only a few years. The eyes of the unfortunate monarch were put out, and he was banished to Ludhiana, where he became a pensioner of the British Government.

The new ruler, by his misgovernment and cruelty, however, soon raised up a host of enemies, and in 1826 he fled his country after brutally murdering his Prime Minister, whom he suspected of treachery. Then it was that Dost Mohammed, the son of the Prime Minister, a native prince, but not of the Royal line, seized the vacant throne, and founded the dynasty of the Barakzai, the present reigning house of Afghanistan.

Dost Mohammed, whose rule dates from 1826, was the first Amir of Afghanistan. The word is of Arabic origin, and means commander. Originally it was a title given to provincial Governors under the Caliphs, but subsequently it was adopted as a name to denote the principal prince of a small but independent State. It is not as dignified a title as Shah, and yet it is considered as more honourable than Prince.

Afghanistan, during the early days of Dost Mohammed's rule, was divided into three or four petty kingdoms, over which the Amir was only nominally King. Strictly speaking, his Royal authority was limited to Ghazni on one side of Kabul, his capital, and Jellalabad on the other. The country thus ruled over was but a fraction of the original independent Afghanistan, but yet it was a compact and powerful little kingdom.

It was during the reign of Dost Mohammed that the English first interfered actively in the affairs of Afghanistan. The Amir was coquetting with the Russians, who were supposed to be desirous of conquering India, and who were seeking to secure the ruler of Afghanistan as an ally. The Indian Government in 1837 sent their first Resident to Kabul in the person of Sir Alexander Burnes, and that official was instructed to seek to counteract the influence of the Russians over the Amir, and to show the latter that his best interests lay in an alliance with the English.

Dost Mohammed proving obdurate, the Indian Government took up the cause of his rival, Shah Shuja, the brother of the blinded Prince Shah Zaman, who had received hospitality at Ludhiana on his dethronement. War was declared against the Amir, whose armies were defeated, and who, seeing the hopelessness of a struggle against the British power, fled beyond the Hindu Kush.

On the 8th of May, 1839, Shuja was crowned at Kandahar, and declared, with great pomp and ceremony, the rightful heir of the Afghan Empire. In August the British entered Kabul, and there set the Shah on the throne of his ancestors, and promised to support him against all foes, in the hope of his proving a loyal ally and effective buffer against the Persians and Russians. Dost Mohammed shortly afterwards surrendered himself to the Indian Government, and was sent as a pensioner of the State to Calcutta.

The hopes of the English that matters had now been satisfactorily settled in Afghanistan were speedily doomed to disappointment, and the eyes of the world were opened, by an awful event, to the native treachery and fanaticism of the Afghans. Dr. Bellew says : " As a people, they have always been evilly notorious for their faithlessness, lawless-ness, treachery, and brutality, so much so that the saying, ' The Afghan is faithless,' has passed into a proverb among neighbouring peoples ; and, oddly enough, is acknowledged by themselves to be a true count, not only in their dealings with the stranger, but among themselves too." All Mohammedan nations hate the Feringhees, or Christians ; but the intensity of such religious hate is nowhere so deep as amongst the Afghans, who are completely carried away by their zeal or fanaticism, and shrink from no deed of treachery or darkness against those whom they consider to be the enemies of their faith. The English have learned this truth by years of terrible experience. It might have been expected that Shah Shuja would be grateful to the British for placing him on the musnud of Afghanistan, but the fact is that the Prince was totally unworthy of the con-fidence reposed in him ; and as soon as he was settled at Kabul, he began to intrigue with other chiefs for the

S

expulsion of the English from the country.   In November,
1841, an insurrection broke out, and Sir Alexander
Burnes, the Resident, was the first victim of the uprising.
The Residency was attacked by a mob, with shrill
yells and fierce imprecations, and the unfortunate Burnes,
while seeking to escape disguised as a native, was
recognized, and in an instant was literally hacked to pieces
by Afghan knives.   The retreat of the British army from
Kabul in January, 1842, on the plighted word of a sanguin-
ary enemy, and its destruction in the Kyber Passes, is a
matter of history, over which I cannot now linger.   It is
enough to say that every oath, though sworn on the
Koran, was broken.   Neither escort nor provisions were
supplied by the Afghan leaders, and the severity of the
season increased the misery of the retreat.   " The fanatical
tribes of the district harassed the flanks and rear of the
army, and slew women and children, as well as men.   Out
of a host of 26,000 only one man, Dr. Brydon, escaped to
carry the dismal tidings to General Sale, who still held his
position at Jellalabad."

On the destruction of the British army, dissensions arose
in the Court of the Shah, and the faithless monarch was
brutally murdered by his still more faithless people.   Then
anarchy reigned supreme.   In September of the same year,
however, the might of the British arms was upheld, for an
avenging army, under Pollock and Nott, occupied the
capital, and, after punishing offenders, dictated terms to the
whole country.   Brighter days now came for the Afghans,
for Dost Mohammed, the pensioner of the Indian Government, was released, and allowed to return to his native land,
where he was received with open arms, and once more
recognized as Amir.   By stern, repressive measures, and by
untiring vigilance and labour, he brought order out of
chaos, and at his death in 1868 he left Afghanistan no
longer a country divided amongst a few petty chieftains,
but united under one strong and stable government.

In addition to military matters, Dost Mohammed took a

deep interest in religion, and encouraged the spread of
education in the country, by endowing schools and colleges,
with the result that the Afghans have now a schoolmaster in
every village and camp, who is maintained by a piece of
land allotted to him, and by a small contribution which he
receives from his scholars.

The children of Afghanistan begin their letters when they
are four years, four months, and four days old, as commanded by the Prophet; but then their studies are immediately laid aside and not resumed until the little ones
reach the age of six or seven years, when they really learn
their letters, and are taught to read a little poem, which
points out the beauty of virtue and the evil of vice. After
that the Koran is learnt, and the proper duties of a
Mussulman, and then as a rule the book education of an
Afghan ends. Though the people generally are of the
Suni sect, yet there are many Shias in the land, chiefly
Persians, who hold high offices in the State and Royal
household, and who are tolerated on account of their
usefulness. Besides, the Mohammedan religion expressly
allows the Faithful to dissemble, so that as long as it is
considered necessary or wise to do so, a Shia will publicly
avow himself a Suni, while secretly he will attend to the
special regulations of his own sect. There is everywhere
in Afghanistan an appearance of great religious devotion
and enthusiasm. Mr. Elphinstone, speaking of this, says:
"From their conversation, one would think the whole
people, from the King to the lowest peasant, were always
occupied in holy reflections; scarce a sentence is uttered
without some allusion to the Deity, and the slightest
occurrence produces a pious ejaculation. For example,
they never speak of any future event, however certain,
without adding Inshalla, "Please God." They even apply
this phrase to past time, and will answer a question about
their age, "Please God, I am forty-five years old." Many
people have always a rosary hanging round their wrists,
and begin to tell their beads when there is a pause in the

conversation." Thus the Afghans show themselves to be strict Mohammedans, and intensely earnest in their devotion to Allah and his Prophet.

But to pick up the historical thread of our narrative. The dying injunction of Dost Mohammed to Shere Ali, his son and successor, was, to keep on good terms with the British, and hold fast by their alliance ; but on no account, as he valued his throne, to let an Englishman set foot in the country. The new ruler was not a popular man, for he was selfish, wayward, and quarrelsome. " He had fits of vice and piety alternately, with intervals in which his best friends dreaded to meet the whims of his temper. For weeks together he would shut himself up in his harem with drugs and wines, and then for weeks he would be employed with the Moulvis, performing prayers, reading the Koran, and listening to theological dissertations." In 1869 Shere Ali was accorded a most honourable and splendid reception by Lord Mayo, the Viceroy of India, at Umballa, in which he was acknowledged before all the world as Amir of Afghanistan, and the friend of the British Government.

This alliance strengthened the power of the Amir at home, and gradually his kingdom prospered, and his coffers were filled. As affording some idea of the Royal state of Shere Ali, it may be noticed that towards the close of his reign, say in 1877, he had an army of more than 60,000 disciplined infantry, with fully three hundred guns, and 16,000 cavalry. As usual with Afghan chiefs, however, the Amir turned on the hand that had helped him to power, and sustained him in it. He received a Russian but refused a British mission at Kabul, and so strained the friendship of the Indian Government by overt acts of malice, that in 1878 war was declared against him, when the Kyber Pass was once more entered by British troops, and Kabul, after some fighting, was once more occupied by a British army. The Amir, with his Russian guests, fled over the Hindu Kush, and died shortly afterwards in exile.

Later events can be briefly told. Yakub Khan was allowed to succeed his father on the throne of Afghanistan, after agreeing to the English terms of peace, which included the installation of a permanent British Resident at Kabul. That was in May, 1879. However, in September of the same year, the world was startled by another instance of Afghan perfidy. The troops of the Amir surrounded and attacked the British Residency, which fell after a gallant defence, when Sir Louis Cavagnari, his staff, and almost the whole of the Indian Guard, were barbarously murdered. Within one month of the receipt of the tidings of the sad event, a fresh British army was at the gates of Kabul, and Yakub Khan was a prisoner. This brilliant exploit astonished the Afghans, and struck terror into their hearts. The Amir was allowed to abdicate his throne, and in 1880 Abdur-Rahman, a grandson of Dost Mohammed, was proclaimed King in his room. And between the Afghans and the British all has gone as well as can be expected since that date ; and Afghanistan has slowly been recovering from the terrible ravages that were wrought within her borders by years of strife and bloodshed. Yet the future is uncertain, for the people most certainly hate the British, and will lose no favourable opportunity of injuring the Indian Government.

There are some English writers who say that it has been abundantly proved in the past that the Afghans cannot govern themselves or others, and sadly need a master, and the question is asked : "Shall it be Russia or England?" For my part I would say "Neither! Let the Afghans fight out their own quarrels." Though doubtless they are treacherous and fanatical they are not without their virtues, for all who know them are ready to admit that they are a hardy and brave race. A nation is not built up in a day, and we must remember that as yet the Afghans have not had much chance of cultivating the arts of peace. Their country from time immemorial has been overrun by the Persians, the Moghuls, and the British. If the outside world would only let them alone, there might be a chance for them, for we may be sure that a people who have through long centuries fought desperately, and not unsuccessfully, for their independence have in them the making of a fine nation.

It is a pity that the Afghans and Persians cannot unite their forces in temporal things. They are both of the Mohammedan faith, and if they could only sink their little differences with regard to Suni and Shia doctrines, and become one in heart and in aims, they might hold their own against all their enemies, and become, respectively, powerful and enduring Moslem nationalities.

CHAPTER XXVII

DERVISHES

DERVISH is a Persian word, (derived from "*der*," a door,) signifying "poor," or a beggar from door to door, and it corresponds to the Arabic word Fakir. Both the terms, Dervish and Fakir, are widely used in the East to designate an order or orders of Moslem mendicants, who resemble in many respects the monks of Christendom. Fakir is a word which is usually applied to Indian mendicants, and Dervish is almost wholly confined to Persian and Turkish mendicants. In this chapter I shall deal with the latter, and leave the former for a subsequent chapter; and it will be found, when the two are compared, that there are points in which Dervishes and Fakirs differ the one from the other.

It would be difficult to say when orders teaching vows of poverty were first introduced amongst the Mohammedans, for such teaching is certainly against the views of Mohammed, who, though a plain man, and of abstemious habits, yet had no sympathy with the extreme views of religious fanatics in the matter of earthly discomforts. The Prophet believed in a wise and temperate use of the good gifts of God's providence, though he did not always practise what he preached. His immediate successor, Abu Bekr, however, was a man who is said to have delighted in coarse clothing and hard fare. The great Omar also was like-minded. And it is to the one or the other of those two early Commanders of the Faithful that Moslems attribute the origin of religious vows of poverty, and the commencement of Dervish Orders.

If we come to inquire more particularly into the nature of the vows which the Dervishes make, we meet with various answers. Generally speaking, however, these fanatics agree to put themselves to as much misery as they can in this world, in hope of obtaining a richer reward in the next. Some of them will, for example, only take one meal a day, and even then eat very sparingly. Others will fast for days together. Others will wander about the country half-naked, exposed to all weathers, utterly indifferent to cold, or heat, or rain. Others, but Fakirs rather than Dervishes, will inflict upon their bodies horrible torments.

In short, there is an infinite variety in the nature of the vows taken, some orders of mendicants even living in monasteries instead of adopting a roving life. But all alike, if they are genuine Dervishes, will be recognized by their sacred rosaries, their peculiar garb, their appearance of untidiness and uncleanness, and their general air of melancholy, if not misery. It has often been asked, and I would repeat the inquiry, "What can be the reason that in all ages, and in all faiths, the odour of sanctity seems to be associated with filth? How is it that cleanliness and godliness are so often set at opposite poles?"

Among the Dervishes there are said to be thirty-two orders, which are divided into two classes, the Ba-Shara and the Be-Shara. The Ba-Shara, or those "with the Law," are governed by the principles of Islamism; but the Be-Shara, or those "without the Law," are amenable to no religious creed, being a law unto themselves, though in name they claim to be Mussulmans. The principal orders are known by the names of their respective founders, and are as follows:—The Bestamees, established 874 A.D.; the Kadrees, 1165 A.D.; the Rufaiyees, 1182 A.D.; the Maulawees, 1273 A.D.; the Nakshibandees, 1319 A.D.; the Bakhtashees, 1357 A.D.; the Gulshanees, 1533 A.D.; the Shamshees, 1601 A.D.; and the Jamalees, 1750 A.D. I have given this list for the benefit of those who are curious, and who like exactitude.

The only two orders in which I am personally interested are the Kadrees and the Maulawees, and these are better known by the names of the Howling and the Dancing Dervishes. It was my privilege to see and hear representatives of these famous orders on one occasion in the Mosque of Mohammed Ali at Cairo. The occasion was an anniversary of the death of some great Dervish, and so important was it considered that the Khedive of Egypt was present, and it was my good fortune to obtain admittance the same evening. It was a sight, to be sure! The great and magnificent Mosque was filled to overflowing with thousands of the Faithful, who had eyes and ears for nothing but the shouts and antics of their Howling and Dancing compatriots. There might be fifty of the saintly men present, and they were allotted a clear, square place for their performances. The Dancing fraternity had peaked caps on their heads and flowing garments from the waist, which, as they whirled themselves round in the dance, assumed the forms of inflated balloons. The Dancers, with extended arms, capered about, independently of each other, like madmen, twirling themselves round and round in a way that was wonderful to behold. After keeping up the exercise with great vigour for a time, they at length stopped suddenly, thoroughly dizzy and exhausted.

The Howling Dervishes were a still more extraordinary set of men. In their case the head was uncovered, but the hair had been encouraged to grow thick and long, so that with most of them it reached below the girdle, and in some instances almost touched the ground. These performers stood in a row, and at a given signal began to bend the body slowly towards the earth, and to straighten themselves up again. Gradually they increased the speed, while they gave a jerk to the head, thus throwing their long hair over their faces, and again over their backs. At the same time they began to chant in a low, monotonous tone, which, as they proceeded and got warmed up to their work, became a loud noise, and eventually turned into a howl. At the time I heard those Howling Dervishes I did not know what they were saying, but I have since found out that they were performing what is called Zikr, or the repetition of certain syllables or phrases in which occurs the name of God. The syllables they were repeating were these, " La-il-la-ha " and " Il-lal-la-ho," the interpretation thereof being, " There is no God but God." The latter syllable was said with each inhalation of the breath, and the former with each exhalation, and I have only to repeat them to myself to recognize the familiar sound at once. If any reader will practise the exercise for five minutes he will find that it is most trying to the throat, and weakening to the frame. Yet those Dervishes in the mosque kept it up with increasing vigour; and with a perfectly deafening noise, for the space of half an hour or more. Indeed, I wearied of listening to them long before they thought well to stop their religious performance. The poor fellows, like their brethren the Dancing Dervishes, must have been dizzy and exhausted. It was very hard work, and they were very enthusiastic over it ; but I felt sorry for them, and wished they had a more worthy cause in which to display their faith and zeal.

Of course, not all Dervishes are given to such violent exercises in the way of religion. Some orders are quiet enough, and are of a secluded and meditative turn of mind. Yet the dancing and howling communities are great favour-ites amongst the devout, and are held in high honour by all Moslems. It is a matter of history that at least one King, and a great and famous King too, became either a Howling or a Dancing Dervish. I refer to Sultan Murad, of Adrianople, one of the bravest and noblest men that ever sat on the throne of the Ottoman Turks. An Eastern writer says of this Prince : " He was just and valiant, of a great soul, patient in labours, learned, merciful, religious, charitable, a lover of the studious, and of all who excelled in any art or science, a great general, and a good Emperor." Nor is the picture overdrawn.

And yet this renowned Sultan, after twenty years of

Royal state, gladly resigned his throne and kingdom to his son, Mohammed the Second, and retired to the society of saints and hermits. Gibbon says : " The Lord of nations submitted to fast and pray, and turned round in endless rotation with the fanatics who mistook the giddiness of the head for the illumination of the spirit."

The influence that Dervishes have exerted in Persia and Turkey, and in the East generally, over others, even over the great ones of the earth, is truly astonishing. It has been due largely to the real or supposed sanctity of their lives, and to the words of wisdom which the more thoughtful and cultured amongst them have uttered when appealed to, as they often are, for advice and guidance in the affairs of life. Let me give a few specimens of their wise sayings. To a King who through a treacherous deed had brought trouble upon himself and his kingdom, a plain-spoken Dervish said : " Whosoever doeth good shall experience good, but he who committeth evil shall suffer evil." To a person who was despondent over his plain looks, though God had richly endowed him with the gift of song, another Dervish consolingly said : " A sweet voice is better than a beautiful face." To a meddlesome character who had come to grief in too readily interfering with the quarrels of others, a shrewd Dervish remarked : " My son, when you see fighting be peaceful, for a peaceful disposition shuts the door of contention." Another wise Dervish, who was found one day suffering distress from poverty, and who at the same time was diligently mending his worn-out garments, remarked to a friend who urged him to be up, and begging : " Nay, friend, I am content with a dry loaf and ragged garments, for it is better to bear the weight of one's necessities than to suffer the load of obligation from mankind." And is not the following saying, uttered by a Dervish on a sick bed, most instructive. Asked what his heart desired, he replied : " Only this, that it may not desire anything."

There are three short stories told of Dervishes in connection with sleep, which are worth recording. On one occasion, when a party of travellers stopped their caravan in the desert to rest for the night, a certain holy man would not sleep nor let others sleep with comfort, for the loud cries which he made.

When expostulated with in the morning by a saintly brother, he remarked, " I heard the nightingale on the trees, the partridges on the mountain, the frogs in the water, and the brutes in the desert, uttering their plaintive notes ; and I reflected that it did not become a human being to be asleep whilst all other creatures were celebrating the praises of God." " Thou fool ! " was the reply, " thou shouldst have reflected that to disturb man is not to please God ! "

The second story is that of a Dervish who boasted that on one occasion he passed a whole night in eating to repletion, while at the same time he read through a dozen long chapters of the Koran. A companion to whom he told the tale, dryly remarked, " To have eaten half a loaf of dry bread, and slept, would have been much more meritorious."

The third story is one that the famous poet and Dervish, Sadi, tells of himself. He says, " I remember even when a youth I was very religious. I regularly rose in the night, and was punctual at all my devotions. One evening I had been sitting in the presence of my father, not having closed my eyes for hours, with the holy Koran on my lap, while all around me other members of the community were fast asleep. Looking towards my beloved parent I said, somewhat proudly, ' Not one of these lifteth up his head to perform his genuflections ; they are so fast asleep that they seem as dead.' The reply I received I shall never forget. In a voice of love, yet of sorrowful reproof, the words were uttered, ' My son, it were better if you also were asleep, if you have nothing better to do than to point out the faults of mankind.' "

Dervishes, as a rule, make a great point of teaching to all the grace of compassion. " Be merciful," they say, " and you shall obtain mercy." They inculcate kindness to animals, to all weak things, and especially to poor people. It is recorded that on one occasion, when Sadi was sitting in the great Mosque at Damascus, a certain King of Arabia, notorious for his cruelty, happened to enter. The King was on pilgrimage to the tomb of the Prophet Yahiya, on whom be peace! After performing most earnestly his devotions, the great man glanced around, and saw the learned and saintly Sadi, whom he knew well by repute.

Advancing towards the Sage, the King made a profound reverence, and said, " Holy man, thou hast power with God, and canst prevail. Unite thy prayers with mine, for I am in dread of a powerful enemy." Sadi promptly replied, " O King, suffer a word of exhortation. Act justly, and, like myself, thou wilt fear no man. Show mercy to the weak peasant in thy country, and thou wilt have no occasion to dread a strong enemy." What the King replied is not recorded ; but it is to be hoped that he took to heart the sound advice of the faithful Dervish.

Not all Dervishes, however, are like Sadi. There are not a few rogues and vagabonds in the ranks of the so-called saints. Altogether, in the Turkish and Persian dominions, there are said to be at least fifty thousand persons who have devoted themselves to a life of religious mendicancy; and of these, probably the majority have adopted the calling or profession because, generally speaking, it is a quiet, easy, lazy life. It is the few, and not the many, who actually practise painful austerities. The rest live in poverty, it is true, and from hand to mouth, yet they are sure of receiving from the Faithful enough to keep body and soul together. And the life is considered in Mohammedan countries a worthy and honourable one.

I might recount many other anecdotes of the Dervishes, illustrative of their ways of life, and of the influence they exert in the East, but one more must suffice. It is a noble story, often told to travellers, and relates to Hassan Ben Omar, the son of a rich merchant, who by years of riot and luxury dissipated the wealth his father had left him. One day Hassan was seen outside the walls of Bassora, prostrate on the ground, in the wild Eastern fashion, tearing his hair, reproaching Allah, blaspheming the Prophet, bemoaning his fate, charging his friends with ingratitude, and loudly calling upon Death to release him from his misery. His old servants approached and tried to comfort him, but he drove them away with abuse and blows, and dashed himself again upon the earth. Suddenly, while he was moaning and weeping, a voice, pleasant and cheerful, sounded in his ears, saying, " Listen, Hassan Ben Omar ! Allah intends thee good."

Hassan sat up, and saw before him a venerable Dervish, who was regarding him with looks of compassion. " Begone, old man ! " he cried, "unless thou canst work a miracle for my relief ! " " A miracle, indeed ! " was the reply. " The Prophet has sent me to serve thee. What wouldst thou have ? " " Give me my possessions again— my vineyards, my fields, and my gold ! " shouted the despairing Hassan. The Dervish quietly answered, "And what would it avail thee if I were to do this ? When they were thine, thou hadst not the wisdom to keep them ; in three years thou wouldst be as wretched as now. But attend, Hassan Ben Omar ! Reform thy life, govern thy passions, moderate thy desires, hate the wine-cup, labour for thy bread, eat only when thou art hungry, and sleep when thou art weary ! Do these things for one year, and thou shalt be monarch of a mighty kingdom ! "

Having so said, the Dervish withdrew, and left Hassan to consider his ways. Deeply impressed by the words of his saintly visitor, the disappointed man rose from the ground with new resolves and nobler purposes in life. Invoking the aid of Allah, he joined a caravan of merchants, and set out on a long journey without delay. He began to rise early, and to labour with diligence. Plain water and a few dates formed his simple meal, and at night he lay down by the side of the camels, and enjoyed sweeter repose than he had ever known before. Thus for a year he lived a frugal, patient, active, blameless life, following to the letter the exhortations of his friend the Dervish, and at the end of the appointed months, he journeyed back to Bassora, and going outside the city walls, prostrated himself on the earth as aforetime, and prayed earnestly, saying, " Now, Allah, fulfil thy promise made by thy servant the Dervish, and give me the kingdom."

Suddenly a voice, the voice of the Saint, was heard, and it said, " Hassan Ben Omar, thou hast done well ! Behold, thy kingdom is thyself ! Allah hath taught thee to rule it ! Be wise, and be happy ! " Hassan started up and looked around, but in vain, for the speaker. No one was near. It was a mystery. A miracle ! " Behold, thy kingdom is thyself ! " exclaimed the voice once more. And Hassan, pondering over the saying, received it as a revelation from God, and departed with a contented heart. For many years after that event he lived—busy, prosperous, and happy—and was known far and wide as Hassan the Good and the Wise. And to the Holy Dervish, under Allah, he gave the glory ! To his dying day he was thankful that he had been taught the truth that " a man's kingdom is himself ! "

CHAPTER XXVIII

MOGHULS OF INDIA

THE immense country of India, with its one million and a half of square miles, and nearly three hundred millions of inhabitants, has been ruled by many nationalities, and not the least prosperous and famous period of its history was when the Mohammedans reigned supreme in the land, and the Court of the Great Moghul was held either at Agra or Delhi, the ancient capitals. The term Moghuls is an incorrect form of Monghols, and designates the race or races of warriors and adventurers, originally from the spacious highlands between China and the Caspian Sea, who overran the greater part of Asia, carrying the terror of their arms wherever they went, and founding mighty empires even in China and in India, as well as in Western Asia. The Moghul Empire in India was founded in the first part of the sixteenth century, but long before that time Mohammedans had made inroads into the land, and had conquered considerable tracts of country. As early as 711 A.D., within a hundred years of the death of Mohammed, an adventurous Arab chief named Kasim had cast longing eyes towards the rich and fertile plains of India, and had advanced into Sind, and, after a brilliant campaign, had settled himself in the Indus valley. But at Kasim's death the Moslems were driven out. However, again and again on subsequent occasions such attempts were renewed, and one of the most famous of the leaders of those predatory armies was the Afghan chief Mahmud of Ghazni, who made the first of his seventeen raids into India in 1001 A.D. Mahmud was a brave but ferocious warrior, and being a most fanatical Mussulman, he was the scourge and terror of the idol-worshipping peoples of India.

The story of the sack of the ancient city of Somnath, and of the destruction of the stone idol called Soma, by Mahmud, is one that is told by the Hindoos even at this day. Somnath was situated at the extreme point of the peninsula of Guzerat, now known as the island of Diu, and it was regarded by the people of India as the most holy of all their cities, because there resided the god Soma, who was believed to possess the absolute disposal of the souls of men, and had the regulation of the successive transmigrations through which human beings had to pass before they were deemed worthy to share eternity with Brahma.

A place of such sanctity in the eyes of the Hindoos did not escape the notice of Mahmud, and he resolved to earn everlasting renown by capturing it and destroying its famous idol. The task was a difficult one, however, for Somnath was a strong city, and stubbornly defended. At length, after many attacks, the valour of the Moslems triumphed, and the city was taken and plundered.

The story goes, which Dr. Hunter, however, declares to be a myth, that the priests of the Temple of Soma offered a fabulous sum of money to Mahmud if he would spare their god from destruction, but the fanatical Prince scoffed at their lamentations and prayers, and swore by the Koran that not for ten thousand times the money would he have his name handed down to posterity as "the sparer of idols." His true name, he declared, was "the Idol Smasher," and at the word he brought down his battle-axe with a mighty blow upon the nose of the graven image. His soldiers speedily followed such an excellent example, and, amidst the groans and supplications of an agonized multitude, the destruction of the idol was completed. Sir Edward Sullivan, writing of this episode in his "Princes of India," says : "Now was the true object of the relentless zeal of Mahmud and the costly supplications of the priests exposed. The

T

image was hollow, and filled with the accumulated treasures of centuries. All the wealth hitherto acquired by the Mohammedans was nothing compared with that now yielded by this prolific god. Piles of diamonds and sapphires, a ruby weighing upwards of six pounds, thousands of pounds' weight of pure gold and precious stones were, to the dismay of the crestfallen priests, brought to light by the triumphant soldiers. The booty was nine millions sterling."

I think there can be little doubt that as in Mahmud's case, so in the case of other Moslem Generals who invaded India from the north, the desire to obtain the wealth of the land, the report of which had travelled far, was the chief motive for their warfare, though they spoke very grandly of zeal for the religion of Allah and his Prophet as spurring them on to conquest. Muhamed, of the Afghan Princedom of Ghor, was the first Moslem chief to obtain a permanent footing in India. One of his Generals, in 1193 A.D., conquered for him the city of Delhi, the seat of the strongest Hindoo power, and at the news Muhamed himself marched into Hindostan through the Kyber Passes at the head of an army of 100,000 men, composed of Turks, Persians, and fierce Afghans. That strong force overran the northern provinces of India as far as Benares, and in the latter city alone 50,000 Hindoos were slain, and more than a thousand heathen temples were pillaged and destroyed. The victorious Prince returned to Ghor with immense spoil, leaving a lieutenant at Delhi to govern India in his name.

At Muhamed's death the Empire he had built up fell to pieces, but the Indian provinces still remained Mohammedan, for they were retained by the Viceroy Kutab, who had himself declared King, and who was thus the first monarch of an independent Moslem kingdom in Northern India. Kutab had started life as a Turki slave, and as most of his successors for two or three generations were of the same low origin, the dynasty which he founded in 1206, and which endured till 1290, was called the "Slave Dynasty." In 1290 the Slave Dynasty was succeeded by the Kilji

Dynasty, which lasted just thirty years, and was in its turn followed by the Tughlak Dynasty, which endured for ninety-four years. It was during the rule of the latter that Tamerlane, the scourge of the East, swept through the Afghan passes at the head of the united hordes of Tartary, and captured and sacked Delhi. That was in 1399. The Tughlak Dynasty fell in 1414, and was followed by the Sayyid Dynasty, and the latter in 1450 by the House of Lodi. Nothing of any special moment happened in those years, so we need not linger over their history, but push on to the year 1526, which ushered in the famous Dynasty of the Moghuls, which for more than two centuries ruled over the greater.part of India with great power and illustrious splendour.

Baber, born in 1482, a descendant of Tamerlane, was the founder of the Indian Moghul line. Driven from Samarkand, the city of his fathers, by rebellion, he seized the kingdom of Kabul in 1504, and having established his power in Afghanistan, he turned his thoughts towards India, and pouring a vast army through the mountain passes, he defeated the last Prince of the House of Lodi on the Plain of Panipat, in 1526, and entered Delhi in triumph. His co-religionists in the country acknowledged him as their Prince, but he was stoutly opposed by the Hindoos, who thought the time favourable for an attempt to throw off the Moslem yoke. The might of Baber's arms, however, prevailed; and when he died at Agra in 1530, he left an empire which stretched from the river Amur in Central Asia to the borders of the Gangetic delta in Lower Bengal. His son, Humayun, succeeded him in India, but lost the other dominions of the Empire. Then misfortune followed misfortune, and the Emperor, with his Moghul retainers, was forced to retire from Hindostan, but only to return again in 1556, and at that date the Moghul Empire was firmly established in the land. Humayun, however, only enjoyed the sweets of recovered power a very short time, for six months after his return to Delhi he was killed by

an accident.   It happened thus : One day when he was
descending from the terrace of his library he heard the
crier from the adjoining Mosque calling to prayers. Pausing
according to custom, Humayun repeated the Moslem creed,
and seated himself on the steps until the crier had ceased
his summons, when, rising suddenly, he slipped and fell
heavily down the stairs, and was taken up injured unto
death.   The poor king truly deserved the cognomen of
" Unfortunate."

Akbar was only fourteen years of age when he succeeded
his father, but he was possessed of wisdom beyond his
years, and had natural abilities of a very high order.   And
he had a grand field for the exercise of his talents, for India
was seething with discordant elements which needed a
master-mind to bring unity and strength out of them.
After ten years of constant warfare the young Emperor was
an Emperor indeed, for he had reduced all the petty
Moslem States to provinces of Delhi, and he had broken
the power of the Rajput Princes, and brought them into
political dependence to his authority.   At twenty-five years
of age Akbar reigned without a rival over the vast Indian
territory first overrun by his ancestor Baber, and had earned
for himself the titles of the "Victorious" and the "Great."
Great in peace as in war, Akbar pursued a policy of con-
ciliation towards the Hindoo States, and abolished the poll-
tax which had hitherto been imposed on all non-Mussul-
mans.   He sought, also, to make wise and just laws for all
his people, irrespective of their race and creed, and gave
the most enlightened encouragement to men of learning of
every sect.   Prosperity consequently followed.   "Thirty
millions sterling composed the magnificent revenues of this
mighty Prince.   Three hundred thousand cavalry, the same
number of infantry, and a thousand elephants constituted
the standing army that curbed the dangerous ambition of
his powerful nobles, and enforced the friendship of foreign
Powers."   The reign of Akbar in India may be compared
with the reign of Queen Elizabeth in England for success

in war, for prosperity in peace, for the encouragement of men of learning, for reverence for religion, and for all that really makes a nation great. And, strange to say, the two reigns were contemporaneous, for Akbar ascended the throne in 1556 and died in 1605, while Queen Elizabeth reigned from 1558 to 1603.

The next Moghul ruler was Jahangir, who adopted the boastful title of "Conqueror of the World." Of this Prince, Dr. Hunter says, in his "Imperial Gazetteer of India," "His reign of twenty-two years was spent in reducing the rebellions of his sons, in exalting the influence of his wife, and in drunken self-indulgence."

The wife referred to was the charming Noor Jahan, who, though born in great poverty but possessed of extraordinary beauty, won the love of Jahangir in his early youth, and retained it till his dying day. For nearly twenty years this remarkable woman practically ruled the Moghul Empire, for her husband complied with her slightest wish as if it were a divine command. In 1611 the coin of the realm was stamped with the Queen's image, or at any rate with this inscription: "Gold has acquired a hundred degrees of excellence in receiving the name of Noor Jahan."

It cannot be said that Jahangir personally reflected much glory on his illustrious house, though during his reign the Moghul Empire grew stronger and more prosperous. He was fonder of talking than of doing, and of seeming religious rather than of being religious, and yet in his folly he is reported to have said: "The prophets of all nations were impostors, and that he himself, should his indolence permit, could form a better system of religion than any yet imposed on the world."

In January, 1628, Shah Jahan ascended the Moghul throne when he was thirty-six years of age. He was a brave, a wise, and a victorious Prince, and by his private actions as well as public deeds added to the already powerful name of his royal race. "He was just to his people, blameless in his habits, a good financier, and as economical as a magnificent court, splendid public works, and distant military expeditions could permit."

It was under this Prince that most of the fine buildings were erected in Northern India which now form the grandest memorials of Mohammedan rule in India. In a later chapter on "Architecture" the reader will find described some of the beautiful mosques, tombs, and palaces which are to be seen in Agra and Delhi, and elsewhere in the East.

Like his father, Shah Jahan was blessed with a good wife, called Mumtaz Zamani, "the most Exalted of the Age." This lady is said to have united in her mind and person much of the exquisite beauty and fascination of her aunt, Noor Jahan. She was the Emperor's guardian angel, and while she lived he had no other spouse. For more than twenty years Shah Jahan was that almost imaginary being of Mohammedan history, the husband of but one wife. And when the great and noble lady died the Emperor was inconsolable. Sir Edward Sullivan, referring to this matter, says : "Shah Jahan was amongst the number of those who at the end of life are brought to acknowledge that of all the good gifts that Providence has spread in their path, the love of woman has been the most delicious, the most intoxicating, the most durable, and the least deceitful."

To the memory of his idolized wife the Emperor erected a tomb, the Taj Mahal at Agra, which is a perfect vision of loveliness, and which is counted by competent judges as the most perfect specimen of Saracenic architecture in the world.

The latter days of Shah Jahan were not only clouded by the death of his wife, but made bitter by the ingratitude of his numerous sons, who rose in rebellion against him, and waged war one with another. Aurangzebe proved the most powerful, and having defeated and murdered his brothers, he dethroned his father, who, after eight years of secluded life in the fortress of Agra, died in 1666, in his seventy-fifth year, almost his last words being : " Fathers have been dethroned by their sons, but to insult the misfortunes of a parent was left for Aurangzebe."

The heartless Prince, however, cared nothing for the reproaches of his sire, but had himself proclaimed Emperor as early as 1658 with the high-sounding title of the "Conqueror of the Universe." Foreign powers at once recognized Aurangzebe as the greatest potentate of the Eastern world. "The Shah of Persia, the Sheriff of Mecca, the Emperor of China, and even the Sovereigns of Europe, sent to congratulate him upon his achievements, and to solicit his friendship." How true it is that "nothing succeeds like success!"

For nearly half a century Aurangzebe ruled India with a rod of iron, and added to the dominions of the Moghuls in the south, annexing, after long years of war, the five Mohammedan kingdoms of the Deccan which had hitherto preserved their independence under petty chiefs. He had to do battle also with the rising Hindoo powers, the Marathas and the Sikhs, and to put down various rebellions in the Rajput States. Begun in blood, his reign was continued in blood. If power and wealth could bring happiness Aurangzebe ought to have been the happiest man on earth, but he was probably one of the most miserable. His sins had found him out! On his death-bed he wrote mournfully to his son Azim: "I came a stranger into the world, and a stranger I depart. I know nothing of myself — what I am, nor for what I am destined; my life, passed in power, has left only sorrow behind it. Though I have a strong reliance on the mercies and bounties of God, yet regarding my actions fear will not quit me. I die! I die! Come what may, I must launch my vessel on the waves! Farewell! Farewell! Farewell!"

The rest of our story must be briefly told. After Aurangzebe the Moghuls had no great Emperor. Puppet followed puppet on the throne, and the Empire, pressed hard by the Afghans, the Rajputs, the Marathas, the Sikhs, the French, and the English, rapidly fell to pieces. In less than a hundred years the Moghul power was nothing but a name, for province after province had been lopped off the parent tree of Delhi, and even the capital itself was, at the close of the eighteenth century, possessed by the Marathas, who allowed a Prince of the Moghul royal line to reign, but not to rule. In 1804 the English took the place of the Marathas, and for fifty years Delhi enjoyed almost uninterrupted tranquillity under the protection of the British, and the Great Moghuls were pensioners of the East India Company. Then came the Mutiny of 1857, when the ancient capital revolted, and the Moghul Empire was once more set up, and a semblance of the past power and glory of the Imperial House was regained. It was, however, of short duration, for at the close of that dread year of mutiny Delhi was recaptured, the Royal Princes were slain, and the Emperor Mohammed Bahadur, the last of his line, was tried, found guilty of rebellion and of the massacre of certain English people, and transported as a State prisoner to Rangoon, where he died in 1862. Thus ended the government of the Moghuls in India, just three hundred and thirty-two years from the time that the victorious Baber had set up the Royal House!

But with the fall of the Moghuls only the supreme temporal power of the Mohammedans ceased in India. There are still Moslem principalities in the land. Moreover, the British have never interfered with the religious beliefs of the people of India, whether Hindoo, Sikh, Jain, Parsee, or Mohammedan: so that Islamism still raises its head, and indeed flourishes numerically. The census informs us that there are over fifty millions of Moslems in the Indian Empire. As a matter of fact, Mohammedanism is stronger in India to-day than in any other part of the world; and there are more followers of the Prophet under the rule of Queen Victoria than there are under the rule of the Sultan of Constantinople, the great head of the Mussulman Faith.

CHAPTER XXIX

FORBIDDEN, OR QUESTIONABLE THINGS

In the Mohammedan religion, as in the Jewish and Christian religions, there are certain rules or laws which may be characterized as negative precepts. In addition to the exhortation "Thou shall" there occurs the command "Thou shalt not."

In previous chapters we have seen that the Moslem creed says : "Thou shalt not kill ;" "Thou shalt not steal ;" "Thou shalt not commit adultery ;" "Thou shalt not perjure thyself," and so on, but in addition to these grave offences there are certain other matters which come under the dictum of Forbidden, or, at any rate, Questionable Things.

Let us begin with Intoxicating Drinks, about which the Koran speaks very plainly, and altogether in condemnation. There was a time in Arabia when the drinking of wines and various spirits was a common occurrence, and was indulged in to excess.

But Mohammed set his face as flint against it, and sought to discourage the drinking habits of his countrymen, by showing them that intoxication was injurious to themselves and displeasing to God.

Matters were brought to a climax on one occasion, when a follower of the Prophet, Abdur-Rahman Ibn Auf by name, gave an entertainment to which he invited many of the leaders amongst the Faithful. At that convivial gathering so much wine was drunk, that when the hour of evening prayer arrived, very few of the guests were in a fit state to attend properly to their devotions.

However they essayed the task, but one of the party in reciting a passage from the Koran, made a shameful blunder, being so overcome with the libations he had taken. When Mohammed heard of the incident he was very indignant and spoke sharp words of reproof, and even inserted a command in the Koran against the free use of wine, which runs thus : " O true believers, come not to prayers when ye are drunk, until ye understand what ye say."

The exhortations and warnings of the Prophet, though they effected much, did not altogether stay the evil, however, so he resolved at last absolutely to forbid the use of intoxicating drinks as a beverage.   It was not that Mohammed thought wines or spirits were without good properties, but his conviction was that, as a general rule, the use of such drinks did much more harm than good.

Take, for example, two or three references in the Koran. In the 2nd sura it is written : " They will ask thee concerning wine.   Answer : In it there is sin, and also something of use, but its sinfulness is greater than its use."   Then in the 16th sura it is said : " Of the fruits of palm-trees and of grapes ye obtain an intoxicating liquor and also good nourishment.   Verily, herein is a sign unto people who understand."

What the Prophet wished to be understood was, that notwithstanding the acknowledged good properties of certain drinks, yet men would act wisely in leaving them alone altogether, for death was in the cup.

And to make his views still clearer, Mohammed wrote in the 5th sura : " O true believers, surely wine is an abomination of the work of Satan, therefore avoid it, that ye may prosper.   Satan seeketh to sow dissension and hatred among you by means of wine, and to divert you from remembering God, and from prayer : will ye not therefore abstain from it ?   Obey God, and obey His Apostle."

And to set the minds of those at ease who had offended in the past, these words were added : " It is no sin in those who believe that they have tasted wine before they were forbidden, if now they fear God and do good works, for God loveth those who do good."

For the most part it may be said of the Faithful that they have obeyed the command of the Prophet and have abstained entirely from the use of intoxicating drinks. At least this may be said of Indian Moslems, who, as a general rule, are sober men, carrying their aversion to wines and spirits to the extreme of refusing even in illness to take a single drop of the forbidden things.

There are exceptions, however. I remember, when in Delhi, there was pointed out to me, in a Mohammedan burial-ground, the beautiful marble tomb of Prince Mirza Jahangir, who was banished for a time by the British Government from his native city, on account of his wild life, and his many attempts to murder his elder brother, and to excite insurrection.

The dissolute prince eventually killed himself by drinking cherry-brandy, of which liquor he used to swallow a glass an hour, limiting himself to that amount in order to protract the pleasure and delay intoxication.

Other Moghul princes of India were addicted to the same unlawful practice. It is a matter of history that Prince Danial, the eldest son of Akbar the Great, died, at the age of thirty, a drunkard's death. His case was a sad and remarkable one.

When Akbar knew that his son had undermined his constitution by too frequent libations, he placed him under arrest at Berhampore, in Bengal, and gave strict orders that no drink should be given to him. However, Danial could not do without his usual beverage, and tried to bribe his attendants to smuggle some into the palace which was his prison.

For a time he could find no one to listen to his overtures, for the displeasure of Akbar was greatly feared. At length, however, one servant was won over by the promise of a large sum of money to gratify the unnatural cravings of the wretched prince.

Danial had a favourite gun which he had christened the "Bier," because it had killed so many foes; and, strange to say, it was in the barrel of that gun that the brandy was hidden which was to kill the prince himself. A few debauches brought on a severe attack of *delirium tremens*, from which the poor victim of intemperance had not strength to rally. In great agony he died.

I am afraid, amongst both high and low in India at the present day, that the custom of drinking intoxicating drinks is on the increase, and that intemperance amongst Moslems is becoming more and more evident.

But what is, after all, a comparatively rare thing in India, is a common thing in Turkey and Persia. In the latter countries the Prophet's prohibition against wines and spirits is now very much a dead letter.

In a book, recently published, of "Travels in Asiatic Turkey," the author, Henry C. Barkley, says: "Drunkenness is almost as common among the Turks as it is with us, and they have apparently got over thinking it a sin and disgrace, for it is both openly indulged in and openly talked of. Few of the upper classes abstain, and many make it a rule to go to bed drunk every night. As far as possible a Turk does everything in the reverse way to a European, and in getting drunk he makes no exception. We sit over our wine after dinner: the Turk before. With us drinking before dinner takes away appetite: but with the Turk it has the opposite effect, and the more he drinks the more hungry he gets. If, after eating, the fumes of the wine are ousing out of his head, he takes a fresh bumper, and then, in nine cases out of ten, tumbles back where he sits, falls fast asleep, and is wrapped up by his servants, and left all night to sleep himself sober. We found drunkenness everywhere in Asia Minor."

What a sad testimony! The spread of the drink mania

is one of the pressing evils of the nineteenth century in Mohammedan as well as Christian countries.

Turning from drinking to eating, it should be noted that certain animals are regarded as unclean, and are forbidden as food to good Mussulmans. A distinction with regard to meats has, for ages, prevailed in the East, and I think there can be little doubt that Mohammed, in making his laws on this matter, not only studied the idiosyncrasies of taste of his own people, but consulted also the Scriptures of the Jews.

In the 5th sura of the Koran it is written: "O true believers, ye are allowed to eat the brute cattle, other than what ye are commanded to abstain from." Later in the same sura, the exceptions are given, and they are as follows : "Ye are forbidden to eat that which dieth of itself, and blood, and swine's flesh, and that on which the name of any god hath been invoked, and that which hath been strangled or killed by a blow, or by a fall, or by the horns of another beast, and that which hath been partly eaten by a wild beast, and that which hath been sacrificed unto idols."

However, in cases of absolute need, where a man may be in danger of starving, the Mohammedan law allows the use even of prohibited meats, according to that saying of the Prophet : "He who is forced by necessity, it shall be no crime in him if he eat of those things, for God is gracious and merciful."

Swine's flesh has been mentioned in the foregoing list, and this is perhaps the most notable of the Forbidden Things with respect to meat. Moslems have a perfect horror of pork, and regard with loathing all those who can bring themselves to eat such unclean food.

And to sprinkle the blood of swine on the walls of a Mosque is a deadly insult that must be avenged. Many have been the quarrels and even wars that have been occasioned in the East by the Hindoos provoking the Moslems in that particular way.

It should be borne in mind also that the great Indian Mutiny was brought to a head by what was supposed to be, on the part of the British Government, a deliberate disregard of the feelings and convictions both of Mohammedans and Hindoos in the matter of forbidden meats.

It happened thus: Towards the close of 1856 the British authorities determined to replace the old infantry musket by an improved firearm with a grooved or rifled bore, and which could not be easily loaded without the greasing of the cartridge. Early in 1857, when the manufacture of cartridges for this new Enfield rifle was proceeding briskly at Dum-Dum, near Calcutta, a low caste workman asked a soldier of the 2nd Grenadiers, a high caste Brahmin, for a draught of water from his drinking-vessel. The soldier declined, whereupon the workman, in mischievous spite, remarked: "Wait a little, you who think so much of your caste, the Christians will soon make high and low on an equality, for cartridges smeared with beef fat and hog's lard are being made up in the magazine, which all Sepoys will be compelled to use."

As beef fat was the abomination of the Hindoos, and hog's lard of the Moslems, we can imagine the consternation the slanderous speech caused. There was not a word of truth in it, but it sounded plausible, and the credulous soldier believed it, and is said to have rushed out of the Arsenal at Dum-Dum in a perfect agony of shame and wrath. Like wildfire the news spread amongst the other soldiers, and was carried by word of mouth and by letter all over India; and in a few weeks the country was ablaze with indignation. It was useless for the English to deny the statement: both Moslems and Hindoos were convinced, or professed to be, of the truth of the report, and openly declared that the Christians were basely attempting to undermine their respective creeds.

The Mohammedans especially were loud in their cries of religious hatred, and clamoured for revenge, which nothing but the lives of all the hated English in the country, they declared, could satisfy. Thus in a wrangle over forbidden meats arose the awful Sepoy Mutiny which deluged the fair land of India with the blood of Christians, Hindoos, and Mohammedans!

Another forbidden thing, on which Mohammed laid great stress in his teaching, was usury, or exorbitant interest, in the business affairs of life. The Prophet advocated fair trading and honest gains, deprecating all endeavours to obtain riches by taking advantage of the pressing needs of our fellow-creatures.

I do not know that any code of laws contains a more striking denunciation of usurers than the Koran. In the second sura it is written: "They who devour usury shall not arise from the dead but as he ariseth whom Satan hath infected by a touch: this shall happen to them because they say, truly selling is but as usury; and yet God hath permitted selling and forbidden usury. He therefore who, when there cometh an admonition from his Lord, abstaineth from usury for the future, shall have what is past forgiven him, and his affair belongeth unto God. But whoso returneth to usury they shall be the companions of hell-fire, for they shall continue therein for ever."

Students of the Bible will call to mind the fact that usury was forbidden also to the Jews in the laws of Moses; but there was this great difference between the Moslems and the Jews—the latter were allowed to exact usury from those who were not of their faith, but the former were forbidden to take it from any man on the face of the earth.

The result has been that, at the present day, there are no such grasping usurers to be found anywhere as the Jews, while Moslems have in this matter a clean record and a good name. It is certainly to the credit of the followers of the Prophet, that while they are ever ready to bestow alms, they absolutely refuse to lend money or goods on usury.

Mohammedanism also entirely repudiates gambling, and speaks of it as a vice only indulged in by the very wicked.

In the 5th sura of the Koran it is written: "O, true believers, surely wine, and lots, and images, and divining arrows, are an abomination of the work of Satan, therefore avoid them." Moslem commentators agree that by "lots," the Prophet meant all games of chance, such as dice, cards, and gaming-tables. Sale says that these games "are reckoned so ill in themselves, that the testimony of him who plays at them is, by the more rigid, judged to be of no validity in a court of justice."

Chess is the only game that Mohammedans will play at, and some even consider this unlawful; but the less strict maintain that there can be nothing wrong or sinful in chess, for it is a game that depends wholly on skill and management, and not at all on chance. Even in chess, however, it is stipulated that no one must play for money or any other thing, and that no betting on results must be indulged in by on-lookers. "Mohammedans comply with the prohibition of gaming much better than they do with that of wine; for though the common people among the Turks more frequently, and the Persians more rarely, are addicted to play, yet the better sort are seldom guilty of it." In this respect Mohammedans compare very favourably with Christians, and with the adherents of Buddha and Confucius.

Strange to say, the simple and refreshing beverage called coffee is regarded by some Mohammedans as a forbidden or questionable thing. Sale says that "this drink, which was first publicly used at Aden in Arabia Felix, about the middle of the fourteenth century, and thence gradually introduced into Mecca, Medina, Egypt, Syria, and other parts of the Levant, has been the occasion of great disputes and disorders, having been publicly condemned and forbidden, and again declared lawful and allowed."

Wonderful treatises have been written on this subject, and many subtle arguments used to show that coffee comes under the same condemnation as wines and spirits, "because the fumes of it have some effect on the imagination." At the present day, all the same, coffee, and very strong coffee too, is used everywhere in the East in Moslem countries. And tea also, "the cup that cheers but not inebriates," is slowly winning its way into Moslem homes.

Who ever met a Mohammedan who did not smoke? and yet I suppose such a curiosity is to be found, for smoking is another questionable, if not forbidden, thing. It is asserted that Mohammed had a revelation vouchsafed to him of what should be in the days to come, and that he condemned in advance the modern practice of smoking. The tradition with regard to the Prophet, which, if it were true, would prove him to have been a Prophet indeed, runs, that he once said: "That in the latter days there would be men who would bear the name of Muslims, but would not really be such, and that they would smoke a certain weed which would be called tobacco."

This questionable or forbidden thing, however, is dearly loved by Mohammedans, and travellers in the East are always struck with the elaborate arrangements that are made for the comfort of those who would indulge in the weed. How picturesque are the pipes, called *nergilehs*, in the Turkish dominions, and the *hukkas* in our great Indian dependency! The Egyptians have a saying that "a dish of coffee and a pipe of tobacco are a complete entertainment;" and the Persians have a proverb to the effect that, "Coffee without tobacco is like meat without salt."

Another questionable thing is opium, which, though not mentioned in the Koran, is regarded by rigid Mussulmans as unlawful, because it has a tendency to intoxicate and disturb the understanding even in a more extraordinary way than wine. Those who partake of this drug very freely, and, alas! there are many that do so, are regarded as men of loose character, and are described by their countrymen as debauchees.

There are two approved ways of taking opium—the one is by eating, or rather swallowing, a number of small pills, and the other by smoking a certain quantity of the poison

U

in a semi-fluid form in a pipe of tobacco. And there is a difference between the opium eater and the opium smoker, for the former usually indulges in the weakness in the privacy of his own home, while the other has to frequent one of the all-too-numerous places of public resort called opium dens.

The taking of opium, whether by pill or pipe, is a habit which, when once formed, it is almost impossible to break off. I have heard of an old decrepit Moslem addicted to the vice who said: " It is useless trying to give up the custom. It cannot be done. I have smoked for over forty years. During that time it has been my master, and I its very humble and obedient slave."

A very small quantity of opium, which costs less than one halfpenny, is enough to intoxicate a strong man.

Opium is smoked thus: " The pipe commonly used consists of a straight piece of bamboo, about a foot in length, to which is attached a round hollow earthenware ball, pierced by a small hole at the side. In this hole a little of the semi-fluid is placed by an attendant. The smoker reclines near a dirty lamp, over the flame of which he holds the hole, and inhales the smoke by a rapid succession of seemingly painful inspirations. Not the least sign of smoke is seen till the opium is exhausted. Then the smoker stops and blows out a huge cloud from mouth and nostrils. More is quickly applied, and the smoking repeated till the small amount bought is exhausted. Intoxication ensues, and the miserable victim drops off into a heavy sleep, described as a succession of dreams, weird and foolish, which may or may not be pleasurable."

Just as intoxicating drinks have grown to be the curse of Western nations, so the intoxicating opium has become the curse of Eastern nations. Mohammedans are right in regarding opium as a questionable thing, and the pity is that they cannot agree in placing upon its use the ban of religious condemnation. It would be a great mercy for Moslems if opium eating and smoking became definitely and strictly " Forbidden things " of their faith or creed !

There are other matters which come under the heading of " Forbidden, or Questionable Things," but we need not linger over them as they are not of present-day interest.

It is enough to say that Mohammed condemned the old practice of divination by arrows or by any other method ; and also that he put a stop to that inhuman custom of burying their daughters alive, which once prevailed amongst the desert Arabs.

There cannot be a doubt that the Prophet showed wise statesmanship in many of his laws or rules of conduct, and Moslems would find it to their highest advantage if they gave diligent heed to the negative as well as positive precepts that are embodied in their Sacred Scriptures—the Koran.

CHAPTER XXX

THE CRUSADES

OUR studies in Mohammedanism would be incomplete if we did not touch, however briefly, on the great subject of the Crusades, by which, of course, is meant those military expeditions undertaken by Christian Powers in the eleventh, twelfth, and thirteenth centuries for the recovery of the Holy Land from the Mohammedans.

It was in the year 636 A.D. that Jerusalem was besieged and captured by the armies of Omar, the second Commander of the Faithful, and that Palestine passed completely under Moslem rule. To the credit of Omar it has to be said that he treated the Christians with consideration, and let them dwell in the land in safety on payment of tribute.

And under the Governments of all the early Caliphs the followers of Christ in Palestine, and more particularly in the Holy City, were granted full protection of their life, property, and even religion. But as the years passed by, and the country became a province of the Caliphate of Damascus, and then of the Caliphate of Bagdad, there arose princes and rulers who ignored the early treaties made with the Christians, and began to persecute all who named the name of Christ.

In Jerusalem the Moslems gradually usurped three-fourths of the city, and confined the Christian Patriarch with his clergy and people to a small area around the ancient Church of the Holy Sepulchre.

And as each year Christian pilgrims arrived at the Holy City from all parts of the West, as had been the custom for centuries, the Mohammedans threw every obstacle they could in the way of their visits to the sacred sites. Yet the crowd of pilgrims seemed to increase rather than decrease, for the persecution they met with from the Moslems only fanned their religious zeal ; and the more dangerous the pilgrimage became the more meritorious it was considered to be.

The object of such pilgrimages was chiefly to visit the spots hallowed by particular association with Christ, but a secondary aim was also to find relics. " If a pretended fragment of the Holy Cross was not to be met with, the pilgrims could at least bring away an olive branch, a phial of Jordan water, a garment dipped in the holy stream, and thereby rendered an invulnerable panoply against demons ; or sometimes he would content himself with a handful of earth picked up at Jerusalem, or a rose or a palm branch cut in the oasis of Jericho. And on his return home the pilgrim's staff was hung up over the hearth as a family relic."

Very popular, indeed, such pilgrimages became in the tenth and eleventh centuries; but the more determined the Christians of Europe were to keep up their old custom the more bitter waxed the enmity and opposition of the Mohammedans of Palestine and the neighbouring countries. And the chief cause of offence in the eyes of the Moslems was the belief of the Christians that in worshipping Christ they were worshipping God.

Gibbon, touching on this point, says : " Had the Christian pilgrims been content to revere the tomb of a prophet, the disciples of Mahomet, instead of blaming, would have imitated their piety ; but these rigid Unitarians were scandalized by a worship which represents the birth, death, and resurrection of a God : the Catholic images were branded with the name of idols : and the Moslems smiled with indignation at the miraculous flame which was kindled on the eve of Easter in the Church of the Holy Sepulchre."

In 969 A.D. Palestine passed for a time from the Abbasides of Bagdad to the Fatimites of Egypt. At first this change seemed beneficial, for the new rulers were liberal-minded men. However, early in the eleventh century the Caliph, known as Hakem the Mad, poured out the vials of religious fanaticism on Jerusalem, and the followers of Christ therein suffered terrible persecutions, and all pilgrimages to the city were interdicted. Hakem carried his insensate zeal so far as to order the destruction of the Church of the Resurrection, which was demolished to its foundations; and he even sought, but in vain, to destroy the natural cave in the rock, which properly constitutes the Holy Sepulchre.

When news of these sacrilegious acts reached Europe, Christian nations were astonished, afflicted, and enraged, and there were rumours of great armaments being prepared to avenge the insults to the tomb of Christ, and to the city which was the cradle of the Christian faith. But the matter was allowed to drop, though the set time for the Crusades was brought perceptibly nearer by the persecutions and unwise deeds of the Sultan Hakem.

At the death of the Mad Caliph the maxims of religious toleration once more prevailed, and the Christians of Jerusalem, aided by their co-religionists of other lands, rebuilt the Church of the Holy Sepulchre; and, "after a short abstinence, Christian pilgrims returned with an increase of appetite to the spiritual feast."

From 1076 to 1096 Palestine was in the possession of the Seljuk Turks of Damascus, and under these new masters the persecution of Christians was resumed, and became so bitter that life was a burden to the oppressed. But in the hour of despair relief came from an unexpected source.

About the year 1095 Jerusalem was visited by a pilgrim-hermit of the name of Peter, a native of Amiens in France.

This good man's sympathy was called out by the distresses he himself endured, and by the persecutions which he saw the inhabitants of Jerusalem were subjected to. He is said to have mingled his tears with those of the Patriarch, and earnestly inquired if no hope of relief could be entertained from the Greeks of Constantinople. When the Patriarch answered sadly, " No !" the bold and enthusiastic hermit exclaimed : " I will rouse the martial nations of Europe in your cause."

And Peter was as good as his word, for on his return home he sought at once an interview with the Pope, Urban the Second, and spoke so feelingly and earnestly of the sufferings of the Christians in Palestine, that the Pontiff adopted his views and commissioned him to preach throughout the West an armed confederation of Christians, for the deliverance of the Holy Land from the accursed sway of the Moslems.

Peter is described as of small stature, and of somewhat mean, if not contemptible, appearance, but "his eye was keen and lively, and he possessed that vehemence of speech which seldom fails to impart the persuasion of the soul." From city to city, from province to province, and from country to country, the hermit wandered, preaching a Crusade against the Mohammedans with all the enthusiasm of his marvellously ardent nature.

Milman says of him : "He rode on a mule with a crucifix in his hand, his head and feet bare, his dress was a long robe, girt with a cord, and a hermit's cloak of the coarsest stuff. He preached in the pulpits, on the roads, and in the market-places. His eloquence was that which stirs the heart of the people, for it came from his own heart. His preaching appealed to every passion—to valour and shame, to indignation and pity, to the pride of the warrior, to the compassion of the man, to the religion of the Christian, to the love of the brethren, to the hatred of the unbeliever, to reverence for the Redeemer and the saints, to the desire of expiating sin, and to the hope of eternal life."

And the results of Peter the Hermit's appeals were extraordinary. All France was stirred to its depths by his preaching, and the princes and people called loudly for the Pope to give the word for a march towards Jerusalem. Other countries were also deeply moved, and expressed their readiness to join in any expedition against the Moslems.

In 1095, at a council at Clermont, the First Crusade was decided upon, and the Pope himself delivered a stirring address to a vast audience of clergy and laymen, in which he spoke rapturously of the merit and glory of the deliverance of the Holy Land. As he proceeded, the pent-up emotions of the crowd burst forth, and cries of *Deus vult*, "God wills it," rose simultaneously from the whole audience. "It is indeed the will of God," replied the Pope, "and let these words, the inspiration purely of the Holy Spirit, be adopted as your cry of battle, to animate the devotion and courage of the champions of Christ— *Deus vult !*"

The recommendation of the Pope was readily and enthusiastically adopted, and *Deus vult* became the war cry of the Crusaders ; and every one, moreover, who took part in the Holy War wore as a badge on his breast or shoulder a red sign of the Cross—hence the name Crusade from the French *croisade*, and the Latin *crux*.

Directly it was known that Pope Urban had publicly sanctioned the enterprise, thousands upon thousands of enthusiasts from all parts of Europe flocked to the Holy Banner. That ancient chronicler, William of Malmesbury, says : "The most distant islands and savage countries were inspired with the ardent passion. The Welshman left his hunting, the Scotchman his fellowship with vermin, the Dane his drinking-party, and the Norwegian his raw fish." It is estimated, but doubtless with exaggeration, that in the spring of 1096 not less than six million souls were in motion towards Palestine.

We cannot linger over the stirring events that took place

by the way. The various armies, with one of which journeyed Peter the Hermit, went by land, *via* Constantinople. Many of the Crusaders were mere military adventurers, and others were the very scum of the countries from which they came, only a remnant being impelled forward by religious motives and genuine interest in the fate of Jerusalem and the Holy Land. It is, therefore, not surprising to find that the vast host fell to pieces as it moved forward, and that tens of thousands died from quarrels amongst themselves, and from strife with the people through whose territories they passed.

Thousands also fell in Asia Minor at the siege and capture of Nice, which was bravely defended by the Sultan Soliman. Thousands, moreover, perished at the siege of Antioch, in Syria, which held out against the Christians for seven months. Thus the ranks of the Crusaders were thinned, and when they at length reached the Holy Land, but a remnant, not more than 40,000 men, remained to wrest Jerusalem from the Moslems. And yet this small army of desperate warriors sufficed for the enterprise. The leaders of the Christian forces were Godfrey of Bouillon, Robert of Normandy, a son of William the Conqueror, Count Robert of Flanders, Tancred, the favourite hero of the Crusades, and Count Raymond of Toulouse.

It was on a bright summer morning in the year 1099 that the Christian forces obtained their first glimpse of Jerusalem, and, as may be imagined, the emotion was intense, and the scene sublime.

Tasso, in his " Jerusalem Delivered," thus describes the feelings of the Crusaders :—

> " With holy zeal their swelling breasts abound,
>   And their winged footsteps scarcely print the ground,
>   When now the sun ascends th' ethereal way,
>   And strikes the dusty field with warmer ray.
>   Behold Jerusalem in prospect lies !
>   Behold Jerusalem salutes their eyes !
>   At once a thousand tongues repeat the name,
>   All hail Jerusalem with loud acclaim.

At first transported with the pleasing sight,
Each Christian bosom glowed with full delight ;
But deep contrition soon their joys opprest,
And holy sorrow saddened every breast.
 Scarce dare their eyes the city walls survey,
 Where clothed in flesh their dear Redeemer lay ;
 Whose sacred earth did once their Lord enclose,
 And when triumphant from the grave He rose."

The thought that the Sacred City was in the hands of the sworn foes of Christianity, and had been for many a century, was a sore trouble to those zealous Crusaders, and they pressed the siege with all the enthusiasm of religious passion.

But the naturally strong place was courageously defended. The Fatimite Caliphs of Egypt had a trusty lieutenant named Aladin at the head of the Moslem garrison, which consisted of at least 40,000 Turks and Arabians, who fought like heroes. But Moslem valour on this occasion availed naught against the determined zeal of the Christian, and "on a Friday, the 15th July, 1099, at three in the afternoon, the day and hour of the Passion, Godfrey of Bouillon stood victorious on the walls of Jerusalem. His example was followed on every side, and about 460 years after the conquest of Omar the Holy City was rescued from the Moslem yoke."

And now was seen a remarkable display of the fiercest and most tender passions on the part of the victorious Crusaders.

They fairly wept for joy at the glorious success of their enterprise, and yet their hearts were filled with hatred towards the discomfited Mohammedans. The city, sad to say, was given up to pillage, for the Christians in the hour of their triumph forgot the Christian grace of mercy, and thought of nothing but revenge, and spared neither age nor sex. About 70,000 Moslems were put to the sword, and for three days a promiscuous massacre was indulged in throughout the whole extent of the Holy City.

Even the wretched inhabitants who took refuge in the Mosque of Omar and claimed the sanctuary of a sacred

place, were slain in cold blood. The victors are said to
have boasted that "in the great Mosque whither they
pursued the fugitives they rode up to the knees of their
horses in the blood of Saracens."

Then the fierce mood of the Christians changed—the
lions became as lambs, and they meekly took part in a
thanksgiving service in the Church of the Holy Sepulchre.
" Bareheaded and bare foot, with contrite hearts and in a
humble posture, they ascended the hill of Calvary, amidst
the loud anthems of the clergy : kissed the stone which
had covered the Saviour of the world ; and bedewed with
tears of joy and penitence the monument of their redemption."

Jerusalem, thus conquered by Christians, was retained by
them for more than half a century. Godfrey of Bouillon
was chosen as the first King, and in his short reign of a
single year he added the whole of Palestine to his crown,
and ruled a kingdom as large, but not as thickly populated,
as that once possessed by David, King of Israel, or Solomon
his son.

When in 1100 Godfrey died, his body was interred near
where his Saviour was crucified, and I think one of the
most interesting things that is pointed out to pilgrims to
Jerusalem at the present day is the spot where that noble
Christian hero was buried.

Godfrey was succeeded by the two Baldwins, his brother
and cousin, and they in their turn were succeeded by
Malisenda, the daughter of the second Baldwin. Days of
weakness for the Christian State now set in, of which the
Mohammedans of the neighbouring countries were not slow
to take advantage.

A famous Moslem warrior, named Saladin, was the leader
of the revolt against the Christian power. This prince, the
chief of a Kurdish tribe, was declared ruler of Egypt on
the fall of the Fatimites, and he soon gathered round him
an army of Moslems eager to win back Palestine, and
especially Jerusalem, to the religion of Islam. Saladin is

described as a brave, a wise, and a chivalrous prince.
Though possessed of enormous wealth he spent little on
himself, but gave with lavish generosity the most costly
gifts to those who deserved his favour. "The garment of
Saladin was a coarse woollen; water was his only drink.
Both in faith and practice he was a rigid Mussulman.
He ever deplored that the defence of religion had not
allowed him to accomplish the pilgrimage to Mecca;
but at the stated hours, five times each day, he devoutly
prayed with his brethren: and his perusal of the Koran
on horseback between approaching armies may be
quoted as a proof, however ostentatious, of piety and
courage."

And perhaps more remarkable still in an Eastern
monarch, it is recorded that "the justice of his divan was
accessible to the meanest suppliant against himself and his
ministers: and it was only for a kingdom that Saladin
would deviate from the rule of equity."

Such was the Moslem Sultan who turned his arms
against the Christian kingdom of Jerusalem. He invaded
Palestine, took town after town, and finally, in October,
1187, compelled the Holy City to capitulate, after a siege
of fourteen days. Happily, the Christians, though not
strong enough to retain Jerusalem, were able to secure for
themselves terms of capitulation by which the lives of all
the inhabitants were spared.

The terms were these: The Greek and Oriental Christians were permitted to remain, and live under Moslem
rule; but within forty days all the Franks and Latins
were commanded to depart to the seaports of Syria and
Egypt. Also it was arranged that of those who remained,
ten pieces of gold should be paid for each man, five for
each woman, and one for each child as a ransom, and
if any were not able thus to purchase their freedom, their
doom was to be perpetual slavery.

When the news of these reverses to the Christian arms in
Palestine reached Europe, fresh Crusades were organized,

for the enthusiasm of Western nations on behalf of the Holy Land yet glowed with a fervent heat.

The Second Crusade, however, was practically a failure, and so was the Third, though it was made famous by the fact that three great kings took part in it, viz., Frederick I., Emperor of Germany, Philippe Auguste, King of France, and Richard Cœur de Lion, King of England. Richard performed prodigies of valour, and earned the respect and admiration of Saladin and the Moslems. Gibbon says that "at the distance of sixty years, the memory of the lion-hearted prince was celebrated in the East by proverbial sayings amongst the grandsons of the Turks and Saracens, against whom he had fought; his tremendous name was employed even by Syrian mothers to silence their infants; and if a horse suddenly started from the way, his rider was wont to exclaim, 'Dost thou think Richard is in that bush?'"

The Crusaders under such renowned leadership reached Bethlehem, and captured it; but then, instead of advancing to Jerusalem, they retreated towards Jaffa, partly owing to dissensions in their own ranks, and partly to the strength of the forces of Saladin, which made the siege of the Holy City seem an almost hopeless enterprise. Yet, if the rest would have essayed the task, the gallant Richard would have ventured on the perilous enterprise. Indeed, so grieved was he of the lion-heart with what he considered the cowardice of his fellow-Crusaders, that he is said to have ascended a hill from which Jerusalem could be seen, but instead of looking at it he covered his face with his hands, and exclaimed through his tears, "O Lord God, we are not worthy to behold Thy Holy City, seeing that we are either unwilling or unable to rescue it from the hands of Thy enemies." .

It was in October, 1192, that Richard turned his back on Palestine, and set sail for Europe.

There were in all seven great Crusades, but only the First Crusade effected anything proportionate to the outlay of money and the immense sacrifice of human life. The last six were merely records of failure upon failure, for the Moslems held tenaciously to the Holy Land, and if partly despoiled of it for a time, they soon returned with recruited forces and revived fanaticism to reconquer it.

It is worthy of notice that Edward the First of England was the last of the Crusaders, and when he left Palestine, towards the end of the thirteenth century, the hopes of the Christians had reached the lowest ebb, and they gradually lost all their possessions in the East. " In 1291 Acre capitulated to the Mohammedans, other towns quickly followed, and the Templars and military knights were glad to quit the country, and disperse themselves over Europe in quest of new employment, leaving Palestine in the undisturbed possession of the Saracens."

And at the present day the Holy Land is in the hands of the Moslems. Palestine is under Turkish rule, and is governed by Pashas. Jerusalem is under the Pashalic of Damascus.

It has to be said, however, that there is now little or no persecution of Christians in the Holy Land, for religious liberty is granted to the adherents of all creeds. The Jews have their synagogues, the Christians their churches, and the Moslems their mosques. When in Jerusalem, I was much struck with this fact of religious toleration, and though I am not an admirer of Turkish rule anywhere, I would give credit where it is due. I think it every way likely, moreover, that as long as the followers of Mohammed have the wisdom to refrain from persecuting the followers of Christ, they will be allowed by Western nations to retain possession of the home of the Christian faith.

Crusades are not a feature of the nineteenth century; but though we Christians have now no ambition to organize military expeditions for the conquest of Palestine, yet the land is dear to us as a place of pilgrimage, and our feelings of reverence and enthusiasm for the sacred sites are as deep as ever were the feelings of the most vehement Crusaders.

Yes ! with Shakespeare we can speak with love of

> " Those holy fields,
> Over whose acres walked those blessed feet
> Which fourteen hundred years ago were nailed,
> For our advantage, on the bitter cross."

CHAPTER XXXI

FAKIR is derived from the Arabic word *fakhar*, which means "poor," and Fakirs are to India what Dervishes are to Arabia, Egypt, Persia, and Turkey. Fakirs are an order of religious mendicants who take upon themselves vows of poverty which cut them off from the cares of the world, and enable them, as they think, to give themselves entirely to contemplation of the Deity.

Whatever was the origin of the Orders of the Dervishes amongst the Arabians, there can be little doubt that the Mussulmans of India got their ideas of Fakirism from the Hindoos.

For almost countless ages vows of poverty have been taken in India, and Orders of religious penitents have been known to exist in the land. The fact is that the climate of India, a country of flowers, fruits and sunshine, is conducive to meditation, and seems to call to seclusion, if not to a life of idleness. And tens of thousands of the people of Hindustan have given way to the seductions of the climate, and have sought in a hermit's cell to pass a life of quiet and ease.

The Mohammedans, when they conquered India, seem to have been strangely drawn towards the devotees who dwelt in the land, and who were known as Saints or Sanyassis. The intense religious feeling of the Moslems saw in such hermit life a fitting way to express their zeal for holy things; and, with enthusiasm, numbers of them speedily imitated the example of their Hindoo neighbours, and filled the country with hermitages.

With the Moslems came in the new name Fakir, which now prevails in the East to characterize the religious mendicants of every sect and creed. To the Mohammedans is largely due also, I think, the excessive rigour which many Fakirs have shown in the observance of their vows of poverty. Abstinence was encouraged to degenerate into mortification and self-torture, and the belief became general amongst the Fakirs that the more painful their deeds of asceticism were, the better pleased God would be with them.

These fanatics took to living in holes, and caves, and dens of the earth, and under banian-trees in the neighbourhood of mosques, practising their penances and mortifications, sometimes openly, but usually in the loneliness of their hidden retreats. The nature of the vows that the more extreme among the Fakirs take may be understood if we bear in mind that some have been known to remain for life in one position, others have been seen dragging heavy chains or cannon balls, or crawling upon their hands and knees for years; others have been found lying upon iron spikes for a bed, and others have been known to swing for months before a slow fire with an Indian sun blazing overhead.

Nor do these horrible torments satisfy the unnatural Eastern taste for asceticism, for the brotherhood is constantly on the look-out for some new method of self-torture. Elphinstone, in his "History of Cabul," tells with dry humour a tale of Haji Mecan, one of the most famous Fakirs of Peshwar, who sent a special messenger to Kabul, begging the English resident to let him know as a favour what severities were practised by Saints in Europe.

The messenger was a Persian of the Shia sect, and as the Fakir was a devotee of the Suni persuasion, the servant was only too delighted with his errand. Elphinstone says:

"Accordingly, when I told him that our clergy performed no austerities, but thought they recommended themselves to God by leading a virtuous and religious life, he begged me not to disappoint the holy man, his master, but to favour him with a few penances in which he might indulge his zeal. I then replied that there were other parts of Europe where the devout exposed themselves to great sufferings, and I mentioned all I could remember of hair-shirts and flagellation. The Persian thanked me with a mischievous smile, and said he was sure the Haji, his master, would be sensibly obliged to me, and took his leave, evidently pleased with the amusement he had procured for his employer."

Fakirs may be divided into certain classes, and at the head I would place those who may with truth be described as men of *saintly character*. I have met a few, and I believe there are many such in India. Their ethical code consists in love for God and man, and in the observance of truth, chastity, and inward purity of thought.

Mrs. Meer Hassan Ali, in her book on the "Mussulmans of India," mentions one saintly Fakir called Shah Jee, who lived at Delhi. This man, it seems, spent the principal part of each day in silent prayer and meditation, when no one ever ventured to intrude within his small sanctuary, though hundreds would assemble outside the building to wait for the appearance of the Saint, whose habit it was to appear publicly for an hour or so, and speak gracious words to all who would listen. When the time drew near for this good man to die, it is said that he foretold the event by twenty days, and speaking to his wife and children about it, he urged them to be resigned to the will of God, and not unduly mourn his loss.

As may be supposed, however, the sorrowful family greatly bemoaned the coming event, for the Fakir had ever been kind, affectionate, and even indulgent in his domestic life. To such an extreme did his relatives carry their grief that the holy man was displeased with them, and gently

upbraided them with their folly, and when they would not
modulate their bewailings, he is said to have remarked:
"Well, well, my dear wife and children, since you cannot
live without me, I will offer my prayers to the gracious
Giver of all good that He may be pleased to permit you all
to bear me company in death."

But that was not what the sorrowful relations desired, so
they hushed their grief and allowed the old man to die
in peace. The parting words of the Saint were: "This
life hath no joys to be compared with those which the
righteous man's hopes lead him to expect in the world
beyond the grave. Farewell! until we meet again in a
blessed eternity."

Some Fakirs have not only displayed great holiness, but
have shown great wisdom, and have been the revered guides
of princes and monarchs. One of the most famous of
these *wise Fakirs* was Shah-ood-Dowlah, who lived in the
reign of Shah Jahan, and whose tomb is worshipped by
the Faithful even at the present day.

This Fakir's fame was great in the land before he met the
Moghul Emperor, and the latter had often wished to see
the wise man, and converse with him. At length the event
came to pass quite unexpectedly. As the King was seated
one day on the roof of his palace at Agra, with some of
his most eminent courtiers, one of them suddenly exclaimed:
"See, there, just before us in the open plain, is Shah-ood-
Dowlah, the famous Fakir!" The monarch ordered that
the Saint should be hailed and invited into the Presence.

The Fakir answered the call readily, and expressed his
willingness to meet the King. Whereupon a basket was
let down from the roof by a strong rope, and the Saint on
entering it was speedily drawn to the top. Shah Jahan
received the Holy Man most graciously. "Pray be
seated, my friend," he said, leading his visitor to the most
honoured part of the royal carpet.

The Fakir, to the astonishment of the assembled courtiers,
obeyed without a moment's hesitation. Then Shah Jahan

remarked : " I have long desired this happiness, that I might converse with thee, for I have heard much of thy great virtue and good life from my subjects." The Saint modestly replied : " They do but flatter me, O King, for none can tell what passes in my heart when they view only my face. I am but a poor and sinful Fakir."

Next the King said : " Thou art reputed wise, Shah-ood-Dowlah—wise as well as good. Wilt thou answer me a question ? " " Willingly, if I can, O Protector of the World," was the response. " Then tell me this : How is it that God hath so enlightened thee, and that thou livest so near to Him ? "

The Holy Man, smiling, said : " Listen, your Majesty, to what I have to say. Thou thyself wast desirous of becoming known to me, one of the humblest of thy subjects. The opportunity arrived, and thou didst condescend to let down a rope to assist me into thy presence. With equal condescension thou hast seated me by thy side. These things I could not have won by right; they are all of grace. So it is with God ! Allah draws those whom He will unto Himself. He sees into the hidden recesses of the human heart, and knows every working of mortal minds, and He is all-powerful, so that He can draw to Himself with the cords of love our heart, and soul, and mind, with infinitely less effort than thou hast exerted to draw my mortal body within thy palace. It is God who in mercy throws the line to man ; happy that soul who accepts the offered means by which he may ascend. For my part, I have done nothing but respond to the calls of Allah, and He has filled me with His spirit, which some call the spirit of wisdom."

Shah Jahan was delighted with the beautiful answer of the Fakir, and from that day forward they were firm friends and true, and the influence of the aged Saint over the King was ever on the side of justice, truth, and mercy.

The Emperor Akbar, however, was not as fortunate as Shah Jahan in his relationship with Fakirs, for though he received many favours from these holy men, they usually ended by treating him churlishly. Loneliness, it is known, does not tend to sweeten the temper, and when austerities are added to loneliness we cannot wonder that some Fakirs have developed a very *churlish disposition.*

History tells us that Akbar the Great, in the early days of his glorious reign, was greatly troubled because the sons and daughters born to him all died in infancy. At length some one suggested for the Royal comfort that perchance a pilgrimage to the shrine of the holiest Fakir in India, who resided in Ajmere, might win the favour of Heaven. It has always been an article of faith amongst Moslems that the prayers of Saints ensure the birth of healthy and strong children. Akbar closed readily with the suggestion, and set off with his favourite wife on the long journey.

" It was a journey of more than three hundred miles, and it was necessary to perform it on foot. Yet must the Begum be shielded from the too curious gaze of chance passers-by. So long screens of cloth were stretched on either side of the carpeted road, which was made ready for the Imperial pilgrims in stages of six miles, at each of which they halted for the night, and these spots were thenceforward marked by the building of high towers."

On their arrival at Ajmere, however, the most holy Saint bade them retrace their steps to a place called Sikri, where lived another Fakir named Sheikh Salim ; and it was intimated that the latter would plead the cause of the King with Allah. Akbar piously complied with the directions given him, and at length stood in the presence of Salim, who promised him all that his heart desired. "Accordingly the Begum took up her abode in a humble dwelling near the Fakirs, and in due time she became the mother of the future Emperor Jahangir."

Let the rest be told in the words of C. F. Gordon Cumming, who refers to the incident in her charming book " In the Himalayas and on the Indian Plains " :—

" 'The grateful Akbar took up his abode permanently

within reach of the counsels of the all-prevailing Saint. So at Sikri he built a beautiful palace, and all his courtiers, his Prime Minister, and other great men, likewise built themselves houses and palaces. They made gardens and wells, the hill was crowned with a lovely white marble mosque, and its rocky sides were laid out in terraces. In the plain below a great artificial lake was formed, twenty miles in circumference, and the beautiful new city, which covered a circle of six miles in diameter, was fortified with strong ramparts and battlements. But, alas! all the fuss and bustle attendant on this busy court life disturbed the devotions of the hermit, who at last could bear it no longer, and sending for the Emperor, informed him that one of them must forthwith depart. Akbar was grieved for the fate of his fair new city, but his duty was clear. The aged Saint must be left to pray in peace, so court and courtiers, great and small, departed straightway to the banks of the Jumna, and there built that glorious city of Akbarabad, the modern Agra."

At the present day the deserted city of Fatehpur Sikri is one of the sights which all visitors to Northern India should see : and there, in the centre of the great cloistered quadrangle, stands as beautiful a tomb as ever Eastern taste devised, which is sacred to the memory of the churlish Fakir, Sheikh Salim, who gave an Emperor to the world and ruined a city.

From churlish to *vengeful Fakirs* is but a step. And I am afraid there are many such in India. Tales are being constantly told of the spitefulness and savagery of men who professedly are holy and saintly. It is a common thing for Fakirs of the baser sort, when they are refused alms, to curse those who refuse them, and to imprecate the vengeance of Heaven upon such. The people of India stand in mortal dread of many of their most famous saints, and by timely gifts seek to propitiate them, and thus avert misfortune or disaster.

One of the most remarkable cases of vengeance on record

is that of the Fakir who compassed the capture of Suraj-ood-Dowlah, the Nabob of Moorshedabad, when he was fleeing from the English who had defeated his army on the field of Plassey. Suraj-ood-Dowlah had not only incurred the enmity of the British by the awful tragedy of the Black Hole at Calcutta, but he had disgusted many of his own subjects by his savage manners and cruel deeds. The Fakirs of Bengal especially were incensed against him because he had brutally treated one of the fraternity by cutting off his ears.

When the Nabob in his flight from Moorshedabad towards Patna became oppressed one night with hunger, and landed from his boat opposite Rajmahal, and took shelter in the hut of a poor Fakir, he little thought that in the strange irony of fate he had entered the abode of the very man whom thirteen months before he had maltreated and spurned from his presence. Yet so it was! The Fakir, who had been brooding over his wrongs, at once recognized his oppressor notwithstanding his disguise. Then hospitality and vengeance strove for the mastery in the breast of the Saint. Mercy and hate struggled hard the one with the other for power, and hate conquered.

The spirit of the Fakir was simply wild for vengeance, and though he pretended to receive the fallen Monarch hospitably he sent off a friend privately to Moorshedabad to reveal the fugitive's hiding-place, and before the night wore out Suraj-ood-Dowlah was a prisoner, and ere many more nights had passed the deposed Nabob was numbered with the dead, stabbed to the heart by the son of Meer Jaffer, his successor. Thus did a poor Fakir compass his vengeance on a powerful foe! And the deed increased the fear, if not the respect, of the Moslems of India for the brotherhood of the so-called Saints.

It seems a paradox to speak of *wealthy Fakirs*, and yet it is a fact that many of these holy men have amassed considerable fortunes by fair means or by foul. And numbers who do not become wealthy yet gather together a competency, and are enabled to indulge in all kinds of riotous living.   Clever rogues soon found out that Fakirism might be made to pay financially.   One writer says : " The halo which from the first surrounded Fakirism, and the ready worship offered by the people, attracted to its ranks at a very early date many whose motives were anything but pure, and who under a garb of humility and mendicity collected fabulous treasures."

Even in recent years instances have been known of Fakirs greedily gathering together that wealth which they profess to despise and renounce.   Mrs. Meer Hassan Ali tells a curious story of a holy brother whom she knew well.   When the last King of Oude but one, she says, was a young man and not on the throne, he met outside the city of Lucknow a Fakir clothed in rags, who spoke to him and predicted a great future for him.   The Prince, greatly pleased, promised the holy man, if his predictions came true, that he would reward him in any way he wished.

Years passed by and the Fakir wandered in foreign parts, but at length he turned his face once more towards Lucknow, and found, as he had predicted, that the Prince had become King of Oude.   The Saint lost no time in making himself known to his Majesty, and in claiming his promised reward.   The King was glad to see him, and granted his request for five cowries daily from every shop-keeper in the city of Lucknow.   His Majesty, moreover, gave him a good house to reside in, and an elephant on which he might ride to collect his revenue.

Five cowrie shells make only one-seventeenth part of a pice or half-penny, and yet the Fakir knew what he was doing when he made his request, for he was aware of the large population of Lucknow; and it is said that he was for the rest of his life in receipt of a very handsome daily allowance from the inhabitants of the capital of Oude. For many years the strange sight was witnessed every morning in Lucknow of a Saint riding on an elephant to gather in his riches, which he spent every evening in anything but a saintly manner. At the present time there are, it is estimated, in India over a million Fakirs, tens of thousands of whom live a roving life in companies, and the appearance of the roving fraternity is usually disgusting in the extreme. "Some bedeck themselves with the skins of serpents, some with human bones, while others array themselves in the garb of women. Their fearful shrieks, and the hideous rolling of their eyes, add to the disgust of their appearance. Imitating madmen, they generally end by becoming madmen."

Bishop Heber in his Diary mentions meeting mad Fakirs on more than one occasion. Let me give an interesting extract. Writing on July 23, 1824, from his boat, in the vicinity of Dacca, the good Bishop says : " In the course of our halt this morning a singular and painfully interesting character presented himself in the person of a Mussulman Fakir, a very elegantly-formed and handsome young man of good manners, but with insanity strongly stamped in his eye and forehead. He was very nearly naked, had a white handkerchief tied as an ornament round his left arm, a bright yellow rag hanging loosely over the other, a little cornelian ornament set in silver round his neck, a large chaplet of black beads, and a little wooden cup in his hand. He asked my leave to sit down on the bank to watch what we were doing, and said it gave his heart pleasure to see Englishmen, that he himself was a great traveller, had been in Bombay and Cabul, and wanted to see all the world, wherein he was bound to wander as long as it lasted. I offered him alms, but he refused, saying he never took money—that he had had his meal that day, and wanted nothing. He sat talking wildly with the servants a little longer, when I again asked if I could do anything for him. He jumped up, laughed, and said ' No pice ! ' Then he made a low obeisance, and ran off singing. His manner and appearance nearly answered to the idea of the Arab Mejnoun when he ran wild for Leila."

In drawing this description of Fakirs to a close I cannot

but reflect that they are, as a community, a strange mixture
of wisdom and folly, of goodness and evil.   But the evil
preponderates over the good, and the folly over the wisdom.
The Fakirs of India indeed are a standing menace to the
peace and prosperity of the land.

In the past the British Government has had on occasion
to seek to put them down with a strong hand, and such a
course will probably have to be adopted again and again.
What with Hindoo and Moslem Fakirs, it is estimated that
a force of three millions has to be reckoned with.   That
country is to be pitied that has within its borders such a
large army of lazy, good-for-nothing, fanatical people, living
solely on charity, and very often on the fat of the land !

And yet certain Western enthusiasts, who know not what
they say, advise Missionaries going out to labour in the
East to become Christian Fakirs.   It cannot be !

CHAPTER XXXII

BARBARY is an extensive region of Northern Africa comprising the countries known as "Barca, Tripoli Proper, Fezzan, Tunis, Algeria, Morocco, together with the half-independent province of Sus. It stretches from Egypt to the Atlantic Ocean, and from the Mediterranean to the Deserts of Sahara." Geographers tell us that Barbary is not specially African in its characteristics, but in climate, flora, fauna, and geographical configuration, belongs to that great region which forms the basin of the Mediterranean. However, the people of the land are distinctly Eastern in their appearance, habits, and customs.

As early as the year 647 Barbary was overrun by the Arabs, and in less than a century the greater part of the Native tribes were forcibly converted to the faith of Islam, and ever since they have remained faithful followers of the Prophet Mohammed. Arabic is the general language of commerce and intercourse, and the population at the present day of the whole country is estimated at about eleven millions.

The history of Barbary from the seventh century to the seventeenth had nothing in it of special interest for the world, though the country was the scene of many wars and dynastic changes, which affected both Egypt and Spain. However, at the close of the sixteenth century, there occurred an event, viz., the expulsion of the Moors from Spain by Ferdinand and Isabella, which wrought a marvellous

change in the history of Barbary, and directed towards the
land the eyes of all European nations.

If the Christians of Spain had acted wisely in the day of
victory, they would have granted the Moors, who were
skilful artisans and agriculturists, permission to stay in the
country, and have given them freedom of religious worship.
But the intense bigotry of their Catholic Majesties could
not bear the thought of permitting even a single Moslem to
live in Spain, so on the fall of Granada the Mohammedans
who were not slain were ignominiously driven forth to find
a home where best they could. It is stated that no less than
three millions of Moors were banished between the fall of
Granada and the first decade of the seventeenth century.

And many of those exiles sought refuge with their co-
religionists on the coasts of Barbary, and there, not being
wanted to till the ground, they determined to "plow the
sea," and to turn their daring and energies towards the
harassment and spoliation of their enemies and persecutors,
the Spaniards. Thus arose the powerful communities of
Moslem pirates at Tunis, Morocco, and especially Algiers,
which came to be designated the Barbary Corsairs, and which
for nearly three centuries were the scourge of Europe.

Mohammedans, as a rule, have a very strong aversion to
the sea. The early Arabs knew nothing of it except by
repute, and from all they heard they regarded it as a terrible
monster which loved to destroy human life. It is related
of the Caliph Omar that on the conquest of Egypt he wrote
from Medina to his General Amr, at Alexandria, requesting
him to give a description of the ocean. Amr wrote briefly
but forcibly, saying : "The sea is a huge beast which silly
folk ride like worms on logs." Thereupon the Caliph,
greatly impressed, and confirmed in his objections to a sea-
faring life, issued a decree forbidding all Moslems to
voyage on the great deep without the special sanction of
the Commander of the Faithful.

Subsequent Caliphs, however, revoked that decree, and
the Omiades of Damascus, wise in their generation, directed

their lieutenants on the shores of Egypt and Barbary to endeavour as far as possible to compete with other nations on the sea as well as on land. Tunis was the first city to become a Moslem seaport. There the Arabs formed an arsenal and dockyard and began to collect a fleet. The work was carried on, however, very half-heartedly, for the Mohammedans could not bring themselves for generations to like the sea, and it became a common saying amongst them : "Allah has not given us command over the ocean."

The advent of the Moors on the Barbary coast in the seventeenth century wrought a change, at any rate for a season, and seemed to promise fair to turn Moslems into sailors. The new-comers were men of surpassing bravery, and were filled with a fierce hatred against the Spaniards, and as the only way to cause the latter to feel the weight of their hate seemed to be to attack them on the sea, to the sea, then, they determined to go.

The Moors established their headquarters at Algiers, a town so far almost unknown, and gathering kindred spirits around them from the tribes of Barbary, they built little brigantines, and ere long sallied forth to try their strength with their foes, whose big ships offered grand prizes to the reckless and daring. Stanley Lane-Poole, writing of these things, says : "What joy more fierce and jubilant than to run the light brigantine down the beach of Algiers, and man her for a cruise in Spanish waters. Drawing little water, a small squadron of brigantines could be pushed up almost any creek, or lie hidden behind a rock till a galleon hove in sight. Then oars out, and a quick stroke for a few minutes, and they are alongside their unsuspecting prey, and pouring in their first volley. Then a scrambling on board, a hand-to-hand scuffle, a last desperate resistance on the poop under the captain's canopy, and the prize is taken, the prisoners ironed, a jury crew sent on board, and all return in triumph to Algiers, where they are received with acclamations."

Thus for a time the Moorish pirates carried everything

before them, and grew rich, and their strong places on the Barbary coast became populous and well garrisoned. At last, however, the Spaniards roused themselves in earnest, and Cardinal Ximenes despatched a small fleet to bring the Corsairs to book. The pirates fought well and bravely, but their old enemies were too strong for them, and succeeded in crippling their power, though not in utterly destroying them. The Algerines were compelled to promise to give up piracy, and to see that they kept their promise, the Spaniards built and garrisoned a fort at the entrance to Algiers to prevent the Moorish brigantines from sallying forth.

The Corsairs were not long silenced, for relief came to them from an unexpected source. In the Levant there lived a Turkish sea-captain called Uruj, who afterwards was named Barbarossa because of his red beard. This man, having heard rumours of the successes of the Moorish pirates, and the rich treasures they had gathered by their capture of Spanish galleons, resolved that he also would turn Corsair, and win for himself riches and renown. So with a crew of bold comrades he left the Levant in search of adventures.

Barbarossa's vessel was a stout galleon of eighteen banks of oars, and the first enterprise in which he engaged was off the Island of Elba against two vessels belonging to his Holiness Pope Julius the Second, richly laden with goods from Genoa and bound for Civita Vecchia. These two galleons represented four times the strength of Barbarossa's one ship, yet the latter forced them to strike their colours, and sailed away with them as prizes to Tunis. We are told that never was such a sight seen there before, and the name of Barbarossa at once became famous throughout the East and the West as a most valiant, enterprising, and successful Commander.

From Tunis the daring Commander sailed for Algiers to free his co-religionists from the power of the Spaniards. He had now a force of sixteen galleons and six thousand

men, and with this army he wrought wonders. The
Spaniards were defeated, Algiers was taken, even the Moors
were subjugated, and Barbarossa captured stronghold after
stronghold both on the coast and inland, until the whole of
what was called Middle Barbary was at his feet, and his
dominions coincided with modern Algeria. Thus was
Barbary retained as the stronghold of pirates, whose depredations on the sea were more numerous and disastrous than
ever.

Barbarossa was the very *beau idéal* of a Corsair, bold,
daring, venturesome, profusely liberal, and never so happy
as when engaged in hand-to-hand contests with the enemies
of his faith. Morgan says of him : " He was highly beloved,
feared, and respected by his soldiers and domestics, and
when dead, was by them all most bitterly regretted and
lamented. He left neither son nor daughter. He resided
in Barbary fourteen years, during which the harm he did to
Christians is inexpressible."

At the death of Barbarossa, in 1518, his brother, Khyr-
ed-din, a man of equal bravery, and of greater prudence
and statesmanlike intelligence, succeeded him. His position seemed very insecure, for the Spaniards were pressing
the Corsairs hard, and hoped to destroy their power now
the great Barbarossa was dead. The new ruler proved
himself equal to the emergency, however, by sending an
Ambassador to Selim, the Sultan of Constantinople, begging
his Majesty's favour and protection.

The reply was gracious. Selim had just conquered
Egypt, and was glad to add Barbary, if only nominally, to
the Turkish crown. The Corsair was assured of the speedy
succour of 2,000 Janissaries, he was appointed Governor-
General of Algeria, and invested with the Turkish insignia
of office, viz., the horse and scimitar and horse-tail banner.

Thus strengthened, Barbarossa the Second was able to
drive off his Spanish assailants, to subdue all internal rebellion, and to strengthen his garrisons along the coast.
Then, like his brother, he devoted himself to "a life on the

ocean wave," and spent his days in scouring the seas in
search of prey of every land and nation. "The season for
cruising began in May and lasted till the autumn storms
warned vessels to keep the harbours, or at least to attempt
no distant expeditions. During the summer months the
Algerian galleons infested every part of the Western Mediterranean. Nothing was safe from their attacks : not a vessel
ran the gauntlet of the Barbary coast in her passage from
Spain to Italy without many a heart quaking within her.
The Scourge of Christendom had begun, which was to keep
all the nations of Europe in perpetual alarm for three
centuries. The Algerian Corsairs were masters of the sea,
and they made their mastery felt by all who dared to cross
their path."

The success of the Pirates was truly astonishing. Everything they took in hand seemed to prosper. "The fleet of
Barbarossa the Second increased month by month, till he
had thirty-six of his own galleons perpetually on the cruise
in the summer season : his prizes were innumerable, and
his forces were increased by the fighting men of the seventy
thousand Moriscos whom he rescued in a series of voyages
from servitude in Spain. The waste places of Africa were
peopled with the industrious agriculturists and artisans
whom the Spanish Government knew not how to employ.
The foundries and dockyards of Algiers teemed with busy
workmen. Seven thousand Christian slaves laboured at
the defensive works and the harbour, and every attempt to
rescue them and destroy the pirates was repelled with
disastrous loss."

In 1535 Barbarossa was tempted away from Algiers by
the Sultan of Constantinople, who offered the renowned
Corsair the post of High Admiral of the Ottoman Empire.
The Turks were desirous of founding a naval power, and
they rightly judged that no one was so well fitted to foster,
encourage, and strengthen the sea-faring spirit in Mohammedans as the brave Algerian captain, who was called by
friends and foes alike "the Chief of the Sea."

The withdrawal of Barbarossa was almost the destruction of Algiers, for the Spaniards, ever on the watch to find an opportunity to subjugate their inveterate enemies, thought their hour had come. The Emperor, Charles V., invincible on land, resolved to add to his triumphs by utterly destroying the nest of pirates who had so long ruled on the sea off the coasts of Spain. In 1541 an immense flotilla or armada started for Algiers, and it was expected that the Corsair city, without the great Corsair in it, would capitulate at the mere sight of such an overwhelming force.

But the Spaniards reckoned without their host. Though Barbarossa was gone, he had left behind him gallant sea-captains, named Dragut, Reis, and Sinan, who had scarcely ever known defeat, and who were ready to meet any odds. The odds in this case were enormously heavy, for on October 19, 1541, "over five hundred sail, manned by twelve thousand men, and carrying a land force of twenty-four thousand soldiers, entered the roads of Algiers."

The city, which stands on a rocky promontory, was strongly built, and was surrounded by a high wall with many towers, but the garrison consisted only of a force of eight hundred Turks, and perhaps five thousand Arabs and Moors, so that, humanly speaking, its fate seemed sealed. However, the forces of Nature came to the rescue. No sooner had the Emperor Charles landed his troops than the rains descended and the winds blew and beat upon his army, till the wretched soldiers were ready to drop with exhaustion and misery.

Then the Corsairs sallied forth, and caused immense destruction amongst the invaders. A lull in the storm gave the Spaniards hope, but on the 25th a very hurricane sprang up, and the cause was lost. The flotilla in the bay was at the mercy of the winds and waves. "Anchors and cables were powerless to hold the crowded jostling ships. One after the other they broke loose and keeled over to the tempest till their decks were drowned in the seas. Planks gaped ; broadside to broadside the helpless hulks crashed

Y

together.   Many of the crews threw themselves madly on
shore.   In six hours one hundred and fifty ships sank.
The rowers of the galleys, worn out with toiling at the oar,
at last succumbed, and fifteen of the vessels ran on shore,
only to be received by the Berbers of the hills, who ran
their spears through the miserable shipwrecked sailors as
soon as they gained the land."

The next day the storm cleared off, but it had done its
work, for the Spanish army was thoroughly demoralized,
and even the determined Charles saw the necessity for
retreat.   So the camp was struck, and the dejected army
started on foot for the Bay of Temandefust, where the
remains of the fleet were lying at anchor.   The Corsairs
hovered on the flanks of the retreating enemy, and cut
off thousands by the sword.   Only a remnant reached
the ships, and when the thoroughly cowed Spaniards
sailed away, it is said that the great Emperor, who
would fain have held Europe in the palm of his hand,
sadly took the crown from off his head, and casting it into
the sea, said : " Go, bauble, let some more fortunate prince
redeem and wear thee."

It was a most famous victory for the Corsairs.   So great
were the spoils taken that even the poor people of
Algiers became rich, and so many were the captives that it
was a common saying, that "a Christian slave was scarcely
a fair barter for an onion."   Thus the Barbary Corsairs
waxed stronger and more defiant.

For generations this state of things continued, and even
after the age of the great Corsairs had passed, petty pirates
reigned in Tunis, Tripoli, Morocco, and Algiers, to the
disgrace of Christendom, for certainly in the eighteenth
century any one of the Christian kingdoms could have
burnt out the hornets' nests if there had been a free hand
allowed by the other kingdoms.   However, an insane
jealousy of each other kept all from acting, and thus the
pirates were left to carry on their unlawful trade with impunity.   Fridays and Sundays were the favourite days for

the sailing of the Corsair vessels, which set forth to the sound of guns. "God speed us!" shouted the crews. "God send you rich prizes!" replied the crowds on the shore.

The ships of all nations were attacked, and there were in the prisons of Algiers thousands of captives—English, French, Spanish, Dutch, Italian, and Portuguese. Speaking of the English, Stanley Lane-Poole says: "Four hundred British ships were taken by the pirates in three or four years before 1622. Petitions went up to the Houses of Parliament from the ruined merchants of the great ports of England. Touching letters arrived from the poor captives, seamen and captains, or plain merchants. In the fourth decade of the seventeenth century there were three thousand husbands and fathers and brothers in Algerine prisons, and it was no wonder that the wives and daughters thronged the approaches to the House of Commons and besieged the members with their prayers and sobs."

But little was done, however, until the nineteenth century, to stop the iniquity, and the United States of America can claim the honour of striking the first blow, which was virtually the stroke of doom to the Barbary Corsairs. The Americans refused to pay tribute to the Rovers, that tribute which all other nations had basely and meanly paid for permission for their vessels to pass the coasts of Barbary in safety. The tribute had never been very efficacious, for the pirates evaded its terms whenever they pleased. The Americans, however, declared that whether efficacious or not they would not pay it, and if the Corsairs attacked any of their ships they would do it at their peril. And that the United States meant what they said was made abundantly clear when, on an insult to their flag, they attacked Tripoli, and in June, 1805, obtained from the Corsairs a treaty by which American vessels should be for ever free from the depredations of the Rovers.

The English, shamed by the success of the Americans, sought to cripple the power of the Algerines, and in 1827 actually bombarded their capital, destroyed their fleet, and forced them to terms. All slaves were set at liberty, and good behaviour was promised for the future. By these reprisals the Dey of Algiers was humbled and weakened, though only for a time. In a few years the scourge began again, and it became abundantly evident that nothing but downright conquest would stop it.

In 1830 the French Government took the Pirates in hand, and they did their work thoroughly. A fleet sailed for Algiers, the French landed in strong force, and though the Corsairs fought game to the last, they were overpowered and utterly defeated. In July, 1830, the Dey, with his family and attendants and belongings, sailed for Naples in a French frigate, and Algiers had seen the last of its Mohammedan rulers.

And with the destruction of the Moslem power at Algiers, and the substitution of a Christian power in its place, the reign of the Barbary Corsairs was ended. Tunis now also is practically under French control. Of the Barbary States Morocco alone remains purely Mohammedan in its government. This century has seen a great change for the better along the African coast. The wonder is that the Christian States of Europe endured so long the dreadful curse of piracy at their very doors ! It is marvellous in how many ways the followers of Mohammed have been the scourge of Christendom ! Happily on the sea the Moslem supremacy has been utterly destroyed by the fall of the Barbary Corsairs.

CHAPTER XXXIII

LITERATURE

AMONGST the Mohammedans there has been from the earliest days considerable literary culture. Even before the time of Mohammed the Arabs were noted for the composition of simple and natural poetry which celebrated the feuds of tribes and sang the praises of heroes and fair women. Some of the works of those early poets have of late years been translated and published in Europe, and critics declare that "they are remarkable for their pathos, soaring conceptions, richness of imagery and phraseology, free and unconstrained spirit, and the glow of their love and hate."

Mohammedanism, which owes so much to its founder, owes this also to the Prophet, that he, by his marvellous work, the Koran, introduced a new style in literature, and gave an impetus to the study of noble thoughts and sublime truths.

All scholars agree in stating that the Koran is a marvellous literary production, and I must say from my own diligent study of it, of late years, that I have been astonished at its wealth of diction, and the majestic swing of the sentences, which, apart from the teaching, carry one away with admiration of the talents of the Prophet. Sale, in his "Preliminary Discourse," speaking on this subject, says: "The Koran is universally allowed to be written with the utmost elegance and purity of language, in the dialect of the tribe of Quraish, the most noble and polite of all the Arabians, but with some mixture, though very rarely, of other dialects.

It is confessedly the standard of the Arabic tongue." And there can be no doubt that the noble diction and transcendental teaching of the Koran have had untold influence over subsequent literary efforts in all Moslem countries.

In the days immediately succeeding the demise of the great Prophet, wars and rumours of wars interfered with the widespread cultivation of Belles-Lettres, but the desire to study and compose was strong in many minds, and of Ali, the son-in-law of Mohammed, we read that he was the first Caliph to protect and encourage national literature. This Prince was a scholar himself, and many of his wise maxims and shrewd proverbs have been preserved and published in a book called "The Sentences of Ali." It is a remarkable work, and deserves to be more widely known and read in the West. Let me give a few quotations, which are chosen very much at random :—

"Opportunity is swift of flight, slow of return."
"Your victory over your enemy is your forbearance."
"Despair is a freeman, hope is a slave."
"A wise enemy is better than a foolish friend."
"Thankfulness engenders increase."
"Life is the shadow of a cloud—the dream of a sleeper."
"A man's behaviour is the index of the man : and his discourse is the index of his understanding."

It was only when the Mohammedan world passed under the rule of the Abbasides of Bagdad, A.D. 750, that literature, arts, and sciences were sedulously fostered and cultivated on a wide and generous scale, and that, properly speaking, the Moslem age of learning, which endured for five hundred years, set in. The Omiades of Damascus during the previous century had not been unmindful of the claims of learning, but they had encouraged chiefly the study and interpretation of the Koran, and confined their flights of poetic eloquence to religious subjects. With the Abbasides it was different, however. While not neglecting the study of the Perspicuous Book, they had regard to other books, and read widely of the literature of the Latins, the Syrians, the Persians, and the Greeks.

Writers of power and merit now sprang up on every side, and Moslems of many lands wrote works dealing with geography, history, philosophy, medicine, physics, and mathematics. Learned men were invited from many countries, and remunerated for their labours with princely munificence. It is related of the Caliph Al-Mamun, who reigned from 813 to 833, that he offered to the Greek Emperor five tons of gold and a perpetual treaty of peace if he would permit Leo the Philosopher, who afterwards became Bishop of Thessalonica, to proceed to Bagdad for a season to give instruction in the Moslem schools and colleges : and when the Emperor refused, Mamun declared war against him, but did not in the end succeed in gaining possession of the Philosopher. However, the incident showed the zeal of the Caliph for knowledge, from whatever source it might come. The same Commander of the Faithful once placed a Christian at the head of a Moslem college in Damascus, and when expostulated with on the strange act, answered: " I chose this learned man not as my guide in religious affairs, but as my teacher in science."

Harun-al-Rashid, the greatest of the Abbaside Caliphs, also was a patron of learning, as well as being himself a diligent student and fine scholar. The name of this prince suggests a reference to that wonderful storehouse of Eastern literature—the " Arabian Nights Entertainment." The Caliph Harun figures prominently in some of the tales, as also do his Prime Ministers—the famous but unfortunate Barmecides, who encouraged men of learning to make their homes at Bagdad.

Few books have been translated into so many languages, or have exerted so great an influence over literature in all parts of the world, as the " Arabian Nights." When the tales were written, or by whom, no one knows, though they are undoubtedly of Saracenic origin. As one writer has said : " Here are found depicted with much simplicity and great effect the scenes of the town-life of the Moslem ; the prowess of the Arab Knight, his passion for adventure, his dexterity, his love and his revenge, the craft of his wives, the hypocrisy of his priests, and the corruptibility of his judges, are all dramatically delineated—far more vividly represented, in fact, than is possible in a book of travels ; while gilded palaces, charming women, lovely gardens, and exquisite repasts captivate the senses of the reader and transport him to the land of wonder and enjoyment.   And besides entertaining the mind with the kaleidoscopic wonders of a teeming and luxurious fancy, which is their most obvious merit, they present a treasure store of instruction upon life in general, and Oriental life in particular."

As examples of the poetry or rhyme which prevailed in the days of the Abbasides, I would quote from three poets.   The first quotation is in rebuke of Harun-al-Rashid, who, it is said, was ever fond of going on pilgrimage to Mecca, but not always of acting as a devout Moslem. On the occasion of one of his pilgrimages a poet addressed to him these outspoken words :—

> " Religious gems can ne'er adorn
>   The flimsy robe by pleasure worn ;
>   Its feeble texture soon would tear,
>   And give those jewels to the air.
>
> Thrice happy those who seek the abode
>   Of peace and pleasure in their God ;
>   Who spurn the world, its joys despise,
>   And grasp at bliss beyond the skies."

The second quotation is an epigram which was addressed by a poet to the somewhat cruel Persian General Tahir, who was ambidextrous and blind of one eye.   Tahir was at the time, the year 812, in Bagdad.   A poet, struck with the General's peculiarities of body and mind, sent to him the following rather sarcastic message :—

> " A pair of right hands and a single dim eye,
>   Must form not a man, but a monster, they cry ;
>   Change a hand to an eye, good Tahir, if you can,
>   And a monster, perhaps, may be changed to a man."

The third quotation is a short poem composed by the Caliph Radi, one of the last of the Abbasides. This ruler, though young, had known much trouble and sorrow, and he expressed his somewhat morbid sentiments with regard to human life in the following not unpleasing lines :—

> " Mortal joys, however pure,
>   Soon their turbid source betray ;
>   Mortal bliss, however sure,
>   Soon must totter and decay.
>
>   Ye who now with footsteps keen
>   Range through hope's delusive field,
>   Tell us what the smiling scene
>   To your ardent grasp can yield.
>
>   Other youths have oft before
>   Dreamed their joys would never fade,
>   Till themselves were seen no more—
>   Swept into oblivion's shade.
>
>   Who with health and pleasure gay,
>   E'er his fragile state could know,
>   Were not age and pain to say—
>   Man is but the child of woe."

The Fatimites of Egypt and the Moors of Spain vied with the Abbasides of Bagdad in the pursuit of learning. They founded grand colleges, and collected vast libraries in the interests of education. Gibbon speaks even of a private professor who refused the invitation of a Sultan of Bokhara to proceed to his court because the carriage of his books would have required four hundred camels.

It is estimated that "the royal library of the Fatimites consisted of one hundred thousand manuscripts elegantly transcribed and splendidly bound, which were lent without jealousy or avarice to the students of Cairo." And at Cordova, in Spain, it is said the Moors had formed a library of six hundred thousand volumes, forty-four of which were employed in the mere catalogue.

The monarch in Spain who was most famous for his encouragement of learning was Hakam the Second, who reigned towards the close of the tenth century. This monarch was called the bookworm on account of his insatiable appetite for gathering together vast quantities of literature. Stanley Lane-Poole, in his work on the " Moors in Spain," says that " Hakam had agents in all parts of the East to buy rare manuscripts and bring them back to Cordova. His representatives were constantly searching the booksellers' shops at Cairo, Damascus, and Bagdad, for rare volumes for the Sultan's library. When the book was not to be bought at any price, he would have it copied, and sometimes he would even hear of a book which was only in the author's brain, and would send him a handsome present, and beg him to send the first copy to Cordova."

It seems also that Hakam was not merely a collector but a reader of books, and was accustomed to annotate them as he proceeded. "So learned was he, that his marginal notes were greatly prized by scholars of after times, and the destruction of a great part of his library by the Berbers was a serious loss to Arab literature." Spain in the Middle Ages was for some generations the centre of European culture, and students journeyed thither from all parts of Europe to study under the Moslem doctors in all the branches of the arts and science, and especially in botany, architecture, astronomy, and medicine.

If from Spain we journey in thought to Persia we find the same interest taken by Mohammedans in the cultivation of literature. In the eleventh century Mahmud of Ghazni was famous not only for his exploits as a warrior but for his true and deep sympathy with authors in their literary efforts. His capital was the great rendezvous of scholars from all parts of Asia, and the sum of £9,000 sterling was annually voted from the civil list for the encouragement of poets and men of letters.

The greatest epic poet of Persia was Firdausi, and his master work was the composition of a history of the Persian kings in verse, which labour of love occupied him during thirty years. This famous "Book of Kings" contains 60,000 double lines. One writer says of it: "Without going so far as many critics have gone, we may fairly rank it among the greatest epics of all nations—the Iliad, the Mahâbhârata, the Nibelungen. Truth and fiction, history and fairy lore, all the most gorgeous imagery of the East and its quaintest conceits, together with the homeliest and most touching descriptions of human joy and sorrow, of valour and of love, the poet has formed into one glowing song."

For this wonderful literary effort Mahmud from the first promised the poet that when it was completed he would give him a gold dirhem for every line in it. However, when the hour arrived for payment, the Sultan, whose love for the poet had been undermined by jealous enemies, only sent 60,000 dirhems of silver instead of gold. Firdausi was at a public bath when the messenger arrived with the money, and so angry was he with the conduct of the Sultan, that he refused to accept the dirhems for his own use, but divided them into three portions, and gave them away, one portion to the messenger, another to the bath keeper, and the third to a man who had brought him a glass of sherbet.

Then the poor poet, whose brain was turned with disappointment and rage, penned a most bitter satire on his royal master, which he forwarded to him by a favourite slave, with the sarcastic message that the King should read it in an hour of despondency. Mahmud was greatly incensed, and if Firdausi had not fled to Bagdad and sought the protection of the Abbasides, it would have fared ill with him.

As it was, the poet was a proscribed man, and went daily in fear of his life, for the hatred of the Sultan followed him even in exile. At length, however, after thirteen years of enmity, the feelings of Mahmud were softened towards his illustrious subject, and he repented of the way he had treated him, and sent a caravan loaded with the costliest goods to Shedab, where the poet was residing in great poverty, entreating forgiveness and reconciliation. Such overtures arrived too late, however, for, sad to say, as the Sultan's messengers entered one gate of the city, the poet's bier was carried out to its last resting-place at the other. Thus lived and died the renowned Moslem, Firdausi, one of the greatest geniuses of the world, and one of the most unfortunate.

In Persia, more than in any other Mohammedan country, we find that literature was fostered and encouraged, and in the twelfth, thirteenth, and fourteenth centuries there appeared a galaxy of famous authors. Firdausi but led the way, and after him came Anwari, the satirist, Nizami, the founder of the romantic school, and Jami, Attar, and Rumi, all mystics. The Sufistic or mystic poetry of Persia was greatly enjoyed by the Faithful, for it represented in glowing songs of love and wine the mystery of Divine love, and the union of the human soul with God.

In 1291 died Sadi of Shiraz, the unrivalled didactic poet of the East. The catalogue of this author's works comprises twenty-two different kinds of writings in Persian and Arabic. "The Gulistan; or, Rose Garden," is the most famous. It is a work in prose and verse, consisting of eight chapters on Kings, Dervishes, Contentment, Taciturnity, Love and Youth, Decrepitude and Old Age, Education, and the Duties of Society. It is a charming production, which one never tires of reading, and from which may be gathered much instruction and edification.

Everywhere in the East Sadi's memory is idolized, and his own countrymen say of him that he was "the most eloquent of writers, the wittiest author of either modern or ancient times, and one of the four monarchs of eloquence and style."

The last of the superlatively great writers of Persia was Hafiz, who was born at the beginning of the fourteenth century, and who lived to its close. His poetry was chiefly lyrical, and he sang of wine and love, of nightingales and flowers, and of things beautiful in every form. He occasionally also wrote in praise of Allah, and of

Mohammed the Prophet. Hafiz was a Dervish, but there was no hypocritical devoutness about him. He believed in enjoying to the full the good things of this world, so far as was consistent with purity and honour, and in some of his poems he speaks with withering contempt of professional piety, of mock humility, and of religious sanctimoniousness. The lyrics of Hafiz were of such exquisite sweetness, that he received the name of Shakkar-lab, or Sugarlip. This poet's works have been translated into many languages.

The other Moslem countries, viz., India, Afghanistan, and Turkey, have not produced writers of such eminence as those geniuses already mentioned, but, nevertheless, each has had its " men of light and leading " in the realm of literature. They have all, however, been greatly influenced by the master-minds of Persia, so that in Mohammedan countries generally we find a wonderful similarity in thought and style.

As a rule Europeans do not find the study of Mohammedan literature very attractive, for its prose, with but few exceptions, is bombastic, and its poetry bristles with verbal tricks and mannerisms that give a forced and unnatural air to the style. Then the subject-matter is often trivial, sometimes foolish, and not seldom inclined to wantonness. Moslem literature is also very wordy, and a great deal has to be waded through before much useful information can be gathered. Still, for my part, I hold that the best of the literature of the Mohammedans is well worthy of our serious study, and that the world owes a debt of gratitude to the followers of the Prophet who, at any rate, in a period of mental darkness in Europe, held up the torch of learning to humanity.

It was an Eastern writer, Abulferaj, who said, and with his words I would close this chapter : " They are the elect of God, His best and most useful servants, whose lives are devoted to the improvement of their rational faculties. The teachers of wisdom are the true luminaries and legislators of a world which, without their aid, would sink into ignorance and barbarism."

CHAPTER XXXIV

ARCHITECTURE

TRAVELLERS in Eastern lands cannot but have beheld with admiration the simplicity and beauty of Moslem architecture, which is in truth usually the most striking feature of an Eastern city.

I have used the phrase Moslem architecture advisedly, for it is a curious fact that architecture is usually moulded more by a religion than by a country. Whether we travel in Turkey, Arabia, Egypt, Syria, India, or indeed wherever Mohammedanism has spread, there we find evidences of an architecture not so much peculiar to the land as to the religion of which Mohammed was the Prophet. This architecture may in one country be called Arabian, in another Moorish, in another Saracenic, in another Moghul, but there is a general style about it which at once leads the traveller to say: "That is Moslem!"

The ancient Arabs had no architecture that was peculiarly their own, and it was only after Mohammed had founded his religion at Medina and Mecca that there began to appear in the East a style of architecture that won a place for itself as like and yet unlike what already existed. It may therefore be said with truth that Mohammedanism has made its mark in the world by its architecture as well as by its creed.

And this architectural growth was, strange to say, altogether undesigned and unconscious. Neither Mohammed nor his successors the Caliphs deliberately set themselves to found a school of religious art, but gradually, as the years came and went, the Moslem style became noticeable.

In the early days of the Faith the most unpretentious square or oblong buildings were erected in which to worship God, and the main object kept in view was size rather than shape. At Medina, where the first Mosque was erected by the Prophet himself, there stands now, it is true, a most beautiful structure, called Al-Haram, the Sacred, but it is of comparatively recent erection. The old Mosque was simple even to plainness.

Arthur Gilman, in his book on "The Saracens," referring to that first architectural essay of Mohammedanism, says: "One of the first duties of Mohammed was to begin the erection of a place of worship, and his plans were of the simplest nature. Trees were cut down at the place where his camel knelt for him to descend; walls of earth and brick were built; and trunks of palms were used to support a roof which was framed of their branches and thatched with their leaves. In this structure, which was of ample proportions to accommodate a good congregation, the Prophet was wont to preach, standing on the ground and supporting himself against one of the palm-trees, until, after a time, a pulpit was constructed for his use."

As the Moslems grew strong and wealthy, however, they desired more substantial religious edifices, and in some measure they copied the ecclesiastical buildings of their neighbours, the Christians. In the second century of the Hegira they even sent to Constantinople for Christian architects to help them in designing their Mosques, the result being that Moslem places of worship resembled Greek churches of the plainer type. It was then that the dome or cupola was introduced, which has since been a settled feature of Mosques.

Another feature, which indeed may be said to be strictly Eastern, is that of minarets. Here originality came in, and by minarets Moslem places of worship were at a stroke differentiated from all other sacred edifices. A minaret is a tall turret, and the conception of this turret was due to the custom which the Prophet introduced of calling the Faithful to prayers by the human voice, rather than by bells or any other musical instruments.

With Christians, bells doubtless led to the idea of towers, and with Moslems the call to prayers by the human voice led to minarets. It was necessary that the Muezzin, or Crier, should call from an exalted station, so that his voice might be heard far and wide over the city. And what more simple than to build him a tall turret on which to stand while performing his allotted task. Thus with the Moslems in this matter of minarets, necessity was the mother of invention.

A minaret contains a staircase, and is divided into several stories with balconies from which the Muezzin sends forth his pleasing call, and the structure is crowned with a spire or ornamental finial. A minaret may be part of a Mosque, or it may adjoin a Mosque, and there cannot be a doubt that it is one of the most beautiful features of Mohammedan architecture. Perhaps the most perfect specimens are to be found in Egypt. I remember, when in Cairo, marvelling greatly at the prodigious height and wonderful beauty of the elegant minarets that adorn the Mosques of that charming city.

In Northern India, at Delhi, there is to be seen a variety of the minaret which is not to be met with elsewhere. I refer to the famous Kutub Minar, which it was once my privilege to ascend. It is not exactly a minaret, that is to say, it is not now, if it ever was, connected with a Mosque, but it is a lofty turret or tower which is called a Minar. Until recently it was regarded as the highest tower in the world, but Mohammedans can no longer claim pre-eminence in that department of architecture. High buildings in Western lands are now the fashion, and the Kutub Minar has to take a second or third place for height, though it may still perhaps hold its own for beauty.

Sir Edwin Arnold, referring to this grand tower in his "India Revisited," says: "You arrive at last at the group of ancient buildings, in the midst of which the Kutub Minar lifts its lofty beauty to the sky, a pillar of fluted masonry, two hundred and forty feet high, embellished at each of its tapering stories with inscriptions in the Tughra character of Arabic, which is so ornamental. The second story of the marvellous pillar is completely belted with the ninety-nine beautiful names of Allah. The three lowest stories of this pillar of victory are made of warm red sandstone, the upper ones of white Ulwur marble. Sultan Altamsh completed it in 1230 A.D. No one can imagine the effect of this conical column, with its deep-cut flutings and diminishing cones, soaring, blood-colour and snow-white, into the blue—twice the height of the Duke of York's column, and adorned with flowing deep-cut Arab scripts, with sculptured lamps, bells, and bosses."

Truly the Kutub Minar is a fine memorial of Moslem architecture in the special and unique line of minarets !

The absence of all pictures, statues, and representations of living creatures in association with Mohammedan buildings is very noticeable. Christians have delighted in all manner of animal figures on the walls of their prominent buildings, and so have the Hindoos and the Bhuddists, but with the Mohammedans it has been different. The command of the Prophet that his followers were not to make unto themselves any graven image has led to exceeding great plainness on the walls of their mosques and palaces, and has indeed been an enemy to plastic art amongst the Moslems.

Yet when the Faithful began to take a true interest in architecture, their architects did what they could to attain elegance of form and harmony of colour without infringing the Prophet's commands or offending the religious scruples of the strictly orthodox, and with what result our great art critic Ruskin has well shown in his "Stones of Venice." Let me quote the passage. Mr. Ruskin says :—

z

" It was contrary to the religion of the Arab to introduce any animal form into his ornament, but although all the radiance of colour, all the refinements of proportion, and all the intricacies of geometrical design were open to him, he could not produce any noble work without an abstraction of the forms of leafage, to be used in his capitals, and made the ground plan of his chased ornaments. But I have already noted that colouring is an entirely distinct and independent art ; and in the 'seven lamps' we saw that this art had most power when practised in arrangements of simple geometrical form : the Arab therefore lay under no disadvantage in colouring, and he had all the noble elements of constructive and proportional beauty at his command : he might not imitate the sea-shell, but he could build the dome. The imitation of radiance by the variegated voussoir, the expression of the sweep of the desert by the barred red line upon the wall, the starred inshedding of light through his vaulted roof, and all the endless fantasy of abstract line, were still in the power of his ardent and fantastic spirit. Much he achieved, and yet in the effort of his overtaxed invention, restrained from its proper food, he made his architecture a glittering vacillation of undisciplined enchantment, and left the lustre of its edifices to wither like a startling dream, whose beauty we may indeed feel, and whose instruction we may receive, but must smile at its inconsistency, and mourn over its evanescence."

The " abstraction of the forms of leafage," mentioned by Mr. Ruskin, suggests a reference to what is known as Arabesque, or a peculiar kind of fantastic decoration in Moslem architecture. Forms of animals not being allowed by their creed, the Mohammedans had to fall back upon the imitation of vegetable productions, varied by geometrical patterns and inscriptions.

The result, though fantastic, was pleasing. In Cordova at the present day may be seen some exquisite specimens of Arabesque panelling, in which are most curiously and elaborately intertwined the foliage, flowers, fruit, and tendrils of plants and trees. It was a branch of architecture in which the Spanish Moors excelled, and which they are supposed to have introduced into modern Europe.

Another very marked characteristic of Moslem architecture is that of archways. The finest specimens that the world contains are indeed to be found in Mohammedan countries. There is the pointed arch, the trefoil, and the quatrefoil, and these styles, which are now common enough in Europe, originally came from the Arabs. The earliest example of the use of the pointed arch in Christian architecture belongs to the twelfth century; but Parker, in his "Glossary of Architecture," maintains that amongst the Mohammedans it was known as far back as 780 A.D. Then there is the horseshoe arch to be found to-day in the Moslem ruins of Spain, and also in the buildings of Morocco and Algiers. Judging by engravings I have seen of these arches, I consider them to be extremely beautiful, and yet, strange to say, it is a style of archway almost unknown in Christian lands.

What magnificent archways there are in India! For example, take the four which admit to the grounds in which stands, at Secundra, near Agra, the grand tomb of Akbar, the greatest of the Moghul Emperors. The principal gateway is built of red granite, and is inlaid with white marble. Even taken by itself it is worth a visit, and will repay most diligent study. Then at the entrance to the famous Taj Mahal, in Agra, there is another beautiful archway. But the grandest of all is to be found at Fatehpur Sikri, about ten miles away.

Fatehpur Sikri is the deserted city in which the aged Saint Salim lies buried, whose history has already been referred to in the chapter on Fakirs. Akbar built a chaste white marble tomb in memory of the Saint, which is to be found in a quadrangle some five hundred feet square, and surrounded by a wall. The entrance to the lovely tomb is through a colossal gateway, one hundred and twenty feet in height and the same in breadth. The span of the arch is forty feet broad by sixty feet high, and it is undoubtedly the most magnificent archway in the world. As Sleeman, in his " Rambles," says of it : " It is an archway under which ships might sail."

Bishop Heber, also, in his " Journal of Indian Travel," speaks rapturously of the noble archway, and referring to it in its choice surroundings, he writes : " The impression which the whole view produced on me will be appreciated when I say that there is no quadrangle either in Oxford or Cambridge fit to be compared with it, either in size, or majestic proportions, or beauty of architecture." A very interesting thing about the famous archway at Fatehpur Sikri is an inscription which has been found on it, one section of which has been translated as follows : " Said Jesus,* on whom be peace ! the world is a bridge, pass over it, but erect no building thereon : he who hopeth for an hour may hope for an eternity : the world is but an hour, spend it in devotion : the rest is unseen. Know that the world is a glass where the favour has come and is gone : take as thine own nothing more than what thou lookest upon."

Mohammedan architecture in association with tombs must not be overlooked, for over the bodies of saints, princes, and kings some very beautiful buildings have been erected. Saint Salim's tomb at Fatehpur Sikri is considered a choice specimen of Moslem skill and taste. Miss C. F. Gordon Cumming, referring to it in her book, " In the Himalayas and on the Indian Plains," says : " Over the dust of the Fakir stands as lovely a tomb as ever Eastern taste devised, a tomb of pure white marble, all inlaid with mother-of-pearl gleaming with iridescent rainbow hues. Rich hangings are there, and holy books, and the whole is enclosed by screens of white marble, latticed and carved like the finest lace."

[* Other authorities state that the word read Jesus (Christ) is really *Chisthi*, the name of the Fakir at Ajmere (*see* p. 309) who was the spiritual father of Saint Salim.]

Around innumerable tombs in India I have noticed exquisite marble trellis-work, and I regard it as one of the most beautiful features of Mohammedan architecture.

A fine specimen of early Moghul architecture is to be seen at Delhi in the tomb of Humayun, which is also the last resting-place of many kings, queens, and princesses. When the illustrious but unfortunate Humayun died, his faithful wife, Haji Begum, began the erection of a noble sepulchre to commemorate the name and fame of her husband. This tomb, which took sixteen years in building, was finished by Akbar, the son of Humayun.

It is a large square building with a dome, estimated to be three-fourths the size of that of St. Paul's, London. The termination of the dome is marked by a firmly-moulded cornice, which gives to it a bold and graceful curve. General Cunningham says that in the tomb of Humayun we first see towers attached to the four angles of a main building, and this innovation in Moslem architecture was gradually improved upon and developed until it culminated in the beautiful Minars which are the glory of the Taj ·Mahal at Agra.

The Taj Mahal is the queen of tombs. There is nothing like it indeed in the whole world. It stands in a garden, by which a river flows, and it is built of pure white marble inlaid with all manner of precious stones. How to describe this lovely square structure, with its grand central dome, its lofty and graceful minarets, its superb archways, and its exquisite inlaid work, I cannot tell. Fergusson, in his " History of Indian and Eastern Architecture," remarks : " No building in India has been so often drawn and photographed as this, or more frequently described, but with all this it is almost impossible to convey an idea of it to those who have not seen it, not only because of its extreme delicacy, and the beauty of the materials employed in its construction, but from the complexity of its design."

This tomb was built in memory of Mumtaz Zamani, the beloved wife of the Emperor Shah Jahan, and it is said

that twenty thousand men were employed upwards of seventeen years in its construction, and that it cost somewhere
about three millions of English money. The plinth of
the Taj is over one hundred yards each way, and it
lifts its golden pinnacle two hundred and forty-four
feet into the sky. There the lofty structure stands, in
its charming surroundings, a thing of beauty and a joy for
ever !

The Taj Mahal is one of those rare buildings of which
the visitor never speaks disparagingly, for he is never
disappointed in his expectations. Bishop Heber when he
saw the tomb frankly confessed that its beauty exceeded,
rather than fell short of, his dreams. Sir Edwin Arnold, in
his " India Revisited," remarks that it is impossible to judge
the peerless edifice dispassionately, for its loveliness fairly
carries the soul away in an ecstasy of delight. Sleeman, in
his " Rambles and Recollections," says : " I asked my wife
when she had gone over the building what she thought of
it." She answered : ' I cannot tell you what I think, for I
know not how to criticize such a building, but I can tell
you what I feel. I would die to-morrow to have such
another over me.' "

Thus all who have seen this wonderful tomb agree in
regarding it as a masterpiece of human ingenuity and skill.
It has been well said, and by a native of India too : " The
Taj is in architecture what the Venus de Medici is in
sculpture, or Shakespeare in poetry."

But turning from tombs to palaces, Mohammedans
have erected some magnificent buildings in Spain, Egypt,
and India, buildings which, though now chiefly in ruins,
are the wonder of the world. How famous the Moorish
architecture of Granada is ! The Alhambra, or Red Palace,
has been the favourite theme of art students and lovers of
the beautiful for centuries. That ancient palace of the
Moorish kings was begun in 1248 and finished in 1348.
The portions still standing are ranged round two oblong
courts, one called the Court of the Fish-pond, and the

other the Court of the Lions. They consist of porticoes, pillared halls, cool chambers, small gardens, fountains, and mosaic pavements. The lightness and elegance of the columns and arches, and the richness of the ornamentation, are unsurpassed. Charles the Fifth, as he looked upon the splendid architectural remains of Granada, said of the unfortunate Boabdil, the last of the Moors: "Ill-fated was the man who lost all this!"

The same might be said of the last of the Moghuls, as we gaze upon the splendid ruins of palaces in the grand old city of Delhi which the Moghul princes erected some three centuries ago. Dr. Hunter, in his "Imperial Gazetteer of India," says: "The great palace at Delhi, now the fort, covered a vast parallelogram 1,600 feet by 3,200, with exquisite and sumptuous buildings in marble and fine stone. A deeply-recessed portal leads into a vaulted hall rising two stories, like the nave of a gigantic Gothic cathedral, 375 feet in length, the noblest archway to any existing palace. The Diwan-i-Khas, or Court of Private Audience, overlooks the river, a masterpiece of delicate inlaid work and poetic design."

Nothing in Imperial Rome, Sir Edwin Arnold says, ever exceeded the magnificence of the Royal Palaces of Delhi. And even now in its ruins the architectural display of the famous city of the East will bear comparison with any city in the world. The proud boast which a Moslem architect engraved on one of the marble palaces of Delhi remains true to this day:—

"If on the earth there be a bower of bliss,
That place is this, is this, is this, is this!"

Thus we fitly bring our survey of Moslem architecture to a close. The Mohammedans have in the past shown great skill in all manner of architectural designs, and have erected some exquisite public buildings. To quote a famous saying of Bishop Heber: "They designed like Titans and finished like jewellers."

It is doubtless true, as Ruskin has said, that the style of architecture of the Moslems is evanescent, but no one can deny its beauty, and its general effect wherever it is found is to brighten all the surroundings, and to delight the eye of the beholder. For my part, I count Moslem architecture to be the glory of the East!

CHAPTER XXXV

ADMINISTRATION OF JUSTICE

MOHAMMEDANISM, it has to be borne in mind, is not only a system of belief, but a rule of practice : it not only gives to the Faithful a theological creed, but laws of jurisprudence. In a very literal and true sense, Church and State in Moslem countries are one and indivisible.

The Koran is the great authority, not merely as to what a man shall believe and what he shall do, but also as to what punishment in this world, as well as the next, shall follow unbelief and unworthy deeds. The administration of justice is, in fact, very much in the hands of the teachers and preachers of the Sacred Scriptures ; and at the present day in Constantinople the chief ecclesiastical functionary is the chief legal officer or magistrate.

At the commencement of Mohammedanism the Prophet himself was for some time the Judge of the people in the civil as well as religious affairs of their life; but, like the great Jewish legislator, Moses, he found the task too heavy for him, and at length appointed a number of officers who were Readers of the Law, chosen from his most devoted adherents, to assist him in his labours. Still, he reserved to himself the right of overruling the decisions of his subordinates, thus practically forming in his own person what we call a Court of Appeal.

The successors of Mohammed also for many generations exercised the power of Supreme Judge, and seemed to delight in the work thereby involved. One of the most

noted of these Caliph-judges was Omar, the Second Commander of the Faithful. The probity and justice of this
great prince were proverbial, and he laboured night and
day in the settlement of difficult cases.

It is related of Omar that he was the first judge to put
into use a scourge with twisted thongs for the correction of
minor offences, amongst which he included satire and
scandal. So potently was this new instrument of punishment applied that it speedily passed into a proverb throughout the Caliph's dominions : " Omar's twisted scourge is
more to be feared than his sword." The scourge is still
widely used in the East.

Another favourite Mohammedan instrument of punishment is the bastinado. This name is derived from the
French baston or bâton—a cudgel. The name was given
by Europeans to the Eastern custom of chastising offenders
by administering sharp blows with a stick, generally upon
the soles of the feet, but sometimes upon the back. The
bastinado is held in great and reverent awe by all Moslems,
who, on account of its efficacy in keeping the people in
order and within the bounds of duty, declare that it came
down from heaven, having been sent by Allah Himself.
The earliest mention of the bastinado I can find was in
the time of Omar, when its use was strongly recommended
by Ali, the son-in-law of Mohammed. Let me give the
incident. One day news reached the Caliph from the seat
of war, which was Damascus, that some of his soldiers,
carried away by the luxuries they found in Syria, were
beginning to indulge in the juice of the grape, like their
adversaries the Christians.

General Abu Obeidah, who sent the news, declared that
he was scandalized at the discovery, and sought the advice
of the Commander of the Faithful as to what he should do
to bring the offenders to their senses and stop the evil.
Omar, thus appealed to, called a Council of State, and the
matter was very gravely discussed in Medina as to what
should be done with those wine-bibbers at Damascus.

Ali at length raised his voice, and said : " Let the Commander of the Faithful and all the Council listen to me. Let him who breaks the Prophet's command and drinks wine receive twenty bastinadoes on the soles of his feet. I have spoken."

The Caliph promptly replied : "Thou hast well spoken, Ali, the Lion of God, and it shall be as thou hast said." Consequently a messenger was sent off post-haste to Damascus with the royal decision. The General in command thereupon summoned his troops to a public parade, had the offenders called out of the ranks, and saw the sentence carried out with the utmost rigour. Washington Irving, commenting on this strange incident, says : "Abu Obeidah, moreover, took the occasion to descant on the enormity of the offence, and to exhort such as had sinned in private to come forward like good Moslems, make public confession, and submit to the bastinado in token of repentance." It is recorded that many took the advice of the General, and had their consciences set at ease by a good drubbing on the feet.

Mohammedan judges pride themselves on being no respecters of persons, but as a matter of fact the claim will not hold good. The general consensus of opinion in the East, as well as in the West, is that in the administration of justice the Moslem cadis are freely open to bribes, and that the influence of wealth goes a very long way with them in deciding the merits of a case. Very often a poor man stands no chance of obtaining redress of grievances. Indeed the crying iniquity of the Turkish Administration for many centuries has been the general failure of justice. With the Turks, as with other Moslems, there has been too much of—

" They should take who have the power,
    And they should keep who can."

Yet, in simple fairness, it must be noted that from Moslem countries there have come some striking cases of impartial judgment which reflect great honour on the parties concerned.

For example, there is a story told of Omar's rigid determination to execute righteous judgment, no matter at what cost. The case was as follows: The Commander of the Faithful was on pilgrimage to Mecca, and had in his train one Jebalah, who was king of a neighbouring State that had given in its adhesion to the Caliphate. As Jebalah was performing the religious ceremony of walking seven times round the Kaaba, the skirt of his ihram, or pilgrim scarf, was accidentally trodden on by a poor Arab. Unfortunately the scarf was dragged off the king's shoulders, and he thereupon turned fiercely upon the Arab, and without listening to any explanation, buffeted him in the face, bruising him sorely, and beating out four of his teeth.

The ill-treated man at once went into the presence of Omar and besought justice from the Caliph on his princely assailant. The Commander of the Faithful called for Jebalah, and asked him whether the charge was true. " Perfectly true," was the bold answer ; "this rascal trod on my scarf and uncovered my back in the sacred house of God." " But it was an accident !" remarked Omar, sternly. " I care not," was the defiant answer ; "and had it not been for my reverence for the Kaaba and for the prohibition to shed blood within the sacred city, I would have slain the offender on the spot, instead of merely thrashing him."

These answers greatly displeased Omar, though he had a friendship for Jebalah and valued his powerful alliance. The Caliph thought for a moment, and then being determined to do right, he said : " Jebalah, thou hast confessed thy fault, and unless forgiven by thine adversary, thou must submit to the law of retaliation, and be beaten by him in return." The surprised prince answered proudly : " I am a king, and he is but a peasant ! " But Omar rejoined : " Ye are both Moslems, and in the sight of Allah, who is no respecter of persons, ye are equal." The utmost that Jebalah could obtain from the inflexible justice of Omar was that the execution of the sentence should stand over until the next day. When the morrow arrived, however, the king was not to be found, for he had made his escape during the night, and fled to Constantinople, where he abjured Mohammedanism and embraced Christianity. Thus Omar lost a powerful ally, but he preserved his integrity, and won an enduring name for executing righteous judgment.

Another very remarkable case of impartiality in the administration of justice is related of the renowned conqueror, Mahmud of Ghazni, who reigned in the eleventh century. On one occasion a poor subject appeared before him and complained bitterly of a certain prince or omrah, who disturbed the peace of his married life by visiting him in his home and turning him out into the street for the night. Having heard the story, Mahmud seemed greatly upset, but answered : "Suspend your clamours : inform me of the next visit of the omrah, and in my own person I will come and punish the offender."

Three days later the visit of the prince was repeated to the house of the poor man, whereupon the latter went in all haste for the king, who shortly arrived with the sword of justice in his hand. He at once ordered the lights to be put out, and then entering the house he slew the intruder with one stroke of his sword. Calling for the lights to be re-kindled, he looked eagerly on the face of the dead, then fell on his knees in prayer, and rising, demanded food, which, being placed before him, he devoured with the voraciousness of hunger.

The poor man, astonished at the actions of the king, ventured to beg an explanation, and the monarch replied : "I had reason to suspect that none, except one of my own sons, would have dared to perpetrate such an outrage as this, and I had the lights extinguished that my justice might be blind and inexorable. My prayer was a thanksgiving when I saw that the guilty man was not a son of mine. And as for my demand for bread, the truth is, so painful has been my anxiety during the past three days that not a morsel of food has crossed my lips since I saw you last."

That most famous Caliph, Harun-al-Rashid, of Bagdad, was also a just man. We read in the "Arabian Nights" how, many a time, he went about his capital in disguise, seeking adventures, and redressing grievances. History tells us a story of an interview he had with a poor woman, who complained that some of his soldiers had pillaged her house and laid waste her goods. The Caliph desired her to remember that the Perspicuous Book said that "When princes go forth to battle, the people through whose fields they pass must suffer." "True!" replied the woman, who showed an intimate acquaintance with the contents of the Koran, "but it is also written in the same Book that the habitations of those princes who authorize such injustice shall be made desolate." This bold and just reasoning had a powerful effect on the righteous Caliph, who commended the poor woman, and ordered immediate reparation to be made to her.

Many other stories of a similar character might be told of Caliphs and Cadis in Moslem countries who prided themselves on the purity of their administration of justice. However, it is to be feared that such noble instances were the exception and not the rule.

One great weakness of the administration of justice in Mohammedan countries is that there is no powerful public opinion to hold the judges in check, or to support their decisions. Uprightness in a Cadi is not so often extolled as cleverness or cunning, and as whatever is done is rarely questioned, the officers of the law are apt to become despotic, and they are nearly always erratic. It is almost impossible for the most observant onlooker to tell on what principle the Cadi decides his cases, whether on that of law, right, or expediency. A little irrelevant matter will often change the whole character of a trial, and lead to condemnation or acquittal according to the fancy of the judge.

And even after a sentence has been passed, it has often been known to be commuted for the most trifling reason. Take a case in point. It is recorded that in the time of Muawiya, the first of the Omiades of Damascus, a notorious robber and murderer was condemned to death by a Cadi after a long and careful trial. The shrewd rascal, however, appealed from the judge to the Caliph, who was a great lover of poetry, in a copy of verses in which he pleaded very pitiably that poverty and want had driven him to crime. Touched by the poetry, Muawiya, though he knew the robber was a reckless character and deserved to die, reversed the death-sentence, set the man at liberty, and gave him a purse of gold, that he might have no plea of necessity for repeating the crime. Poetry, not justice, carried the day in that case. Let us hope that the robber sinned no more.

There is one form of punishment amongst Mohammedans seldom resorted to, which is considered the most disgraceful and degrading of all punishments. It is that of depriving a man of his beard. Both by precept and example Mohammed, the Prophet of God, taught the Faithful the duty of cultivating a beard, and such importance did this matter assume, that hair on the chin came to be considered as one of the necessary passports of admittance into the Sacred House at Mecca.

It may be conceived, then, that to be deprived of this manly appendage was a loss and a disgrace indeed. A very prominent instance of such a dreadful punishment occurred under the short Caliphate of Ali. The enemies of Ali were many, and amongst the rest was Ayesha, the favourite wife of the dead Prophet. Though related by marriage to Ali, she yet hated him, and when Othman, the Governor of Bassora, one of the most devoted adherents of the Caliph, fell into the hands of Ayesha's party, the wrathful lady sought to vent her anger against Ali on the person of his faithful follower.

So she called the unfortunate Governor into her presence, and had him bastinadoed before her eyes, and then she commanded her attendants to pluck out his beard hair by hair. His eyebrows were served in the same fashion, and then he was contemptuously set at liberty. It is related that when Othman appeared before Ali he was so overcome with the humiliation of his disgrace that he burst into tears, and uttered the exceeding bitter cry : " Oh, Commander of the Faithful, when you sent me to Bassora I had a beard, but now, alas ! I have not a hair on my chin ! Woe is me ! woe is me !"

Generally speaking, the Koran is very stern in its punishment of evil-doers, and even for somewhat trivial offences it commands harsh measures. At first the Faithful rigidly carried out the extreme sentences of the law, but as the centuries passed by somewhat milder counsels prevailed, and the judges did not in all cases exact "an eye for an eye, or a tooth for a tooth." The letter of the law, I believe, at the present day in legal matters is not considered so much as the spirit of it.

Sale, in his " Preliminary Discourse," refers to this change in public feeling. He remarks : " Notwithstanding the Koran is by the Mohammedans in general regarded as the fundamental part of their civil law, and the decisions of the Sunnat among the Turks, and of the Imams among those of the Persian sect, are usually followed in judicial determinations, yet the secular tribunals do not think themselves bound to observe the same in all cases, but frequently give judgment against those decisions, which are not always consonant to equity and reason."

I think it will be found in practice that law-breakers amongst Mohammedans are not hardly dealt with in the legal sentences passed upon them, or in the carrying out of such sentences, I mean in cases where justice is attempted at all. Judgment may be uncertain, but the penalties are not usually severe, a good bastinadoing often taking the place of a long imprisonment, and in some cases of the death sentence itself. Moslem administration of justice, in short, seems more cruel than it really is !

For example, take the case of apostasy. It is not often that a Moslem renounces the faith of his fathers, but for all who do there is theoretically no hope of mercy in this world or the next. An apostate must die the death of a malefactor, if caught and brought to justice. In India under the English Government, however, the law is a dead letter. So it is in Turkey, for though the penalty is on the Statute Book, there has been a tacit understanding for the last forty years that it shall not be enforced.

There was a time, however, when apostates were shown little if any mercy. I have read of many a case of the death sentence being passed on those who had dared to leave Islamism and embrace Christianity. And even now the feeling on the matter is very strong, and some fanatical Moslems would fain see carried out against all faithless ones the extreme penalty of the law. A wholesome fear of outside Christian Governments, however, tends to keep zealots within bounds, and apostates at the present day are safe so far as their lives are concerned, though they have to submit to social disabilities and the petty persecutions of their kindred and neighbours.

In the Turkish dominions there are five orders of Judges or Doctors of the Law, and with a few words on their respective duties I shall close this chapter. The Sheykh-ul-Islam, or Elder of Islam, stands foremost. His power is very great, as he fills the post of Supreme Judge, which the Caliph himself used to hold as the successor of the Prophet. I have been told that no war can be begun, that no peace can be concluded, that no great public matter of any kind can be determined until the Sheykh-ul-Islam has been consulted and has pronounced the projected undertaking lawful according to the word of Allah as revealed in the Sacred Koran.

A A

Immediately under the Sheykh-ul-Islam are the Kazi-ul-Lasker, or Judges of the Army, whose duty it is to accompany the troops to war, and to settle disputes which may arise amongst the soldiers. One Judge is for Europe, and the other for Asia. Next comes the Istambol Kadisi, or judge of Constantinople, then the Magistrates of the two sacred cities of Mecca and Medina, and then the Judges of the most important cities of the Empire, such as Damascus, Jerusalem, and Cairo. All these belong to the first order of Doctors of the Law.

"The second order consists of the Moolahs, or Magistrates of certain other of the more important cities: the third of a number of officials termed Muftistees, or Inquisitors, whose duty it is to see that the legacies bequeathed to mosques and other religious or charitable institutions are properly administered. The fourth order is that of the Cadis or ordinary Judges of the less important towns: and the fifth and lowest, that of the Naibs or Judge-substitutes."

With all these officials justice ought to be properly administered amongst Moslems!

CHAPTER XXXVI

HOLY DAYS OR FESTIVALS

In all countries, and in connection with all religions, certain Feast Days or Weeks are kept. With Moslems this custom has not been as popular as with Christians, Jews, Hindoos, or Buddhists ; but yet there are a few Holy Days or Festivals of special importance to which reference might be made.

Perhaps the most prominent is the Feast of Sacrifice, which takes place on the tenth night of Dhu'l Hijjah, which is the last month of the Moslem year, and also the month of Pilgrimage. Not only at Mecca, but throughout the Mohammedan world the Feast is kept with great pomp and ceremony, and with the sacrifice of millions of animals.

The Moslem name for the Festival is Buckrah Eade, *i.e.*, Sacrifice Festival, and it had its origin in the well-known circumstance of Abraham offering up his son Isaac in sacrifice to God, only it should be carefully borne in mind that Mohammedans substitute Ishmael for Isaac. The incident is referred to in the 37th chapter of the Koran, where we read : " Abraham said unto his son, O my son, verily I saw in a dream that I should offer thee in sacrifice ; consider, therefore, what thou art of opinion I should do. He answered : O my father, do what thou art commanded : thou shalt find me, if God please, a patient person. And when they had submitted themselves to the Divine will, and Abraham had laid his son prostrate on his face, we cried unto him, O Abraham, now hast thou verified the vision. Thus do we reward the righteous. Verily this was a manifest trial. And we ransomed him with a noble victim. And we left the following salutation to be bestowed on him by the latest posterity, viz., Peace be on Abraham."

To commemorate the faith of Abraham, and the deliverance of Ishmael, the progenitor of the Arabs from death by the mercy of God, Mohammed arranged that the Faithful should keep a feast of sacrifice and thanksgiving on the tenth night of Dhu'l Hijjah, the day of "the ransom." And as Ishmael was ransomed by "a noble victim," it was decreed that wealthy Moslems should, on the anniversary of the event, sacrifice camels, while the poorer members of the community should offer up sheep or goats, or lambs, or kids. It was to be a general feast, and a time of great rejoicing, and it was to be observed throughout Islam for ever.

In some Mohammedan States at the present day Buckrah Eade is taken advantage of for a grand public display. Princes with their nobles and a great gathering of retainers, and sometimes even troops, go in state to the place of sacrifice, where the moolahs or priests read forms of prayers prepared for the occasion, and the throats of the animal victims are cut to the cry of "Peace be on Abraham, on Ishmael, and on their seed for ever and ever!"

This rather gruesome task of sacrifice having been performed, the people give themselves up to pleasure, and keep holy day with zeal and energy. Ladies dress in their most costly jewels and apparel to receive or to pay calls. Gentlemen have their sports, and regale themselves with the sight of an extra good Nautch dance. Little children have their games and amusements. The whole Moslem world seems bent on happiness, so much so that it is now a proverb in the East, "Every one must be cheerful on Buckrah Eade."

Nor are the poor or the unfortunate forgotten. Mrs. Meer Hasan Ali, of Lucknow, who witnessed many a magnificent celebration of the Festival in Oude, says that the most pleasing part of the day's proceedings always was the consideration that was paid to the indigent. She writes : " On Buckrah Eade the rich send presents of goats and sheep to their neighbours and to the poor, so that the meanest of the people are enabled to offer sacrifice, and rejoice in the good things of which they partake : new suits of clothes are also distributed to the dependants of the family and to the poor. In short, on this day there seems to be a spirit of benevolence abroad, which makes rejoicing doubly sweet."

Amongst Moslems Buckrah Eade is also called " the greater Bairám." The term Bairám is Turkish, and signifies a holy day or holiday. There is another feast of almost equal importance, which is characterized by the distinguishing title of " the lesser Bairám." This occurs at the close of the fast of Ramadan, and is sometimes called " the feast of breaking the fast." This feast was briefly referred to in the chapter on " Ramadan, or Lent," but I would now give fuller details. As may readily be imagined, after forty days of fasting, faithful Moslems stand in need of something to cheer their spirits and rouse hope in their hearts. The need has been met by the appointment of a few days' cessation from work, when the exhausted people may rest if they choose, or seek recuperation for the frame in recreation. The majority do the latter, and give themselves up with perfect abandon to merry-making, to secure amends, as it were, for the mortification of the previous month. In Constantinople, and other parts of Turkey, " the lesser Bairám lasts three days, but in Persia it is continued for five or six days, and kept with great demonstrations of public joy.

The first day of the breaking of the fast begins with an early morning breakfast, and in India in innumerable houses exactly the same kind of food is partaken of. It consists of plain boiled rice, with sour curd and sugar. As a dessert dried dates are eaten in remembrance of the Prophet's family, whose greatest luxury was supposed to be dates of Arabia. As the day proceeds greater luxuries are indulged in according to the taste or wealth of the individual or family.

Processions are also arranged to visit the mosques that thanks may be publicly given to Allah for preserving His faithful ones through the month of trial. The processions then march round the town or village to the accompaniment of music, and friends greet each other pleasantly, and everything is done to make the general holiday a most enjoyable one. " The ladies' assemblies on this Festival also are marked by all the amusements and indulgences they can possibly invent in their secluded state. The Zenana rings with festive songs and loud music, the happy meeting of friends, and the distribution of presents to domestics : all is life and joy, cheerful bustle, and delight."

Thus the season of " the lesser Bairám " passes ; and in feasting, music, dancing, and other enjoyments, the people of Islam seek to drown the memory of the previous miserable Ramadan days of aimless bodily self-denial.

Mohammedans keep New Year's Day as a holiday. In India it is called " Nau-Roze," and is a festival that is greatly appreciated by the children and ladies in the Zenana. One special feature about the day is a colour that is worn in the garments of the people, from the princes in their palaces to the meanest ryots in their huts. The colour varies according to the hour of the day or night when the Moslem New Year commences. I ought to say that Mohammedans do not count the hours of the day as we do. The exact period of commencing the New Year is the very moment of the sun's entering the sign Aries, and that moment is calculated by astronomers and announced by criers to the people. If the moment, say, is midnight, then the colour to be worn on New Year's Day would be dark puce ; but if midday, as sometimes happens, then it would be the brightest crimson. Any intermediate moment would be met by a given shade of colour applicable to the time of the day or night.

It is a curious custom, and I have not been able to discover a good reason for it. The people, as might be expected, are most pleased when the hour of the commencement of the New Year justifies them in wearing a bright crimson, as gay colours are most in favour in the East, and indeed seem most suitable to a day of private and public rejoicing.

Another peculiar feature of the Festival of the New Year is, that when it is known that it will commence by daylight the ladies in the Zenana have a custom of preparing for it by placing a fresh rose, which has been plucked from its stalk, in a basin of water. It is asserted that at the very moment the sun passes into the sign Aries the rose turns over of itself. To see this phenomenon is considered very lucky, and not only augurs a happy day but a happy year to the fortunate onlooker. Mrs. Meer Hasan Ali tells us in her " Mussulmans of India " that she often watched Native ladies bending eagerly over the fresh-cut rose floating in a basin of water, but, so far as her experience went, the turning over never occurred.

In truly religious families the New Year is opened by " prayer and praises," and then after a meal has been partaken of, the inmates go forth to visit their friends, and the salutation that passes between all who meet is the pleasant one, " May the New Year be fortunate ! " The day is then devoted to sending presents and to amusements. Children and nurses are specially remembered, and everything is done to make New Year's Day a red letter day in the lives of the little ones, which we will all agree is very commendable.

In some Moslem communities the commencement of Spring time is held as a holiday, and very sensibly so I think. There is something exhilarating in the sight of Nature putting on her new garb, and in the merry songs of the birds. The heart of man responds to the signs of renewed and renewing life around him, and he would fain keep " holy day."

In Northern India the Festival is called Bussunt, or

"Spring Colour." The trees of India, generally speaking, may be said to have perpetual foliage, and yet there is a time of the year when new leaves sprout and young buds force off the old leaves. When the trees are thus clothed in their fresh foliage they look lovely. Usually at the first a yellow tinge is noticeable in the colour, and this is called Bussunt.

In Lucknow, a few years back, it was the custom of the King to appoint a day for a general holiday, and then every one wore the spring colour. The elephants, the horses, the camels, and the bullocks of the people were all ornamented with the same colour, as trappings, and the towns and villages consequently presented a gay and festive appearance. The amusements of the day took the form of attendance at public banquets, and also at sports, which the King arranged for the people on a grand scale. Since the dethronement of the King, however, the Spring Festival has ceased to be a public affair in Oude, though it is still kept up privately by some of the princes and by many of the people.

I am surprised that such a holiday has not appealed more strongly to the whole of Islam, for no season of the year can be considered more suitable for all manner of rejoicings than Spring. It would seem as if amongst Moslems no Festival but an ecclesiastical one stood a fair chance of universal acceptation.

The New Moon is the occasion of a Festival in the family of every good Mussulman. Mohammedans date the new moon from the moment it becomes visible, and not as we do from the moment it changes. The appearance of the new moon is usually announced in a Moslem city by the noise of artillery. I have read also that directly "the ruler of the night" appears many people amongst the Faithful bow the knee to her, though when questioned about it they say that they mean the adoration for God as the giver of the moon, which is such a blessing to mankind.

Amongst devout Moslems there is much preparation in

bathing and changing the dress against the evening the moon is expected to be visible, and when the guns are heard announcing the event the Sacred Koran is at once brought and opened at the place where it is written : " The hour of judgment approacheth, and the moon hath been split in sunder." A small looking-glass is then placed on the Perspicuous Book over the words just quoted, and the Koran is held in such a position that the moon may be first seen by the person reflected in the glass. Thereupon a prayer, expressly appointed for the occasion, is repeated, and that done the members of the family rise and embrace each other, the younger ones making salaams and reverence to their superiors and elders. The servants also come forward to offer congratulations to the heads of the house, and to receive good wishes and something more substantial in return. Then all join in an exclamation to the effect, " May the new moon bring us good fortune ! "

From this account of the Festival of the New Moon it will be seen that it is a private festival rather than a public one, but it is universal all the same, and is entered into very heartily by both young and old, and the night is spent in festivity.

Another festival of very general observance in Moslem countries is that called the Festival of the Full Moon, called Shab-i-Barat, which occurs in the month of Shaban. Every full moon is regarded with attention by Moslems, but the one that is seen in the month Shaban, the eighth of the Mohammedan year, is of special importance. On that night the Faithful believe that the fate of all human beings is fixed in heaven, and that whatever is to be their lot during the year, whether life, health, and prosperity, or sorrow, sickness, and death, is assuredly settled by Allah in the Book of Life and Death. Prayer is consequently offered on the Festival of the Full Moon for grace to meet the will of God whatever it may be.

Mrs. Meer Hasan Ali says : " The religious make it a night of strict devotion : they offer prayers and intercessions for themselves and for the souls of their departed friends, since they imagine that this period of all others is most favourable to prayer, as they believe the heart is more open to the throne of mercy, that prayer is more effectual, that the real penitent suing for pardon on the night of Shab-i-Barat is certainly heard and his sins forgiven."

The singular custom of "drinking the moon at a draught," often takes place on the Festival of the Full Moon. It is a superstitious practice recommended by certain medical professors in nervous cases, and for palpitations of the heart. The way it is managed is as follows :— " A silver basin being filled with water, is held in such a situation that the full moon may be reflected in it ; the person to be benefited by the charm is required to look steadfastly at the reflected image, then shut his eyes, and quaff the liquid at one draught." Many cases of cure in connection with this custom can be vouched for, but one may be allowed to question the reality of the illness or attribute the result to imagination or faith.

It must not be thought that the Festival of the Full Moon is entirely taken up with prayers and faith-healing. Time is also devoted to amusements. And perhaps the most popular element of the occasion is the custom of private and public firework displays. At all seasons of the year Mohammedans and Eastern people in general delight in an exhibition of fireworks, but on the night of Shab-i-Barat Moslems indulge this pleasure to the full. For one thing on such an important night, when the issues of joy or sorrow, life or death, are in question, it is required that no one should sleep, and to keep the Faithful awake no happier suggestion could have been made than to let off fireworks.

I have seen sober-looking Moslems, both young and old, relax their features to a wonderful extent on the occasion of the Full Moon Festival, and throw themselves into their favourite pastime with all their heart and soul. . How the children have shouted with delight at every explosion ;

and the "children of a larger growth" have encouraged them by example and precept ! Of all the Mohammedan festivals I question if any one of them is really more enjoyed than this one of the Full Moon, though at its commencement it seems to have about it an air of sadness. As the night wears on the fun increases, and the excitement reaches fever heat, so that when daylight arrives the general opinion is that the month of Shaban is the happiest month of all the year, and that it augurs well for the future.

Moslems may be said to take their pleasures seriously, for, as has been already hinted, their holidays are nearly all holy days, *i.e.*, connected with religious observances. Islamism, indeed, enters thoroughly into the social life of the Faithful, and moulds their leisure as well as their workday hours. And in one respect the result is eminently satisfactory and commendable, viz., that on Holy Days or Festivals, drunkenness and rowdyism are almost unknown, while there is plenty of quiet enjoyment.

CHAPTER XXXVII

FANATICISM

MOHAMMEDANS have earned for themselves throughout the world the title of "fanatics," as a consequence of their wild words and actions in connection with the Faith, once delivered to them by Mohammed the Prophet. The feeling amongst Moslems has been and is, that they are the chosen of Allah, that they are the appointed instruments of God to bring all men, even by the power of the sword, to the knowledge of the only true faith. Consequently woe be to the individuals, communities, or nations, that will not listen to the call to accept Islamism with all its forms and ceremonies !

It is true that at the present time the power of Mohammedanism, as a conquering religion, is on the wane ; but the desire to conquer still remains, and the old feeling of intolerance and fanaticism is probably everywhere almost as strong as ever it was.

In my researches into the history of Mohammedanism I have met with many instances of fanaticism, some of which I would now mention, as they will help us to understand what Islamism really is in the intensity of its wild faith and zeal. Fanaticism in war may well come first. Mohammed, though in the early days of his career a man of peace, and an advocate of mild measures in the propagation of truth, eventually developed into a man of war, and a stern and enthusiastic propagator of Allah's religion by the sword.

The later books of the Koran teem with passages which

counsel strong measures to be taken with infidels. It is written : " Fight against those who believe not in God until they pay tribute by right of subjection, and are reduced low." And again : " When ye meet the infidels, strike off their heads, until ye have made a great slaughter among them." And then it is added : " As for those who fight or fall in defence of God's true religion, He will not suffer their deeds to die. Verily, God loveth those who fight for His religion." " Paradise," it was declared, " is under the shadow of swords." " The sword," it was asserted, " is a surer argument than books."

Is it to be wondered at that a people thus taught should have grown to love war as the very breath of their nostrils, and to revel in it with a fanaticism that was cruel as the grave ? Even before the Prophet died his terrible injunctions began to bear fruit, and after his death the fighting spirit raged throughout Arabia, and the Moslems went forth conquering and to conquer. From the Caliph to the meanest servant or slave in Islam the fanatical creed was accepted, that " the sword was the Key of Heaven and Hell, that a drop of blood shed in the cause of God, a night spent in arms, were of more avail than months of fasting and prayer."

Fanaticism in war showed itself not merely in the determination to overcome an enemy, but in the ardent wish, if Allah willed it, to die on the field of battle, as thus to be " martyred " in the cause of God was believed to be the most certain way of obtaining the highest joys of eternal life in the world beyond the grave.

Listen, for example, to the words of an Arabian youth, whom a fond mother and sister vainly sought to persuade from adopting the profession of arms. His parting speech to those who loved him was : " Hold me not back, nor grieve that I leave you ! It is not the delicacies of Syria or the fading delights of this world that have prompted me to devote my life in the cause of religion. But I seek the favour of God and His Apostle : and I have heard from one of the companions of the Prophet that the spirits of the martyrs will be lodged in the crops of green birds, who shall taste the fruits and drink of the rivers of Paradise. Farewell ! We shall meet again among the groves and fountains which God has provided for His elect."

I have read of another case of a warrior who on the field of battle fought with reckless fury, raving, as he slashed right and left with his sword, about the joys of Paradise promised to all true believers who fell in the wars of the Faith. " Methinks ! " he cried aloud, so as to be heard above the din of arms, " Methinks I see the black-eyed girls looking upon me ; one of whom, should she appear in this world, all mankind would die for love of. And I see in the hand of another a handkerchief of green silk, and a cap of precious stones, and she beckons me and calls out : 'Come hither quickly, for I love thee ! ' " Scarcely had the fanatic thus spoken when a javelin pierced his heart and despatched him to his vaunted elysium. And these two instances are but types of countless thousands in Islam whose fanaticism has exceeded all bounds in the race for martyrdom in a jihād, or holy war.

Besides the joy of fighting for the Faith, and the incentive of the pleasures of Paradise for the valiant, the fanaticism of Mohammedans has been deepened and strengthened by the doctrine of predestination, as taught by the Prophet, or at any rate as believed by the Faithful. The Koran says in one place : " The fate of every man have we bound about his neck ;" and in another, " No soul can die unless by the permission of God, according to what is written in the book containing the determination of things."

Mohammed inserted these passages after the temporary defeat of his followers at Ohod, to inspire them with fresh courage. He represented to the Faithful that the time of every man's death is decreed and determined by Allah, and that those who had fallen in the battle could not have

avoided their fate had they stopped at home, so there was
no reason to grieve unduly, or to be discouraged and disheartened.

Thus did the Prophet instil into the minds of his soldiers
a belief in Fate, and under this persuasion did Moslems
engage in battle without anxiety or fear, believing that what
would be must be, that no one could die before his time,
and that no human sagacity or foresight could evade the
hand of death if the moment had been preordained. We
can see how such a doctrine of predestination spurred the
Faithful on to deeds of recklessness, and made the early
soldiers of the Crescent men to be dreaded beyond the
ordinary run of adversaries, for they were fanatics.

One of the most remarkable of these warrior-fanatics was
Kaled, who was employed by Abu Bekr and Omar in the
wars in Syria. He was a man who added superstition to
his belief in fate, for he was wont to declare that a special
providence watched over him, and that as long as he wore
a certain cap which had been blessed by Mohammed he
was invulnerable to all the darts of the enemies of Islam.
And truly it seemed as if he bore a charmed life, for
though in every battle he rushed into the thickest of the
fight, and was ever surrounded by dangers, he always
marvellously escaped, and in a good old age died in his
bed.

The exploits of this fanatic in the siege of Damascus are
almost beyond belief. He rushed madly at every antag-
onist, generally singling out the strongest and the bravest,
and he was always conqueror. On one occasion, after a
desperate struggle with a bold Christian General, which left
him exhausted, a fresh adversary spurred his charger to
attack him. A companion in arms, the gallant Derar,
seeing the exhaustion of Kaled, called out to him: "O
Kaled, repose yourself for a moment, and permit me to
supply your place," but the reply he got was: "Not so,
good Derar; if I needs must rest, it will be in Paradise.
He that labours to-day will rest to-morrow." At the word

he sprang upon his foe, and hurled him lifeless to the ground. Kaled by such deeds earned for himself the title of "The Sword of God."

But the doctrine of predestination can influence in two ways: It can make fanatical cowards as well as fanatical braves. And in these latter days it seems in Moslem countries to be producing a weak and degenerate race. The belief in fate is as strong as ever, but it now takes the form of lazy, instead of active, fanaticism, and it is striking at the root of all enterprise and progress. As one writer has said: "Many Moslems positively refuse to exert themselves, while they excuse their natural indolence by declaring: 'Everything is determined: what is to be will be: if God intends that we should become rich we shall become so without any personal exertion: if He intends that we shall be poor, poor we shall have to remain, despite our labour.'" Thus the doctrine of predestination as held by Mohammedans is baneful, whether in war or peace, for when exercised in the sphere of the former it produces a hard and cruel race of warriors, and when in the sphere of the latter, a race of weak and helpless citizens.

Fanaticism has shown itself very markedly in the department of teaching, and especially in the teaching of the truths of the Koran. The verbal inspiration of the Scriptures has ever been part of the orthodox creed of Islamism. Some of the Faithful at various times have questioned the doctrine, and have even striven to show that the Koran contains passages that contradict each other, and therefore cannot be infallible: but such liberal views are far from common.

In every age Moslems, as a whole, have been most dogmatic in their teaching, and perfectly fanatical in their enforcement upon others of what they have conceived to be truth. Take for example the time of the Abbasides of Bagdad. The author of "Islam under the Caliphs of Bagdad," says, "Every one who either in act or word questioned a single syllable of the Koran was regarded as an infidel, and was in peril of being torn in pieces by the devout."

Then to look at an earlier period. Omar, the second Commander of the Faithful, delighted in teaching the law, and would brook no interference from doubters or cavillers. There is a characteristic story told of him when he was on his famous journey from Medina to Jerusalem, when the latter city was subjected by the Moslem arms. The Caliph often stopped by the way as he passed through Arabia and Syria to administer justice and expound the Sacred Koran. Usually a crowd gathered round him to see and hear the grand old man. On one occasion he took for his text a few words from the Koran which assert that those whom God shall lead in the right way are secure from all harm, but that those whom He shall lead in the way of error are doomed to punishment. As Omar enforced these pregnant lessons a grey-headed man in the audience disturbed the flow of the preacher's utterance by remarking aloud, "Tush! God leads no man into error!" The stern, fanatical Caliph deigned no direct reply, but turning to his body-guard, he said: "Strike off that old man's head if he repeats his words!" The preacher met with no further opposition.

One of the most fanatical acts on record is associated with the name of Omar—I refer to the destruction of the Alexandrian Library. I know that the story has been gravely questioned of late years. Gibbon and others have made light of it, but still the tale was believed for centuries, and it has not yet been proved false, and it is certainly just such a deed as a fanatical Moslem prince like Omar might have committed.

"The Alexandrian Library was formed by Ptolemy Soter, and placed in a building called the Bruchion. It was augmented in successive reigns to 400,000 volumes, and an additional 300,000 volumes were placed in a temple called the Serapeon. The Bruchion, with the books it contained, was burned in the war of Cæsar, but the Serapeon was preserved. Cleopatra, it is said, added to it the library of

Pergamus, given to her by Marc Antony, consisting of 200,000 volumes. It sustained repeated injuries during various subsequent revolutions, but was always restored to its ancient splendour, and numerous additions made to it. Such was its state at the capture of Alexandria by the Moslems." The famous library was, in fact, the finest in the world.

The story goes that Amr, the Conqueror of Egypt, and the leader of the Moslem armies, had his attention drawn to the Library by the learned Greek known as John the Grammarian, to whom Amr had granted many favours. John asked that the books might be given to himself, as the Moslems would probably have no use for them. The General was inclined to gratify the wish of the Grammarian, but his rigid integrity refused to alienate anything without the permission of the Commander of the Faithful, to whom he at once wrote. The answer which Omar is generally believed to have sent was inspired by the ignorance and zeal of a fanatic. It ran: "If these writings of the Greeks agree with the blessed Koran, the Book of Allah, they are useless, and therefore need not be preserved ; if they disagree, then they are pernicious, and ought to be destroyed."

Washington Irving, commenting on this extraordinary message, says : "Amr, as a man of genius and intelligence, may have grieved at the order of the Caliph, while as a loyal subject and faithful soldier, he felt bound to obey it." Consequently the command went forth to seize and to destroy, and the valuable manuscripts and books were distributed as fuel among the five thousand baths of the city of Alexandria, and, it is said, so numerous were they, that it took six months to consume them. Thus perished by a deed of Moslem fanaticism much of the learning, the arts, and the genius of antiquity.

Fanaticism in Moslem lands is not confined to men, but is as strong or stronger amongst women. Notwithstanding the disabilities and hardships under which women labour in

Islam, they cleave with blind enthusiasm to the teaching of the Prophet of God, hugging to their breasts the Book which has made their degradation an article of faith and binding throughout the ages.

And little children too are veritable fanatics. Lane, in his " Modern Egyptians," tells us that from their earliest days Moslem boys and girls are taught to hate " infidels " with a perfect hatred. It must be remembered that in the eyes of Mohammedans all are infidels who are not of the true Faith—that is, Islam. Let me quote a prayer that is now in use amongst the children of Moslems. Lane translates it thus : " O God, destroy the infidels and poly- theists, thine enemies, the enemies of Islam ! O God, make their offspring orphans, defile their abodes, cause their feet to slip, and give them and their families, and their children, and their possessions and their race, and their wealth, and their land, as booty to the Moslems." What an awful prayer to put into the mouths of boys and girls ! Little wonder that the rising generation, like all preceding generations in Islam, regards the world with eyes of anger and hate !

A little incident that happened in my own experience may not be unworthy of notice. I was travelling at the time in Palestine, and was drawing near the ancient city of Hebron, once so famous in Jewish history, but now in the possession of Moslems. The day was hot, and I had ridden far, and was suffering from thirst. Suddenly I espied by the wayside a maiden, perchance of seven years of age, tripping gaily along with a waterpot poised on her head in Eastern fashion. I hailed her and made signs for a drink of water. That she understood me perfectly was clear, but to my surprise she was not prepared to grant my request. Now, usually in the East, if the traveller can get nothing else, he can get a drink of water from the people he sees, for it is considered churlish indeed to refuse such a neces- sary of life.

However, the heart of the little maiden at Hebron was

closed against all not of her own Faith. And so insulted and enraged was she that I should have even presumed to ask anything from her, that she put her hands up to her head, and in a tempest of indignation dashed the unoffending waterpot to the ground. Then pointing to the spilt water, she declared, with oaths and curses, so my Dragoman told me, that she hoped that thus would my blood ere many days be spilt and sink into the ground. For the time being the maiden was a little fury, and I was convinced that the fanaticism of the people of Islam was, even amongst the juvenile members of society, something to be carefully watched by travellers, or dangerous results might follow. The inhabitants of Hebron or, as it is now called, El-Khalid, are notorious for their fanaticism, and by their conduct they belie both the ancient and the modern name of their city, which names, being interpreted, mean, " the Friend."

Sometimes the evil results of the fanaticism of Mohammedans have not been confined to strangers, but have made themselves felt within their own borders ; as, for instance, in those sad cases of regicide which have been so common in Moslem countries. As we have seen in the course of these Studies, Omar, Othman, and Ali, three of the Commanders of the Faithful, fell victims to the mad zeal of some of their own followers, who conceived that they were doing God and Islam service by despatching the Caliphs with their daggers.

The truth is fanaticism is an uncertain instrument to use : it is a two-edged tool which it is dangerous to handle. The leaders of Mohammedanism in all generations have found that they have not always been able to control the fierce spirit they have called up, and they have been taught by a terrible experience the truth of that saying : " They that take the sword shall perish by the sword."

I wonder sometimes whether Mohammedans will ever learn that their best interests lie in realizing the great truth of the Brotherhood of Humanity. There can be no peace, no prosperity, and no real happiness in Islam, until the feelings of cruel religious fanaticism nurtured by the Koran have been replaced by feelings of brotherly sympathy and love for all nations and peoples.

CHAPTER XXXVIII

GRAND VIZIERS

Vizier is a word of questionable origin, but some Arabic scholars derive it from *vezan*, to bear or carry, and others from *vesara*, he has advised. The position in the East of a Grand Vizier, which corresponds, to some extent, with that of a Prime Minister in the West, is an office both of "advising" and "bearing," for the Vizier of a Moslem Ruler has to advise his master in all the great affairs of State, and practically to bear the load of government, which is usually a very heavy one.

The first reference to the office of Vizier in the history of Mohammedanism dates as far back as the time of Mohammed himself, even' before the Prophet was generally accepted as a power in the land. It happened thus :—

At the commencement of his religious career Mohammed had few followers, not more than fourteen, it is said, but all the same, he was convinced that he was the Apostle of Allah, and that some day the world would acknowledge his claim. In the fourth year of his teaching and preaching he resolved to assume the prophetic office, so he called together his little band of disciples, and invited other guests with them to a banquet, at which he declared his Divine Mission to teach and to preach concerning Allah. Then he said with great earnestness, looking keenly round the assembly : "Friends and Kinsmen, I offer you, and I alone can offer, the most precious of gifts, the treasures of this world, and of the world to come. God has commanded me to call you to His service. Who among you will support my burden? Who among you will be my companion and my Vizier?"

The guests at first listened, greatly surprised, to the words of Mohammed, then some laughed, some sneered, and some mocked, for it seemed so strange for a man with less than a score of followers to ask for the aid of a Vizier to assist him in ruling them.

The Prophet was thinking of the future, however, when tens of thousands would bow reverently at the mention of his name; and thus one, at least, of the guests understood him, viz., Ali, who afterwards became his son-in-law. At the time Ali was only a youth, but he was full of enthusiasm for the cause of his friend, and jumping up, he declared amidst a scene of wild excitement: "O Prophet, I am thy man; whosoever rises against thee I will dash out his teeth, tear out his eyes, break his legs, and rip up his body. O Prophet, I will be thy Vizier." It was a strange speech, coming from a youth, and it throws a weird light on what was conceived to be the duties of the Prime Minister of a temporal Prince, or an Apostle of God, in the East. Truly the early days of Islam were days of gross ignorance and violent deeds!

It is a most singular thing that after the night of that banquet nothing more was heard of the office of Vizier in Mohammedanism for generations. Whether Ali ever really became Prime Minister to Mohammed we are not told, nor do we hear of any other person being appointed in his place. The probability is that the Prophet found it wiser to have no "second" in place or power, especially as a host of able and valiant men eventually gathered around his banner, any one of whom he could depend upon to help him in the carrying out of his bold plans.

Abu Bekr, Omar, Othman, and Ali himself, the early successors of the Prophet, do not seem to have favoured any more than Mohammed the adoption of Grand Viziers, for they ruled in their own persons, and would brook no close companions in power.

And when we come to the century of Moslem rule at Damascus, when the Omiades sat in the seat of the Caliphs, there is the same silence maintained with regard to the office of Vizier. Doubtless all the Commanders of the Faithful had special favourites in whom they reposed confidence, and on whom they greatly depended for counsel and support in the arduous duties, responsibilities, and cares of their high station, but such favourites were not called Viziers, nor did they occupy the position which Viziers afterwards came to hold in Mohammedan councils of state.

It was not till the year 750 A.D., when the Abbasides began to reign at Bagdad, that we read of Grand Viziers worthy of the name. Indeed some students of history say that Abul Abbas, the first of the Abbasides, originated the proud title of Vizier, and introduced on to the scene of Eastern affairs a race of Ministers who have ever since played a prominent, and on the whole a useful, part in the life of Moslem States.

In the reign of Harun-al-Rashid, or Aaron the Just, there appeared a very noted family of Viziers called the Barmecides, whose career was brilliant yet chequered, and whose star went down in darkness. The most prominent of the Barmecides was Yahya, the Prime Minister and the great favourite of Harun. Wherever the Caliph went the Vizier went, whether on the road of duty or pleasure, and the friendship was a blessing to those who lived

> " By Bagdad's shrines of fretted gold,
>   High-walled gardens, green and old."

It was the Grand Vizier who encouraged trade, who regulated the internal administration of Government in every respect, who fortified the frontiers of the State, and made the provinces prosperous by making them safe.

And a son of Yahya, named Jaafer, governed Syria and Egypt in the interests of the Caliph, as well as holding other great and important posts. The Barmecides, father and son, and indeed all the numerous members of the princely family, were patrons of art, letters, and science, and gathered around them the talent and genius of the East, which, with the willing approval of Harun-al-Rashid, they utilized to beautify and enrich Bagdad. Thus powerful and useful did the Barmecides become! As has been grandiloquently said by one of the Moslem chroniclers of the age: "The family was an ornament to the forehead, and a crown on the head of the Caliph: they were brilliant stars, vast oceans, impetuous torrents, beneficent rains, the refuge of the afflicted, the comfort of the distressed, and generosity itself."

Unfortunately, however, Harun became jealous of his great Ministers, and when he discovered that Yahya had secretly married a princess of the Royal House he decreed their ruin. Gilman says: "With the usual Oriental treachery the different members of the family were taken and imprisoned for life or slaughtered to the last man. In this case, as in many others in the Saracen history, no sentiment of gratitude for all that had been accomplished by the faithful servants of the Crown was taken into account, though Harun is said to have shed tears over the fate of the two children of his sister and Yahya."

Thus miserably perished a noble and brilliant family of Eastern Viziers, to the lasting disgrace of the Caliph whom they served so well!

> "Fallen was the house of Jaafer: and its name
> The high romantic name of Barmecide,
> A sound forbidden on its own bright shores,
> By the swift Tigris' wave. Stern Harun's wrath,
> Sweeping the mighty with their fame away,
> Had so passed sentence: but man's chainless heart
> Hides that within its depths which never yet
> The oppressor's thought could reach."

The sudden and unexpected ruin of the Barmecides suggests the uncertainty of tenure by which the office of Grand Vizier was held in Moslem lands. Indeed the post

has always been one of surprises, sometimes of sudden
elevation, and anon of sudden doom.   It was so under the
rule of the Abbasides of Bagdad, and perhaps still more
markedly so under the Ottoman Turks.

If we pass on to the sixteenth century, and look at the
reign of Selim the Grim, we shall find some striking illustrations of the uncertainty of tenure in the high office of Grand
Vizier.   For example, on one occasion when Selim had
called together his Council of State, which consisted of
six or eight Viziers, he asked the chief of them what should
be done with regard to Egypt, the armies of which country
had hovered on the flanks of the Sultan's army on a recent
expedition against Persia.

The Prime Minister advised forbearance, and the over-
looking of the fault, seeing that the Egyptians had not
actually struck a blow; but such counsel was not what
Selim wanted. The Imperial Secretary, Muhammad, standing by, saw this, and venturing to interpose, remarked
briefly: "War! war!" At the word the Sultan smiled
with delight, and then turning towards his Grand Vizier he
dismissed him at once from his post, and ordered the
Secretary to step into his place. The latter, however,
tremblingly deprecated any such sudden change of offices,
or questionable exaltation, and it was only after the excellent man had been soundly bastinadoed by command of
his master that he consented to accept so dangerous a
dignity as Grand Vizier. It is said, however, that he
worthily filled the office, though he in his turn did not hold
it very long.

Selim was famous for executing his Viziers, and Stanley
Lane-Poole, in his "History of Turkey," tells us that it was
a common form of cursing in the Ottoman dominions for
generations to say "Mayest thou be Selim's Vizier!"

A very good idea may be obtained of the uncertainty of
tenure of the office of Vizier by bearing this table in mind,
viz., that "From the series of one hundred and fifteen
Viziers in the Turkish dominions, from the time of Orkhan

till the siege of Vienna, the high position may be valued at three and a half years' purchase."

The greatest of the Ottoman Viziers was Ibrahim, who was chosen by that grand monarch Suleyman to be his companion, friend, and helper in the year 1523. Ibrahim was the son of a sailor of Parga, and in his boyish days had the misfortune to be captured by Corsairs. After a time of hardship with the Rovers of the Sea, he passed into the hands of a widow at Magnesia as a slave, and from her he was bought by Suleyman when he was but heir-apparent and Governor of Magnesia.

The young man showing fine parts, and especially a wonderful genius for learning, Suleyman treated him with much kindness, and employed him in various offices about his person. He was then made Grand Falconer, and finally, on the accession of the Prince to the throne of Turkey, the favourite was raised to the high position of Grand Vizier. There is an Eastern proverb which says: " When God gives office He gives also the ability to fill it," and it was so with Ibrahim. It was something wonderful how this man, who was simply the son of an ordinary seaman, was able to meet the duties of his exalted office. He is described as great in peace and war, and everything seemed to succeed and prosper in his hands.

And the more Suleyman saw of the great genius and fine character of his Vizier the more he loved him. " Ibrahim was not only a friend, he was an entertaining and instructive companion. He read Persian, Greek, and Italian ; he knew how to open unknown worlds to the Sultan's mind, and Suleyman drank in his Vizier's wisdom with assiduity. They lived together : their meals were shared in common : even their beds were in the same room. At length the Sultan gave his sister in marriage to the sailor's son, who was then at the height of his power."

And for thirteen years that friendship lasted, but at length it was undermined by a jealous and unscrupulous woman and Ibrahim, the dear friend and peerless Minister, was sacrificed by the Sultan in a fit of rage. Bitterly did Suleyman regret the hasty deed, and, it is said, had no more ease of mind. What is more certain is, that the State had thenceforth little peace, and sorely felt the loss of the brilliant genius and firm rule of Ibrahim.

While most Viziers have been deposed or slain by the caprice or jealousy of their masters, a few have been known to sacrifice themselves to save their princes, whom the latter would fain have kept in office and power. The fate of Hafiz the Martyr is a case in point. This Grand Vizier was an able minister, and was dearly beloved by his Sultan, Murad the Fourth, who was the last of the fighting Sultans of the Ottoman race. When Murad ascended the throne he was young in years and experience, and depended greatly upon the services of his able Vizier. Hafiz, however, was not popular with some factions in the State, which sought disorder rather than a firm and settled government. In the ninth year of the Sultan's reign these factions rose in rebellion, and besieged Murad in his palace. They even pressed into the Seraglio and called for the heads of the Viziers, and especially for the head of Hafiz, who, they declared, had advised the Sultan badly.

The occasion was a critical one, for Murad had no troops at hand equal to the emergency, and the insurgents laid before him a choice of evils, either the sacrifice of his Prime Minister or abdication. The Sultan declared he would not do the former, and temporized with regard to the latter, hoping for a favourable turn of events. However, the mutineers insisted upon their request being granted, and the life even of the Sultan was endangered. It was at that moment that the Grand Vizier appeared on the scene, and entreated his master to leave the settlement of the matter with him. The brave man was resolved to sacrifice himself to save his Prince, and said: "Grieve not for me, I have seen my fate in a dream to-day, and I am not afraid to die." And before the sorrowing Sultan could stop him he had stepped forth into the court where his enemies were waiting. They sprang upon him, and though he fought gallantly for his life he fell pierced by seventeen wounds.

The young Prince, powerless to avert the murder, yet vowed to avenge it, and said aloud to the mutineers : " So help me, Allah, ye men of blood, who fear not God, nor are ashamed before God's Prophet, a terrible vengeance shall overtake you ! " And he kept his word ! When free to sally forth from his palace Murad gathered around him what loyal troops he could find, and in every city of his kingdom he sought the insurgents who had foully done to death the man he had loved. " The Bosphorus floated thick with the bodies of the slain, and the death of Hafiz the Martyr was avenged tenfold."

If we pass from Turkey to Spain, and look at the rule of the Moors in the latter country, we find that the office of Vizier there was one that was not, generally speaking, made much of. The Omiades of Spain, like their brethren of Damascus, preferred to rule in person rather than by deputy. However, there were exceptions, and some of the Sultans of Cordova are known to have had Grand Viziers.

I would refer to one Prime Minister in particular, who in the tenth century exercised paramount influence in Spain, and retained it, which is more remarkable still, until his dying day. This Vizier is known in history by the name of Almanzor, or " The Victorious by the grace of God," and he may be said to have been the most able, the most powerful, and the most fortunate Grand Vizier that the Moslem world has ever known. Almanzor started life as an insignificant student at the University of Cordova, and his career is an interesting example of what talent, daring, and selfishness can do in a Moslem State where the road to power has ever been open to all classes of society.

The student ingratiated himself first of all with the servants of the Royal Palace by becoming a professional letter-writer to them : by-and-by he gained the notice of the Grand Chamberlain : and eventually, by his charm of manner and skilful flatteries, he obtained the favour of the ladies of the Harem, and especially of Amina the Queen-Mother, who is said to have fallen in love with the brilliant and handsome young man.

Hisham the Second, a boy of twelve years of age, was Caliph, but he was entirely under the influence of his mother, Amina, and he was led by her eventually to choose Almanzor as his Grand Vizier, and to leave everything in the favourite's hands. Thus the student rose to the highest office in the land, and he filled it with astonishing ability. As a judge he was counted most wise and upright : as a leader of society he was most popular : and as commander of the armies of the Faithful he was simply idolized, for he invariably led his soldiers to victory and to booty.

So completely did both the Caliph and his people trust the Grand Vizier that almost all the important posts in the state passed into his hands. "Almanzor became the virtual ruler of Mohammedan Spain. From his palace in the suburbs of Cordova he governed the whole kingdom : letters and proclamations were issued in his name : he was prayed for from the pulpits, and commemorated on the coinage : and he even wore robes of gold tissue, woven with his name, such as kings only were wont to wear." And for nigh twenty years this extraordinary man held the reins of power, without a rival, beloved at home and feared abroad, and then died quietly in his bed. He is said to have been a perfect terror to the Christians of neighbouring states, who time by time waged war with the Moors, for Almanzor always defeated them with very great slaughter.

The hate of the Christians, and the relief they felt at the news of the death of this great Moslem Vizier, may be gathered from the brief but emphatic entry that has been found in the manuscript of a Monkish annalist, which reads : "In 1002 died Almanzor, and was buried in Hell."

For a moment let us direct our thoughts to India. The great Moghuls had their Viziers, some of whom in the latter days of the royal Baber line became independent princes and monarchs, breaking off, as opportunity presented branches of territory, such as Oude and Bengal, from the parent tree. I would speak, however, of a humbler and more faithful servant, who lived at the commencement of the eighteenth century, and who did a graceful act, the memory of which ought not to be suffered to die.

The incident happened in the year 1739, when Mahomed Shah was on the throne at Delhi, and Nadir Shah, the fierce Persian, had captured and was sacking the Imperial city. The two kings, the conquered and the conqueror, were one day seated in the beautiful Diwan-i-Khas, or Hall of Audience, talking over the terms of peace, when coffee was announced. The servant, who brought it on a gold salver, placed it on a table and retired. It was now the Grand Vizier's duty to hand the beverage to the two Emperors, but to whom should he offer it first, to his own prince or to the stranger? It was a point of etiquette that had never arisen before in his experience, and one that was fraught with danger, even to his life, if a false step were made. The eyes of all in the room were fixed upon the Vizier, but he did not hesitate above a moment, and then advancing with firm step to the side of his beloved but unfortunate master, he handed him the gold salver, saying: "I cannot aspire to the honour of presenting the cup to the king of kings, your majesty's guest, nor would your majesty wish that any hand but your own should do so."

Mahomed Shah, greatly pleased with the adroit move of his Vizier, which honoured himself and did no dishonour to Nadir Shah, took a cup from the salver and presented it to the latter. Even the terrible Nadir had been charmed with the incident, and as he accepted the coffee from his host, he said, with a smile: "Had all your officers known and done their duty like your Grand Vizier, you had never, my good friend, have seen me or my soldiers at Delhi! Cherish this estimable man for your own sake, and get around you as many like him as you can!"

From what has been related in this chapter, it will be at once manifest that the post of Grand Vizier is a most unenviable one to fill. It is no sinecure office, and is the almost certain road to a violent death. That so many have failed to fill it with comfort to themselves, or benefit to the princes or states they have been called to serve, is not to be wondered at. The examples I have been able to give of true, useful, and honourable service are therefore the more precious and the more to be admired.

CHAPTER XXXIX

SLAVERY AND THE SLAVE TRADE

ONE of the most ancient institutions of the human race is that of slavery. In every age almost of the world's history it has been known, and in every land. And wherever it has prevailed it has been a source of national weakness as well as individual misery.

Slavery is an outrage against humanity, and in the long run it is its own avenger in the decay of those nations that foster it. Hannah More has said :—

> " Indignant Nature blushes to behold
> Degraded man himself, tracked, bartered, sold,
> Of every native privilege bereft,
> Yet cursed with every wounded feeling left.
> Hard lot ! each brutal suffering to sustain,
> Yet keep the sense acute of human pain."

At the present day Christian nations, generally speaking, are free from the curse of slavery. It is Heathen and Mohammedan nations that are the offenders, for slavery exists in Turkey, Egypt, Persia, Tunis, Morocco, Madagascar, China, and Afghanistan, and in a very modified degree in the Independent Native States of India.

Amongst Moslems this dreadful institution has existed from time immemorial, and has the sanction of their Sacred Scriptures, the Koran. When Mohammed became the Prophet, Priest, and King of Islam, slavery existed amongst the Arabians, and though he had, at any rate at first, little sympathy with the custom, he forbore to denounce it, and only sought to some extent to mitigate its evils.

Here and there in the Koran references are made to slavery, and it is stated that captives taken in war are the lawful property of those who capture them—property that may be either kept, given away, or sold. Thus the legality of the possession of slaves. by Moslems is placed beyond all doubt, and the abolition of slavery in Mohammedan countries is made an almost impossible task, because to do so would be to abrogate a large part of the teaching of the Perspicuous Book. As a matter of fact, no Moslem state has ever voluntarily abolished slavery, and probably never will.

There are more women than men slaves in Mohammedan countries, and the sanction which the Koran gives to the Faithful to take their women slaves as concubines is one of the chief reasons why slavery has such a hold on Moslems. In the 4th sura of the Koran it is written: "Take in marriage of such women as please you, two, three, or four, and not more. But if ye fear that ye cannot act equitably towards so many, marry one only, or the slaves which ye shall have acquired." This permission to add to the one wife any number of slave-girls, opened not only the floodgates of vice to Mohammedans, but forged a chain of iron about the necks of slaves that has made slavery an enduring national institution in Moslem lands.

Muir, in his "Life of Mahomet," says: "As regards female slaves under the thraldom of Mohammedan masters, it is difficult to conceive more signal degradation of the human species; they are treated as an inferior class of beings. Equally restricted as if they had entered the marriage state, they are expressly excluded from any title to conjugal rights. They are purely at the disposal of their proprietors." We can conceive, then, how strong are the reasons which lead Moslems to cling to slavery, for the abolition of the custom means very largely the abolition of Zenanas.

It has in justice, however, to be said, that, though Mohammed, in his character of Prophet, sanctioned slavery, he strongly urged the Faithful to treat their slaves with consideration and kindness, and make their lot as easy and comfortable as possible.

In some cases the Prophet even advised his followers to marry their slaves. In the 4th sura of the Koran we read : "Whoso among you hath not means sufficient that he may marry free women who are believers, let him marry with such of your maidservants, whom your right hands possess, as are true believers : for God well knoweth your faith. Ye are the one from the other : therefore marry them, with the consent of their masters, and give them their dower according to justice. And when they are married, if they be guilty of adultery, they shall suffer half the punishment which is appointed for the free women. This is allowed unto him among you who feareth to sin by marrying free women ; but if ye abstain from marrying slaves, it will be better for you : God is gracious and merciful."

Not content with urging the Faithful to treat their slaves well, and in some cases to marry them, Mohammed even declared that it was a meritorious act to free slaves, and that those who did so would bring down upon themselves the blessing of Allah. In the 90th sura of the Koran it is written : "What shall make them to understand what the highway of good is? It is to free captives, or to feed in the day of famine the orphan who is of kin, or the poor man who lieth on the ground. Whoso doeth this, and is one of those who believe, and recommend perseverance unto each other, and recommend mercy unto each other, these shall be companions of the right hand."

Then in the 24th sura the words occur : " Unto such of your slaves as desire a written instrument allowing them to redeem themselves on paying a certain sum, write one, if ye know good in them, and give them of the riches of God, which He hath given you."

Doubtless these gracious words and rules of conduct of Mohammed with regard to the treatment of slaves have had some weight with devout Moslems; and if all owners of slaves only lived up to such exhortations slavery would not be the dreadful curse it is. The mistake the Prophet made, however, was to sanction slavery at all! It is a custom that it is almost impossible to regulate. The true cure for the evils of slavery is to abolish the sinful practice altogether.

For many generations the Faithful obtained their supply of slaves through the wars they waged. Every prisoner was a captive, to be redeemed or not at the pleasure of the victor. As a rule, women captives were never ransomed, but retained to swell the ranks of the harem. And this method of obtaining slaves by war was the favourite method all through the centuries of the Damascus and Bagdad Caliphates, and for a time even under the Ottoman rule in Turkey.

The *Times of India*, a Bombay newspaper, in an admirable article in 1890 on the Slave Trade, said: "Up to the beginning of the present century all captives of war taken from Christian nations were enslaved by the Turks, and a Turkish campaign in Hungary or Poland was little more than a gigantic slave raid. Less than 200 years ago 100,000 German and Magyar women and girls were carried off in a single campaign. And even when the decay of the Ottoman military power prevented the Turks from invading Christian countries any more, they still continued raiding and kidnapping. But the supply of captive women became less and less, and the markets of Algiers, Tunis, and Tripoli were closed by the indignation of Europe in 1816."

Moslems will have slaves, however, and when white races failed them, the Persians and the Turks turned their attention to dark races, and entered upon the modern African slave trade, which has assumed such proportions that the decimation of an entire continent is threatened. As the *Times of India* has forcibly said: "The closing of all the other avenues by which women were formerly obtained to replace the drain caused by polygamy has intensified and aggravated the East African slave trade. It is simply a case of demand and supply, and so long as the demand exists it will continue to be supplied, no matter at what risks and hazards short of actual physical impossibility."

The 'dreadful cruelties practised by the Arab slave dealers in Africa cry out to Heaven for punishment. That grand Christian missionary, Dr. Livingstone, was one of the first to call public attention to the evil. Wherever he went in his travels he found sad traces of the trade, which he held to be the sum and substance of all villainy. And missionaries and travellers of the present day tell the same tale.

The slave-hunts are organized in three regions: in the interior of Africa, on the borders of the Upper Nile, and on the coast of the Indian Ocean. Arabs and Turks are at the head of such expeditions. The plan of operations is usually to surround a village, and as the inhabitants at the first sound of alarm rush out, with or without their spears in their hands, the traders shoot them down as fast as they can. In a few minutes the struggle is over, and the men being killed the women and children are gathered into a group. A dreadful scene then ensues. The older women are seized and brutally murdered on the spot, while the younger women and children are tied together with ropes, some having in addition a pole, forked at the end, fastened round their necks, and then they are driven away on their journey to the coast. In the majority of instances the journey covers an extent of land more than twice the length of Great Britain, and it is across the dreadful solitudes of the desert.

The sufferings of the poor slaves are frightful from hunger, thirst and weariness. From time to time one of the miserable company falls to rise no more, but her fellow-captives do not even stop to cover the body with sand.

"When evening draws on the sad groups have often not enough physical strength to drag their wearied bodies to the springs that might slake their parched mouths. Sometimes the wind fills the mouth of the well with sand. When this is the case, some of the poor wretches, not having sufficient strength to wait until the place is cleared, die, and their companions are barely able to remove the corpses."

Fearing ambuscades during the march through the desert, the slave traders often flog their captives to make them move quickly, and when the lash or the club has no longer any effect upon the miserable beings, worn out by fatigue, they are either killed or abandoned without pity in the solitude. Sir Samuel Baker tells of a convoy conducted by Turks in which a woman did not walk quickly enough. As soon as she was overcome with fatigue she was knocked down with a blow from a club on the back of the neck, and all that remained was a body quivering in death.

The Arabs often hang the exhausted ones, and their route to the coast can sometimes be followed by those frightful landmarks. As the caravan of slaves nears its destination, the lot of the captives is generally ameliorated. The merchants from self-interest show less cruelty, and arrange for the weak and fatigued to be carried by those who are stronger and more enduring. But at the best, we are told, and can well believe, that the sight of a caravan when near the coast is horrible and sickening. "The slaves are no longer united, but scattered in groups along the road, tottering and resembling skeletons, their faces expressive of nothing but hunger, their eyes dull and sunken, their cheeks only bone."

It is calculated that 90,000 human beings are carried off every year in Africa, and sold into slavery. And this figure represents but a small section of the evils done by slavery and the slave trade, for it is computed that for one slave that arrives at the slave market ten are slain in the first attack on the village, or die by the way. Thus we reach the awful total of 900,000 souls that are the victims yearly of this infamous traffic in human beings, and all to gratify the selfish and sensual passions of the followers of the Prophet of Islam. Verily Mohammedans have much to answer for to God in this matter of slavery and the slave trade!

I will not linger over the horrors endured by the captives in the slave dhows as they are being transported along the Eastern coast of Africa, nor over the degradation and sufferings in the slave markets. Probably the happiest part of a slave's life is in the homes of the people of Islam; but from the beginning to the end the whole traffic is an abomination, and the conscience of the civilized world is beginning to be touched by the sad tale of Africa's woes; and the nations of Christendom are arousing themselves to battle with this great evil.

The feeling is becoming more general and intense that if Mohammedans will not root out the trade from the inside by abolishing the demand, Christians must stop it from the outside by cutting off the supply. Already in Egypt for a few years, and latterly in Zanzibar, the action of the English has been felt, and slavery has been partially crippled. Sir Evelyn Baring, in a recent report to the English Government on Slavery in Egypt, states that in 1885 there were thirty-two slave dealers in Cairo, but the Khedive was urged to take vigorous measures against them, and now not a single slave dealer is to be found. A very few slaves, it is said, may be occasionally smuggled into the country, and sold privately, but for all practical purposes the slave trade in Egypt is extinct.

It must be clearly understood, however, that slavery is not extinct. Egyptian Moslems have slaves in their households; but every year the number diminishes owing to the difficulty of obtaining fresh ones. As long as England retains Egypt and brings pressure to bear on the Egyptian Government, slavery will be moribund in the Land of the Pharaohs, but as Sir Evelyn Baring significantly says at the close of his Report:—" Of the many abuses, now partially abolished, which would tend to reappear should the influence at present exerted by the British Government in Egypt be diminished, I know of none whose reappearance may be predicted with a greater degree of probability than that now under discussion."

And the same may be said of Zanzibar. Owing to the influence of the British, the Sultan of Zanzibar has declared the slave trade to be illegal in his dominions, and has prohibited all sale and exchange of slaves. These stringent laws, however, are very unpopular, and it is found very difficult to enforce them. News comes from time to time that dealers manage to evade the law, and that the dread traffic goes on to some extent still. It is most earnestly to be hoped that the British Government will continue firm in its attitude, and strengthen the Sultan to uphold his decrees. Zanzibar has been so long the stronghold of the slave-trading communities, that to cripple their power there is to strike a heavy blow at the traffic.

The Church of Rome is to be congratulated on the attitude she has taken up towards the slave trade, and for the vigorous aggressive policy she has inaugurated through that veteran friend of slaves, Cardinal Lavigerie. All the churches of Christ throughout the world should join in a Holy Crusade against the common enemy of mankind—for the slave trade is truly nothing less—until the wide world over slavery is utterly abolished !

The Anti-Slavery Conference held at Brussels in 1890, at which seventeen of the great Powers of the world were represented, it is expected will be fruitful in good results. A general act and declaration was drawn up, which has since been signed by all the contracting parties, which declares that " the powers are equally animated by the firm intention of putting an end to the crimes and devastations engendered by the traffic in African slaves, protecting effectively the aboriginal populations of Africa, and insuring for that vast continent the benefits of peace and civilization."

The wish of every feeling heart is that the seventeen Powers may succeed in their noble but herculean task. As yet little has been done, and it will doubtless be many years before much can be done. Some of the signatories to the "Act and Declaration," it is to be feared, are only half in earnest. Turkey has signed it, and yet Turkey is very greatly the cause of the dreadful traffic. It is futile for the Sultan, who styles himself the Commander of the Faithful, to issue tirades against the slave trade so long as he keeps one thousand women and girls in his seraglio, guarded by eunuchs and governed by the rod.

If only Turkey and other Mohammedan nations could see the evil of their ways in keeping slaves at all, even domestic slaves, then the doom of the slave trade would, indeed, be struck, and Africa would be saved. The prospect is not hopeful from the Moslem side; so we can but look to the vigilance of the Christian Powers to check, diminish, and cut off the supply. This method, however, can work but slowly, so that, humanly speaking, while slavery is now dying, it will probably be a generation or so before it is dead.

CHAPTER XL

ISLAM IN ENGLAND

PERHAPS the last place in the world where we should expect to find Mohammedanism is England, and yet it is a fact that this religion has been established in our land of late years, and, strange to say, by an Englishman.

Mohammedanism can scarcely be said to be a missionary religion like Christianity, for nowhere in the pages of the Koran is there such a passage as, "Go ye into all the world and preach the Gospel to every creature." The nearest approach to a missionary command is that which occurs in the 3rd sura, where it is written : "Let there be people among you who invite to the best religion." This may be construed into a call for missionaries to go forth to propagate the Faith of Islam, and it has been so construed, but not on a large scale, or with any definite system.

It is true we find Mohammedanism established not only in Arabia, the place of its birth, but in India and China, in Sumatra and Java, in Egypt, the Soudan, and Central Africa, and even in Madagascar. But in all these countries, as has been shown in the earlier chapters of this work, it was the power of the sword that won an opening for the Faith rather than the power of truth as presented by missionaries.

However, in the case of England, we are met with an exception to the general rule. Force in these days on the part of Commanders of the Faithful even could do nothing against England's might, so that if Mohammedanism were to obtain a footing at all in our country, the only possible way for it was the way of inward conviction of the superior value of the religion of Allah on the part of Englishmen. And thus it has actually befallen.

The centre of Mohammedanism in England is Liverpool, and Mr. William Henry Quilliam, a solicitor of that city, is the life and soul of the movement. In the year 1884 Mr. Quilliam visited Morocco, and there his attention was drawn to Mohammedanism. His statement is that he was first struck with the apparent sincerity of the followers of Islam, and with the absence in Moslem cities of the vices so prevalent in large centres of population in Great Britain. Then he devoted his spare time to the study of the Koran, and every other work he could procure upon the subject, *pro* or *con*, with the result that he was at last convinced that of all the religions of the world Islamism was the best. Having reached this point, he had the courage of his convictions, and openly confessed himself a convert to Mohammedanism, while he formally renounced Christianity.

Returning to Liverpool, the new convert, filled with zeal, sought to propagate the Faith of Islam amongst his countrymen by means of conversation, but seems only to have been laughed at for his pains. Then he tried lecturing, and with somewhat more encouraging results, for after a year or two he could point to four disciples. Thereupon a Church of Islam was formed in a hall in Mount Vernon Street, and after five hard up-hill years of work, the number of the Faithful increased to over thirty, when it was resolved to move to more comfortable and commodious premises, and bring the religion of Islam somewhat more prominently before the people of England by vigorous meetings, press notices, and various pamphlets and books.

On Christmas morning, 1889, the new premises at Brougham Hall, Brougham Terrace, West Derby Road, were opened by a substantial breakfast given to 230 poor children of the neighbourhood, and the Liverpool Moslem Institute was founded, of which Mr. W. H. Quilliam was made first President. From that date the public services have been better attended, and outside interest in the movement has grown, until the fame of "Islam in England" has gone to the uttermost parts of the earth.

In the autumn of 1891, being in England, I resolved to visit Liverpool and investigate thoroughly Mohammedanism in that city. During the four days of my stay I was the guest of the President, and was treated with much kindness, and shown everything in the Institute, and told all about the inner working of the whole movement, with the clear understanding that I could make public whatever I pleased. I timed my visit so as to arrive on a Friday, the "Day of the Assembly," and at once made my way to the Institute, though doubtful of obtaining admittance, as the services on that day are for the Faithful only.

It was the hour of Evening Prayer when I reached Brougham Hall, and the first thing I saw and heard was the President standing in the balcony of a window, which did duty for a minaret, giving the Azan or Call to Prayer, both in Arabic and English. I had not heard the famous Call since leaving Egypt in the year 1888, and it sounded passing strange to me to listen to it in the street of an English city. ·As the cry was raised "Allah is Great! Allah is Great! I bear witness there is no God but God! I bear witness that Mohammed is the Prophet of God! Come to prayers! Come to salvation! Allah is Great!" a crowd gathered round and listened with considerable curiosity, but without any remark.

The Liverpool Moslem Institute is a large old-fashioned house. On the notice board outside I read these words :

There is no God but God, and Mohammed was His Prophet!

CHURCH OF ISLAM.

Divine Service.   Sunday Morning 11 o'clock.
    „   „   „   Evening 7   „

I called the President's attention to the words "Mohammed *was* His Prophet," and asked whether it was a mistake

or not. I was told that " is " would be at once substituted
for " was," as the Faithful believe that Mohammed not only
" was " but " is " the Prophet of God. The word was an
unfortunate painter's error. Inside the Institute are various
rooms, such as a library, a museum, and a small lecture
hall, where the members meet for the study of the Koran,
for instruction in Eastern languages, and for social meet
ings of various kinds. Though it was the " Day of the
Assembly," the President courteously showed me through
the rooms, and then took me to see the Pro-Mosque where
Divine Worship is held.

The so-called mosque is just an oblong building in the
rear of the Institute, erected in what was formerly the
garden of the house. It will hold, probably, about 150
people, and is fitted up very plainly with somewhat uncom-
fortable benches, the only ornamentation being several
pairs of Burmese curtains, with here and there an Indian
durie, or prayer-mat, on the floor. At one end of the
building is a small platform with a reading-table, on which
rests a copy of the Koran, while at the other end a portion
is railed off as sacred ground where only the Faithful are
allowed to enter, without shoes on their feet, as they wish
to offer prayer and praise to Allah.

On the following Sunday I was present at two public
services. The morning meeting was very thinly attended,
only nine members being in their places, and no outsider
save myself. At the evening meeting there was a congregation of fifty-seven, of whom twelve were Lascars from the
ships in the Mersey.

There is, of course, no priesthood in Islam, though in
the East there are readers of the Koran, and doctors of
the law, who are virtually priests, and who usually lead
the Faithful in their devotions. I was told that in Liverpool the plan is for the Faithful in monthly assembly to
choose certain of the members of the Institute to conduct
the religious meetings for the following four weeks.

The honour is duly shared in turn, and no one receives

payment for service thus rendered. This practice of non-payment is founded upon that passage of the Koran which says: "Whosoever striveth to promote the true religion striveth for the advantage of his own soul, for God requireth not aid from any of His creatures;" and that other passage which declares, "I ask not of you any reward for this my preaching, besides the conversion of him who shall desire to take the way which leads unto his God."

The morning service consisted simply of a few hymns, a short prayer, and the reading of a very long and wearisome *sura* of the Koran, entitled "The Table, Revealed at Medina." The opening words of the *sura* were very good, viz., "O true believers, perform your contracts. . . . . Assist one another according to justice and piety, but assist not one another in injustice and malice." Then, however, the teaching suddenly degenerated, and the Faithful were told that unbelievers would be turned into apes and swine, that Jews and Christians would be cursed with a curse and reserved for hell-fire. Moreover, certain cruel laws were enjoined on true believers, such, for example, as: "If a man or a woman steal, cut off their hands in retribution for that which they have committed: this is an exemplary punishment appointed by God." But I forbear further quotation. I fail to see that the reading of the 5th sura of the Koran will commend Islam to inquirers after "the best religion," who may happen to enter the Pro-Mosque at Liverpool.

The President took no part in the morning service other than as a listener, but in the evening he was a prominent figure, and delivered a vigorous address. Let me give a general outline of the evening service, which will show my readers exactly what occurs week by week in the Church of Islam at Liverpool.

The proceedings opened with a chant—the first sura of the Koran, which is: "Praise be to God, the Lord of all creatures, the most merciful, the King of the Day of Judgment. Thee do we worship, and of Thee do we beg assistance. Direct us in the right way, in the way of those to whom Thou hast been gracious; not of those against whom Thou art incensed, nor of those who go astray." Then a hymn was sung from a very small "Collection of Hymns for use at the Meetings of the English-speaking Church of Islam." Strange to say, the first hymn was "Our God, our help in ages past." Prayer was next offered by Mr. Quilliam, the President. It was such a prayer as is heard doubtless every Sunday in a Unitarian Church, with the exception of the clause in it which asked for the blessing of Allah specially to rest upon his gracious majesty the Sultan of Constantinople, the Head of the Religion of Islam, and the Commander of the Faithful.

After the prayer the beautiful hymn was sung—

> "Take my life, and let it be
> Consecrated, Lord, to Thee."

Then followed a lesson from the 27th sura of the Koran, entitled "The Night Journey." Next came an anthem, excellently sung by the small choir. And then the President stood up to give his usual Sunday evening address or lecture. The subject was "A Moslem View of Christ."

Mr. Quilliam is a thin, somewhat sharp-featured, delicate-looking man, of the medium height, with a good voice, a ready utterance, and a pleasant manner. His delivery is usually quiet and deliberate, but now and again he waxes warm and passionately eloquent. His great fault, however, is his one-sided presentation of truth, even though he knows that something can be said on the other side. In short, he is a solicitor—an advocate in the pulpit as well as before the magistrate's bench.

His text was taken from the 5th sura of the Koran, and consisted of the words: "They are infidels who say, Verily, God is Christ, the son of Mary." Then in strong language but weak logic he proceeded to try to demonstrate to his hearers that Christ was not only not Divine, but a very poor specimen of a perfect man. I made copious notes of the argument, but I need not reproduce them. The chief points that the speaker relied upon to prove his case were, that Jesus often made mistakes, was constantly losing his temper, was a disobedient son, and was of a revengeful disposition, as witness the incident of the cursing of the barren fig-tree.

When I expostulated afterwards with the President for giving us such a caricature of the life of Christ, he smiled, and said that his method of treatment of the subject was the right one for a popular audience and for his purposes. "However," he remarked, "I do not often attack Christ or Christianity, but content myself with teaching and enforcing the moral and spiritual truths of Islam." And it is only fair to say that the subject announced for the following Sunday was "The Four Perfect Women of Islam."

The service concluded with the hearty singing of one of the few hymns in the Moslem Hymnal not taken from Christian sources. Mr. Quilliam himself was the composer of it, I think. It was a hymn of praise, the last verse of which was to this effect :—

> " And when the sands of life have run,
> And all our time on earth is done :
> We pray Thee, O Thou God of love,
> Take us to Thee in heaven above."

After the public meeting a private one for the Faithful, more especially for the Lascars, was held. While I was waiting in the lecture-room, and enjoying a chat with a lady, who before she joined the Moslem Institute was an ardent Theosophist, my attention was drawn to a crowd of street-arabs and roughs outside, who were amusing themselves by throwing stones into the hall of the house, some of which even went through into the mosque itself. The little band of the Faithful did not, however, seem to mind the persecution and disturbance much. I felt, however, that it was a disgrace that such things could be done in an English city with impunity. Where were the guardians of the public peace? Conspicuous by their absence !

Mr. Quilliam, it appears, visited the Sultan of Constantinople by special request in May, 1891. His eldest son, Robert, a boy of ten years of age, accompanied him, and to this lad the Sultan took a fancy. The President had a gracious reception, and returned, of course, to England more pronounced than ever in his attachment to Islamism. His son was made a Colonel in the Household Troops and dignified with the title of Bey. The boy, whether he thought much of the title or not, was evidently delighted with the beautiful Arab steed which the Sultan had given him, and with the regimentals appertaining to his new dignity of Colonel. When fifteen years of age, the young Bey will be expected to take up his quarters in the Turkish capital, and to cast in his lot for good with his Eastern co-religionists. Robert Quilliam is a handsome and gallant boy, and I sincerely wish him a better fate than to spend his days in the Household Troops of a Moslem Prince, even though that Prince be the Sultan of Constantinople.

Mr. Quilliam, senior, is an enthusiast, and seems to me to be killing himself with work. His law practice alone, I am told, is enough to keep any ordinary man busy all the week, yet he is present at various meetings at the Moslem Institute, Sunday and week-day, and is constantly writing pamphlets and books for the enlightenment of the world on this his particular hobby. "Fanatics and Fanaticism" was the first pamphlet he published. It was originally a temperance lecture, but Mohammed was introduced into it, and Islamism eulogized, and by means of "Fanatics and Fanaticism" the President won his first follower.

"The Faith of Islam," a work of forty-nine pages, next appeared. It is published at sixpence, and has reached a second edition. I have read it through very carefully, but do not consider it at all a reliable account of Islamism. As an example of what I mean, I find on page forty-one the statement that a great excellency of the Koran is "the total absence throughout of all impure, immoral, and indecent ideas or expressions . . . . it may be read from beginning to end without causing a blush to suffuse the cheek of modesty itself." Now this is entirely misleading, as I said to the author of the pamphlet when turning his attention to several passages in the "Perspicuous Book" which are decidedly conspicuous for filth. Why, in the 5th sura of the Koran, to go no further, in the chapter which was read in the Pro-Mosque, as already related, there occurred words which made me hot with shame and indignation as they were publicly recited before a mixed audience of ladies and gentlemen.

Take another example of the unreliableness of Mr. Quilliam's "Faith of Islam." On page forty-four it is written : "Islam has never interfered with the dogmas of any faith—never persecuted, never established an inquisition, never aimed at compulsory proselytism. It offered its religion but never enforced it, the maxim of the Mussulmans being the text of the Koran 'Let there be no violence in religion.'"

Does the worthy President of the Liverpool Moslem Institute suppose that any student of Eastern history will accept such wild statements without question ? Why, even the Koran itself is a witness against him. It is perfectly true that in the 2nd sura of the Koran it is written : "Let there be no violence in religion," but if Mr. Quilliam did not reason as an advocate he would have acknowledged in his "Faith of Islam" that Mohammed at a later date abrogated that peaceful decree, and issued another to the effect, as we read in the 76th sura : "Let those fight for the religion of God who barter the present life for the life to come : whosoever fighteth in the path of God, whether he be slain or victorious, we will in the end give him a great reward." Then, was it not Abu Bekr, the first Commander of the Faithful, who declared : "When a people leaveth off to fight in the ways of the Lord, the Lord also casteth off that people." And to this day it is a proverb amongst the Arabs—"The sword is a surer argument than books."

However, so blind to the whole teaching of history on this point is the President of the Liverpool Moslem Institute that he has just issued a somewhat bulky volume in three parts, entitled "The Religion of the Sword," with a view to prove that the Religion of the Sword is not Islamism but Judaism or Christianity. The bias of the writer and the misleading character of his arguments may be gathered even from a glance at the title-page, where we find quotations from the New Testament, the Old Testament, and the Koran respectively. Will it be believed that the quotation from the New Testament which is given as the keynote of Christianity is the saying of Jesus : " I came not to send peace but a sword : I am come to set a man at variance against his father, and a daughter agains the mother ! "

What unfairness this is ! How the words of Christ are wrested from their context, and made to insinuate what they do not mean ! I do not say for a moment that many cruel and wicked deeds have not been done by so-called Christians in the name of Christianity, but I would protest with the whole force of my nature against the teaching that the life or the sayings of Christ in the slightest degree countenance violent deeds. Nay, Christ was essentially the Prince of Peace, and His Kingdom was not of this world ! No student of the New Testament of any nationality can really believe that the above quotation about " not peace but a sword," accurately represents the teaching of Christ or the genius of Christianity.

"Islam in England " has its headquarters in Liverpool, but elsewhere in our country branch societies are to be found. There are said to be 120 Moslems in London, but they are Orientals. Then at Manchester there are forty of the Faithful, but only four of them are English converts. At Woking there is a mosque in connection with an Oriental Institute there, which, however, has only one or two students.

There is some talk of erecting a proper Eastern mosque

with dome and minarets in Liverpool ; and subscriptions are now being received towards this object. The money comes in very slowly, however, and chiefly from India.

The Liverpool Institute has at present only fifty-two members, fourteen of whom are ladies. Now that I have studied the movement on the spot, I consider that the world-wide fuss made over it is altogether beyond its deserts. Apart from the President, I do not think the Institute contains any mental strength or sign of vigorous life.

In my judgment the movement which Mr. Quilliam has inaugurated is a forlorn hope. Islam in England may drag on for some years a feeble existence, but then it will probably die a sudden death.

Islam, indeed, the world over, is a lost cause! Christianity is everywhere in the ascendant. The pale Galilean has conquered ! Of Christianity, and of Christianity alone, can it be said, as I saw engraved on an old wall of the Great Mosque at Damascus, which was once a Christian church : "Thy Kingdom, O Christ, is an everlasting Kingdom, and Thy Dominion endureth throughout all generations."

CHAPTER XLI

CONTRASTED WITH CHRISTIANITY

WE come now to our last chapter on Mohammedanism. Our previous Studies have all been intended to lead up to this point: What think you of Islamism in comparison with Christianity? Which is the better religion? Which contains the nobler creed? Which will do most to elevate and bless humanity?

It is a remarkable thing that at the present moment there is a Moslem Mission in Liverpool, started and maintained by Englishmen, with the direct object of converting us all to the doctrines of Mohammedanism. The enthusiasts who sustain this mission firmly believe that they have found in Islamism a better religion than they had aforetime in Christianity.

It is easy to pooh-pooh such beliefs, and smile at the vagaries of our brethren who hold them, but are we sure that they are wrong; and if they are, can we give sound reasons for our difference of opinion, and for our holding fast to the faith of our fathers? These are practical and important questions. As the result of my Studies in the faith of Islam, I have no hesitation in saying that, if we apply the comparative method in dealing with Mohammedanism and Christianity, we shall inevitably arrive at the conclusion that the religion of Christ is undoubtedly infinitely superior to the religion of Mohammed in every respect. Let us see!

Take first the character of the founders of the two

religions. What have we to say, without prejudice, of Mohammed? Some students of history have spoken very harshly of him ; and it was the fashion ·until recently to style him "the False Prophet." Luther looked upon Mohammed as "a devil, and first-born of Satan." Even the mild and gentle Melancthon considered that " he was inspired by Satan." Prideaux said of him that " he was a wilful and intentional deceiver from first to last, who for the purpose of raising himself to supreme power, invented the wicked imposture which he palmed with so much success on the world." Other eminent critics have even descended to the use of such epithets as " dastardly liar," " blasphemer," " vile wretch," and " antichrist." Now, with all such harsh judgments I have not the least sympathy. If we desire to be fair at all in our criticism we must frankly acknowledge that Mohammed was a man of extraordinary powers and gifts, and we must not judge him by modern commonplace standards. We must bear in mind the age in which he lived, and the work he undertook to do ; and we must not let his opposition to Christianity prejudice us against him.

For my part, while I do not close my eyes to the weaknesses, follies, and even sins, of Mohammed, I hold him to have been for his times a great and a good man. I am even prepared to say: "Take him all in all, the history of humanity has seen few more earnest, noble, and sincere prophets—using the word prophet in the broad, human sense of one irresistibly impelled by an inner power to admonish and to teach, and to utter austere and sublime truths." I hold that Mohammed served his generation well, and that he was the finest and noblest public character of his day. But when we have acknowledged to the full the ability and wisdom of the Prophet, and his amiability, faithfulness, tender-heartedness, and readiness to forgive, what was he compared with Christ—not the Christ of our ardent imagination, but the Christ of history ?

Mohammed, with all his good points, had some very bad

ones, notably his intense worldly ambition and his licen-
tiousness.   His life was not an ideally unselfish one, nor
an ideally holy one, and his frequent lapses from the path
of strict virtue sadly marred his usefulness in his own times,
and have injured Islamism for ever by the power of a bad
example.   How different from Christ, in whom friends and
enemies alike could find no evil; who was holy, harmless,
undefiled, separate from sinners, whose whole life was one
of purity, of lowly service, and of self-sacrificing love.   If
we may judge religions in any degree by the characters of
their founders, then how vastly superior Christianity is
to Mohammedanism !   As Lord Houghton has beautifully
said :—

> Mohammed's truth lay in a holy book,
>   Christ's in a sacred life.
>
> So while the world rolls on from change to change,
>   And realms of thought expand,
> The letter stands without expanse or range,
>   Stiff as a dead man's hand.
>
> While, as the lifeblood fills the growing form,
>   The Spirit Christ has shed
> Flows through the ripening ages fresh and warm,
>   More felt than heard or read.

Now let us contrast the two religions in respect to their
Sacred Scriptures, the Koran and the Bible.   I have no
wish to depreciate the writings of Mohammed on religious
matters.   When we consider that the Koran is the work
of one man, we must acknowledge that it is a unique and
wonderful performance.   And the more I have studied it
the more I have found in it to admire.   At the first, when
we read the Koran we are apt to weary at its peculiar and
involved phraseology and its senseless repetitions ; and we
may also be somewhat disgusted with its childish stories,
its bitter invectives against unbelievers, and its licentious
references to the joys of Paradise ; but when we examine
the book more carefully, and study it more diligently, we

find in its pages here and there passages calculated to instruct, to edify, and to ennoble.

Take, for example, such a saying as this: "Man prayeth for evil as he prayeth for good, for man is hasty." We feel the truth and force of the statement. Again, how noble is the advice: "Bridle thine anger, and be ready to forgive thine enemies, and turn away evil with good." And once more, how sublime is the passage which says: "There is no piety in turning your faces towards the east or the west, but he is pious who believeth in God, and the last day, and the angels, and the Scriptures, and the Prophets; who for the love of God dispenseth his wealth to his kindred, and to the orphans, and the needy, and the wayfarer, and those who ask, and for ransoming; who observeth prayer, and payeth the legal alms, and who is of those who are faithful to their engagements, and patient under ills and hardships, and in time of trouble. Such are pious and fear the Lord!"

Truly the Koran is a book that repays close study! And it may be said to hold a high place amongst the Sacred Scriptures of the world; but it is a poor volume when compared with the Bible—how poor only those know who have carefully read and diligently compared the two! There are, for instance, in the Koran no Psalms of David, with their deep spiritual inspiration and their tender and sweet devotional utterances! There is no book of Job, with its profound thinking, and its grand precepts with regard to life's joys and sorrows! There are no Proverbs of Solomon, with their shrewd insight into human character, and their wise and practical counsels with regard to human conduct in every-day affairs! And there is no Gospel of Christ, there are no Acts of the Apostles, and Epistles, breathing the divinest sentiments of the divinest of men, even the Lord Jesus Christ Himself! The Koran seems so meagre, so poor, so paltry, when compared with the Bible. The Koran is merely one book, and that not of the noblest kind, though noble, while the Bible is a veritable storehouse of sacred books, written or compiled in all ages of human history, and giving the world's profoundest and most spiritual thoughts. And whereas in the Koran the passages of beauty and grace which tend to enlightenment, comfort, and edification are few and difficult to find, in the Bible they abound, and are seen on every page! Thus judged by the comparison of Sacred Scriptures, Christianity is greatly superior to Mohammedanism. But let us take another line of comparison.

Let us judge the two religions by their conception of the Divine Being called Allah and God respectively. Now, the glory of Mohammedanism amongst the religions of the East lies in its teaching with regard to God. Indeed, the mission of Mohammedanism to this world has been to declare and maintain the unity of God. It was a grand truth that Mohammed saw and seized and taught, that "there is no God but God." This truth was the power that enabled Islamism in the early days of her career to carry all before her.

We must never forget the service that Mohammedanism has rendered to humanity in keeping the sublime truth of the unity of God before the eyes of the heathen world steeped in idolatry! Throughout all the ages, since Islamism first appeared in Arabia until now, never for one moment have the Faithful ceased to believe or to teach that "there is no God but God." But what has been the Moslem conception of God? Infinitely better than the heathen idea, I am fully prepared to grant; but it has fallen far short of the Christian conception. Let me quote two or three short passages from the Koran. In one place it is written: "O man of Mecca! serve your Lord who hath created you, and those who have been before you: peradventure ye will fear Him, who hath spread the earth as a bed for you, and the heaven as a covering, and hath caused water to descend from heaven, and thereby produced fruit for your sustenance. Set not up therefore any equals unto God." Again it is written: "Judgment belongeth unto God. With Him are the keys of the secret things, none knoweth them beside Himself: He knoweth that which is on the dry land and in the sea ; there falleth no leaf but He knoweth it : neither is there a single grain in the dark parts of the earth, neither a green thing, nor a dry thing, but it is known to God. It is He who causeth you to sleep by night, and knoweth what ye merit by day. He also awaketh you therein that the prefixed time of your lives may be fulfilled : then unto Him shall ye return, and He shall declare unto you that which ye have wrought."

And once more it is written, in words of stately eloquence: "God! There is no God but He, the living, the self-subsisting; neither slumber nor sleep seizeth Him, to Him belongeth whatsoever is in Heaven and on earth ! Who is he that can intercede with Him but through His good pleasure ? He knoweth that which is past, and that which is to come unto them, and they shall not comprehend anything of His knowledge, but so far as He pleaseth ! His throne is extended over Heaven and earth, and the preservation of both is no burden unto Him ! He is the high, the mighty ! "

In these passages we have the very best that Mohammedanism can give us with regard to the nature and character of " Allah, the Eternal, the Living one, who never dieth, the first and the last." But in Mohammedanism we search in vain for such a passage as this, which is the very foundation of Christianity, viz., " God is love ; " or as this, " God so loved the world that He gave His only-begotten Son, that whosoever believeth in Him should not perish, but have everlasting life." And as for the dear name of " Father," as for the faintest notion of the " Fatherhood of God," it is nowhere to be found in Islamism. Amongst " the Ninety-nine Beautiful Names of Allah " there is no place for that of " Father," which expresses so much to the Christian heart. Dr. J. Cameron Lees, in his St. Giles' lecture on " Mohammedanism," commenting on this point, says truly : " The God of the Arabian Prophet is not a God of love, who desires that His children should become one with Him, and should yield Him their affection.

He is a God of will and power, withdrawn from the
human world, the highest relation to whom, attainable by
man, is expressed in the well-known name the religion
bears : ' Islam, that is resignation.' "

> " One God the Arabian Prophet preached to man,
>   One God the crescent still
> Adores through many a realm of mighty span,
>   A God of power and will.
>
> " A God that, shrouded in His lonely light,
>   Rests utterly apart
> From all the vast creations of His might,
>   From nature, man, and art.
>
> " A power that at His pleasure doth create,
>   To save or to destroy :
> And to eternal pain predestinate
>   As to eternal joy."

But such is not the God of the Christian ! Christianity
gives us a nobler conception of the Divine Being than
Mohammedanism. "The God and Father of Our Lord
Jesus Christ " is a God of tender pity, of manifold compassion, of parental kindness and love. God does not,
like Allah, empower men to propagate His truth with the
sword, but he sends His children forth into the world
with a Gospel of "peace on earth, good-will towards
men." Therefore do we take Christianity to be the nobler
Faith ; and therefore do we cleave to it with all our heart
and soul, and mind and strength !

I shall not linger over other comparisons that might be
profitably dealt with at some length. It will be sufficient
for my purpose just to mention them briefly.

1. There is ethical teaching. Some people have said,
notably our brethen who have turned Moslems in Liverpool, that the ethical teaching of Islamism is superior to
Christianity. I require proof, however, and I cannot find
it in the Koran. The attitude of Mohammedanism to the
drink traffic, it is maintained, is most commendable. I
grant that readily, and I believe it would be a good thing

for Christendom if we could, as a matter of policy, imitate Moslems in the utter condemnation of the use of intoxicating drinks. The gain in morality would be greater than the loss in wealth. But, taking Christianity and Mohammedanism as a whole, in their ethical teaching, I do not believe that there is anything in the latter to compare with the noble laws and rules of life inculcated by Christ, say, in the Sermon on the Mount. It must be borne in mind that intemperance can be shown in many ways besides strong drink. The Moslem creed is lacking in such noble precepts as " Blessed are the pure in heart, for they shall see God."

2. Then there is the treatment of women. Mohammedanism does not shine in this matter. Nay, nowhere on earth will you find woman so degraded as in countries where Islamism reigns supreme ! A Mohammedan regards woman not as a companion and helpmeet for him, but as a plaything, a pretty toy, as soulless almost as his turban, his pipe, and his amber mouth-piece. How blessed is the contrast when we look at Christianity, and think of Christ, who reverenced women, who made them His friends, who chose them as His co-labourers, and who regarded them as heirs with men of the Kingdom of Heaven !

3. Then, lastly, there is the regenerating power of religion to be borne in mind. Whether does Christianity or Mohammedanism tend more to renew the hearts of sinful men, and raise mankind to higher and nobler things ? There can be but one answer ! Christianity has proved itself superior ! It may be said that Mohammedanism has done much to raise heathen nations from the dust. True ! but not as much as Christianity. As Professor Monier Williams has said : " There is a finality and want of elasticity about Mohammedanism which precludes its expanding beyond a certain fixed line of demarcation. Having once reached this line, it appears to lapse backwards—to tend towards mental and moral slavery—to contract within narrower and narrower circles of bigotry and exclusiveness.

But the Christian's course is ever onwards ; his movements are free—he is ever tending towards wider reaches of comprehensiveness, tolerance, and charity. He is ever advancing towards a higher life, towards higher conditions of being, where he may find infinite scope for the development of all that is most pure, most noble, and most spiritual in his nature."

Such are the comparisons that can be made between Mohammedanism and Christianity, and all most certainly and fairly are in favour of the latter. Whether we look at the character of the founders of the two Religions, at the Sacred Scriptures of the two Faiths, at their conception of God, at their ethical standards, at their views of social and family life, or at the relative power of the two Religions to elevate and save humanity, we arrive inevitably at the same conclusion.

I know Mohammedanism and I know Christianity, and by their fruits all men may know the two Faiths, and for my part I say unhesitatingly that Christianity is a thousand times the nobler and better religion. Therefore will I remain true to Christianity ! And may this sublime Faith prevail throughout the world ! It shall prevail !

> " The moon of Mahomet
> Arose, and it shall set,
> While blazoned as on Heaven's immortal noon,
> The Cross leads generations on."

THE END.

INDEX

E E

www.ingramcontent.com/pod-product-compliance
Lightning Source LLC
Chambersburg PA
CBHW032309280326
41932CB00009B/749